IN PRAISE OF NATURAL PHILOSOPHY

In Praise of Natural Philosophy

A Revolution for Thought and Life

NICHOLAS MAXWELL

McGill-Queen's University Press
Montreal & Kingston · London · Chicago

© McGill-Queen's University Press 2017

ISBN 978-0-7735-4902-9 (cloth)
ISBN 978-0-7735-4903-6 (paper)
ISBN 978-0-7735-4904-3 (ePDF)
ISBN 978-0-7735-4905-0 (ePUB)

Legal deposit first quarter 2017
Bibliothèque nationale du Québec

Printed in Canada on acid-free paper that is 100% ancient forest free
(100% post-consumer recycled), processed chlorine free

McGill-Queen's University Press acknowledges the support of the Canada
Council for the Arts for our publishing program. We also acknowledge the
financial support of the Government of Canada through the Canada Book
Fund for our publishing activities.

Library and Archives Canada Cataloguing in Publication

Maxwell, Nicholas, 1937–, author
In praise of natural philosophy: a revolution for thought and life /
Nicholas Maxwell.

This book is an expansion of an article published in *Philosophia* 40 (4),
2012, 705–15.
Includes bibliographical references and index.
Issued in print and electronic formats.
ISBN 978-0-7735-4902-9 (cloth). – ISBN 978-0-7735-4903-6 (paper). –
ISBN 978-0-7735-4904-3 (ePDF). – ISBN 978-0-7735-4905-0 (ePUB)

1. Physics – Philosophy. 2. Science. 3. Philosophy. I. Title.

QC6.M39 2017   530.01   C2016-906502-2
                                      C2016-906503-0

This book was typeset by Marquis Interscript in 10.5 / 13 Sabon.

For Christine van Meeteren

Contents

Acknowledgments

This book grew out of an article with the same title I published in *Philosophia* 40 (4), 2012, 705–15. I am grateful to Asa Kasher and Springer, editor and publisher of *Philosophia*, for permission to reuse the title, and to republish in the present book a few paragraphs from the original article. Part of chapter 3 has been adapted from text published in Nicholas Maxwell, "What Philosophy Ought to Be," in *Death And Anti-Death, Volume 11: Ten Years After Donald Davidson (1917–2003)*, edited by Charles Tandy (Palo Alto, CA: Ria University Press, 2014). Charles Tandy is thanked for permission to republish this text.

Preface

The central thesis of this book is that we need to reform philosophy and join it to science to recreate a modern version of natural philosophy; we need to do this in the interests of rigour, intellectual honesty, and so that science may serve the best interests of humanity.

The book seeks to redraw our intellectual landscape. It leads to a transformation of science, and to a transformation of philosophy, so that these two distinct domains of thought become conjoined into one: natural philosophy. This in turn has far-reaching consequences for the whole academic enterprise. It transpires that we need an academic revolution. We urgently need to reorganize universities so that they become devoted to seeking and promoting wisdom by rational means – as opposed to just acquiring knowledge, as at present.

Modern science began as natural philosophy. In the time of Newton, what we call science and philosophy today – the disparate endeavours – formed one mutually interacting, integrated endeavour of natural philosophy: to improve our knowledge and understanding of the universe, and to improve our understanding of ourselves as a part of it. Profound discoveries were made, indeed one should say unprecedented discoveries. It was a time of quite astonishing intellectual excitement and achievement.

And then natural philosophy died. It split into science on the one hand, and philosophy on the other. This happened during the eighteenth and nineteenth centuries, and the split is now built into our intellectual landscape. But the two fragments, science and philosophy, are defective shadows of the glorious unified endeavour of natural philosophy. Rigour, sheer intellectual good sense, and decisive argument demand that we put the two together again, and rediscover the immense merits of the integrated enterprise of natural philosophy. This requires an intellectual revolution, with dramatic implications for how we understand our world, how we understand and do science, and how we understand and do philosophy. There are dramatic implications, too, for education.

And it does not stop there. For, as I will show in the final chapter, resurrected natural philosophy has dramatic, even revolutionary *methodological* implications for social science and the humanities, indeed for the whole academic enterprise. It means academic inquiry needs to be reorganized so that its basic task becomes to seek and promote wisdom by rational means, wisdom being the capacity to realize what is of value in life, for oneself and others, thus including knowledge, technological know-how, and understanding, but much else besides.

The outcome is institutions of learning rationally designed and devoted to helping us tackle our immense global problems in increasingly cooperatively rational ways, thus helping us make progress towards a good world – or at least as good a world as possible.

IN PRAISE OF NATURAL PHILOSOPHY

I

Triumphs of Natural Philosophy

In this book I set out to expose an intellectual disaster at the heart of our culture – at the heart of our world. It has a multitude of adverse repercussions for the way we think and the way we live. Science and scholarship are adversely affected. Our understanding of our place in the universe is obscured. Our ability to see what is of value in life, and our ability to achieve what is of value, are undermined. Peace, justice, liberty, democracy, sustainability are all compromised. The disaster obstructs attempts to develop institutions and social endeavours that work in our best interests. It sabotages our efforts to make progress towards a good world.

What is this malignant intellectual disaster that spreads its tentacles in such an abundant fashion throughout our world? It is, to begin with, a blunder about the nature of science. But it is also a long-standing blunder about how to understand our human world – the world as we experience it, imbued with consciousness, free will, meaning and value – given the new vision of the universe ushered in by modern science. It is a blunder about the nature of rational inquiry and, perhaps even more important, the nature and desirability of rational living, of rational institutions. Our very psyches are affected, the way we split off reason and intellect from feeling and desire, fact from value, science from art.

It is, at root, a philosophical blunder – or a series of philosophical blunders.[1] At once it will seem absurd to hold that philosophical blunders could have such dire, far-flung consequences. Everyone knows that philosophy is a dry, esoteric discipline, of absorbing interest no doubt to its academic practitioners, but otherwise devoid of relevance to anything else whatsoever.

Academic philosophy as it exists today is however one of the products of the disaster I seek to expose, and correct. The very act of correcting it reveals that philosophy as it should be pursued is far too important, for thought and for life, to be left to its current academic practitioners.

The intellectual disaster that we shall be concerned with in this book threads its way far back into our history. It has its roots in the seventeenth century, with the birth of modern science. That is where we will begin.

I must stress, however, that what follows in this chapter is only a sketch of those elements of the scientific revolution just sufficient to provide a historical background to the blunder about the nature of science (and inquiry more generally) that is the real theme of this book.[2] Towards the end of the chapter, I make a few remarks about what historians of science have said about the scientific revolution in recent decades.

SCIENCE BEGAN AS NATURAL PHILOSOPHY

Modern science began as natural philosophy, or "experimental philosophy," as it was sometimes called. In the time of Isaac Newton, in the seventeenth century, science was not only called natural philosophy. It was conceived of, and pursued, as a development of philosophy. It brought together physics, chemistry, and other branches of natural science as we know it today, with diverse branches of philosophy: metaphysics, epistemology, methodology, philosophy of science – even theology. Science and philosophy, which we see today as distinct, in those days interacted with one another and formed the integrated enterprise of natural philosophy.[3] Its basic aim was to improve our knowledge and understanding of the universe – and to improve our understanding of ourselves as a part of the universe. And around the time of Newton there was this great upsurge of excitement and confidence. For the first time ever, in the history of humanity, the secrets of the universe, hitherto wholly unknown, had been revealed and laid bare for all to understand – or at least, for all those who understood Latin and the intricate mathematics of Newton's *Principia*.[4]

Today we look back at the great intellectual figures associated with the birth of modern science and we unhesitatingly divide them up into scientists on the one hand, philosophers on the other. Galileo,

Johannes Kepler, William Harvey, Robert Boyle, Christiaan Huygens, Robert Hooke, Edmond Halley, and of course Isaac Newton are all scientists; Francis Bacon, René Descartes, Thomas Hobbes, John Locke, Baruch Spinoza and Gottfried Leibniz are philosophers (see table 1 for dates). But this division is anachronistic. They did not see themselves in this fashion. Their work interacted in all sorts of ways, science with philosophy, philosophy with science. They all sought, in one way or another, to improve our knowledge and understanding of the universe, to improve our understanding of how we can acquire knowledge of the universe, and to work out the implications, for our understanding of ourselves, of the new view of the universe that the new natural philosophy had ushered in.

That the distinction we make between science and philosophy is anachronistic when projected back into the sixteenth and seventeeth centuries becomes all the more apparent when one considers the *philosophy* that was done by those natural philosophers we now consider to have been scientists, and the *science* done by those natural philosophers we now regard as philosophers. Thus Galileo, for us a scientist, made a substantial contribution to what we would now regard as philosophy when he drew the distinction between what came to be called "primary" and "secondary" qualities. He writes:

Whenever I conceive any material or corporal substance, I immediately feel the need to think of it as bounded, and as having this or that shape; as being large or small in relation to other things, and in some specific place at any given time; as being in motion or at rest; as touching or not touching some other body; and as being one in number, or few, or many. From these conditions I cannot separate such a substance by any stretch of my imagination. But that it must be white or red, bitter or sweet, noisy or silent, and of sweet or foul odour, my mind does not feel compelled to bring in as necessary accompaniments ... Hence I think that tastes, odours, colours, and so on are no more than mere names so far as the object in which we place them is concerned, and they reside only in the consciousness. Hence if the living creature were removed, all these qualities would be wiped away and annihilated.[5]

Galileo goes on, delightfully, to consider a hand tickling a person and a statue, and points out that we would consider it ridiculous to hold that the tickling is a property of the hand in addition to its motion and touch. The tickling sensation is in the person being tickled, not in the hand that does the tickling; and so it is, Galileo argues, for colour, sound, taste, and odour. He adds, very significantly, that "to excite in us tastes, odours, and sounds I believe nothing is required in external bodies except shapes, numbers, and slow or rapid movements."[6] Galileo is here, of course, elaborating on what Democritus had asserted 2,000 years earlier: "Colour exists by convention; sweet and sour exist by convention: atoms and the void alone exist in reality."[7] Galileo is in effect affirming the key metaphysical tenet of the new natural philosophy: the universe is made up of atoms in motion or, more generally, of physical entities in motion whose physical properties can be depicted in mathematical terms. Galileo is also, implicitly, invoking a key paradox inherent in the new natural philosophy: on the one hand there is the appeal to observation and experiment, while on the other hand, the new (or revitalized) metaphysical vision of the universe – atomism, or the corpuscular hypothesis – tells us that perception is profoundly delusive. This paradox, unresolved, played an important role in driving science and philosophy apart, as we shall see.

Newton, whom we undeniably deem to be a scientist, echoed Galileo's philosophical remarks concerning real physical properties and illusory perceptual qualities, in connection with light. He also put forward many metaphysical theses and speculations about such matters as space, time, the aether, and unknown forces governing physical and chemical phenomena. He engaged in philosophy of science in seeking to characterize scientific method by means of four "rules of reasoning in philosophy," as we shall see below. And he even engaged in theology in arguing that God played an important role in setting up the solar system, and in intervening from time to time to ensure its continuing existence.

Descartes, for us a philosopher, made a vital mathematical contribution to subsequent science by creating what we call "Cartesian coordinates." This made it possible to translate geometrical figures, curves and problems into algebraic equations and vice versa, thus facilitating the mathematical treatment of motion. Descartes was the first person to formulate the correct version of the law of inertia.[8] He put forward laws of reflection and refraction, and proposed what we would today call a physical "theory of everything" intended to account for all phenomena, including those associated with the solar system. According to this theory, what seems to be empty space is really filled with invisible particles that possess extension and motion but no other property. Swirling vortices of these particles sweep the planets around the sun. That this theory turned out to be unworkable,[9] or at least false on empirical grounds, does not negate its scientific character, or its important role in the history of science.

Leibniz, another philosopher, made a vital contribution to science by inventing the integral and differential calculus, independently of Newton, Leibniz's formulation being the one that was subsequently used.

Finally Locke, unquestionably for us a philosopher, declares at the beginning of his *Essay concerning Human Understanding* that he sees his task to be that of an under-labourer of the work of "such masters as the great Huygens and the incomparable Mr. Newton" in "clearing ground a little, and removing some of the rubbish that lies in the way of knowledge."[10]

There were good reasons why, in the seventeenth century, empirical science could not be split off from philosophy. Natural philosophers disagreed about crucial questions of method. Should evidence alone decide which theories are accepted and rejected, or does reason play a role as well? After the work of Galileo and Kepler, and with the work of Descartes and, above all, Newton, it became apparent that mathematics had an important role to play in science, along with observation and experiment. But mathematical truths can be established by reason alone. Reason must therefore have an important role in science. But how? In what way? Some held that all knowledge comes to us via the senses, via experience. Reason, according to this kind of empiricist view, could not establish any knowledge at all independent of experience. The nature of mathematical knowledge became problematic. Others – most notably Descartes and Leibniz – held that reason plays a vital role in natural philosophy, in the enterprise, that is, of acquiring knowledge of the universe. These different views about the roles of experience and reason in science led to different methods in science, and thus had practical consequences for science itself: they had to be discussed as a part of science.

Again, the new natural philosophy ushered in a new vision of the universe: it is made up of colourless, soundless, odourless corpuscles which interact only by contact. This metaphysical view[11] had an impact on what scientific theories are to be accepted and rejected; natural philosophers held different versions of the view, and different attitudes to the influence the view should have on science: all this had to be discussed as an integral part of science. Physics and chemistry could hardly be pursued without some thought being given to the manner in which corpuscles might produce phenomena associated with light, combustion, heat, chemical reactions, gravitation.

Table 1   Some natural philosophers of the scientific revolution

Leonardo da Vinci 1452–1519	Pierre Gassendi 1592–1655
Nicolaus Copernicus 1473–1543	René Descartes 1596–1650
William Gilbert 1544–1603	Robert Boyle 1627–1691
Tycho Brahe 1546–1601	Christiaan Huygens 1629–1695
Giordano Bruno 1548–1600	John Locke 1632–1704
Francis Bacon 1561–1626	Baruch Spinoza 1632–1677
Galileo Galilei 1564–1642	Robert Hooke 1635–1702
Johannes Kepler 1571–1630	Isaac Newton 1642–1727
William Harvey 1578–1657	Gottfried Wilhelm Leibniz 1646–1716
Thomas Hobbes 1588–1679	Edmond Halley 1656–1742

In addition, the corpuscular hypothesis provoked profound philosophical problems about how it is possible for human beings to acquire knowledge of the universe, and how it is possible for people to be conscious, free, and of value if immersed in the physical universe. If everything really is made up of colourless, soundless, odourless particles, how come roses are red, dogs bark, and lavender smells? If our bodies and brains are made up exclusively of these particles, what becomes of our inner sensations, our consciousness? If all our knowledge of the world around us is based on particles of light entering our eyes, other particles bouncing against our eardrums or nostrils, how is it that we know anything about what we think we see, hear, and smell? And if the corpuscles dart about and collide in accordance with precise, mathematical laws, how can we be responsible for our actions? What becomes of free will? Natural philosophers could hardly take the corpuscular theory seriously in what we might today regard as their "scientific" work, and then just ignore the radical and disturbing implications this theory seems to have for human knowledge, consciousness and free will. They did not, as we shall see.

The new science did not just usher in a new vision of the universe. Its birth owed much to the advent of this new vision. One might have supposed, naively, that modern science began when people started to take evidence seriously. Is not modern science based on evidence? What more natural, then, than to suppose that science began when people based the pursuit of knowledge, not on mere tradition or authority, but on evidence?

To be fair, there is an element of truth in the idea – but only an element. Appealing to evidence did not begin with the birth of modern science. And factors other than appealing to evidence were of even greater significance. A key factor was a revolution in philosophy: the downfall of Aristotelianism, and the creation – or recreation – of the corpuscular hypothesis, or the more general view that the universe has some kind of mathematical structure, or that "the book of nature is written in the language of mathematics" as Galileo put it.[12] Kepler, Galileo, Descartes, Huygens, and Hooke all held versions of this view. And their adoption of the view played an essential role in their scientific work – as we should call it today.

Aristotelianism is the view that change comes about because objects strive to actualize their inherent potentialities, much as an acorn strives to actualize its potential to become an oak tree. Objects fall because they have an inherent potential to seek the centre of the earth. The natural world is, in a sense, alive. Purpose, goal-seeking is built into the constitution of things. According to Aristotelianism, a sharp distinction is to be made between terrestrial and heavenly phenomena. The earth is at the centre of the universe. On earth, there is imperfection, change, decay, and phenomena do not observe precise, mathematical laws. In the heavens, by contrast, there is perfection, no decay, and the motions of heavenly bodies do observe precise mathematical laws.

COPERNICUS AND THE DOWNFALL
OF ARISTOTELIANISM

The first step towards the overthrow of Aristotelianism was the Copernican revolution.[13] The earlier theory of Ptolemy put the earth at the centre of the universe, the sun, planets, and stars rotating around the earth in uniform, circular motion. In order to account for deviations from uniform circular motion, Ptolemy was forced to postulate epicycles, and other devices. Thus planets move as if fixed to the rim of a uniformly rotating disk, the centre of which is fixed to the rim of a much bigger, uniformly rotating disk which has its centre at the centre of the earth. By means of a horrendously complex system of epicycles and other such devices, Ptolemy was able to account for the observed motions of the planets, the sun, and the stars.

Copernicus hesitated to publish his new theory of the cosmos (as the solar system was then thought to be) not, it seems, because he feared persecution from the Church, but rather because he feared ridicule from his fellow scholars. It was not until he lay on his deathbed in 1543 that his book *De Revolutionibus Orbium Coelestium* (On the Revolutions of the Celestial Spheres), setting out his new theory, was published.

It was not evidence that prompted Copernicus to put the sun at the centre of the solar system. He may have been influenced somewhat by a tendency towards sun-worship. And he may also have been influenced by Aristarchus, a third-century BC Greek who put forward the heliocentric view. The decisive factor however was simplicity. A sun-centred solar system promised to be much simpler than Ptolemy's complicated system. Evidence, if anything, told against Copernicus's theory. Both theories accounted equally well for observed astronomical motions, but Copernicus's theory faced additional empirical problems. First, there was the problem that if the earth rotates on its axis every twenty-four hours[14] and sweeps at vast speed around the sun, why is this motion not felt? Why does a stone, thrown vertically into the air, not fall some distance away because of the earth's motion during the stone's flight? And if the earth goes round the sun, why do the stars have the same, fixed relative positions at six-month intervals? Stars would have to be absurdly far away for no parallax to be observed.[15]

If planets moved in circles round the sun, Copernicus's theory would indeed have been much simpler than Ptolemy's. But, as Kepler subsequently discovered, they move in ellipses. In order to reduce the motions of the planets to uniform circular motion, Copernicus was obliged to introduce complicated epicycles of just the kind that bedevilled Ptolemy's theory. And in the end, in order to do justice to observations, Copernicus had to stipulate that the planets went round, not the sun, but a point in space some distance from the sun. The beautifully simple idea of Copernicus, or of Aristarchus before him, became somewhat complicated and ugly when developed in detail so as to do justice to observation – although, even in its final, complicated form, Copernicus's theory is still simpler than Ptolemy's.[16]

There is, nevertheless, a beautifully simple idea, which does not quite work, buried in the complexities of Copernicus's actual theory, which does work. It was this beautifully simple idea that subsequently inspired Galileo, Kepler, and a few others.

The Copernican revolution has dramatic implications for Aristotelianism. No longer is the earth at the centre of the cosmos, utterly distinct from the heavens. The earth is thrown into the heavens, one planet among the others that encircle the sun. This may be taken to mean, on the one hand, that the earth, now itself a part of the heavens, partakes of the mathematical precision of the heavens. Apparently wayward, haphazard terrestrial phenomena such as weather, growth, and decay, all occur, perhaps, in accordance with unknown, mathematically precise law. On the other hand, the Copernican revolution may be taken to imply that since the earth is a part of the heavens, and imperfection, change, growth, and decay are everywhere apparent on earth, all this obtains on other heavenly bodies too – the moon, the planets, even the sun. Both these implications came to dominate the thinking and work of Galileo, Kepler, and those that came after them. The implications of the Copernican revolution only came to full fruition, however, with Newton. His laws of motion and law of gravitation apply with equal force to all phenomena, terrestrial and heavenly: to the motion of a stone thrown into the air on earth, and to the motion of the earth and other planets around the sun.

There is a diagram in Newton's *Principia* which vividly depicts the point. It shows the earth. Projectiles are hurled horizontally from a mountain peak with greater and greater force. The projectiles travel further and further around the earth before they crash into the ground. But eventually a projectile is hurled with such force that it goes all the way round the earth and returns to the mountain peak from which its flight began. It is in orbit – like the moon, or, more accurately, like today's satellites. Thus is continuity between the terrestrial and astronomical depicted in graphic terms. But we are getting ahead of ourselves!

The Copernican revolution was not the only reason for a reawakening of the ancient Greek idea that the ultimate nature of the cosmos might be mathematical in character – or such that it could only be depicted employing mathematical ideas. This reawakening came also from the Renaissance, and a renewed interest in the work of Plato, Pythagoras, Euclid, and Archimedes, all of whom can be regarded as holding that the physical universe is mathematical in character. Leonardo, who died before Copernicus's great work was published, nevertheless became convinced that mathematics held the key to understanding nature.[17] Others convinced of the importance of mathematics in this respect include Roger Bacon (1214–1294), Nicholas of Cusa (1401–1464), and Giordano Bruno.

Bruno was an early convert to Copernicus's heliocentric view. Influenced possibly by Nicholas of Cusa, who held somewhat similar views, Bruno argued that the universe is infinite in extent, in both space and time, and homogeneous in that the same four elements – (water, earth, fire, air) are present everywhere. He held that the stars are distant suns with their own planetary systems. Matter, Bruno held, is made up of atoms, but these are living, possessing a kind of intelligence (an idea which does not help much with the universe having a precise mathematical structure at a fundamental level).

In January 1600, after a protracted trial, Bruno was condemned as a heretic, partly for his religious views, partly for his cosmology, and on February 27 of that year he was burned at the stake.

William Gilbert was another early convert to Copernicus's theory. His great contribution to natural philosophy, however, was to investigate magnetism experimentally. He discovered many properties of the lodestone, and discovered, too, that the earth is a gigantic magnet. In life, he fared rather better than Bruno. He was a successful physician, and ended up chief physician to Queen Elizabeth and, briefly, to King James.

The full rich implications of Copernicus's theory only began to emerge, however, with the work of Kepler and Galileo.

KEPLER

Kepler started out studying theology. It occurred to him that he could study God by studying His creation: the heavens. He decided to devote himself to astronomy. And in a flash of inspiration, he thought he might have discovered the secret of the cosmos. If one imagined the five Platonic solids – in a form both gigantic and invisible – being placed one inside the other, centred on the sun, then the planets could be understood as pursuing circular paths around the sun in the spaces within, between and around the five solids. Thus could one explain why there are only six planets (all that were known at the time), and why they are arranged as they are, with their various distances from the sun. (A great triumph of Euclidean geometry is the theorem that there are only five perfect solids, the so-called Platonic solids: the tetrahedron, the cube, the octahedron and so on.[18]) Even though Kepler discovered subsequently that the actual distances of the planets from the sun do not accord with those predicted by his great idea, he never altogether abandoned it.[19] What is really significant for the theme of this chapter is that Kepler's idea is a magnificent exemplification of the thesis that the universe has a mathematical structure. Kepler's first revelation into the structure of the universe amounts to a special (if false) case of the general, profound idea inherent in the birth of modern science, the scientific revolution, and the immense success of science ever since: *some* kind of beautiful mathematical structure is built into the universe, into the way all natural phenomena occur.

This general idea informed all of Kepler's subsequent great astronomical discoveries, his big contributions to science or, rather, to natural philosophy. In essence, these consist of the following three laws of planetary motion:

1 The planets orbit the sun in ellipses, with the sun at one of the two foci of each ellipse.
2 The planets move in such a way that a line joining any planet to the sun sweeps out equal areas in equal times.
3 The time taken for each planet to orbit the sun is such that the square of the time taken is proportional to the cube of the semimajor axis of the orbit.[20]

Kepler's works are packed with many additional numerical relationships concerning the solar system which he regarded as being of equal importance, but the above three laws embody Kepler's great contribution to science – to natural philosophy.

Accurate observation played a major role in Kepler's discovery of these three laws. Kepler was fortunate to meet and, for a time, work for Tycho Brahe, who had amassed a body of observations of the planets of great accuracy for the period.[21] When Tycho Brahe died, Kepler inherited his data, and was employed to work on them. It was Tycho Brahe's observational data that made it possible for Kepler to discover and confirm his three laws.

But if observational data were important, so too was Kepler's metaphysical view of the cosmos, his conviction that it had been created by God to exemplify a magnificent, harmonious mathematical structure. It was Kepler's conviction that the motions and distances of planets must exemplify simple and beautiful mathematical relationships that made it possible for him to discover his three laws, and accept them as representing genuine knowledge when they fitted the facts of observation.

Somewhat analogous considerations apply to Galileo, except that in Galileo's case what is most significant in his work depends even more on observations and experiments he carried out himself than is the case with Kepler.

GALILEO

Galileo, more than any other single individual, was responsible for the demise of Aristotelianism, the adoption in its stead of Copernicanism and what might be called the "mathematical" view of nature, and the creation of the new natural philosophy – or what we now call modern science. Galileo fruitfully developed both implications (mentioned above) of Copernicus's theory that result from the theory hurling the earth into the heavens: first, that heavenly phenomena exhibit change and imperfection just like phenomena on earth, and second, that apparently random, chaotic phenomena on earth actually occur in accordance with precise mathematical law – something hitherto associated with the heavens.[22]

The opportunity to develop the first implication arose when Galileo turned his newly invented telescope to view the skies.[23] He discovered that the moon has mountains and craters, and is far from the perfect sphere of Aristotelian orthodoxy. He discovered, most momentously perhaps, that Jupiter has four moons which rotate around it – an emblematic image of the Copernican vision of the solar system. He discovered that Saturn is not a perfect sphere – the first observational hint of Saturn's rings. He discovered that Venus has phases like the moon, an observation which can easily be explained given Copernicus's theory but which is almost impossible to explain given Ptolemy's. He discovered that the Milky Way is made up of a multitude of stars, an observation that supports the idea of Nicholas of Cusa, Bruno, Gilbert, and others that stars are spread out in an immense space – perhaps an infinite space. And he discovered that the sun has dark spots on its surface which rotate with the rotation of the sun and which come and go, a manifestation of imperfection and change.

Galileo reported these discoveries in *The Starry Messenger*, a book that made Galileo famous all over Europe – indeed, all over the educated world. A translation of the book appeared in China five years after its first publication in 1610.

Galileo worked on developing the second implication of Copernicus's theory, on and off, throughout much of his life. By far the most important of this work was his discovery of laws governing terrestrial motion.[24] His first discovery was made when he was sixteen years old, soon after first becoming interested in mathematics. During a sermon in the cathedral in Pisa, he noticed, using his pulse to measure time, that a swinging chandelier took the same time to complete a swing however wide or gentle its swings might be. Some years later, Galileo confirmed by experiments that the time a pendulum takes to execute one cycle of swings depends only on the length of the pendulum, and is independent of the amplitude of the swinging or the weight of the bob.

Galileo's most famous discovery concerning terrestrial motion is probably that all objects near the earth fall at the same rate whatever their weight may be, and fall with constant acceleration. Legend has it that Galileo dropped balls of different weight from the leaning tower of Pisa to refute Aristotle's claim that the rate of fall is proportional to the weight of the object. There is no evidence that Galileo did drop balls from the leaning tower of Pisa. The experiment was performed, rather, by an Aristotelian opponent to refute Galileo and confirm Aristotle. And that was the result claimed for the experiment: the heavy weight did hit the ground a bit before the light one! Galileo was scornful in his dismissal of this conclusion.[25] Historians of science used to believe that Galileo never did perform the experiment anywhere. But more recently, examination of Galileo's papers has revealed that he performed the experiment many times, noting the results with considerable accuracy. Galileo also sought to confirm his discovery that objects fall with constant acceleration by measuring the time balls take to roll down inclined planes – experiments which again, it seems, Galileo really did perform.[26]

Another achievement of Galileo is his discovery of the law of inertia: in the absence of friction or other forces, a body continues in its state of uniform motion in a straight line (and does not gradually come to rest as Aristotelianism holds). Closely associated with this is Galileo's enunciation of what, today, is called "Galilean invariance": laws governing motion – or, more generally, all laws – are the same with respect to all bodies as long as they are moving with uniform velocity in a straight line. In his *Dialogue concerning the Two Chief World Systems* published in 1632 (which in effect argued for Copernicus and against Ptolemy, and got Galileo into trouble with the Catholic Church), Galileo considers a ship travelling smoothly through a calm sea. He argues that no experiment performed in the cabin of the ship would be able to tell that the ship was in motion. Exactly the same results would be obtained as experiments performed at rest on land.

As I have indicated, these Galilean laws of terrestrial motion are of decisive importance when it comes to rebutting what were, at the time, standard objections to the Copernican theory. These laws explain why, for example, a stone thrown vertically into the air returns to the point from which it was thrown even though the earth is hurtling through space round the sun.

The law of inertia and Galilean invariance subsequently became key components of Newtonian physics and were not revised until the advent of Einstein's theory of special relativity in 1905.[27]

Galileo made clear that his laws of terrestrial motion ignored air resistance and friction. And indeed a feather falls as fast as lead shot in a vacuum.

Galileo did not succeed quite in enunciating the law of inertia in the form I have just stated it. He considered a ball rolling on a smooth plane and realized it would move in a giant circle as it travelled round the earth. For Galileo, inertial motion is circular motion, not motion in a straight line. It is possible that he hoped that his version of the law of inertia would somehow explain what he took to be the circular motion of the planets round the sun, the motion of the moon round the earth, and the motion of the moons of Jupiter. But any such idea neglects, of course, that these bodies are subject to the force of gravitation, and thus are not exhibiting inertial motion.

As I have already mentioned, it was Descartes who first articulated the law of inertia in its correct form: bodies continue in their state of rest or uniform motion in a straight line unless a force is impressed upon them.[28]

Galileo also discovered that projectiles trace out parabolas as they fly through the air – neglecting air resistance. (A parabola is an ellipse with one focus moved to infinity.) That projectiles do move along parabolas is a consequence, as Galileo demonstrated, of two of his other discoveries: the law of inertia, and the law of free fall with constant acceleration. It is because a thrown stone continues to have the motion it acquired when it left the hand, and at the same time falls towards the earth with constant acceleration, that it executes the path of a parabola as it flies through the air.

Galileo's achievements are remarkable, both for *what* he achieved, and for *how* he achieved it. More than any other of his contemporaries, Galileo strikes one as doing science in the way that scientists do it today. He is the first modern scientist – as well as a great natural philosopher! Not only does he exploit the telescope brilliantly to obtain observational results highly pertinent to the key cosmological problem of the time: Ptolemy or Copernicus? Even more strikingly, he performs experiments to test, to falsify or corroborate, theoretical conjectures. And he derives consequences from theories and tests them against the results of experiments.

Galileo was not, however, an out-and-out empiricist. He is quite clear that physical objects and natural phenomena exhibit mathematical structure. And not just any mathematics, but rather in essence *simple* mathematics. Thus it emerges that objects move in accordance with mathematically *simple* laws once one puts aside inessential complications due to friction and air resistance. The intrinsically simple mathematical structure of the universe makes it possible for us to discover what this structure is – as long as we acknowledge that it does have such a structure and develop, as a result, conjectures and theories that reflect this mathematical reality. There are, in short, two crucial components in Galileo's conception of scientific method. There is, first, the appeal to observation and experiment. But equally, there is the appeal to a quite definite metaphysical view of the universe: the book of nature is written in the language of mathematics – ultimately *simple* mathematics. Both play essential roles in Galileo's discoveries, not just psychologically, but methodologically.[29] As for Kepler, so for Galileo: *evidence* and *metaphysics* are both essential – the metaphysics being that the universe has some kind of underlying simple mathematical character.

One astonishing feature of Kepler's and Galileo's achievements is that the somewhat different astronomical and terrestrial motions that they discovered are both examples of conic sections. Conic sections are curves produced by the intersection of a plane with a circular cone. Imagine the cone stands upright on a table. If the intersecting plane is horizontal, the resulting curve of intersection is a circle. Tilt the plane, and the curve of intersection becomes an ellipse. Tilt the plane further so that its slope is as steep as the slope of the cone's side, and the curve of intersection becomes a parabola. Tilt the plane even further so that its slope is even steeper than the sides of the cone, and the curve of intersection becomes a hyperbola (or a pair of straight lines if the plane intersects the apex of the cone). The elliptical paths of planets, and the parabolic paths of stones thrown on earth, though different, nevertheless belong to a common class of curves. Even more astonishingly, conic sections were first identified and studied by ancient Greek mathematicians, Menaechmus, Apollonius, and others, almost 2,000 years before Kepler and Galileo discovered that planets in the heavens and stones hurled on earth travel along conic sections. We have here a dramatic example of something that has occurred on a number of occasions in the history of science: mathematicians exploring mathematical ideas with no thought whatsoever for applications to the physical universe nevertheless come up with discoveries which turn out to depict the way physical phenomena occur with incredible accuracy. It is as if mathematicians' minds are attuned, in some mysterious way, to the inner workings of nature. This capacity of pure mathematics to anticipate subsequent physics has baffled scientists and philosophers.[30] An explanation will be proposed in chapter 5 (note 17)!

NEWTON

The next great natural philosopher for us to consider is Isaac Newton. Building on the contributions of his great predecessors – Copernicus, Kepler, Galileo, and Descartes – Newton produced a kind of triumphant synthesis of their work. But it was much more than a synthesis of his predecessors. Newton laid the foundations for classical physics, which met with ever-expanding empirical success until the theories of relativity and quantum theory in the twentieth century. And even today, long after the advent of these twentieth-century theories, it is still Newtonian physics that is used to calculate the paths of spaceships and artificial satellites. Newton put forward the first fundamental dynamical theory of physics ever – his theory of gravitation.[31] There are only six successful fundamental dynamical theories in physics, and Newton's was the first.[32] To some of his contemporaries and immediate successors, it seemed that Newton had done something almost miraculous. He had discovered the secret of the universe. He had put his finger on what it is that causes the earth, the moon, the planets and the stars to move as they do throughout the universe, for all time. There is a sense in which, with Newton, modern science comes of age. But, as we shall see, though Newton was clearly a natural philosopher himself, his work nevertheless played a key role in the demise of natural philosophy – its disintegration into science and philosophy.[33]

What, in a bit more detail, did Newton achieve? First, he created the differential and integral calculus, mathematics required to describe motion and change more generally, and essential for the subsequent development of physics.[34] But it is in the three Books of his *Principia*,[35] published in 1687, that Newton laid the foundations of classical physics and demonstrated how his universal law of gravitation was able to predict and explain the motions of the planets, moons, and comets of the solar system, together with a wealth of other phenomena as well. In the preface to the first edition of the *Principia*, Newton makes clear what he sets out to do – and even specifies clearly the research programme for the future of physics.

The whole burden of philosophy seems to consist in this – from the phenomena of motions to investigate the forces of nature, and then from these forces to demonstrate the other phenomena; and to this end the general propositions in the first and second Books are directed. In the third Book I give an example of this in the explication of the System of the World; for by the propositions mathematically demonstrated in the former Books, in the third I derive from the celestial phenomena the forces of gravity with which bodies tend to the sun and the several planets. Then from these forces, by other propositions which are also mathematical, I deduce the motions of the planets, the comets, the moon, and the sea. I wish we could derive the rest of the phenomena of Nature by the same kind of reasoning from mechanical principles, for I am induced by many reasons to suspect that they may all depend upon certain forces by which the particles of bodies, by some causes hitherto unknown, are either mutually impelled towards one another, and cohere in regular figures, or are repelled and recede from one another. These forces being unknown, philosophers have hitherto attempted the search of Nature in vain; but I hope the principles here laid down will afford some light either to this or some truer method of philosophy.[36]

Newton's suspicion – the conjecture he expresses here about the nature of the physical universe and the path physics would take in the future – has turned out to be substantially correct, even if Newtonian principles have had to be revised along the way. Three forces in addition to gravitation suffice in principle to account for all the known phenomena of Nature – properties of matter, electromagnetic, chemical and nuclear phenomena.[37]

In Book 1 of the *Principia*, after defining crucial notions such as "quantity of motion" (mass times velocity, or momentum), Newton formulates the following three laws of motion, the basis for classical mechanics:

> I Every body continues in its state of rest, or of uniform motion in a right line, unless it is compelled to change that state by forces impressed upon it.
> II The change of motion is proportional to the motive force impressed; and is made in the direction of the right line in which that force is impressed.
> III To every action there is always opposed an equal reaction: or, the mutual actions of two bodies upon each other are always equal, and directed to contrary parts.[38]

The second of these laws in effect asserts that the force, F, on a body is equal to the mass, m, times the acceleration, a, of the body, that is: $F = ma$.

Newton then goes on in Book 1 to prove a great number of propositions and theorems, many, but by no means all, related to the tasks of establishing his universal law of gravitation and using it to explain the System of the World – that is, the solar system – to be taken up in Book 3. Thus the first theorem proves that a body attracted by a force to a fixed point moves in such a way that the line joining the body to the fixed point sweeps out equal areas in equal times – echoes of Kepler's 2nd law! Theorem 2 establishes the converse: if a body moves so that a line joining it to a fixed point sweeps out equal areas in equal times then it is attracted to the fixed point by a force. Proposition 11 establishes that a body moving in an ellipse experiences a force directed at a focus of the ellipse, the strength of the force being inversely proportional to the square of the distance. Newton goes on to establish similar results for bodies moving in hyperbolas and parabolas. He then goes on, in Proposition 17, to prove the converse of these results, namely that if a body moves under the influence of a force directed towards a fixed point, the force varying inversely as the square of the distance, then the body will move in a conic section – an ellipse, parabola or hyperbola.

Book 2 is in the main concerned with the motion of bodies through fluids. It may have been written in part to refute Descartes' vortex theory of the solar system, according to which invisible swirling matter in space sweeps the planets round the sun (a modified version of which was also held by Huygens).

Book 3, exploiting the results of Book 1, sets out to establish Newton's universal law of gravitation and explain the System of the World. First, Newton makes explicit his conception of what we would today call "scientific method" in what he calls "Rules of Reasoning in Philosophy":

Rule 1: We are to admit no more causes of natural things than such as are both true and sufficient to explain their appearances.

Rule 2: Therefore to the same natural effects we must, as far as possible, assign the same causes.

Rule 3: The qualities of bodies, which admit neither intensification nor remission of degrees, and which are found to belong to all bodies within the reach of our experiments, are to be esteemed the universal qualities of all bodies whatsoever.

Rule 4: In experimental philosophy we are to look upon propositions inferred by general induction from phenomena as accurately or very nearly true, notwithstanding any contrary hypothesis that may be imagined, till such time as other phenomena occur, by which they may either be made more accurate, or liable to exceptions.[39]

Newton goes on to specify six "phenomena" – six regularities of the solar system – that form the empirical basis for arriving at the law of gravitation. These are that the moons of Jupiter and Saturn obey Kepler's 2nd and 3rd laws of planetary motion, and so too do the planets other than the earth in their motion round the sun; and our moon, in its motion round the earth, obeys Kepler's 2nd law.

We come now to the central claim of the *Principia* – a claim that was to have profound consequences for the subsequent development of science. Newton sets out to derive his law of gravitation from the phenomena by induction, appealing at various points to his laws of motion, theorems, and rules of reasoning.

Newton first proves, in Proposition 1, that the moons of Jupiter move subject to a force directed towards the centre of the planet that is inversely proportional to the square of the distance to the centre (i.e., $F \propto 1/D^2$, where D is the distance from the centre of the moon to the centre of Jupiter). He goes on to establish the same for the moons of Saturn and, in Proposition 2, the same for the planets (D in this case, of course, being the distance to the centre of the sun). The moon too is shown to obey the inverse square law (in Proposition 3). Then, invoking his first two rules of reasoning, Newton argues, in Proposition 4, that the force to which the moon is subject is the force of gravity – the very same force we feel on Earth and call gravity, responsible for bodies falling near the earth's surface. Likewise (Proposition 5), the moons of Jupiter are drawn towards Jupiter by the force of gravitation – as are the moons of Saturn towards Saturn. Indeed "there is a power of gravity tending towards all the planets." "And," Newton goes on, "since all attraction (by Law III) is mutual, Jupiter will therefore gravitate towards all his satellites, Saturn towards his, and the earth towards the moon, and the sun towards the planets." And "all the planets do gravitate towards one another" which means, Newton points out, that Jupiter and Saturn, when closest together, will sensibly disturb each other's motion, as the sun disturbs our moon's motion, and the sun and moon disturb our seas (causing the tides). Then (in Proposition 6), Newton sets out to establish that "all bodies gravitate towards every planet," weights of bodies, at any given distance from the centre of the planet, being proportional to the quantity matter (i.e., the mass). Newton then establishes in Proposition 7 that "there is a power of gravity pertaining to all bodies, that is proportional to several quantities of matter which they contain." Then, in Proposition 8, we have the theorem that, given two homogeneous spheres attracting each other by gravitation, the force on either towards the other "will be inversely as the square of the distance between their centres." Newton then establishes that the centre of the solar system is, not the centre of the sun, but rather the centre of gravity of the solar system, the sun being somewhat in motion with respect to this centre as it is tugged this way and that by the gravitational attraction of the planets. Newton then derives Kepler's laws for the planets *a priori*, as he puts it – the planets only moving precisely in ellipses, however, if gravitational forces between planets are neglected, and the sun is assumed not to move.[40]

Newton goes on to derive various consequences from his law of gravitation and what has been established so far. He discusses the flattening of the earth and other planets at the poles because of their rotation; variation in weight at different latitudes on the earth; gravitational attraction of the moon and sun producing the tides; the motion of the moon, affected by gravitational attraction of both the earth and sun (a difficult three-body problem which cannot be solved exactly); and the motion of comets, which are shown to be along conic sections (approximately parabolas close to the sun).

What Newton does in the *Principia* is extraordinarily impressive. It really does seem that Newton derives his universal law of gravitation from the phenomena, just as he claimed he had done. First, there are the purely mathematical theorems: bodies that move so as to obey Kepler's laws must be deflected from uniform motion in a straight line by a force that varies inversely as the square of the distance. Then, observation tells us that moons and planets do actually move so as to obey Kepler's laws. Therefore they must be subject to a force that varies inversely as the square of the distance. And since we can move, by degrees, from the motion of a stone thrown on earth to the motion of the moon round the earth, this force must be the force of gravitation, of which we are so familiar here on earth. Granted that every body in the universe gravitationally attracts every other body, it is clear that the motions of the moons and planets must deviate slightly from perfect Keplerian motion due to mutual gravitational attraction – the final, devastatingly convincing evidence in support of Newtonian theory.

The contrast with Kepler and Galileo is striking. Newton does not appeal to the metaphysical thesis that the universe has some kind of mathematical structure – or does not do so explicitly. He is quite clear. In a famous passage in the *Principia* he declares: "I have not been able to discover the cause of [the] properties of gravity from the phenomena, and I frame no hypotheses; for whatever is not deduced from the phenomena is to be called an hypothesis; and hypotheses, whether metaphysical or physical, whether of occult qualities or mechanical, have no place in experimental philosophy. In this philosophy particular propositions are inferred from the phenomena, and afterwards rendered general by induction."[41]

Newton, subsequently, was taken at his word. He became a hero of the Enlightenment. The *Principia* was seen as revealing what one has to do to secure knowledge. First, phenomena have to be reduced to precise regularities; then laws and theories can be inferred by induction, just as Newton had done, and had himself affirmed. No longer do natural philosophers need to engage in fruitless debate about metaphysics, philosophy, epistemology, and methodology. That could be left to the philosophers.

Newton's *Principia*, the moment of high triumph of the new natural philosophy also, paradoxically, spelled its downfall. It was Newton's *Principia* that led, eventually, to a decisive split between science and philosophy, and thus to the death of natural philosophy.

EPILOGUE: SCIENCE, PROGRESS, AND HISTORY

In this chapter I have argued that science began as natural philosophy, and this brings together two crucial elements: first, a new metaphysical vision of the universe (it is made up of atoms; it is governed by precise mathematical laws); and, second, associated with this, the empirical method of careful observation and experimentation. Both are essential. The second element stems, in part, from the first. New theories, in order to be acceptable, must meet two requirements: they must accord sufficiently well with the new metaphysical view of the universe, and they must meet with sufficient empirical success.

This picture of the origins of science and the scientific revolution has been expounded and defended by a number of notable historians of science: A.E. Burtt, Alexandre Koyré, Herbert Butterfield, Richard Westfall,[42] and others. But some historians of science have called aspects of this orthodox picture into question. Pierre Duhem[43] argued that there is far more continuity in the development of science than the orthodox picture allows; research conducted in medieval times anticipated aspects of the work of Galileo and his contemporaries. Other historians of science have pointed out that some of those who contributed to natural philosophy around the time of Galileo did not accept atomism or the mathematical view of nature, and may have seen the world in Aristotelian terms. This is true of both William Gilbert and William Harvey. Others have denied that there is anything unique or distinctive about the scientific revolution, or even that it existed at all.

Burtt and Koyré seem to be out of fashion. This may be, in part, because both stressed the importance of so-called "internal" factors – intellectual and methodological factors – in the emergence of modern science. These days, "external" factors – social, institutional, cultural, economic, political – are all the fashion among many historians of science, and internal factors are regarded as somewhat passé. In fact we need to attend to both.[44] Modern science has institutional, social, cultural, economic, and political aspects: in order to tell how it arose and evolved, all these features need to be appealed to. But science is also an intellectual endeavour; it seeks to improve our knowledge and understanding of the universe, and of ourselves and other living things as a part of the universe, and in that endeavour it has met with astonishing success. In order to understand how that intellectual success has come about, we need to attend to the intellectual and methodological aspects of science just as much as its social, political, and economic aspects. Indeed, there are grounds for holding that the intellectual leads the way. It was because natural philosophy began to be astonishingly successful *intellectually*, that it was able to attract support, social status, and funds.

Many contemporary historians of science seem incapable of doing intellectual history of science because such history would be of an enterprise that seeks, and achieves, intellectual progress, which in turn would mean – they believe – that it would inevitably be disreputable "Whiggish" history.[45] But that is nonsense. As Popper argued decisively long ago, all history is of something more or less specific: "the history of art; or of language; or of feeding habits; or of typhus fever."[46] There is no such thing as "total" history – history of everything that has happened. One entirely legitimate specific topic for history is any endeavour that seeks to make progress or, more specifically, *science construed as an endeavour that seeks to make progress in knowledge*. In writing history of science so construed, one should not, of course, just assume that progress is inevitable, or even that it has occurred; nor should one write propaganda on behalf of science and its claims to have made progress. It does mean, however, that one selects out for attention those past episodes, contributions, events, that in retrospect constitute steps in the progress of scientific knowledge and understanding. In order to tell the history of science properly, it is vital to consider blind alleys, failed efforts, theories, and research that may have seemed promising at the time but led nowhere.

And it is important to consider what past contributions, research, and debates meant at the time, not just what they mean to us today. The crucial point to appreciate, however, is that intellectual history of science as an endeavour that seeks, and achieves, progress in knowledge lies at the heart of the discipline of history of science. The idea that such history must be "Whiggish" in some intellectually disreputable sense is an elementary blunder. Those who make the blunder render themselves incapable of writing history of science as a progress-achieving endeavour. The fundamental problem of the history of science – how and why scientific progress has come about – disappears from view.[47]

There is a more specific reason why Burtt and Koyré are out of fashion. Both held, I think it is fair to say, that modern science emerged from a new, significant intellectual and methodological discovery: *how to do science*.[48] This tends to be denied by a number of contemporary historians of science. I now consider the views of two such historians: Steven Shapin and Stephen Gaukroger.

Shapin begins his book *The Scientific Revolution* (1998) with the inflammatory sentence: "There was no such thing as the Scientific Revolution, and this is a book about it." He goes on to claim that science did not exist in the seventeenth century. Instead, there was "a diverse array of cultural practices aimed at understanding, explaining and controlling the natural world." It is doubtful, Shapin declares, that there is any such thing as scientific method, and even more doubtful that its origins are in the seventeenth century. There was no revolution in knowledge and understanding. On the contrary, natural philosophy displays continuity "with its medieval past."[49] In opposition to most of this, in this book I argue that natural philosophy, if not science, certainly did exist in the seventeenth century. There may well have been "a diverse array" of approaches to understanding nature, but this does not in any way challenge the profound significance of the work of Galileo, Kepler, Newton, and others associated with the new natural philosophy that led eventually to modern science. No one, surely, has thought that *everyone* was doing the new natural philosophy! In chapters 3 and 5 we will see that there very definitely *is* such a thing as scientific method, and its roots are to be found, above all, in the work of Galileo and Newton. A profound revolution in our knowledge and understanding of nature took place in the sixteenth and seventeeth centuries, associated with the work of Copernicus, Kepler, Galileo, Newton, and others. Continuity with medieval science is only apparent if we ignore the revolutionary character of the discoveries and methods of seventeenth-century natural philosophy.

Lurking behind Shapin's claims there is perhaps the "social constructivist" view that there is no such thing as scientific progress – or at least history of science must be conducted as if it does not exist.[50] If scientific progress does not exist, then of course the unprecedented progress made by Galileo, Newton, and others disappears, and *the* reason to acclaim their work by calling it "the scientific revolution" disappears as well. Take scientific progress seriously, and it is at once obvious that the scientific revolution exists and is of profound significance.

The idea that there is no such thing as scientific progress may gain sustenance from the long-standing failure of philosophers to explain how it is possible. That source of sustenance is removed by this book. As my argument unfolds, it will become abundantly clear, I trust, how progress in science – or rather in natural philosophy – is to be understood.

Stephen Gaukroger is more modest in his denial of the profound intellectual significance of the scientific revolution. He does not deny it exists, but holds that it was just the latest in a series of similar earlier revolutions. In his *The Emergence of a Scientific Culture* (2006) – a work of magnificent sweep and scope, rich in detail – he declares, "There have been a number of civilizations that have witnessed a form of 'scientific revolution.'" What distinguishes *the* scientific revolution from these earlier ones is its "uninterrupted and cumulative growth that constitutes the general rule for scientific developments in the West since that time."[51] It is the *persistence* of the science that emerged from *the* scientific revolution that distinguishes it, in Gaukroger's view, from earlier scientific revolutions in Europe, China, and the Islamic world. These earlier revolutions all exhibit a "pattern of slow, irregular, intermittent growth, alternating with substantial periods of stagnation, in which interest shifts to political, economic, technological, moral, or other questions."[52] Thus the persistent, accumulative character of modern science, stemming from *the* scientific revolution, does not come, for Gaukroger, from any new intellectual or methodological discovery; it comes, one might say, from persistent effort, a refusal to be distracted.

But all this is a mistake. Modern science does emerge from a new intellectual and methodological discovery: how to marry metaphysics and method, a specific view of the universe and a method of experiment and observation – experimentation linked to the new metaphysical view. (This has antecedents, of course, that go back to the ancient Greeks, to Democritus, Aristarchus, Eratosthenes, Archimedes, and Euclid.) This idea is all but encapsulated in the title of one of Koyré's books: *Metaphysics and Measurement*. There is a reason why *the* scientific revolution led to "uninterrupted and cumulative growth": a key discovery had been made about how to acquire knowledge progressively, not made by earlier "scientific revolutions."

In one respect I may differ from the views of Burtt and Koyré. I hold that the new methodological discovery, that led to modern science, never got properly articulated and understood. The natural philosophers who created modern science made a crucial discovery in scientific *practice*, but failed to make this discovery lucidly explicit. And this failure lingers on down to the present. Scientists today take for granted an untenable view of science that fails to do justice to what actually goes on in scientific practice – fails to do justice to what is responsible for the growth of scientific knowledge.[53]

It may be that it is this long-standing failure to get the progress-achieving methods of science properly into focus that is in part responsible for the failure of many historians of science to see that there is anything novel, methodologically, about the new natural philosophy. If *empiricism* is all that characterizes the methods of modern science then one may well hold that there is nothing especially distinctive *methodologically* about the scientific revolution, or the science that came from it.

A central concern of this book is to demonstrate that empiricism is not enough. Science needs evidence *and metaphysics*. Once this is appreciated, it becomes clear that we need a new conception of science which acknowledges explicitly metaphysical assumptions of science so that they can be critically assessed and, we may hope, improved. In chapters 3 and 5 I expound, argue for, and spell out implications of, this new conception of science, which I call *aim-oriented empiricism*. This view provides methods designed to facilitate the articulation, critical assessment, and improvement of metaphysical assumptions of science.[54] It is the methodological framework for synthesizing metaphysics and empiricism, science and philosophy, and thus recreating something close to seventeenth-century natural philosophy.

Scientific progress has been possible because scientists have managed to come close to implementing aim-oriented empiricism in scientific practice, even though they have not understood their scientific work in this way. Science would become even more successful, in both intellectual and humanitarian terms, I shall argue, in chapters 5, 6, and 8, if it put aim-oriented empiricism consciously and explicitly into practice.

But is it conceivable that *what scientists do* is at odds with *what they think they are doing*? One rather well-known scientist thought so – a scientist who made profound contributions to science as a result of implementing methods close to those of aim-oriented empiricism, and came close to *advocating* aim-oriented empiricism explicitly. That scientist is Albert Einstein.[55] And he remarked on one occasion, "If you want to find out anything from the theoretical physicists about the methods they use, I advise you to stick closely to one principle: don't listen to their words, fix your attention on their deeds."[56]

In this chapter and the next I attend only to the bare minimum required to sketch the story of the fundamental *intellectual* blunder, traceable back to Newton, inherent in our current conceptions of science – a blunder all historians of science known to me ignore. I might add that histories of science which ignore the intellectual and methodological aspects of science thereby deprive themselves of even the possibility of uncovering damaging intellectual blunders inherent in the birth and evolution of modern science. The very possibility of *criticizing* aspects of modern science vanishes. The fundamental *problem* of the history of science disappears as well – the problem of improving our understanding of how science has made such astonishing intellectual progress.

Fortunately, there is a recent, magnificent account of the rise of modern science that does do justice to the intellectual and methodological issues involved, and explores them in rich and fascinating detail: H. Floris Cohen's *How Modern Science Came into the World* (2010). Cohen fully appreciates just how extraordinary the great discoveries of the scientific revolution are – and how astonishing subsequent scientific progress has proved to be. But Cohen, like other historians of science, fails to point out that the scientific community even today still fails to get the nature of the progress-achieving methods of science sharply into focus. We are not really in a position to tell the story properly of how humanity discovered how to do science until we get clear about *what it was that humanity did discover*!

2

Emergence of Science

As I indicated towards the end of the last chapter, Newton in the *Principia* proceeds in a way that is dramatically different from his great predecessors. Kepler and Galileo appealed to both evidence and metaphysics. Observation and, in the case of Galileo especially, experiment, were of decisive importance. But so was the metaphysical thesis that the universe has some kind of harmonious mathematical structure, motion – whether terrestrial or astronomical – thus obeying simple mathematical laws. Neither claimed to have derived the laws they discovered solely from the phenomena by means of induction. Both assumed that the metaphysical thesis that the "book of nature is written in the language of mathematics" gives one an assurance that simple mathematical laws govern motion. The role of observation and experiment is then to select out those simple laws which nature has chosen to adopt.

But Newton, as we have seen, abjures any such metaphysical assumption. He makes the amazing claim to have derived his law of gravitation solely from the phenomena by induction. It was this, together with the immense success and prestige achieved by Newton's work, that led to the quiet death of natural philosophy and to the emergence of science. In this chapter I write the obituary of natural philosophy. I show how it died, and gave way to natural science.[1]

The first point to appreciate is that Newton did *not* do what he claimed he had done: derive his law of gravitation from the phenomena without recourse to metaphysical hypotheses. Indeed, Newton makes this clear himself in the *Principia*.

Newton's "derivation" of his law of gravitation appeals at various points to one or other of his four rules of reason,[2] and these rules all concern simplicity or unity and in effect make implicit metaphysical assumptions concerning the simplicity or unity of nature. As far as the first three rules are concerned, Newton makes this point quite clear himself in his comments. He makes it clear that adopting each rule amounts to making a big assumption – in effect a metaphysical assumption – about the nature of the universe.

Thus, in connection with rule 1 he declares that "Nature is pleased with simplicity, and affects not the pomp of superfluous causes."[3] Rule 1 is a good rule to adopt if Nature is indeed pleased with simplicity, but it would be a bad rule to adopt if Nature adored the pomp of superfluous causes. Adopting the rule as a rule of reasoning in natural philosophy thus amounts to accepting a big, highly problematic metaphysical conjecture about the nature of the universe.

Rule 2, it may be remembered, asserts that "to the same natural effects we must, as far as possible, assign the same causes," which Newton illustrates by remarking: "As to respiration in a man and in a beast; the descent of stones in Europe and in America; the light of our culinary fire and of the sun; the reflection of light in the earth, and in the planets."[4] Here again, this is a sensible rule to adopt if the universe is such that, on the whole, similar effects do have similar causes – that is, if the metaphysical doctrine asserting this is true. But in a perversely wilful universe which loves to assign quite different causes to similar effects, it would be a bad rule to adopt. And much the same holds as far as rule 3 is concerned.

For these rules to be good rules to follow in natural philosophy, ones which lead to authentic knowledge, the universe must be such that the same laws govern phenomena everywhere, so that, for example, it is reasonable to generalize from terrestrial phenomena to phenomena everywhere. If Aristotle had been right, and there is a fundamental distinction between terrestrial and heavenly phenomena, Newton's rules would have been exactly the *wrong* rules to adopt. Nothing could illustrate more clearly the point that Newton's four rules of reasoning make metaphysical presuppositions about the nature of the universe.[5]

That Newton's law of gravitation cannot be selected (let alone established) on the basis of evidence alone is decisively established by the fact that any number of theories different from Newton's can be formulated which predict, just as successfully as Newton's theory does, all the phenomena known to Newton and his contemporaries. One such rival might postulate additional forces which do not apply to the solar system but which do apply to stars and other heavenly bodies far away, which gravitate towards one another in accordance with laws different from Newton's, but not so that the difference would be observable to Newton or his contemporaries. Such a theory (and endlessly many could be concocted along these lines) successfully predicts all the phenomena known to Newton, and which his theory predicts. Another rival theory asserts: all bodies move in accordance with (Newton's) laws of motion and law of gravitation except for Mercury, whose perihelion advances at 42.98 arcseconds per century in excess of that predicted by Newtonian theory. This grossly ad hoc rival fits the phenomena even better than Newtonian theory! Another rival predicts that everything occurs as Newtonian theory predicts except for solid gold spheres of mass greater than 1,000 tons; for such spheres, the gravitational force between them obeys, not Newton's inverse square law, but an inverse cube law.

On what grounds are these theories to be excluded? Not because they are not as empirically successful as Newtonian theory, but because they all clash with Newton's first three rules of reason; they are to be excluded on that ground. But in invoking these three rules, one thereby appeals, implicitly, to metaphysical hypotheses about the nature of the universe, as Newton himself acknowledges. Newton's claim that his law of gravitation is derived from the phenomena by induction without recourse to hypotheses, metaphysical or physical, collapses. Evidence alone does not suffice to determine acceptance of Newton's law of gravitation. One needs evidence *plus metaphysical hypotheses implicit in Newton's first three rules of reason.*[6]

Nevertheless, as we saw towards the end of the last chapter, Newton is explicit and emphatic in his claim to have derived his law of gravitation from the phenomena without recourse to hypotheses "whether metaphysical or physical."[7] And yet, paradoxically, Newton himself acknowledges, in his comments on at least three of his four rules of reasoning – rules that play an essential role in his "derivation" of his law of gravitation from the phenomena – that employing these rules involves making "metaphysical hypotheses" about the nature of the universe. The very process of "deriving" the law of gravitation from the phenomena contradicts Newton's claim to make no metaphysical hypothesis – and Newton is quite explicit himself that metaphysical hypotheses are involved and required![8]

All this raises fascinating questions. Was Newton himself aware that he had contradicted himself in his comments on his first three rules of reasoning, where he had made it quite clear that his derivation of his law of gravitation from the phenomena did make metaphysical hypotheses about the nature of the universe? Was Newton perhaps well aware that he could not possibly claim to have derived his law from the phenomena *alone*, without recourse to metaphysical hypotheses? Could it even be that Newton here knowingly practised something like a confidence trick? Could he have hoped that his comments on his first three rules would be interpreted to be nothing more than rhetorical flourishes, not to be taken seriously at all? Could he have hoped that, in this way, he would succeed in concealing his essential reliance on metaphysical hypotheses in "deriving" his law from the phenomena? If so, he was extraordinarily successful in pulling off this confidence trick, as we shall see below.

It could be that when he wrote and first published the *Principia*, Newton was unaware of the issue. Perhaps it only dawned on him subsequently. In fact, a number of changes made to the first edition, in the second and third editions of the *Principia* published in 1713 and 1726, indicate strongly that Newton consciously sought to eliminate *hypotheses* and *metaphysics* from the derivation of the law of gravitation from the phenomena. In the first edition of 1687, instead of the *rules of reasoning* and *phenomena* of the second edition, there are nine propositions, all baldly entitled *hypotheses*. The first two of these *hypotheses* become the first two *rules of reasoning* of the second and third editions, and the last five *hypotheses*, which concern the solar system, become the *phenomena* of later editions. *Hypothesis* III of the first edition disappears altogether in later editions,[9] while hypothesis IV, which asserts that the centre of the solar system is immovable, is tucked away, after *Proposition* X, *Theorem* X of Book III, as *Hypothesis* I. An additional *hypothesis* of the first edition, a rather strange proposition concerning the earth being replaced by a rotating ring, becomes in subsequent editions *Hypothesis* II, again tucked away, this time after Lemma III of Proposition XXXVIII of Book III. Newton also added the third rule of reasoning in the second edition, and the fourth rule was added to the third edition.[10] Newton is clearly determined to remove all trace of "hypothesis" from the crucial initial assumptions of his "derivation" of his law of gravitation from the phenomena.

Furthermore, in editions subsequent to the first, Newton does what he can to tone down or eliminate the idea that his "derivation" in any way appeals to metaphysics. Thus, in the first edition, in connection with *hypothesis* I – later to become *rule of reasoning* I – Newton asserts: "For nature is simple and does not luxuriate in superfluous causes of things." This bald metaphysical statement of the first edition becomes, in Koyré's translation from the Latin of the second edition, "To this purpose, the philosophers say: Nature does nothing in vain, and it is in vain to do by more that which can be done by fewer."[11] The bald metaphysical proposition of the first edition has become a proposition merely about *what philosophers say* in the second edition!

Even more strikingly, Newton's very strong statement that he derived his law of gravitation from the phenomena without recourse to hypotheses "whether metaphysical or physical," quoted towards the end of the last chapter, was only added to the second edition of the *Principia* published twenty-six years after the first edition.[12] In the third edition, there appeared for the first time Newton's fourth rule of reasoning, concerning induction from phenomena in general.[13] Newton's comment on this rule, quite unlike his earlier comments on his first three rules, makes no reference to metaphysical hypotheses about the nature of the universe at all. He says merely, "This rule we must follow, that the argument of induction may not be evaded by hypotheses."[14] Far from explicitly stating, as earlier, that the rule makes a metaphysical hypothesis, Newton, quite to the contrary, explicitly states that the rule must be followed so that hypotheses are *not* made. It is these additions to later editions of the *Principia*, then, which seem specifically designed to create the impression that the law of gravitation is derived by means of induction solely from the phenomena without any appeal being made to metaphysical hypotheses.[15]

Newton's fourth rule of reasoning does not succeed in doing this, of course. Generalizing from observed phenomena to all phenomena everywhere, as this fourth rule tells us to do, is only sensible, and will only meet with success, if the universe exhibits the required kind of uniformity, so that what goes on for a highly restricted range of phenomena, for a highly restricted region of space and period of time – all we can ever observe – is relevant to what goes on everywhere, throughout all time and all space, for all the vast reaches of the universe. Even though, in his comment on rule 4, Newton fails to draw attention to the metaphysical presuppositions implicit in the rule, nevertheless metaphysical presuppositions are there, despite Newton's failure to acknowledge them (or his deliberate intention to conceal their presence and inevitability).

Thus Newton does not forego metaphysical hypotheses. The transition from Kepler and Galileo to Newton amounts to a surreptitious slide from metaphysics to methodology. Instead of metaphysics being openly acknowledged, from the second edition on it is smuggled in by a sleight of hand, implicit in "rules of reasoning in philosophy" – at least as far as the argument for the law of gravitation and its role in explaining the system of the world is concerned.

This is not a gain in rationality. It is rational to acknowledge openly and explicitly assumptions that one is making – for that exposes one's assumptions to possible criticism, and to improvement, if it is needed. Progress in knowledge and understanding is facilitated. Smuggling in assumptions in a surreptitious fashion is anti-rational precisely because such assumptions may be hard to detect, and thus hard to subject to critical scrutiny and, where required, improvement.

Thus, despite the appearance that Newton's arguments in the *Principia* meet far higher standards of rigour than arguments to be found in Kepler and Galileo, in one all-important respect this is not the case at all – at least as far as the second and third editions are concerned. Kepler and Galileo, in openly acknowledging background metaphysical assumptions, were more rigorous than Newton, who sought to conceal such assumptions – or at least did conceal them.

Newton had powerful motives for attempting to convince his readers that his law had been derived solely from the phenomena. Presenting his work in that light provided the strongest possible grounds for holding the law to be decisively established, beyond all doubt and controversy. Newton would have wanted to do that in an attempt to forestall criticism, whether anticipated or received. He was fully aware of the fact that his law of gravitation, apparently postulating the existence of a force operating across empty space, without any agency to convey it, would be found by some to be thoroughly objectionable. And his law did indeed encounter opposition, just as he must have anticipated. Thus Huygens in a letter to Leibniz declared, "Concerning the Cause of the flux given by M. Newton, I am by no means satisfied [by it], nor by all the other theories he builds upon his Principle of Attraction, which seems to me absurd ... I have often wondered how he could have given himself all the trouble of making such a number of investigations and difficult calculations that have no other foundation than this very principle."[16] Huygens in fact agreed that Newton had shown that planets move so as to be subject to a force that varies inversely with the square of the distance to the sun. What he rejected was the Newtonian thesis that every particle of matter attracts every other particle in the universe in accordance with Newton's law of gravitation.[17] The action-at-a-distance aspect of Newton's theory meant that he was accused of reintroducing old, discredited Aristotelian "occult" qualities into natural philosophy. There was a failure to distinguish between a teleological thesis, which seeks to account for the actions of a body as striving to attain some distant goal, and a thesis of physical law, which specifies in precise, mathematical terms how a body moves, or accelerates.

There is a sense in which Newton agreed with Huygens's doubts about the force of gravity, as he indicates in the remark: "That gravity should be innate, inherent, and essential to matter, so that one body may act upon another, at a distance through a vacuum, without the mediation of anything else ... is to me so great an absurdity, that I believe no man who has in philosophical matters a competent faculty of thinking can ever fall into it."[18] In a certain sense, Newton rejected his own law of gravitation! Newton, like Huygens and other Cartesians, found the idea that a force could act at a distance across empty space without anything to mediate it utterly "absurd." The big difference between Newton and Huygens was that, whereas Huygens thought there had to be a Cartesian explanation for the force of gravity in terms of invisible, whirling particles of aetherial matter filling space and interacting by contact, Newton was apparently much more open-minded about what the ultimate explanation for the force of gravity might be. Huygens could not imagine that there could be a Cartesian explanation for the universal law of gravitation – one that could account for every particle in the universe attracting every other particle in accordance with the inverse law. His commitment to Cartesianism compelled him to reject the universal law of gravitation. Newton, on the other hand, opposed as he was to Cartesianism, in part probably on religious grounds, was more open-minded about the ultimate explanation for the force of gravitation, and so he was able to accept his universal law of gravitation, not as an ultimate explanation, but rather as a description of how particles and bodies do in fact move under the influence of gravity.

Newton's attempt to establish his law so decisively that it was beyond all doubt had another, more personal motive. Notoriously, Newton hated controversy.[19] Whenever he became embroiled in it, as he did in effect with Leibniz over questions about the nature of space and who had first invented the calculus, Newton got his supporters to present his side of the matter for him. Newton may have hoped that his claim to have derived his law solely from the phenomena would mean the law would not become a matter of controversy. He may have made his claim that he did not appeal to metaphysical hypotheses much more explicit in later editions of the *Principia* in part at least to combat criticism he had already encountered.

There is, however, another consideration to bear in mind when pondering Newton's failure to acknowledge the role that metaphysics played in his argument for his universal law of gravitation in the *Principia*. Newton *rejected* the metaphysical view of nature espoused, in slightly different forms, by Kepler and Galileo (and Descartes, Huygens, Gassendi, and others). He *rejected* the thesis that the universe has a harmonious mathematical structure, and that all natural phenomena are the outcome of particles interacting in accordance with precise physical law. As it happens, he is quite explicit about this in the *Principia*. In the famous General Scholium added to the second edition of the *Principia*, Newton declared, "This most beautiful system of the sun, planets, and comets, could only proceed from the counsel and dominion of an intelligent and powerful Being."[20] Newton seems to have held that God actively intervenes in the physical world, adjusting positions or velocities of planets from time to time to ensure the stability of the solar system.[21] He may even have held that God is ultimately responsible for the force of gravity, from instant to instant as it were. In a letter of 1692, Newton said, "When I wrote my treatise about our system, I had an eye on such principles as might work with considering men for the belief of a Deity; and nothing can rejoice me more than to find it useful for that purpose."[22] If there is a purely *physical* explanation for gravity, why should the *Principia* persuade "men for the belief of a Deity"? Newton may have regarded God as being actively in charge of and responsible for natural phenomena from moment to moment, the physically inexplicable character of gravitation being for him welcome, for it would mean that, in the end, everyone would be obliged to acknowledge that God must ultimately be in control.

Newton is, in many ways, a complicated and paradoxical figure. His weirdly medieval outlook meant that he did not share the metaphysical views of the cosmos of many of his contemporaries and great predecessors. He both exploits and rejects the views of his predecessors. His work implicitly presupposed and required a metaphysical outlook similar to that of Kepler and Galileo, and his work is inconceivable without the example of their great prior work. At the same time, Newton's rejection of the metaphysics associated with the new natural philosophy freed him to entertain possibilities which even his great contemporaries, Huygens and Leibniz, could not take seriously.

Could Newton really have consciously set out to deceive his readers into thinking no metaphysical hypotheses were involved in his derivation of his law of gravitation from the phenomena? Who knows? What is beyond doubt, as we have seen, is that even though Newton acknowledged openly and fully the vital role of *metaphysical hypotheses* in the first edition of the *Principia*, he removed all trace of "hypotheses," and especially *metaphysical* hypotheses, from basic assumptions required to derive the law of gravitation in the later editions. Furthermore, in the second and third editions, Newton states strongly that he derives his law of gravitation from the phenomena by induction without recourse to hypotheses, whether metaphysical or physical; and in the third edition he adds his fourth rule of reasoning, to be employed "so that the argument may not be evaded by hypotheses."

All this looks to me like a conscious cover-up. Even though the *Principia* began as a great work of natural philosophy in the manner of Kepler and Galileo, Newton deliberately set out to obscure the hypothetical and metaphysical dimensions of his work in later editions, so as to mislead his audience into thinking his law was derived by induction solely from the *phenomena*, solely from *evidence*.

Certainly there were strong motives to do it, as I have indicated. And certainly Newton could be mean enough to do such a thing. He was not exactly the noble figure the Enlightenment liked to think of him as being.[23] To give just one example, Robert Hooke seems to have been the first person to have the key idea as to how the solar system works: bodies free of forces move in straight lines and therefore the planets must be attracted towards the sun by a force to cause them to move in ellipses around the sun.[24] Hooke published this idea before anyone else, and Newton got the idea from Hooke: it was in a letter Hooke wrote to Newton in 1679.[25] Furthermore, Hooke arrived at the idea of universal gravitation independently of Newton, and the inverse square law,[26] and was the first person to publish the law.[27] Granted all this, one would think that Hooke deserved to be mentioned by Newton in his *Principia*. When Hooke discovered he was to receive scarcely any mention at all in the *Principia*, he pleaded with Halley – on good terms with Newton – to ask Newton to do his work justice. Newton's response was to remove what reference there was to Hooke's contributions! And down the centuries, Hooke's contribution has been forgotten – until quite recently.[28]

NEWTON VERSUS DESCARTES

The publication of the *Principia* led, eventually, to the death of natural philosophy and the rise, in its stead, of natural science. But this way of describing what happened is, in a way, highly misleading. Before I go into details, I must first make a few general clarifying remarks about what actually occurred.

First of all, everyone involved continued to speak of natural philosophy, for a century or so. Not till the nineteenth century did "natural philosophy" largely disappear, the term "science" coming into general use instead.[29] And even today there are some universities in Scotland that still speak of "natural philosophy" rather than "science" or "physics."

Second, natural philosophy in the sense in which we are speaking of it here – *authentic natural philosophy*, as we may call it, the endeavour pursued by Kepler, Galileo, Huygens, and even Newton, that included science, metaphysics, philosophy, epistemology and methodology – died very quietly indeed, almost unnoticed.[30] One might suppose that there was a great debate between proponents of natural philosophy and proponents of science. Nothing of the kind took place. No one sprang to the defence of natural philosophy. No one noticed its demise.

Instead, after the publication of the *Principia*, there was a quite different dispute. Natural philosophers split into two camps: on the one hand, the supporters of Newton, the empiricists, in the main in England; and on the other hand, the supporters of Descartes, the rationalists, in the main in France. As Voltaire put it decades later in his *Lettres Philosophiques*:

A Frenchman arriving in London finds things very different, in philosophy as in everything else. He has left the world full, he finds it empty. In Paris they see the universe as composed of vortices of subtle matter, in London they see nothing of the kind ... For your Cartesians everything is moved by an impulsion you don't really understand, for Mr. Newton it is by gravitation, the cause of which is hardly better known.[31]

This dispute between supporters of Descartes and Newton, or, more generally, between supporters of rationalism and empiricism (Descartes the hero of rationalism, Newton the hero of empiricism), is related to, but is not at all the same thing as, a possible clash of views about the relative merits of natural philosophy and science. Rationalism is not at all the same thing as natural philosophy as we have been considering it, practised by Kepler, Galileo, and others. Rationalists hold that there are some metaphysical propositions about the world whose truth can be established decisively by reason alone, independently of evidence. Natural philosophy adopts, as an unproven *conjecture*, the metaphysical thesis that the universe is made up of one kind of physical entity – corpuscles or atoms perhaps – which interact in accordance with simple mathematical laws, the universe having some kind of simple, harmonious mathematical structure. Laws and theories of natural philosophy are to be accepted when (a) they are compatible with the basic metaphysical conjecture of mathematical harmony, and (b) accord with the results of observation or experiment.

After the publication of Newton's *Principia* there ought to have taken place a great debate concerning the relative merits of natural philosophy, as just characterized, and Newton's conception of natural philosophy, which held that all laws and theories are to be derived by induction from phenomena without recourse to hypotheses, "whether metaphysical or physical." If such a debate had taken place, one can only think that Newton's *physics* would have been triumphantly accepted but his *methodology* would have been rejected. It would have been rejected for the reasons already indicated: the very rules of inductive reason that Newton specifies in effect make metaphysical conjectures. Indeed, in connection with the first three, Newton makes this point emphatically himself! (Although he did later contradict himself, as we have seen.) Natural philosophy would have flourished, incorporating Newton's physics and Kepler's and Galileo's methodology.

But none of this occurred. No one sought to distinguish Newton's *physics* from his *methodology*. Instead these two very different elements came as one package. No one sprang to the defence of what might be called the Kepler-Galileo conception of natural philosophy. Instead, the great battle was between Newton and Descartes. Natural philosophy, just at the moment of its greatest triumph, faded away unnoticed, unsung and unlamented.

Paradoxically, then, science emerged not by defeating natural philosophy – that which gave it birth – but rather as a result of the defeat of Descartes and rationalism.

Descartes differed from Newton in two absolutely fundamental ways. He put forward a physics, an account of the solar system, a cosmology, that differed profoundly from Newton's, as the quotation from Voltaire indicates (and as we saw briefly in the last chapter). And he propounded an epistemology and methodology that differs dramatically from Newton's.

Whereas Newton was (or was taken to be) an out-and-out empiricist, Descartes was a rationalist, in that he held that reason can establish knowledge about the world – with some help from experience. Descartes' rationalism was, however, born of a ferocious skepticism. And Descartes seemed to have very good reasons for his skepticism.

As we saw in the last chapter in connection with Galileo, there is a deep underlying paradox inherent in the new natural philosophy: on the one hand it appeals to observation and experiment, while on the other it calls these into question, in that the new (or re-vitalized) metaphysical vision of the universe – atomism, or the corpuscular hypothesis – tells us that perception is profoundly delusive. If the universe really is composed exclusively of corpuscles – or of the physical particles of modern physics – physical entities that are without colour, sound, smell and other sensory qualities, then our ordinary perceptual experiences of the world around us must be almost wholly delusive. The world is in reality wholly different from the way we ordinarily perceive it to be. Furthermore, the corpuscular hypothesis, or our modern physical theories, when applied to the processes of perception, may well seem to imply that our ordinary perceptions must be delusive because what we really see is not objects external to us, but rather the outcome of a long, complicated chain of events. When I perceive a red rose, light of such and such a range of wavelengths (or photons of such and such a range of energies), emitted from the rose, enters my eyes and causes chemical processes to occur in cells in the retinas of my eyes, which in turn cause cells of my optic nerve to fire, which in turn cause neurons of my brain to fire – and only then do I have the visual experience of seeing the red rose. Whether one conceives of this process in the way Descartes would have conceived of it, in terms of seventeenth-century corpuscular ideas, or in terms of the science of the twenty-first century, the conclusion may well be held to be the same: the visual experience of seeing the red rose is quite different from the physical object in the world which we dub "the rose." Given the long chain of transformations that occur between the physical rose and my perception of it, we seem to have good reasons to hold that what I appear to see differs radically from the external cause – the physical rose.[32]

It is thus not surprising that Descartes, upholding a version of the corpuscular hypothesis, and well aware of the kind of considerations I have just indicated, should come to have serious doubts about the truthfulness of observation, the capacity of perception to deliver authentic knowledge about the world.[33] The extraordinary optimism of the new natural philosophy, its immense confidence that it will be able to acquire entirely new knowledge and understanding of the universe of great depth and scope, comes with it very strong reasons for being highly skeptical of the capacity of our eyes and ears to provide us with reliable knowledge.

Descartes is confronted by a very real problem of skepticism, of how knowledge is possible at all. He rose to the challenge. He decided to doubt everything that it was possible to doubt, in the hope of arriving at a nugget of secure knowledge which could not be doubted. His senses might deceive (indeed almost certainly did deceive!); and reason, too, might deceive, but he could not doubt that he was doubting or, in other words, thinking. Hence Descartes's famous foundation of certainty for his entire philosophy: *I think, therefore I am*. Having established beyond doubt that his conscious mind exists, Descartes then argues that he can entertain the idea of a Being more perfect than himself. This Being must exist since, if He did not, He would lack perfection. Having established the existence of a beneficent God in this way, to his own satisfaction, Descartes argues that God would not wickedly deceive us. Hence, whatever is clear and distinct must be true. This means, Descartes argues, that the universe is made up of corpuscles that have just one property: extension. The universe is to be understood exclusively in the clear and distinct ideas of geometry.

There is no such thing as empty space. The vacuum is filled with invisible, intangible corpuscles. These, whirling about in space in vortices, cause the planets to move around the sun. Descartes did not entirely discount the role of experiment and observation in natural philosophy, but he relegated them to a rather minor role. One may need to appeal to evidence to decide between rival specific corpuscular mechanisms for some specific natural phenomenon.

Today, after over three centuries of empirical science stemming from Newton, Cartesian rationalism seems a somewhat absurd position to adopt. But in Descartes's time, there were considerations which led to it seeming much less absurd. First, the metaphysics of the new natural philosophy, as we have just seen, cast doubt on the capacity of experience to deliver knowledge. Second, mathematics must have seemed then to provide us with definite knowledge established by reason without recourse to evidence – and mathematics, of course, had a vital role to play in the new natural philosophy. The distinction we draw today between pure and applied mathematics – only the latter being about the world and therefore conjectural, and dependent on experience for confirmation – did not really exist. Finally, Euclidean geometry would have seemed to be a paradigmatic example of a branch of mathematics established by reason that embodied significant knowledge about the nature of physical space. From a few simple and undeniable axioms, a wealth of theorems had been derived depicting facts, it would have seemed, about the nature of space. (Not till the advent of Einstein's general theory of relativity did it emerge that Euclidean geometry, interpreted as a physical theory about the nature of space, is false!)

It is even possible to think of Cartesian physics and cosmology as a slight extension of Euclidean geometry. Descartes's theory is usually interpreted as asserting that the universe is full of matter – there being no such thing as empty space. But since, according to Descartes, the only properties which particles of matter possess are extension and relative motion, one might also characterize the theory as asserting that everything is made up of empty space – space itself being made up of tiny spatial bits in relative motion. Looked at in that way, Descartes's theory could be thought of as an extension of Euclidean geometry that postulates, in addition to Euclid, that space consists of spatial bits in relative motion. The whole of physics might just be an extension of Euclidean geometry, it being possible to derive all the laws of physics from the axioms of Euclidean geometry plus a few equally elementary and obvious axioms covering the relative motions of bits of space. This even seems to be the way Descartes himself viewed the matter. In a letter to Mersenne, Descartes wrote, "There is nothing in my Physics that is not in geometry."[34]

One needs also to take into account Descartes's religious argument for the knowability of the universe. Today, the argument seems somewhat absurd. The argument for the existence of God is invalid, and as for the argument that God would have created a universe that can be readily known to us as long as we attend to "clear and distinct ideas," well, the difficult and profound mathematical structure of modern theoretical physics hardly seems to bear this out. In Descartes's time, however, this religious argument would have seemed to many far more convincing than it does to us. Many of those associated with the creation of modern science were inclined to believe that it must be possible to acquire knowledge of the nature of the universe on the grounds that a beneficent God would have created it that way. For the founders of modern science, Christianity provided a justification for science, and ought not to be at loggerheads with science.

There is an additional factor to take into account. Natural philosophers of a Cartesian persuasion, in Paris and elsewhere, fully accepted the need for observation and experiment. They were empiricists, in other words. They thought an acceptable theory had to satisfy *two* requirements. It had to be empirically successful; but it also had to accord with the Cartesian idea that natural phenomena are the outcome of the motion and impact of extended particles. A theory which failed to comply with this Cartesian requirement – such as Newton's law of gravitation – was, for the Cartesians, unintelligible and unacceptable, however empirically successful it might be. After three centuries of science, we may see the Cartesians as lamentably dogmatic and benighted. But in one respect, the Cartesians were more enlightened than out-and-out empiricist Newtonian opponents. The Cartesians were absolutely correct to demand that physical theories must comply with metaphysical principles (in addition to empirical considerations) in order to be acceptable. It was just that the Cartesians committed themselves too dogmatically to a metaphysical thesis that is false and much too restrictive.

If we take these considerations into account, it becomes clear that Cartesianism was a more reasonable position to adopt, at the time, than it may seem to us today. Nevertheless, once Newton's *Principia* had been published in 1687, Cartesian physics and cosmology hardly stood a chance. The immense empirical and explanatory success of Newtonian science, together, no doubt, with Newton's claim to have derived his law of gravitation solely from the phenomena, meant that Descartes could hardly compete. All the more surprising, then, that Cartesianism lingered on, mainly on the Continent, for decades after the publication of the *Principia*.

Up until around 1730, there was no real contest between Cartesianism and Newtonianism.[35] In England, it was taken for granted that Newton was vastly superior to Descartes. On the Continent, and especially in Paris, those able to understand what Newton had done took his contributions to the mathematics of motion very seriously. Mathematicians such as Pierre Varignon (1654–1722) and the Marquis de l'Hôpital (1661–1704) in Paris, and Johann Bernoulli (1667–1748) in Basel – influenced by the Cartesian and rationalist philosopher Nicolas Malebranche (1638–1715) – contributed to the mathematical study of motion, building on Newton's work but employing Leibniz's formulation of the calculus. But Newton's contributions to *physics* and *astronomy* – his claim to have established his universal law of gravitation – were simply ignored as obviously untenable, clashing as they did with the basic precepts of Cartesianism. Descartes's physics and cosmology were successfully promoted and popularized by Bernard Le Bovier de Fontenelle, an influential figure in Paris, who, born in 1657, lived to the ripe old age of 100. He was for many years Secretary to the Royal Academy in Paris, a position that enabled him to exercise considerable influence over the way mathematics and physics developed in Paris.

The Newtonian wars were triggered in part by a fierce priority dispute between Leibniz and Bernoulli on the one hand, and British mathematicians and natural philosophers close to Newton, such as John Keill (1671–1721), on the other hand. The dispute was about who had first invented the infinitesimal calculus, and whether Leibniz had plagiarized Newton.[36] (As I have already mentioned, Newton's work on the calculus came first, but Leibniz was the first to publish, and it was his version and notation that came to be generally used and developed.)

Out of this dispute, which was at its most intense during the years 1710 to 1720, another one arose, which took the form of an exchange of letters between Leibniz and Samuel Clarke (1675–1729) which continued up until Leibniz's death in 1716, and which was published by Clarke in 1717. Leibniz accused Newton of associating God too closely with nature, and mocked Newton's idea that God might have to intervene in nature now and again. "God Almighty wants to wind up his watch from time to time; otherwise it would cease to move," Leibniz scoffed. "He had not, it seems, sufficient foresight to make it a perpetual motion."[37] And Leibniz went on to pour scorn on the idea that there could be an attractive force of gravitation acting at a distance through empty space. Clarke, in close consultation with Newton, defended Newton against these Leibnizian attacks.

Perhaps partly in response to criticisms of Newton by Leibniz and Bernoulli, British Newtonians, such as John Harris, Francis Hauksbee, and John Keill, became more belligerent in their defence of Newton, more explicitly scornful of the "vain hypotheses" of the Cartesians. A similar emphasis is to be found in Roger Cotes's preface to the 1713 edition of Newton's *Principia*, in John Theophilus Desaguiliers's *Physico-mechanical Lectures* (1717), and in Henry Pemberton's *A View of Sir Isaac Newton's Philosophy* (1728). Newtonianism was also taken up in Holland by Jean Le Clerc and Willem Gravesande.

Finally, in the 1730s, two Frenchmen took up the task of promoting Newton in France. In 1732, a young, wealthy natural philosopher, mathematician and member of the Royal Academy in Paris, Pierre-Louis Moreau de Maupertuis (1698–1759)[38] published *Discours sur les différentes figures des astres*.[39] In 1734 Voltaire published *Lettres Philosophiques* in Rouen (published one year earlier in English in London with the title *Letters concerning the English*). Maupertuis's book was not so much a defence of Newton as a diplomatic criticism of Cartesian criticisms of Newton. Voltaire's book praised Bacon, Locke, and Newton at the expense of Descartes, created an uproar, and led to the French Enlightenment.

Both Maupertuis and Voltaire had visited London. Maupertuis visited London for three months in 1728, and got to know many of the leading Newtonians of the time, including Clarke, Desaguiliers, and Pemberton. He was even admitted to the Royal Society. Voltaire, given the choice of prison or exile, chose exile and left Paris for England in 1726. While in London, Voltaire met many literary and scientific figures, including key Newtonians such as Clarke and his associates. He returned to France in 1929, and was given permission to re-enter Paris.

In his 1732 book, Maupertius gave an exposition of Newton's work that was designed to appeal as much as possible to French mathematicians and natural philosophers. In chapter 2 he challenged the Cartesian idea that Newton's attractive force of gravitation was monstrous and unintelligible. He pointed out that Newton did not claim to have an explanation for gravitation: he held merely that bodies moved in accordance with such a force, whatever the explanation might be. Maupertuis cunningly went on to consider whether impulsion might be, in reality, just as mysterious as attraction. The proper procedure, he concluded, is to be open-minded about the question, and let the phenomena of nature decide the matter. Significantly, Maupertuis asserts that, as far as attraction in nature is concerned, "one must freely inquire into whether the phenomena prove it or not … It is in the system of the universe that one must look in order to determine whether it is a principle which holds in nature."[40] One has here in effect a statement of the basic creed of *science* (as opposed to natural philosophy): evidence alone must decide what theory is to be accepted. In chapters 3 and 4 Maupertuis went on to compare the relative successes of Descartes's and Newton's theories in accounting for the phenomena. He was able to show that, whereas Newton was able to account for the phenomena brilliantly and in great detail without departing at all from the extreme simplicity of his basic laws, Cartesian vortex theory became increasingly complex and implausible as it struggled to do justice to the phenomena.

In one important respect, Maupertius modified Newtonianism to make it more palatable to French Cartesians. He presented Newtonianism as the view that celestial phenomena unfold in accordance with precise physical law – in particular, of course, the laws of Newtonian mechanics – without God ever intervening. In the *Principia* Newton had suggested that God does intervene from time to time.

Maupertuis's book was well-received. Maupertuis gathered about him young mathematicians and natural philosophers associated with the Royal Academy who supported the Newtonian cause. On the other hand, Cartesian opposition to Newton stiffened. In the years 1733 to 1738, Joseph Privat de Molières published a four-volume tome that gave a thoroughly Cartesian, vortex account of terrestrial and astronomical phenomena: the book claimed to have established decisively its Cartesian principles. Strikingly, however, Privat de Molières accepted Newton's inverse square law – as Huygens had done before him, to a limited extent. Another work propounding and defending Cartesian vortex theory and criticizing Newton was published in 1740 by Étienne-Simon de Gamaches, who became increasingly vehement in his defence of Cartesianism.

Rather oddly, the debate between Cartesianism and Newtonianism began to concentrate on the question of the shape of the earth. Cartesians held that the poles were elongated, like a lemon; Newtonians that they were flattened, like a grapefruit. It so happened that Huygens had claimed to have derived such a flattened shape from Cartesian principles, so the shape of the earth would not seem to have been a very good crucial observation to decide the debate between Newtonians and Cartesians. Nevertheless, Maupertuis led an expedition to Lappland to make careful observations, and came back with the finding that the earth is flattened. Newtonians were right, and Cartesians were wrong! His findings were hotly contested, but eventually Maupertuis won the day. His main opponent, the Cartesian astronomer Jacques Cassini, did not acknowledge defeat, but his son, Cassini de Thury, did concede in 1740 that the earth is flattened at the poles, but claimed that this fact had been established by careful measurements by him and his associates, and not by Maupertuis. Nevertheless, a victory of sorts for the Newtonians! Then, in the same year, a pamphlet was published anonymously which gave a masterly, impartial account of the debate. It became a sensation, in part because the author was unknown. Around three years later, with the publication of a second edition, it became known that the author was Maupertuis himself – all of which assisted the Newtonian cause.

Meanwhile Voltaire struggled, most of the time independently of Maupertuis, to launch his campaign on behalf of English empiricism, Newton, and freedom. On his return from London to Paris, Voltaire asked Maupertuis, in the humblest of terms, for help in composing the Newtonian sections of his *Lettres Philosophiques*. As Voltaire sought to obtain permission to publish from the censor, copies of the book went on sale in Paris, London, and elsewhere without Voltaire's permission. The book was condemned, a copy was ceremonially burnt on the order of Parlement, and Voltaire had to flee into exile to avoid being imprisoned in the Bastille. In sharp contrast to Maupertuis, Voltaire was extravagant in his praise of Francis Bacon, John Locke, and above all Newton – the latter, he suggested, being the greatest genius of the last ten centuries. Voltaire cast Bacon as the founding father of English empiricism, and even claimed he had anticipated Newton's law of gravitation. But it was Voltaire's praise of Newton that was, perhaps, the most noteworthy feature of the book, and it led eventually to Newton becoming the sanctified hero of the Enlightenment.

Exile for Voltaire was not too bad. He set up house with Emilie de Breteuil, Marquise du Châtelet, in her chateau at Cirey-sur-Blaise in northeastern France. They were lovers. Emilie's husband did not seem to mind.[41] Voltaire and Emilie du Châtelet pursued their interests in natural philosophy, performed experiments, and each contributed an essay on fire to an Academy competition on the subject, both receiving an honorable mention. In 1735 a young Italian Newtonian, Francesco Algarotti, visited and showed the couple dialogues on Newton, almost certainly drafts of his *Newtonianism for Ladies*, published in Italian in 1737, and widely discussed at the time. This may have triggered Voltaire's determination to write his own introductory book on Newtonian mechanics. He was much helped by Emilie du Châtelet, who knew far more about the subject than did Voltaire. Her independent contributions to the Newtonian cause were important in their own right. Her translation of Newton's *Principia*, together with her notes on the text, was published in 1756 after her early death in 1749. It remains the only translation of the *Principia* into French to this day.

Voltaire's treatise, *Eléments de la Philosophie de Newton*, was finally published in 1738, together with an unauthorized, error-filled version which appeared slightly earlier in Holland and sold wildly, provoking much discussion. Voltaire did what he could to correct the errors of the Dutch edition. Emilie du Châtelet weighed in with an anonymous review of Voltaire's book, partly critical, but ultimately full of praise for Newton and for Voltaire's exposition of him.[42]

The debate became lively – even vicious. There were reviews for and against Voltaire and Newton. Voltaire entered into a particularly fierce dispute with Pierre-François Desfontaines, man of letters and journalist. Anonymous pamphlets were published in which charges of irreligion, licentiousness, and depravity were hurled, in both directions.

In 1740 Emilie du Châtelet published *Institutions de physique* (*Lessons in Physics*) which sought to synthesize Newton and Leibniz, the latter being in some respects superior to the former, in du Châtelet's view. The book received long and respectful reviews. Voltaire responded with *La métaphysique de Newton*, published in 1740, in which he criticized the arrogant rationalism of Leibniz,

Descartes, and Malebranche, and argued for the superiority of Newton's approach, based on observation, experiment, and mathematics. The book did not so much defend Newton's metaphysics as his empiricism, and his lack of any need for metaphysics.

Then in 1743 the young and then unknown Jean d'Alembert published *Traité de dynamique* to much acclaim by mathematicians and natural philosophers of the Royal Academy. This treatise provided a mathematically sophisticated formulation and development of Newtonian theory and, incidentally, put to rest a controversy that had raged between Newtonians and Leibnizians for decades. Cartesians and Newtonians, for once in agreement, held that momentum, mass times velocity (m.v), is conserved as physical systems evolve in time, whereas Leibniz held that it is *vis viva* – or, as we would say today, *kinetic energy*, that is conserved, given by $m.v^2$ (or $^1/_2 \, m.v^2$). d'Alembert quietly dissolved the controversy by pointing out that both are required, both being conserved.

Just eight years later, d'Alembert published his *Preliminary Discourse*, the introduction to the first volume of the *Encyclopédie*, edited by Denis Diderot (and initially by d'Alembert too). Diderot's *Encyclopédie*, consisting eventually of seventeen volumes published during the years 1751 to 1765, formed something like the backbone of the French Enlightenment. In his *Preliminary Discourse*, d'Alembert spelled out the manifesto for the Enlightenment. Descartes and Leibniz were praised for their contributions, but criticized for their rationalism. It was the empiricists, the heroes of the Enlightenment, that received unstinting praise: Francis Bacon, John Locke, and Isaac Newton.

In *The Structure of Scientific Revolutions*, Thomas Kuhn approvingly quotes Max Planck as declaring that "a new scientific truth does not triumph by convincing its opponents and making them see the light, but rather because its opponents eventually die, and a new generation grows up that is familiar with it."[43] This seems to have been a factor in bringing the French Newtonian revolution to a conclusion. Hard-line Cartesians were not converted. They retired, and died, leaving the field open for the empiricists and Newtonians. Privat de Molières died in 1742. Fontenelle retired from the Academy in 1740, and Jean-Jacques Dortous de Mairan, another prominent Cartesian Academician, went into semi-retirement three years later. In the first edition of his *Traité de dynamique* of 1743, d'Alembert wrote that the Cartesians "are a sect that is very much weakened." In the second edition, published fifteen years later in 1758, he declared, "The Cartesian sect barely exists anymore."[44]

One might have thought that the fact that mathematicians and natural philosophers on the Continent (aside from the Dutch) took nearly seventy years to come round to full acceptance of Newton's *Principia* would mean that they would lag far behind the British in developing Newton's work. In fact it was, if anything, all the other way round. In the *Principia* Newton had employed what rapidly became a rather old-fashioned kind of mathematics, based on geometry. His British successors were constrained by their adoption of it. In order to develop and apply Newton's work, it was essential to recast it in terms of Leibniz's version of the calculus. This was done in the main by Continentals: Varignon, l'Hôpital, Johann Bernoulli, Maupertuis, d'Alembert, and the great German mathematician Leonhard Euler (1707–1783) who, amongst other things, developed the crucial notion of a mathematical function. This work led to the crowning achievements of Joseph-Louis Lagrange (1736–1813) and Pierre-Simon Laplace (1749–1827).

THE QUIET DEATH OF NATURAL PHILOSOPHY AND THE TRIUMPH OF SCIENCE

With the defeat of Descartes and the triumph of Newton, and Newtonian empiricism, in France around 1750, modern science was well on its triumphant way (even if it was still called "natural philosophy"). What matters in science, it came to seem, is observation and experiment, measurement and mathematics. The endless, esoteric, fruitless subtleties of philosophy, metaphysics, epistemology, and other purely speculative thought can be ignored. Metaphysicians, in building their mighty axiomatic systems of thought, peddle mere dreams. Science has a proven method for acquiring knowledge – the inductive method of Newton – or at least the empirical methods of science to be associated loosely with Newton.[45] And so the great divide between science and philosophy began to open up. Science, it seems, makes such astonishing progress in knowledge, understanding, and technological know-how precisely because in science everything is in the end based on evidence, and philosophy is repudiated as irrelevant.[46] That, at least, is how most "scientists" came eventually to view the matter – as natural philosophers came to be called from the nineteenth century onwards.[47]

The tale I have sketched of the seventy-year-long battle between Newtonians and Cartesians creates the impression that the most serious opposition and rival to Newtonian empiricism, from an intellectual standpoint, was the rationalism of Descartes and Leibniz. Newton's opponents in reality had no hope whatsoever before the astonishing empirical and explanatory success of Newton. What is surprising is that it took so long for Newtonianism to triumph.

But what this conventional picture leaves out entirely is the endeavour that had achieved so much success before Newton, which led up to Newton's work, and upon which the *Principia* was based. I refer of course to what I have called *authentic natural philosophy* – natural philosophy as pursued by Kepler and Galileo, intermingling empirical science and metaphysical conjecture, and including discussion of epistemology, methodology, philosophy, and even theology. Despite its achievements, despite its role in initiating the so-called scientific revolution and making Newton's *Principia* possible, despite its greater intellectual rigour (as a result of making metaphysical conjectures explicit) – despite all this, authentic natural philosophy was nevertheless ignored and forgotten amidst the sound and fury of the Newton/Descartes debate. And when Newtonianism eventually triumphed around 1750, authentic natural philosophy had vanished from the scene. Even the fact that the first edition of Newton's *Principia* is itself a great work of authentic natural philosophy could not save it from extinction. The emphatic assertion in the second edition of 1713 that no metaphysical hypotheses are associated with the derivation of the law of gravitation from the phenomena; and the emphatic inductivism of the third edition of 1726 with the addition of rule 4 of reasoning in philosophy; and the whole way in which the *Principia* came to be understood, especially after the defeat of Cartesianism; all of this ensured that Newtonian empiricism dominated subsequent scientific developments, and authentic natural philosophy became all but invisible.

In chapters 3, 5, and 6, I will argue in more detail that all this was a mistake. Not only is authentic natural philosophy more rigorous than science based exclusively on evidence; it does better justice to actual scientific practice, and its explicit implementation would lead to greater intellectual success, and to a kind of science more intelligently responsive to human need. We need to resurrect authentic natural philosophy.

This plea faces, however, a monumental, multiple difficulty. Natural philosophy (or science) pursued in the empiricist spirit of Newton from around the middle of the eighteenth century onwards, has achieved success after astonishing success in a wholly unprecedented manner – unprecedented in that no previous age witnessed anything comparable. Since the middle of the eighteenth century we have discovered that all the myriad different substances there are on earth, and many in the heavens, are made up of no more than ninety-eight elements.[48] We have discovered that elements are composed of atoms, each atom a tiny solar system composed of protons and neutrons in a minute nucleus in the centre surrounded by a cloud of electrons. The atom of each element has its own specific number of positively charged protons in the nucleus (and the same number of surrounding, negatively charged electrons, if the atom is electrically neutral overall). We understand why atoms combine together in specific ways to form molecules, the constituents of chemical compounds. We know why substances, in appropriate conditions, form gases, liquids, and solids. We have a good understanding of why different compounds have the diverse properties they do. We have discovered that electricity and magnetism are two aspects of one force, the electromagnetic force. We have discovered that light is just waves in the electromagnetic field of force, these waves being light of different colours from red to violet, or a vast range of invisible rays, from radio waves, infrared rays, ultraviolet rays, x-rays to gamma rays, as we go from very long to very short wavelengths.

We have discovered that all of life on earth has evolved by means of the Darwinian mechanisms of inherited variations and natural selection during some 3.8 billion years from some original, primitive cell. We have vastly enhanced our knowledge of the millions of diverse species living on earth, and our knowledge of extinct species alive in the past, and of how evolution has taken place. We have transformed our knowledge of processes taking place in living things. We have a good understanding of the workings of muscles, nerves, the eye, the ear, the immune system, and so on, and we understand electronic and molecular processes associated with photosynthesis. We know that all living things, apart from viruses, consist of cells, the nucleus of each cell consisting of DNA that determines the characteristics of the individual in question. We know what the composition and structure of the DNA molecule is, and what the mechanisms are that translate information from the DNA molecule to specific proteins that go to make up multi-cell plants and animals – why, in plants, some cells form leaves, others roots, others stems, and why, in animals, some cells form muscles, others skin, others bone, and so on. We know what occurs when a new individual mammal or person is conceived, and what goes on in the womb to transform the fertilized egg into an infant. We have vastly increased our knowledge of disease, whether infectious like polio, or non-infectious like cancer, and we have transformed our capacity to cure and prevent disease. We have discovered a great deal about the structure and history of the earth. We know the continents float on semi-molten rock and slowly move with respect to each other, creating oceans when they move apart, and pushing up mountains when they collide. We know why there are earthquakes and volcanoes. We know that conditions on earth have changed dramatically over billions of years: there have been ice ages, and times of tropical heat. We know that the oxygen in the atmosphere was created in the distant past by algae as a result of photosynthesis. We have discovered that our solar system belongs to a galaxy – the Milky Way – a great spiral disc of 300 billion[49] stars, some 120,000 light years[50] across, our galaxy one among some 170 billion spread across space. We have discovered that this vast cosmos, at least 90 billion light years across, was once packed into a space smaller in volume than the nucleus of an atom: it exploded some 13.8 billion years ago in the so-called big bang which, after a period of rapid expansion, led to the formation of stars, galaxies, and the universe we find ourselves in today – which is still expanding, possibly at an increasingly rapid rate. We know how the elements were formed: hydrogen, some helium, and traces of lithium in the big bang, and all other elements as a result of the death throes of stars. We know much about the different types of stars that exist, how they evolve over time, and how they die, as white or brown dwarfs, neutron stars, and black holes. Recently, we have discovered many planets orbiting around stars other than our sun.

And we have discovered physical theories that correct and surpass, in predictive and explanatory power, even the extraordinarily successful theory of Newton. The first hint that Newtonian theory might not be correct came from the observation that Mercury's orbit does not conform precisely to what the theory predicts. Then, in 1905, Einstein put forward his special theory of relativity which reveals that Newtonian conceptions of space, time, and motion require radical revision. Einstein's general theory, when confirmed, revealed that Newton's theory of gravitation, at the theoretical level, is fundamentally wrong. According to Einstein, thrown stones, moons and planets move as they do, not because they are pulled by a force, but because they move through space curved by the presence of matter. Matter (or energy more generally) curves space-time, and curved space-time tells matter to move along geodesics – what straight lines become in a curved space. (On the curved surface of the earth, geodesics are great circles, the shortest distances between any two points.) Einstein generalizes Newton's first law of motion – every body continues in its state of rest, or of uniform motion in a right line, unless a force is impressed upon it – so as to take into account motion through curved space (or, more accurately, in curved space-time), and that suffices to account for the force of gravitation. Newton's law of gravitation and, in a sense, the force of gravitation, are eliminated. They are not required. Einstein's revised version of Newton's first law of motion suffices to account for gravitational effects, all the outcome of the curvature of space-time.[51] One fascinating consequence of Einstein's theory is that there are gravitational waves – waves of curvature of space that travel through space at the velocity of light. Gravitational waves have even, recently, been detected!

An even more radical revision of Newton took place with the advent of quantum theory. According to this theory, electrons, protons, atoms, even molecules, exhibit wave-like features, and wave-like entities such as light exhibit particle-like features too. (The particles of light are called photons.) In sharp contrast to Newton's and Einstein's theories, quantum theory in general makes *probabilistic*, not deterministic, predictions. There is no other theory in physics that predicts phenomena over such a vast, diverse range with such accuracy – and yet the theory is marred by somewhat defective, paradoxical features.[52]

We have discovered that the proton, like the neutron, is composed of three particles called *quarks*, fractionally charged and bound together inseparably in pairs (to form mesons), or in threesomes (to form particles like the proton or neutron). The quantum field theory of electrons, neutrinos, quarks, and the forces between them – electromagnetism, the weak and strong forces (with their associated particles, the photon, the vector bosons, and the gluon) – is known as *the standard model*. It is not altogether satisfactory, in that it has all the defects of standard quantum theory, has too many particles associated with it, and fails to predict some of their properties, such as mass, and does not say anything about dark matter. It nevertheless makes astonishingly accurate predictions and, in principle, if not in practice, predicts almost all known phenomena apart from those associated with gravity (and dark matter). The standard model and Einstein's theory of gravitation are the two current fundamental theories of physics (if one discounts string theory,[53] which has yet to make any successful predictions).

Associated with this astonishing record of scientific progress, there has been equally astonishing progress in technological know-how. This has led to modern industry, agriculture, transport, communications, medicine – and, in short, to the modern world.[54]

My suggestion that empirical science lacks rigour clearly faces a serious difficulty when confronted by this record of massive, cumulative success. Can empiricist natural science really be seriously defective in conception, if it has achieved such incredible success? Can lack of rigour matter if science is so incredibly successful? What possible greater success could be achieved by a science reformed to become authentic natural philosophy? These questions will be tackled in chapter 5.

One final question for this chapter. I have blamed the unnoticed demise of authentic natural philosophy on Newton and Descartes, and on the fierce debate between those who followed them. But suppose neither Newton nor Descartes had existed. Suppose both are plucked from history. Are we to suppose that, in that case, authentic natural philosophy would have flourished?

I think not. There is a broader reason for the demise of authentic natural philosophy. Without Descartes and Newton, natural philosophy, authentic or otherwise, would nevertheless have flourished initially. Much of what is in Descartes can be found in Galileo, Kepler, and Fermat. Some of Newton's contemporaries, men like Hooke and Wren, suspected that the inverse square law of gravitation governed the solar system, and Hooke may well have given Newton the basic idea of the *Principia*, as we have seen. But then, as science began to flourish, without Descartes and Newton, there would have been a strong tendency to overestimate the *certainty* of the knowledge acquired. There would be a profound temptation to interpret the great predictive and explanatory success of science as an indication of its security, its proven character. We see this tendency in both Descartes and Newton, as it is. Descartes held that basic principles about the nature of the universe could be proved by reason alone – by arriving at clear and distinct ideas. And Newton claimed to have derived his law of gravitation by induction from the phenomena without recourse to hypotheses "whether physical or metaphysical." Newtonian science came subsequently to be held to be even more firmly established than Newton had held it to be.

The astonishing success of science is very likely, in other words, to lead to a kind of epistemological overconfidence in a wide range of circumstances, and quite independently of the particular influence of the views of Descartes and Newton. It is the all-too-human tendency to suppose that success implies certainty that is the real enemy of authentic natural philosophy – for the latter, of course, is based on the idea that scientific knowledge is dependent on a profound, highly problematic *conjecture* about the nature of the cosmos. There is, in a way, something almost touchingly ludicrous in the idea that tiny human beings have the power so to subjugate the entire universe that it has not the power to prove our scientific knowledge to be lamentably, appallingly fallacious. No doubt this will not happen. But we cannot *know for certain* that it will not. As Karl Popper devoted his life to trying to establish, all our scientific knowledge ultimately has the status of fallible conjecture. Some of it may well be true, but we cannot *know* this to be the case with anything approaching certainty.

3

Failures of Philosophy, Part I

Over the centuries, from Newton's time to our own, a gulf has opened up between science and *philosophy*. Science has made extraordinary progress, the outcome, it would seem, of attending to *evidence*, and repudiating all that which cannot be assessed by means of evidence – philosophy, metaphysics, epistemology, theology. Philosophy, in glaring contrast, seems to have failed to make progress at all. Classics in the field of philosophy have been published as the centuries have rolled by, but these disagree with one another, and hardly add up to overall intellectual progress, in the manner of science. Furthermore, whereas in the seventeeth century, science and philosophy intermingled in the unified enterprise of natural philosophy, as time passed some philosophical traditions became indifferent to science or even hostile to it. The great success of science, and the failure of philosophy, is something philosophers have themselves noted and lamented. The contrast between the two has even led to anguished questions about what on earth philosophy could legitimately be. Indeed, far from advancing and growing over the centuries, philosophy seems to have dwindled and become increasingly insignificant. Instead of advancing, philosophy has gone into reverse. Philosophers sometimes account for the present impoverished state of their discipline in the following terms.

Once upon a time, philosophy reigned supreme, just below theology. Then, as some part of philosophy began to achieve intellectual success, it broke away and established itself as a separate discipline, distinct from philosophy. This happened again and again, each time diminishing philosophy until it became the impoverished thing that it is today. First, physics and astronomy became astonishingly successful, and established themselves as independent sciences. Then chemistry, biology, geology. And then the social sciences: economics, anthropology, psychology, sociology, political science. Finally, logic and linguistics broke away, and established themselves as successful independent disciplines. The moment a bit of philosophy becomes successful, it ceases to be philosophy! Only the unsuccessful residue persists as philosophy.[1] By the 1930s it had become uncertain as to what was left, what philosophy could possibly be, given that so much of its former territory had declared independence. One influential, early twentieth-century view was that the proper task of philosophy is *conceptual analysis*. Its task is to analyze such concepts as: mind, matter, causation, science, reason, perception, free will, democracy, and so on. Adopted and pursued by Bertrand Russell, G.E. Moore, Ludwig Wittgenstein, and Gilbert Ryle, amongst others, this became a widely influential approach in the English-speaking world from around 1905 onwards, and is still a powerful influence in academic philosophy today. Below I shall argue that this amounts almost to anti-philosophy. It constitutes a disgraceful betrayal of what philosophy ought to be.

What, then, ought philosophy to be? What is there that needs to be done that is not done by science, other academic disciplines, or good journalism, that could be done by philosophy, and that would not do violence to the whole intellectual tradition of the subject? How can academic philosophy be turned into an intellectually worthwhile discipline?

One possibility is to take seriously the original meaning of "philosophy": friend or lover of wisdom. I am not unsympathetic to this suggestion, as will become clear in chapter 8. Here, however, I want to discuss a different idea, a related idea as it will turn out to be.

The proper task of philosophy is to keep alive awareness, in the public domain, of our most fundamental problems, our fundamental problems of knowledge and understanding, and our fundamental problems of living, personal, social, and global – especially those that are most important and urgent. The task is to articulate, and try to improve the articulation of, such problems, and to assemble and assess critically the best, and perhaps the most influential, attempted solutions. Philosophy should also, of course, attempt to *solve* our fundamental problems – or at least improve attempted solutions, encourage others to do just that, or depict what needs to be done to solve our problems of living. The proper task of philosophy, in short, is to create and keep alive a socially influential tradition of tackling our fundamental problems *rationally* – that is, imaginatively and critically.

Furthermore, philosophy has the task of keeping alive awareness of the important role that fundamental problems, and our attempts at solving them, have in all aspects of life and thought. Implicit in the way we think and act there are invariably more or less inadequate assumptions about how fundamental problems are to be solved. Such assumptions are implicit in science,[2] politics, economic activity, art, education, law, and so on, whether we recognize them or not. The more or less defective character of these assumptions has more or less adverse consequences for life and thought as a result. It is worthwhile trying to improve assumptions we make about how fundamental problems are to be solved because, apart from anything else, this may enable us to improve our lives as well. It is worth doing for its own sake, and for the sake of everything else. Philosophy as intelligent thinking about how to solve our fundamental problems matters in its own right and because of the impact it can have on the rest of life.

It is crucial to this conception of philosophy that it does not have its own particular intellectual territory, its unique *field* of expertise. The whole idea of this kind of philosophy is to encourage everyone to become philosophers, in this sense. The very young do not need encouragement: they are instinctively philosophers. Three-year-olds have had to ponder ultimate questions, in one way or another, in order to have concocted for themselves, without formal instruction, a view of the world, and a view of human life.[3] Their elders may, however, have forgotten, and may need to be reminded of, their infant passionate, profound philosophical selves, their endless asking of: Why? Why? Why? Adult life, and all adult activities, however formal or institutional, however individual, haphazard or idiosyncratic, need to have at least a scrap of philosophy, an openness to, and readiness to engage with, some pondering of fundamental problems. Nothing in human life should be wholly immune to philosophy. Love, war, dying, work, politics, religion, parenting, play, art, science: all need some philosophy sometimes.

Professional philosophers, in encouraging everyone else to engage in a bit of philosophy now and again too, need to speak and write in a way that is engaging, lively, witty, and lucid, but also in a way that retains full intellectual responsibility. Philosophy is for everyone, and the task of the professionals is to help make it so, without deviating one iota from intellectual integrity – from the basic task of enhancing our general awareness of what our fundamental problems are, what we need to think and do to solve them. Both kinds of problems are the concern of philosophy – fundamental problems of knowledge and understanding, and fundamental problems of life, of action. Both kinds of question, "What are we to *think*?" and "What are we to *do*?," are equally important. And a basic task of global philosophy is to get into social life the habit of tackling problems of *thought* and *life* in cooperatively rational ways, in so far as circumstances permit.

I should perhaps make clear that this proposal to reform philosophy – so that its basic task is to keep alive awareness of our fundamental problems of thought and life – is put forward as a preliminary step towards the basic proposal of this book: we need to reform both philosophy *and* science, and put them together to recreate a modern version of natural philosophy. Of the two, it is *philosophy* that needs the most radical reform. My argument for bringing together science and philosophy to recreate natural philosophy does not begin to make sense without the prior reform of philosophy along the lines indicated in this chapter and the next. In chapter 5 I develop the argument for the reform of science.

I also need to make clear that the above is intended to indicate the proper *basic* task of philosophy. In pursuing the above task, philosophers will also need to tackle rather more specialized problems. An important task, indeed, is to explore the multitude of ways in which our fundamental problems, and our attempted solutions, interact with research pursued in other disciplines – physics, biology, cosmology, mathematics, neuroscience, engineering, social inquiry – and interact with personal and social life – politics, economics, global problems, education, the law, well-being. Interactions in both directions need attention: the way more specialized problem-solving in other fields of thought and life has implications for the way we understand and seek to solve our fundamental problems, and vice versa, the way thinking about our fundamental problems and how to solve them has implications for research in other fields, and for our personal and social lives.

It may be asked: when I declare that the basic task of philosophy is to keep alive awareness of fundamental problems, what do I mean when I say a problem is *fundamental*? A part of what I mean can be put like this: problem P_1 is more fundamental than P_2 if the solution to P_1 in principle solves P_2, but not vice versa. This is a rather weak notion of *more fundamental*, because it might just mean *more general*. Can we distinguish "more fundamental" from "more general" – the former being stronger? It can be done like this. We can declare that P_1 is more fundamental than P_2 if the solution to P_1 solves P_2, but not vice versa, and the solution to P_1 is unified or coherent in some significant, substantial sense of these terms, and not just a jumble of disconnected items. An example of a unified or coherent solution is a unified physical theory that solves a range of diverse problems in physics.[4]

Our fundamental problem of all of thought and life can, in my view, be put like this:

How can our human world, and the world of sentient life more generally, imbued with perceptual qualities, consciousness, free will, meaning, and value, exist and best flourish embedded as it is in the physical universe?[5]

I interpret this in such a way that it encompasses all of academic thought, from theoretical physics, mathematics, and cosmology, via the biological and technological sciences, to social inquiry and the humanities. It also encompasses all practical problems of living – problems facing individuals, groups, institutions, societies, nations, and humanity as a whole.[6] In living we all seek to achieve what is of value, however misguided or clear-sighted we may be about what is of value.

It is clear that this fundamental problem contains a host of baffling, unsolved, just slightly less fundamental problems. What is the ultimate nature of the physical universe? If everything, including ourselves, is made up of fundamental physical entities (perhaps just one kind of entity) interacting and evolving in accordance with precise physical law, what becomes of free will? What becomes of the world as we experience it, full of colour, sound, tactile properties, meaning, and value? How can there be sentience and consciousness? How can we know anything if the entire world we experience is no more than an illusion? How can anything of value exist if everything is just physics? What becomes of such things as democracy, justice, art, science, friendship, love? How is any life of value possible? What kind of good, civilized human world can we hope to create? What, ultimately, is of value? Even science itself becomes problematic if everything is just physics! Philosophy has the task of keeping alive awareness of such somewhat less fundamental problems; it has the task of revealing how both academic thought and life can be enriched by such awareness.

There are those, of course, who reject the idea that the ultimate reality of the natural world is physical in character. Many hold that it is God. In order not to exclude such views in an *a priori* fashion, as it were, we need a broader formulation of the above problem:

How can our human world ... exist and best flourish embedded as it is in the real world?

In what follows, I take the first, narrower formulation, stated above, to be the correct formulation of the problem. I will, in a moment, argue that there are very good reasons indeed for holding that our human world is embedded in the physical universe! This is the key argument of this book.

This, then, is what philosophy in my view ought to be, *global philosophy*,[7] that discipline which seeks to keep alive awareness of our fundamental problems, especially our most fundamental problem of all, as formulated above, and the nest of nightmare dilemmas it contains. This means that a basic proper task of philosophy is to help solve a multitude of intellectual problems, and problems of living, that arise as a result of taking seriously what it is that modern science tells us about the universe – and ourselves. Global philosophy is, from the outset, inextricably linked to modern science – provoked by, even at times at odds with, in conflict with, the view of the world ushered in with science.

What grounds are there for holding that this is what philosophy ought to be? There are at least four.

First, we do clearly need to take very seriously the way in which the scientific view of the world seems to threaten the very existence of so much of what we cherish and value in life – the whole character of the world as we experience it, the world in which we live out our lives, or suppose that we do. What we experience, our inner feelings and thoughts, our capacity to act in the world and be responsible for what we do, our very being, all seem to drain away and become nothing before the onslaught of physics, the physical view of the universe.

This onslaught of physics against everything we experience and hold dear cannot be left to scientists to combat or resolve. The problems concern subjective experience, consciousness, our inner being, poetry, love, meaning, and value, things that lie beyond the scope of factual, objective science. It cannot be left to science, or scientists, to reconcile these conflicts between the way we ordinarily understand ourselves and the world we live in, and the way it is understood by physics.[8]

Second, global philosophy, as I have just characterized it, very much accords with what philosophy once was, both in the ancient and the modern world. The ancient Greeks, the Presocratics, Plato, and Aristotle, did philosophy in this sense. And so did philosophers associated with the rise of modern science, Descartes, Locke, Spinoza, Leibniz, and others. Cartesian dualism is indeed, quite clearly, an attempt to solve in outline our fundamental problem, as indicated above.

Third, there is clearly a profoundly important need for philosophy in this sense. It is essential if academic inquiry is to be *rational*. Whatever else academia may be, a proper basic task that it has is to solve, or help solve, *problems*. In considering the rationality of academic inquiry, then, what we need to consider is how well, or ill, it puts basic *rules of rational problem solving* into practice. There are four elementary, uncontroversial rules of rational problem-solving that we need to consider.

1 Articulate, and seek to improve the articulation of, the fundamental problem to be solved.
2 Propose and critically assess possible solutions.
3 If the fundamental problem to be solved proves intractable, specialize. Break the basic problem up into subordinate problems. Tackle analogous, easier-to-solve problems, in an attempt to work gradually to the solution to the basic problem.
4 But if one engages in specialized problem-solving in this way, make sure that specialized and fundamental problem-solving interact, so that each influences the other (since otherwise specialized problem-solving is likely to become unrelated to the fundamental problems we seek to solve).[9]

In order to improve attempts at solving our fundamental problem, we need to put rule 3 into practice. We need to specialize. Most of the time it is highly specialized bits, versions or aspects of the above fundamental problem that we are concerned with, in any case. Most of us most of the time are concerned with problems that are specific to us, to our particular environment and activity, our particular desires and goals.

However, we also need to put rules 1, 2, and 4 into practice. We need to articulate, and improve the articulation of, our fundamental problems, at greater and lesser levels of generality, and we need to propose and critically assess possible solutions in such a way that these may influence and be influenced by more specialized problem-solving, in accordance with rule 4. If we do not do these things the danger is that we will lose our way in the maze of specialized problem solving. We will forget what our fundamental purposes are. Rules 1, 2, and 4 are just as vital for rationality as rule 3.

But it is just the task of global philosophy, as I have characterized it above, to put rules 1, 2, and 4 into practice, and to encourage others to do that as well. Global philosophy is thus vital for the rationality, the intellectual integrity, of academic inquiry.

Of course if scientists and scholars, who are *not* professional philosophers, take care of the vital tasks 1, 2, and 4, as it is, without any help from academic philosophy, then the case for global philosophy rather collapses. In that case, non-philosophers would keep alive global philosophy in a perfectly satisfactory way. There would be no need for professional philosophers to get involved.

This brings me to my fourth reason for holding that global philosophy is what philosophy ought to do and be. Global philosophy is urgently needed to counteract dire consequences that stem from rampant specialization.

During the last century or so, a massive process of specialization upon specialization upon specialization has taken place. Academia as it is today consists of an intricate labyrinth of ever more specialized disciplines. This development has been driven in part, no doubt, by the need to put rule 3 into practice. But it has also been driven by extra-rational needs having to do with academic careers and status. One way to further careers and establish status is to found and promote a new specialization, with its own journals, research groups, professional bodies, and so on. None of this would matter too much if this repetitive implementation of rule 3 had been counteracted by influential implementation of 1, 2, and 4. But this has not taken place.

The problem of almost endless specialization with not much to counteract it is an old one.

As I reported in an article on the subject published long ago in 1980,[10] Aldous Huxley, writing over forty years earlier in 1937, put the matter like this:

The mass of accumulated knowledge [in contemporary science] is so great that it is now impossible for any individual to have a thorough grasp of more than one small field of study. Meanwhile, no attempt is made to produce a comprehensive synthesis of the general results of scientific research. Our universities possess no chair of synthesis. All endowments, moreover, go to special subjects – and almost always to subjects which have no need of further endowment, such as physics, chemistry and mechanics. In our institutions of higher learning about ten times as much is spent on the natural sciences as on the sciences of man. All our efforts are directed, as usual, to producing improved means to unimproved ends. Meanwhile intensive specialization tends to reduce each branch of science to a condition almost approaching meaninglessness. There are many men of science who are actually proud of this state of things. Specialized meaninglessness has come to be regarded, in certain circles, as a kind of hall-mark of true science. Those who attempt to relate the small particular results of specialization with human life as a whole and its relation to the universe at large are accused of being bad scientists, charlatans, self-advertisers. The people who make such accusations do so, of course, because they do not wish to take any responsibility for anything, but merely to retire to their cloistered laboratories, and there amuse themselves by performing delightfully interesting researches.[11]

But the problem is even older than that, as Aldous Huxley has also remarked.

My grandfather, T.H. Huxley ... did a lot to turn London University into a modern university, that is to say into a university with a high degree of specialization in various fields. The interesting thing is that by the early 1890s he was already deeply preoccupied with the problem of excessive specialization. About three years before he died he actually worked out a plan to co-ordinate the various specialized departments in the University of London so as to create some kind of integrated education.

I need hardly add that my grandfather's plans were never put into effect and that the problem of integrated education remains exactly as it was – despite the fact that it is a problem which concerns everybody in the field, and despite a number of attempts that have been made to solve it.[12]

Serious attention was given to the problem by some scientists and other academics in the 1960s, '70s and '80s. One idea was to create "bridging" disciplines, such as biochemistry and biophysics, in an attempt to facilitate communication between existing disciplines. But this only made matters worse. It created further barriers between disciplines, and drove them further apart. More recently, interdisciplinarity, intra-disciplinarity and multi-disciplinarity have been advocated: bring academics from different disciplines together to work on problems that require contributions from different disciplines.[13] Initiatives such as these have met with only very partial success in combating the sins of unmitigated specialization.

What no one has appreciated is that the problem has arisen because philosophy has failed in its basic task: to keep alive awareness of fundamental problems and our best attempts at solving them. Not even academic philosophers themselves have seen the long-standing failure to combat rampant specialization as a failure of *philosophy*.[14] Philosophy has become so enfeebled that it has occurred to no one that it could or should take on such a task. No one takes philosophy to be responsible for the current situation.[15]

To sum up. The view of the universe that comes from modern science seems to annihilate everything we value in life, the very world we experience, our very beings. This unresolved conflict needs attention, and cannot be left to science to solve. Global philosophy, as I have characterized it, accords with what philosophy has been in the past. It is urgently needed. Academic inquiry, devoid of it, becomes so grossly irrational in a wholesale, structural way that it violates *three* of the four most elementary rules of rational problem-solving one can think of – rules 1, 2 and 4. Finally, the long-standing failure to put global philosophy into practice has led to modern universities falling victim to just this disastrously irrational state of affairs. Relentless, unmitigated specialization has produced a situation such that our fundamental problem is scarcely considered at all in the university, and certainly is not given the prominence, in research and education, that it needs. Three of the four most elementary rules of reason are indeed violated. This grotesque structural irrationality of academic inquiry has had disastrous consequences, both intellectual and humanitarian, as we shall see in what follows. Most serious of all, the capacity of humanity to learn how to make progress towards as good a world as possible has been severely undermined, as we shall see in chapter 8.

What needs to be done to put this dire situation to rights?

A part of what is required is a revolution in what goes on in departments of philosophy. There are contemporary philosophers who seek to do global philosophy. But, for historical reasons, there has been a massive failure of academic philosophy to keep global philosophy alive – even to construe the task of philosophy in such terms. This is an issue I will discuss in the rest of this chapter, and in the next. I will argue that, even though academic philosophy has failed to establish our fundamental problem as one that ought to be of some concern for the whole of the academic enterprise – has failed even to conceive of the task of philosophy in such terms – nevertheless, in recent decades there have been substantial improvements, and many philosophers do indeed explore aspects of our fundamental problem. First steps have been taken towards global philosophy, but much more needs to be done.

However, in order to bring global philosophy back to life to cure academia of its structural irrationality, far more is needed than a change in what goes on in philosophy departments. All schoolchildren need to encounter global philosophy as a standard part of their education. They need to be encouraged to ponder, to discuss imaginatively and critically fundamental problems – including the most fundamental of all – as a standard part of education, there being some exposure to the best of the ideas that have been developed in response to these problems.[16] And just this needs to become a standard, influential part of the university. Every student course, whether undergraduate or postgraduate, needs some exposure to, some engagement with, our fundamental problem. Every discipline, every department, needs one or two academics alive to questions about how the discipline, the work of the department, contributes to and is affected by ideas about how to solve our fundamental problem. All specialists, ideally, need some awareness of these fundamental aspects of their specialized concerns. Every university needs a "global seminar," devoted to exploring fundamental problems and their connections with problems of more specialized research – a seminar that meets on a regular basis, open to both students and staff, and capable of influencing and being influenced by specialized research, thus implementing rule 4. And schools and universities need to take up the task of promoting imaginative and critical exploration of fundamental problems in personal and social life – in the workplace, politics, the media, and so on.

Could academic philosophers bring these changes about? Probably not. What is required is a comprehensive intellectual and institutional revolution in schools and universities, one which needs active support from a wide range of scientists, scholars, educationalists, administrators, staff, students and pupils, if it is to succeed. The proper job of professional philosophers is to spell out, in a variety of contexts, what the revolution would involve and why it is so urgently required. They need both to *do* global philosophy themselves, and urge others to do it too.

THE PROBLEM OF INDUCTION

How and why has modern philosophy failed to do what it most needs to do?

The first point to make is that it has not entirely failed. Some modern philosophers have made important contributions to global philosophy.

The most striking example of such a philosopher is Karl Popper. In his first four books in particular, Popper tackled fundamental problems concerning science, reason, freedom, and civilization, and proposed solutions of great originality and power with fruitful implications for a wide range of fields: science, education, art, politics, economics, social science, and the humanities.[17] Science makes progress, Popper argues, not by *verifying* theories, which cannot be done, but by *falsifying* them. All knowledge is conjectural in character. Scientific knowledge is distinct from the rest in its extraordinary imaginative boldness, its vulnerability to empirical falsification, its submission to sustained and ferocious attempts at falsification, and its success in surviving! Science is a special case of something more general of very great importance: rationality. This consists of seeking to learn, to solve problems by imaginatively proposing and critically assessing possible solutions. This notion of critical rationality is relevant to all that we do, to all aspects of life. It is especially relevant to politics, to the great, ancient, heartrending task of learning how to make progress towards a freer, more just, more civilized world – a more open society, as Popper put it. One might think a rational society would be a highly uniform, organized one, dominated by rules and regulations, a sort of totalitarian state with reason as the supreme authority. All this is transformed once Popper's notion of critical rationality is accepted. The rational society becomes the society that values, and learns by means of, criticism. But criticism is only possible in a society that is able to sustain a variety of beliefs, values, and ways of life. Thus the rational society *is* the open society, the society best able to allow and encourage a diversity of ways of life to flourish.

Not only did Popper *do* global philosophy, in an exemplary way, with great clarity, simplicity, and intellectual integrity. He argued that it *should* be done, again with great clarity and simplicity. Furthermore – and this is especially significant for the basic theme of the present book – Popper sought in his work to contribute to natural philosophy, or to *cosmology* as he tended to call it, a synthesis of science and philosophy. Here, however, there is a paradoxical element in Popper's contribution, for Popper most famously argued that science is to be sharply demarcated from philosophy, in that science consists of that which is falsifiable, whereas philosophy does not. This key component of Popper's philosophy, quite widely accepted by scientists themselves, a sort of twentieth-century update of Newtonian empiricism, has done much to preserve the long-standing distinction between science and philosophy, and thus prohibit the recreation of natural philosophy.[18]

Many others – scientists, philosophers, authors with a variety of backgrounds – have made valuable contributions to global philosophy, especially in recent decades. It is an enterprise that is not quite dead. Nevertheless, academic philosophy during the last one hundred years or so has failed to do what global philosophy most needs to do: keep alive awareness of our fundamental problem and our best attempts at solving it. I now consider how and why this has come about. Two factors have been crucial, namely:

1　The failure of philosophy over the centuries to solve the problem of induction – and thus the failure, as we shall see, to establish that science cannot proceed without metaphysics. The failure to make out the case, in short, for the need to bring together science and philosophy to re-create natural philosophy.

2 The failure of philosophy adequately to articulate, let alone solve, our fundamental problem (as formulated above).

In the rest of this chapter I will discuss the first failure, and how to put it right – how to solve the problem of induction and thus provide the key argument for the need to recreate natural philosophy. In the next chapter I will discuss the second failure, the way in which it has stifled global philosophy, and what needs to be done to put matters to rights.

Let us now consider the problem of induction. In 1739 David Hume published *A Treatise of Human Nature,* in which he pointed out, in effect, that science (or natural philosophy) cannot establish laws or theories by means of evidence. For however empirically well-established a theory may be (Newton's law of gravitation, for example), it must always be possible, for all that we can know for certain, for the course of nature suddenly to change in such a way that the predictions of the theory become dreadfully false. It is no good arguing that this has not happened in the past and that we therefore have no reason to suppose it will happen in the future, for what is at issue is precisely this question of whether we can know that the past is a good guide to how the future will be. We cannot even argue that the future will *probably* resemble the past.

The book fell, in Hume's phrase, "still-born from the press." Hume tried again, first with an anonymous pamphlet published in 1740, then with the collection of essays *An Enquiry concerning Human Understanding* in 1748. Not till 1778, two years after Hume's death, did a serious response come, in the form of a highly obscure work in German called *The Critique of Pure Reason* by the famously obscure Immanuel Kant (1724–1804). Kant argued, in effect, that in order to escape from Hume's conclusion we must assume that some of our knowledge about the world can be known to be true with certainty entirely independently of experience or evidence. How is this possible? Because conscious experience is only possible if our experiences exhibit order. We can know for certain that the world we experience will exhibit order because if it does not, we cannot experience it – it precludes the possibility of conscious experience.

Kant's attempted solution fails. Even if we grant Kant his main point that conscious experience is only possible if experiences exhibit a certain degree of order, this does not suffice to solve Hume's problem. The world might begin to behave in a way that refutes Newton's law and, now and again, all other laws, and yet might still, most of the time, exhibit sufficient order for conscious experience of it to be possible.[19]

Kant did help, however, to put Hume's problem of induction on the philosophical map. Since Kant's day, down to the present (2016 at the time of writing), thousands of papers and books have been published attempting to solve the problem. Not one succeeds.[20]

We see here yet another example of the striking contrast between science and philosophy. As natural science forges ahead and makes astonishing progress in improving our knowledge and understanding of the universe, philosophy, despite massive effort, fails hopelessly to make sense of this manifest scientific progress. For two centuries or so, there seemed to be no progress whatsoever in the philosophical effort to solve the problem of induction.

What is absolutely extraordinary about the flood of literature attempting and failing to solve the problem is that almost all of it takes for granted that the orthodox view that science is based exclusively on evidence, and verifies theories by means of evidence, is fundamentally sound. Hume appears to have shown that it cannot be. But it is. So there must be something wrong with Hume's simple argument. It is just a question of finding out where the argument goes wrong.

Not till Karl Popper, in 1934, did a philosopher have the courage to conclude that Hume is right, and scientific theories cannot be verified, or rendered probable, by any amount of evidence in support of them. As I have already indicated, Popper holds that science makes progress by means of a process of conjecture and refutation.

Popper made an important contribution towards solving the problem of induction but, despite claiming to have solved it,[21] he did not in fact succeed.[22]

I now outline how the problem is to be solved. This is the key argument of this book. For, out of the solution to the problem of induction emerges a conception of science that requires science to incorporate elements of metaphysics, methodology, philosophy, epistemology. The solution requires us, in other words, to transform *natural science* into something like pre-Newtonian *natural philosophy*. It is this argument, in short, that is the backbone of my case for the need to recreate natural philosophy. Elsewhere, I have spelled out this argument in much greater detail:[23] here, I expound the argument in as succinct a way as I can.

First, I must delineate a bit more precisely the orthodox empiricist conception of science, stemming from Newton, that, in my view, must be rejected if we are to solve the problem of induction and make rational sense of science.

According to this view – which I call *standard empiricism* – it is *evidence* that decides what theories are to be accepted and rejected in science. Non-empirical considerations such as the simplicity, unity, or explanatory character of a theory may influence choice of theory as well, for a time at least, but not in such a way that nature herself, or the phenomena, are presupposed to be simple, unified, or comprehensible. *In science, no factual thesis about the world, or about the phenomena, can be accepted as a part of scientific knowledge independently of empirical considerations.*

Standard empiricism, as I have just characterized it, is widely, almost universally, taken for granted by scientists, philosophers of science, and the public alike. Versions of the view began to be taken for granted after the triumph of Newton and the collapse of Cartesianism in the mid-eighteenth century. It is a central component of almost all views about science that philosophers of science have come up with, from the logical positivists in the 1930s to the views of Popper, Thomas Kuhn, and Imre Lakatos,[24] and others in more recent times.

Not everyone accepts standard empiricism. Newton rejects it in the first edition of the *Principia*, as we have seen, in that he makes clear that his first three rules of reasoning make metaphysical assumptions about the nature of the universe, not based on evidence. It is only in what is added to the third edition, in 1726, in his fourth rule of reasoning, and in his claim to have derived his law of gravitation from the phenomena by induction without recourse to hypotheses "whether metaphysical or physical," that Newton expresses his allegiance to standard empiricism. Kant rejected standard empiricism, as we have seen. J.S. Mill rejected it, in holding that science accepts the uniformity of nature – a metaphysical principle.[25] Bertrand Russell rejects it in one of his later books, in which he formulates a number of metaphysical principles implicitly taken for granted in his view when scientists arrive at theories from evidence by induction.[26]

Standard empiricism is, however, unthinkingly taken for granted by the vast majority of working scientists to such an extent that it is rather rare to find the doctrine being explicitly formulated, let alone defended. Scattered throughout the writings of scientists one can, nevertheless, find affirmations of the view. Thus Planck once remarked that "experiments are the *only* means of knowledge at our disposal. The rest is poetry, imagination."[27] Or, as Poincaré put it, "Experiment is the sole source of truth. It alone can teach us something new; it alone can give us certainty."[28] Millikan expressed it like this: "the distinguishing feature of modern scientific thought lies in the fact that it begins by discarding all *a priori* conceptions about the nature of reality – or about the ultimate nature of the universe ... and takes instead, as its starting point, well-authenticated, carefully tested *experimental* facts ... In a word, modern science is essentially empirical."[29] Popper put it slightly more succinctly: "in science, only observation and experiment may decide upon the *acceptance or rejection* of scientific statements, including laws and theories."[30] Most recently, the President of the Royal Society in 2016 put it like this: "Science is simply the systematic accumulation of knowledge based on evidence."[31]

It is general acceptance of (one or other version of) standard empiricism that keeps science and philosophy apart. Philosophical doctrines are not empirically testable; hence, given standard empiricism, they have no significant role within science.

Scientists do not just take standard empiricism for granted; they do what they can to ensure that science conforms to the doctrine. As a result, it exercises a widespread influence over science itself. It influences such things as the way aims and priorities of research are discussed and chosen, criteria for publication of scientific results, criteria for acceptance of results, the intellectual content of science, science education, the relationship between science and the public, science and other disciplines, even scientific careers, awards, and prizes.[32]

Despite all this, standard empiricism is untenable, unworkable, and irrational. It is this doctrine that must be rejected to save science from Hume. But, in order to do this, we must first, paradoxically, strengthen Hume's argument.

Hume argued that, however overwhelmingly scientific theories may have been verified by evidence, nevertheless at any moment, for all that we can ever know, the course of nature may suddenly change so as to falsify any or all of these theories. This idea of nature changing course can be captured by saying that we can always think up rivals to our accepted theories that are, so far, just as empirically successful as our accepted theories, but which predict that, from some time in the future, phenomena occur that differ dramatically from the predictions of our accepted theories. These rival *aberrant* theories, as we may call them, postulate that dramatic changes occur in the future but, up to that future moment, are just as empirically successful as our accepted theories.

There are, furthermore, infinitely many such empirically successful aberrant theories – reflecting the point that the course of nature might change in infinitely many different ways.

Suppose we take our accepted theory, T, to be Newton's law of gravitation, $F = Gm_1m_2/d^2$. (Here, G is a constant, m_1 and m_2 are the masses of two bodies, d is the distance between them, and F is the attractive force between them due to gravitation.) We can now concoct a rival, aberrant theory, T_1, which asserts: up to the last moment of 2050 (Greenwich Mean Time), everything proceeds in accordance with Newton's law; after that moment phenomena occur in accordance with $F = Gm_1m_2/d^3$. Up until the last moment of 2050, the two theories, T and T_1, are equally successful empirically. On the face of it, there is just as much evidence in support of T_1 as T, just as much evidence for holding that drastic changes will occur on the first moment of 2051 as there is for holding that no such changes will occur.

No doubt when the first moment of 2051 arrives, T_1 will be resoundingly refuted. The trouble is that there will always be infinitely many such unrefuted, aberrant rivals to Newton's theory, since infinitely many moments always stretch off into the future at which point an aberrant theory may declare the law of gravitation to change.

And we can concoct infinitely many aberrant rivals to Newton's law, not by changing the future date on which theoretical predictions begin to differ, but by sticking to the last moment of 2050, let us say, and changing what the aberrant theory predicts for phenomena after that date. The aberrant theory might predict that Newton's law becomes $F = Gm_1m_2/d^N$, where N is any real number. (There are infinitely many real numbers between any two integers, 2 and 3 say.) Or the force of gravitation might become abruptly repulsive, again in infinitely many different possible ways. The constant G might change in infinitely many different possible ways. And the functional relationship between force, mass, and distance might come to differ from that specified by Newton's law in infinitely many much more drastic ways.

So far we have only considered aberrant theories that postulate an abrupt change in physical law at a specified *time*. But there are other dimensions of variation along which laws may abruptly change. They might change in *space*. We can concoct theories which agree with accepted theories for all observed phenomena, but which disagree dramatically for phenomena occurring now in regions of space not yet observed (because light from these regions has not yet reached us, for example). Infinitely many empirically successful aberrant theories can be concocted which make predictions quite different from accepted theories only for kinds of physical system not yet observed (and such, perhaps, that they never will be observed). One such theory might agree precisely with Newtonian theory except for systems consisting of spheres of pure gold of over 1,000 tonnes moving in space in a spherical region no larger than 1,000 miles in diameter: for such systems, $F = Gm_1m_2/d^N$, where N is any real number, plus or minus, other than 2.[33] Or we may take any familiar experiment that has verified some theory, T, endlessly many times, and change it in some bizarre, irrelevant way – painting the apparatus red, for example, or sprinkling diamond dust around it in a circle. Here, the aberrant theory, T_1, agrees with T for all phenomena and all experiments, except for this specific, bizarrely modified, unperformed experiment, for which our aberrant theory, T_1, predicts – whatever we like. Endlessly many aberrant theories can be concocted in this way that are just as empirically successful as accepted theories – until we set out to refute them.

We have vastly increased ways in which "the course of nature" might change over what Hume had in mind. It is not just with the passage of time that such changes could occur. They could occur as other variables are varied: distance, mass, relative velocity, kind of substance, temperature, or kind of experiment (kind of phenomenon). Furthermore, we have an infinity of aberrant theories, just as empirically successful as accepted theories, which nevertheless yield dramatically different predictions for phenomena not yet observed.

It is worth noting that in all practical contexts which exploit the predictions of physical theories – building bridges or aeroplanes, for example – we must always assume that such empirically successful aberrant theories (and the empirically *more successful* aberrant theories to be discussed in a moment) can be ignored. No individual bridge or aeroplane is quite like any other. There will be infinitely many aberrant theories, so far just as empirically successful as accepted theories, which predict that just for this bridge, this aeroplane, quite different laws will come to operate. It is not *evidence* that rules out these aberrant theories, but some kind of underlying assumption of uniformity or unity.

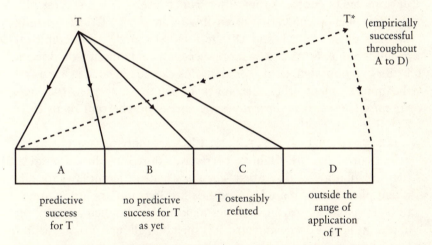

Figure 1 Given any accepted physical theory, T, there is always an empirically more successful (but disunified) rival T*

Now matters become considerably more serious. Each one of these infinitely many aberrant theories that are just as empirically success-ful (so far) as our accepted theory, T, can be modified further to become *even more empirically successful* than T. Any accepted fun-damental physical theory, T, successfully predicts a range of phenom-ena, A (see figure 1). But there will be phenomena, B, which come within the scope of the theory but which cannot be predicted because the equations of the theory cannot (as yet) be solved. T is also almost bound to face some empirical difficulties, and thus be, on the face of it, refuted – by phenomena C. And there will be other phenomena, D, that fall outside the scope of the theory altogether. We can now take any one of the infinitely many equally empirically successful aberrant rivals to T, T_1 say, and modify it further so that the new theory, T_1*, agrees precisely with T as far as phenomena A are concerned, but differs further from T in predicting, in an entirely ad hoc way, that phenomena B, C, and D occur in accordance with empirically established laws L_A, L_B, and L_C, T_1* is the same as T as far as phenomena A are concerned, but consists of laws L_B, L_C, and L_D as far as phenomena B, C, and D are concerned. T_1* successfully predicts all that T has successfully predicted; T_1* (like T_1) makes predictions concerning unobserved phenomena that differ from those of T; T_1* successfully predicts phenomena C that ostensibly refute T; and T_1* successfully predicts phenomena B and D that T fails to predict. On empirical grounds alone, T_1* is clearly more successful and thus, it would seem, better corroborated, than T. And all this can be repeated as far as all the infinitely many other aberrant rivals of T are concerned, to generate *infinitely many empirically more successful* aberrant rivals to T: $T_1*, T_2*, ... T_\infty*$.[34]

But even though all of $T_1*, T_2*, ... T_\infty*$ are more successful empirically than T, they are all, quite correctly, ignored by physics because they are all horribly disunified. They postulate different laws for different phenomena in a wholly ad hoc fashion, and are just assumed to be false. But this means physics makes a big, implicit assumption about the nature of the universe: it is such that all such grossly disunified, aberrant, "patchwork quilt" theories are false.

If physicists only ever accepted theories that postulate atoms even though empirically more successful rival theories are available that postulate other entities such as fields, it would surely be quite clear: physicists implicitly assume that the universe is such that all theories that postulate entities other than atoms are false. Just the same holds in connection with unified theories. That physicists only ever accept unified theories even though endlessly many empirically more successful, disunified rival theories are available means that physics implicitly assumes that the universe is such that all such disunified theories are false.

It may be objected: unified theories are inherently more likely to be true; they are such that they are better verified by a given body of supporting evidence, than disunified rivals. Thus, even if aberrant rivals are empirically more successful, the unified theory is actually better verified.

I have two replies to this objection. First, many disunified theories can be approximated, arbitrarily closely, by unified theories.[35] The line between unified and disunified theories is not always as sharp as the considerations developed so far might lead one to suppose. But second, even if we restrict our attention to theories that are either obviously unified or disunified, it is only in a certain kind of universe, with an appropriate kind of underlying unity, that empirically verified *unified* theories would be more likely to be true than empirically verified *disunified* ones. In a universe that has underlying *disunity*, the reverse would be the case. This shows decisively that to hold that unified theories are inherently more amenable to verification than disunified ones amounts to adopting (or favouring) a metaphysical thesis about the universe concerning underlying unity.

It may be objected, again, that only those predictions of a theory can be trusted, or taken seriously, that come from that part of the theory that is unified and has already been empirically confirmed. Predictions that come from a disunified bit of the theory that has had no confirmation have no credence whatsoever. But this objection falls to the same criticism. First, many disunified theories can be mimicked arbitrarily closely by unified theories: in these cases, predictions that come from the disunified bit of an aberrant theory can be mimicked arbitrarily closely by a theory that is unified. Secondly, even if we restrict our attention to theories that are either clearly unified or disunified, in some kinds of disunified universes, it will be the predictions of certain kinds of disunified bits of aberrant theories that will meet with success; corresponding predictions of unified theories will tend to fail. Whether this is the case or not depends on what kind of universe we are in.

The argument so far might be summed up like this. Physics cannot proceed on the basis of evidence alone. Infinitely many different theories will always successfully predict all the evidence we have accumulated. In deciding what theories to accept and reject, two kinds of methods need to be employed: (1) empirical methods, which determine what theories are to be accepted and rejected on the basis of empirical success and failure; (2) ostensibly non-empirical methods which determine what theories are to be accepted and rejected on the basis of theoretical unity, simplicity, explanatory character, and other such characteristics of theories. We need both. The second may even override the first, as we have seen. Whatever specific form (2) takes – whatever we decide to mean by theoretical "unity" – inevitably this amounts to selecting out, from the domain of possible theories compatible with available evidence, a highly restricted domain of acceptably unified theories. Infinitely many empirically successful theories are excluded; and some are permitted, how many depending on how broadly or narrowly theoretical "unity" is defined. Adoption of any specific method of type (2) inevitably amounts to making some kind of assumption about the nature of the universe[36] – a highly problematic assumption, almost bound to be more or less false because it is a sheer conjecture, no more than a *guess* about that of which we are most ignorant, the ultimate nature of the universe.

Philosophers have always been aware of the possibility of invoking some kind of metaphysical principle of the unity or uniformity of nature in order to solve the problem of induction. But this approach has almost always been ridiculed as nonsensical. As Bas van Fraassen has put it, "From Gravesande's axiom of the uniformity of nature in 1717 to Russell's postulates of human knowledge in 1948, this has been a mug's game."[37] It has been assumed that, if this approach is to succeed, it must be possible to provide a justification for the truth, or the probable truth, of the principle in question.[38] As no such justification seems conceivable, the whole approach is laughed out of court.

And thereby the philosophy tradition has profoundly missed the point, and incidentally condemned itself to triviality and impotence. For, the whole point of acknowledging the inevitable presence of the metaphysical thesis is to appreciate that it is both highly *influential* and highly *problematic*, a mere *conjecture*, and thus strongly in need of being explicitly articulated within physics, so that it can be critically assessed, so that alternatives can be developed, proposed, and criticized, in the hope that the thesis that is accepted as the best available can be *improved*. It is the very absence of any hope of any kind of justification of the truth of the metaphysical principle which demands that the principle be acknowledged explicitly, so that attempts can be made to improve it. The philosophical tradition could not have more monumentally missed the point.

What is being appealed to here is a quite basic principle of rigour or rationality, which can be stated like this:

Rationality requires that assumptions that are influential,
problematic, and implicit be made explicit so that they can be
subjected to imaginative and critical scrutiny, in an attempt
to improve them.

Thus, a kind of physics which acknowledges fully the metaphysical principle implicit in persistent preference for unified theories is thereby more *rigorous*, more *rational*, than a kind of physics which does not – and this applies especially if the principle in question is no more than an unjustifiable conjecture! In other words: *authentic natural philosophy is more rigorous than standard empiricist science.* We have here the nub of the argument of this book.[39]

The philosophical tradition, in failing even to consider the possibility that the metaphysical principle of the unity of nature is a sheer conjecture, reveals thereby just how decisively natural philosophy disappeared from view during the great battle between Newton and Descartes depicted in the last chapter. Empiricism versus Rationalism is a well-known debate within philosophy. Natural philosophy versus standard empiricist science is not.

What all this reveals is that a profound dilemma lies at the heart of science, the very existence of which is obscured by standard empiricism. It deserves to be called *the fundamental dilemma of science.*[40] It can be put like this. Science must make some kind of conjectural assumption about the ultimate nature of the universe (evidence alone is not enough). It is crucially important to adopt a good assumption, since only then can there be any hope of scientific progress: a bad assumption will lead scientists to adopt bad methods, develop the wrong kind of theories and assess them in the wrong kind of way. And yet it is just here, concerning the ultimate nature of the universe, that we are most ignorant, are only able to guess, and are almost bound to get things disastrously wrong. Paradoxically, science must assume it already knows (in outline) just that of which it is most ignorant, and seeks ultimately to discover!

This dilemma helps explain why humanity found it so difficult to create science in the first place. We have learned that in order to create and pursue science successfully so that real theoretical knowledge and understanding is achieved, it is necessary to adopt some version of physicalism – or, at least, implement methods that presuppose physicalism: roughly, the view that precise physical laws govern the way natural phenomena occur.[41] Most people, for most of history, have accepted versions of a very different view, namely that spirits, demons, gods, or God govern the way natural phenomena occur. Given a view of this kind, it will be quite rational to adopt such methods as prayer, sacrifice, consultation of prophets, oracles, omens and dreams. Theories will be put forward which seek to explain phenomena in terms of the purposes, moods, and desires of the gods – exactly the wrong kind of theories granted that impersonal physical law governs the way events unfold. Metaphysics determines methodology – and bad metaphysics determines bad methodology, which may well lead to failure of a peculiarly persistent kind. There will be some apparent successes, as when the tribal witch doctor apparently succeeds in curing disease or causing rainfall by calling upon the gods; these successes will help to keep the basic doctrine alive. Many failures need not at all, however, cast doubt on the basic doctrine, for the doctrine will contain explanations as to why such failures should occur: anger of the gods at undisclosed crimes or evil thoughts within the tribe, for example.[42] Indeed, if the doctrine determines the methodology whereby beliefs are developed and assessed, beliefs that clash with, or cast doubt on, the basic doctrine will be excluded *a priori* as it were. In this way, it may be very difficult indeed to escape from a bad choice of basic metaphysics, even though it leads to a programme of improving knowledge and control of natural processes that meets with only very limited success.[43]

In order to create science it is essential to adopt a very different metaphysical view of the universe: a view which holds that impersonal, precise regularities govern natural phenomena.[44] Or, at least, it is essential to adopt methods which presuppose such a metaphysical view. Locked into the view that nature is controlled by gods or spirits, humanity has found it extraordinarily difficult to accept that mere impersonal regularities govern natural phenomena.[45] The ancient Babylonians made very precise astronomical observations, but failed to develop astronomy: their view of the heavens made it impossible. More significantly, China, over the centuries, made a wealth of technological discoveries,[46] but failed to develop science. Almost everything required for science to be possible was present in China, perhaps as long ago as the tenth century A D, or even earlier. The one element missing was the vital metaphysical view of physicalism – or, a bit more generally, the view that precise regularities govern natural phenomena. Why did such a metaphysical view become one that philosophers could adopt in Europe in the sixteenth and seventeeth centuries? In part because of the influence of ancient Greek philosophy and mathematics, in part because religious views made a sharp distinction between God and nature, which in turn made it possible to think of nature as a vast mathematical machine created by God to be knowable by humans. Christianity did more to promote than to retard the birth of modern science, despite the way the Catholic church treated Bruno and Galileo.

If standard empiricism is accepted, it becomes something of a mystery as to why China did not create modern science long before Europe: this mystery is known as "the Needham question."[47] Grant the viewpoint of what I have called authentic natural philosophy, and there is no mystery.[48] Accept physicalism, and at once there is an enticing invitation to do science, or natural philosophy rather; to discover *what* regularities govern natural phenomena. This metaphysical view holds out the promise of progressive improvement of predictive and explanatory knowledge, although it does not guarantee it. The view that the world is governed by gods or spirits holds out no such promise or, insofar as there is some such promise, it is one that is fraught with disappointment and failure, on its own terms.

AIM-ORIENTED EMPIRICISM

Once it is accepted that physics makes a big, persistent, metaphysical assumption about the nature of the universe, two crucial questions immediately arise. What ought this metaphysical thesis concerning the unity of nature to be? How can we best go about improving it?

The answer to these two questions is a view of science that I have called *aim-oriented empiricism*. This is the view that paves the way for the resurrection of natural philosophy.

As I have expounded and argued for aim-oriented empiricism in great detail elsewhere,[49] here I will be as brief as I can. The basic idea is that, in order to give ourselves the best chance of improving the metaphysical assumption accepted by physics, we need to represent this assumption in the form of a hierarchy of assumptions which become, as one goes up the hierarchy, less and less substantial, and more nearly such that their truth is required for science, or the pursuit of knowledge, to be possible at all. In this way we create a relatively unproblematic framework of assumptions and associated methodological rules high up in the hierarchy, below which much more substantial, problematic assumptions and associated methodological rules, low down in the hierarchy, can be critically assessed and, we may hope, improved, in the light of the empirical success they lead to, and their compatibility with assumptions higher up in the hierarchy (see figure 2).

At the top there is the relatively insubstantial assumption that the universe is such that we can acquire some knowledge of our local circumstances. If this assumption is false, we will not be able to acquire knowledge whatever we assume. We are justified in accepting this assumption permanently as a part of our knowledge, even though we have no grounds for holding it to be true. As we descend the hierarchy, the assumptions become increasingly substantial and thus increasingly likely to be false. At level 6 there is the more substantial thesis that there is some rationally discoverable thesis about the nature of the universe which, if true and if accepted, makes it possible progressively to improve methods for the improvement of knowledge. "Rationally discoverable," here, means at least that the thesis is not an arbitrary choice from infinitely many analogous theses. At level 5 we have the even more substantial thesis that the universe is *comprehensible* in some way or other, whether physically or in some other way. This thesis asserts that the universe is such that there is *something* (God, tribe of gods, cosmic goal, physical entity, cosmic programme, or whatever), which exists everywhere in an unchanging form and which, in some sense, determines or is responsible for everything that changes (all change and diversity in the world in principle being explicable and understandable in terms of the underlying unchanging *something*). A universe of this type deserves to be called "comprehensible" because it is such that everything that occurs, all change and diversity, can in principle be explained and understood as being the outcome of the operations of the one underlying *something*, present throughout all phenomena. At level 4 we have the still more substantial thesis that the universe is *physically* comprehensible in some way or other. This asserts that the universe is made up one unified self-interacting physical entity (or one kind of entity), all change and diversity being in principle explicable in terms of this entity. What this amounts to is that the universe is such that some yet-to-be-discovered unified physical theory of everything is true.

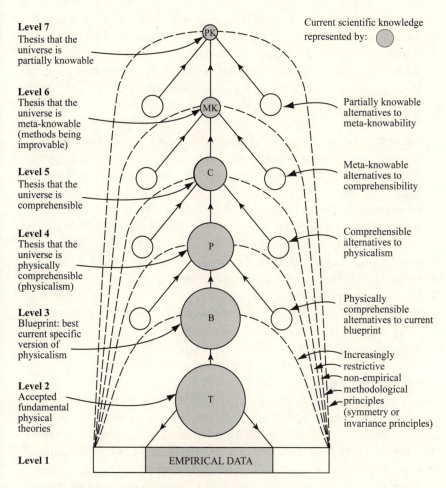

Level 7
Thesis that the universe is partially knowable

Level 6
Thesis that the universe is meta-knowable (methods being improvable)

Level 5
Thesis that the universe is comprehensible

Level 4
Thesis that the universe is physically comprehensible (physicalism)

Level 3
Blueprint: best current specific version of physicalism

Level 2
Accepted fundamental physical theories

Level 1

Current scientific knowledge represented by:

Partially knowable alternatives to meta-knowability

Meta-knowable alternatives to comprehensibility

Comprehensible alternatives to physicalism

Physically comprehensible alternatives to current blueprint

Increasingly restrictive non-empirical methodological principles (symmetry or invariance principles)

EMPIRICAL DATA

Figure 2 Aim-Oriented Empiricism (AOE)

I shall call this thesis *physicalism*. At level 3, we have an even more substantial thesis, the best, currently available specific idea as to how the universe is physically comprehensible. This asserts that everything is made of some specific kind of physical entity: corpuscle, point-particle, classical field, quantum field, convoluted space-time, string, or whatever. Given the historical record of dramatically changing ideas at this level, and given the relatively highly specific and substantial character of successive assumptions made at this level, we can be reasonably confident that the best assumption available at any stage in the development of physics at this level will be false, and will need future revision. Here, ideas evolve with evolving knowledge. At level 2 there are the accepted fundamental theories of physics, currently general relativity and the standard model. Here, if anything, we can be even more confident that current theories are false, despite their immense empirical success. This confidence comes partly from the vast empirical content of these theories, and partly from the historical record. The greater the content of a proposition the more likely it is to be false; the fundamental theories of physics, general relativity and the standard model, have such vast empirical content that this in itself almost guarantees falsity. And the historical record backs this up; Kepler's laws of planetary motion and Galileo's laws of terrestrial motion are corrected by Newtonian theory, which is in turn corrected by special and general relativity; classical physics is corrected by quantum theory, in turn corrected by relativistic quantum theory, quantum field theory, and the standard model. Each new theory in physics reveals that predecessors are false. Indeed, if the level 4 assumption is correct, then all current physical theories are false, since this assumption asserts that the true physical theory of everything is unified, and the totality of current fundamental physical theory, general relativity plus the standard model, is notoriously disunified. Finally, at level 1 there are accepted empirical data, low-level, corroborated, empirical laws.

The idea is to separate out what is most likely to be true, and not in need of revision, at and near the top of the hierarchy, from what is most likely to be false, and most in need of criticism and revision, near the bottom of the hierarchy. Evidence, at level 1, and assumptions high up in the hierarchy, are rather firmly accepted, as being most likely to be true (although still open to revision): this is then used to criticize, and to try to improve, theses at levels 2 and 3 (and perhaps 4), where falsity is most likely to be located.

In order to be acceptable, an assumption at any level from 6 to 3 must (as far as possible) be compatible with, and a special case of, the assumption above in the hierarchy; at the same time it must be (or promise to be) empirically fruitful in the sense that successive accepted physical theories increasingly successfully accord with (or exemplify) the assumption. At level 2, those physical theories are accepted which are sufficiently (a) empirically successful and (b) in accord with the best available assumption at level 3 (or level 4). Corresponding to each assumption, at any level from 7 to 3, there is a methodological principle, represented by sloping dotted lines in figure 2, requiring that theses lower down in the hierarchy are compatible with the given assumption.

When theoretical physics has completed its central task, and the true theory of everything, T, has been discovered, then T will (in principle) successfully predict all empirical phenomena at level 1, and will entail the assumption at level 3, which will in turn entail the assumption at level 4, and so on up the hierarchy. As it is, physics has not completed its task, T has not (yet) been discovered, and we are ignorant of the nature of the universe. This ignorance is reflected in clashes between theses at different levels of aim-oriented empiricism. There are clashes between levels 1 and 2, 2 and 3, and 3 and 4. And the two fundamental theories at level 2, the standard model and general relativity, clash as well. The attempt to resolve these clashes drives physics forward.

In seeking to resolve clashes between levels, influences can go in both directions. Thus, given a clash between levels 1 and 2, this may lead to the modification or replacement of the relevant theory at level 2; but, on the other hand, it may lead to the discovery that the relevant experimental result is not correct for any number of possible reasons, and needs to be modified. In general, however, such a clash leads to the rejection of the level 2 theory rather than the level 1 experimental result; the latter are held onto more firmly than the former, in part because experimental results have vastly less empirical content than theories, in part because of our confidence in the results of observation and direct experimental manipulation (especially after repetition and expert critical examination). Again, given a clash between levels 2 and 3, this may lead to the rejection of the relevant level 2 theory (because it is disunified, ad hoc, at odds with the current metaphysics of physics); but, on the other hand, it may lead to the rejection of the level 3 assumption and the adoption, instead, of a new assumption (as has happened a number of times in the history of physics). The rejection of the current level 3 assumption is likely to take place if the level 2 theory, which clashes with it, is highly successful empirically, and furthermore has the effect of increasing unity in the totality of fundamental physical theory overall, so that clashes between levels 2 and 4 are decreased. In general, however, clashes between levels 2 and 3 are resolved by the rejection or modification of theories at level 2 rather than the assumption at level 3, in part because of the vastly greater empirical content of level 2 theories, in part because of the empirical fruitfulness of the level 3 assumption (in the sense indicated above).

It is conceivable that the clash between level 2 theories and the level 4 assumption might lead to the revision of the latter rather than the former. This happened when Galileo rejected the then-current level 4 assumption of Aristotelianism, and replaced it with the idea that "the book of nature is written in the language of mathematics" (an early precursor of our current level 4 assumption). The whole idea, however, is that as we go up the hierarchy of assumptions we are increasingly unlikely to encounter error, and the need for revision. The higher up we go, the more firmly assumptions are upheld, the more resistance there is to modification.

The idea of representing the metaphysical presuppositions of physics (concerning the nature of the universe) as a hierarchy of theses, increasingly insubstantial as one goes up the hierarchy, gains some support from the fact that something somewhat similar exists informally at the empirical level – level 1 in figure 2 – and for much the same reason. There are, at the lowest level, the results of experiments performed at specific times and places. Then, above these, there are low-level experimental laws, asserting that each experimental result is a repeatable effect. Next up, there are empirical laws such as Hooke's law, Ohm's law, or the gas laws. Above these there are such physical laws as those of electrostatics or thermodynamics. And above these there are theories which have been refuted, but which can be "derived," when appropriate limits are taken, from accepted fundamental theory – as Newtonian theory can be "derived" from general relativity. This informal hierarchy at the empirical level exists for the same reason we need the hierarchy at the metaphysical level: so that relatively contentless and secure theses (at the bottom of the empirical hierarchy) may be distinguished from more contentful and insecure theses (further up the hierarchy) to facilitate pinpointing what needs to be revised and how, should the need for revision arise. That such a hierarchy exists at the empirical level provides some support for my claim that we need to adopt such a hierarchy at the metaphysical level.

Aim-oriented empiricism, as depicted in figure 2, provides physics with a meta-methodology which facilitates improvement of the metaphysical assumptions and associated methods as physics advances, in the light of which of them seem to be the most fruitful empirically, and other considerations. As knowledge in physics improves, so metaphysical assumptions and methods improve as well, or, in other words, knowledge about how to improve knowledge improves.

There is something like positive feedback between improving knowledge of the universe, and improving aims and methods, improving knowledge about how to improve knowledge.[50] Everyone would acknowledge that this kind of positive feedback goes on at the empirical level. New empirical knowledge can lead to new methods, via the development of new instruments, new experimental techniques, which in turn lead to further acquisition of new knowledge. Aim-oriented empiricism provides methods which facilitate such positive feedback at the metaphysical and theoretical level as well. As we increase our scientific knowledge and understanding of the universe, we increase our knowledge of how to increase knowledge – the very nub of scientific rationality which helps explain the explosive, and apparently ever-accelerating, growth of scientific knowledge. We adapt the nature of science to what we find out about the nature of the universe.[51] All this has gone on in science to some extent *implicitly*: what the transition from standard to aim-oriented empiricism does is to make the implicit *explicit* – science becoming even more successful as a result.[52]

A potential objection to what has been said so far is that, since Galileo and Kepler, physics has been extraordinarily successful in developing a succession of theories that satisfy the almost contradictory requirements of (a) enormously increasing the scope of empirical predictions, and simultaneously (b) bringing ever-greater unity to fundamental theory in physics. This immense success has been achieved, for most of the time, with the physics community taking (versions of) standard empiricism for granted. It is just not conceivable that this success could have been achieved with physicists accepting and implementing a conception of science that is untenable, unworkable, and irrational, as I have claimed above. The above refutation of standard empiricism must be invalid.

My reply is that physics has met with such extraordinary success because aim-oriented empiricism has been implicitly put into practice despite official allegiance being paid to standard empiricism. Success has been achieved *despite*, not *because of*, allegiance to standard empiricism. Fortunately, acceptance of standard empiricism has been somewhat hypocritical; it is that which has allowed something close to aim-oriented empiricism to be put into scientific practice, which in turn has made it possible for physics to achieve such astonishing success. But, as I have indicated above, and as I shall point out again in chapter 5, physics would be even more successful if it repudiated standard empiricism and explicitly adopted and implemented, in a thoroughgoing way, aim-oriented empiricism instead. The attempt to keep alive the myth of standard empiricism obstructs, to some extent, the full implementation of aim-oriented empiricism. It is of interest to recall that Einstein, whose mature view of science included elements of aim-oriented empiricism,[53] was aware of a mismatch between what theoretical physicists *say* they do, and what they *actually* do. He wrote, "If you want to find out anything from the theoretical physicists about the methods they use ... don't listen to their words, fix your attention on their deeds."[54]

As I have argued in some detail elsewhere,[55] aim-oriented empiricism almost became explicit with Einstein's discovery of special and general relativity. Both theories arose out of Einstein's search for theoretical unity, the unification of Newton's and Maxwell's theories. In both cases Einstein was led to the new theory via the formulation of general principles: the restricted principle of relativity and the light postulate, in the case of special relativity, and Lorentz invariance and the principle of equivalence in the case of general relativity. Remarkably, Einstein first discovered general relativity in the form of a metaphysical idea: gravitation is the variable curvature of spacetime induced by matter and energy. He then had to work hard to turn this into a precise, testable physical theory. This, according to aim-oriented empiricism, is the manner in which new theories in physics should be created, as we shall see in chapter 5. It is strikingly different from the way Newton and Maxwell created their theories: in these cases, not only did the then-current metaphysical ideas not lead to the new theory[56] – they actually obstructed the correct interpretation of the new theory once it had been formulated. I will argue that this happened too with the discovery and interpretation of quantum theory. It is significant that Einstein believed passionately in the physical comprehensibility of the universe, and this belief played a significant role in his discovery of special and general relativity. He devoted his life to trying to discover how the universe is comprehensible, in the form of a testable, unified theory. And in his later years Einstein almost came to advocate a key component of aim-oriented empiricism: physics cannot be understood without the assumption that the universe is physically comprehensible.[57] Eugene Wigner has pointed out, correctly, that the methods Einstein employed to discover his theories of relativity have had a profound impact on subsequent physics.[58] But Einstein's work has not yet led to the repudiation of standard empiricism and the acceptance of aim-oriented empiricism, as it perhaps should have done. It deserves to be noted, nevertheless, that the roots of aim-oriented empiricism lie in physics, not in philosophy.[59]

There is, however, as we have seen, a decisive philosophical argument against standard empiricism and for aim-oriented empiricism. Standard empiricism is refuted by its abject failure to solve the problem of induction. It cannot even do justice to the way theories are *selected* in physics, ignoring all questions about *verifying* theories, or rendering them *probable*. In physics only *unified* theories are ever accepted, with endlessly many empirically more successful *disunified* rivals invariably being ignored: this means physics makes the big, implicit assumption that the universe is such that all disunified theories are false. That flatly contradicts standard empiricism. Aim-oriented empiricism, by contrast, faces no such contradiction. It openly acknowledges that persistent preference for *unified* theories in physics means that physics accepts a highly problematic metaphysical conjecture concerning the underlying unity of the universe. It is more rigorous intellectually just because it does acknowledge this metaphysical conjecture (which standard empiricism denies). Furthermore, as a result of representing this conjecture in the form of a hierarchy of conjectures, aim-oriented empiricism provides a meta-methodology for the *improvement* of conjectures lower down in the hierarchy – those conjectures being chosen which best promote the growth of empirical knowledge, and best accord with conjectures higher up in the hierarchy. And what is really decisive is that aim-oriented empiricism succeeds in solving the problem of induction. What the long-standing failure of philosophers to solve the problem of induction has been trying to tell us, over the centuries, is that standard empiricist science is untenable, and what we need to develop in its place is aim-oriented empiricist natural philosophy!

In appendix 2 I demonstrate, in outline, that aim-oriented empiricism does indeed provide us with the solution to the problem of induction. I there show that we are justified in accepting, as a part of scientific knowledge, each of the metaphysical conjectures at levels 7 to 3 of figure 2. A more detailed argument in support of the claim that aim-oriented empiricism solves the problem of induction is to be found in my *Understanding Scientific Progress*.[60] The outline of the argument is I hope clear. No attempt is made to prove that any of these conjectures is *true*, or *probably* true. Instead, the argument is that acceptance of these conjectures give us the best hope of achieving scientific progress in knowledge of the truth. A part of the point of distinguishing conjectures at different levels is that different arguments apply at different levels. At levels 7 and 6 the argument is that we will never want to reject these conjectures because their acceptance can only help, and cannot hinder (or can scarcely hinder) the search for knowledge whatever kind of universe we may be in. Arguments in support of accepting conjectures at levels 5 to 3 are based on claims that these conjectures are associated with progress in scientific knowledge at levels 2 and 1, to an extent that no rival conjectures can match.

Some historians and philosophers of science have denied that anything theoretical persists through scientific revolutions.[61] Actually, all theoretical revolutions in physics exemplify the persisting idea that there is some kind of underlying unity of physical law in nature. These revolutions are all great achievements of theoretical *unification.* Thus Newton unifies Galileo's terrestial laws of motion and Kepler's astronomical laws of motion. James Clerk Maxwell's theory of electrodynamics unifies the electric and magnetic forces into the single force of electromagnetism. It unifies optical theory and electromagnetism by revealing that light is just waves in the electromagnetic field. And it further unifies gamma rays, x-rays, infrared rays, ultraviolet rays, and radio waves by revealing that all these are waves in the electromagnetic field, of different wavelengths. Special relativity brings greater unity to Maxwell's theory,[62] unifies energy and mass by means of $E = mc^2$, and partially unifies space and time to form space-time. General relativity unifies gravitation and space-time by absorbing gravitation into a richer conception of space-time. The theory of elements and chemical compounds initiated by Lavoisier brings astonishing unification to chemistry, in reducing millions of different sorts of elementary substances to around 100 elements. Quantum theory and the theory of atomic structure brings massive unification to atomic theory, properties of matter, interactions between matter and light. Instead of nearly 100 elements plus electromagnetic radiation, the theory postulates just four entities: the electron, proton, neutron, and photon. Instead of a multiplicity of laws concerning the chemical and physical properties of matter, there is Schrödinger's equation. Quantum electrodynamics unifies quantum theory, special relativity, and classical electrodynamics. The electro-weak theory of Weinberg and Salam partially unifies the electromagnetic and weak forces. The quark theory of Gell-Mann and Zweig brings greater unity to the theory of fundamental particles: a large number of hadrons are reduced to just six quarks. Quantum chromodynamics brings further unification to the theory of fundamental particles by providing a quantum theory of the strong force. The standard model, the current quantum theory of fundamental particles and the forces between them, partially unifies the electromagnetic, weak and strong force.[63] All theoretical revolutions in physics without exception embody the discovery of greater unity in nature. The whole enterprise of theoretical physics, from Kepler and Galileo down to today, cries out to be interpreted as the progressive discovery of unity in nature, the level 4 thesis of physicalism of AOE. As I have put it elsewhere: "Far from obliterating the idea that there is a persisting theoretical idea in physics, revolutions do just the opposite in that they all themselves actually exemplify the persisting idea of underlying unity!"[64]

Aim-oriented empiricism transforms the idea we may have of the extent to which physics specifically, and science more generally, is making progress. Viewed from the perspective of standard empiricism, the picture can seem rather bleak. Physics staggers, it seems, from one false theory to another. That science will continue to advance in this manner has even been called, by one philosopher of science, the "pessimistic induction."[65] It may not even be clear, in these circumstances, what it can *mean* to hold that physics makes progress. There can be no grounds, it may seem, to hold that physics is making progress. Thomas Kuhn, for one, has declared that we may have to abandon the idea that science does make progress across scientific revolutions.[66]

Accept aim-oriented empiricism, and the situation is transformed. Aim-oriented empiricism implies that physicalism is an item of current scientific knowledge. According to physicalism, as interpreted here, that which determines how events evolve splits into two components, what may be termed the "theoretical component" U, the same everywhere, and the variable component V. Only the true, unified theory of everything can specify *precisely* the nature of U. All dynamical theories restricted in scope specify U at best only inaccurately. All such theories, in other words, are false. Given physicalism, a physical theory can only be precisely correct about how *any* specific phenomenon evolves if it is correct about how *all* phenomena evolve. Thus, if physicalism is true, and physics proceeds by developing theories that apply to more and more phenomena with greater and greater accuracy without applying to *all phenomena*, progress towards the truth – towards the true, unified theory of everything – must involve moving from one false theory to another. That theoretical physics has advanced in this fashion thus provides no grounds whatsoever for pessimism concerning the reality of progress. This is exactly how physics must advance if it is to make progress towards a true, unified theory of everything!

But what does it mean to say of two false theories, T_1 and T_2, that T_2 is closer to the truth than T_1? It would take us too far astray for me to spell out the solution here to this "problem of verisimilitude."[67] It is, however, fully spelled out elsewhere.[68]

Strong grounds for accepting aim-oriented empiricism arise from the fact that the view leads to the solution to five fundamental problems in the philosophy of science that philosophers have struggled and failed to solve for decades, and in some cases, for centuries: the problem of induction; the problem of what it means to say of a physical theory that it possesses simplicity and unity; the problem of how it can be justified to give preference for simple, unified theories in physics; the problem of verisimilitude; and the problem of the nature of scientific method.[69]

Once aim-oriented empiricism is accepted, adopted, and implemented by scientists and philosophers alike, natural philosophy will begin to flourish again. The gulf between science and philosophy will begin to be healed. But before that can happen, philosophy needs to acknowledge and put right its other great failing, the subject of the next chapter.

4

Failures of Philosophy, Part II

OUR FUNDAMENTAL PROBLEM
AND CARTESIAN DUALISM

The primary task of philosophy, I argued in the last chapter, is to keep alive awareness of our fundamental problems, and the importance of trying to improve our attempted solutions to them. Implicit in much that we do and think in life there are answers to fundamental problems, more or less inadequate, having more or less adverse repercussions for what we do and think, the quality of our lives, individual, social, and global. It is important, for its own sake and, to some extent, for the sake of everything else, to keep alive awareness of what our fundamental problems are, and what our best – and our most influential – attempts at solving them are. As we saw in the last chapter, it is vital that academia supports sustained tackling of fundamental problems. If it does not, academic inquiry becomes damagingly irrational, and is likely to lose its way among a maze of specialized research and education.

All this applies straightforwardly to our most fundamental problem of all, which I have stated like this:

How can our human world, and the world of sentient life more generally, imbued with perceptual qualities, consciousness, free will, meaning, and value, exist and best flourish embedded as it is in the physical universe?

But philosophy since Descartes has failed to keep alive awareness of this fundamental problem – as we shall now see.[1]

It all began very promisingly. Cartesian dualism quite clearly attempts to solve this problem – *the human world/physical universe problem*, as we may call it. The material world is ultimately physical in character. It is made up exclusively of fundamental physical entities – corpuscles, point-particles, a unified field, quantum strings, or physical entities not yet thought of – which interact in accordance with precise physical law. Everything that cannot in principle be reduced to physics – colours, sounds, smells, tactile qualities as we perceive them, sentience, consciousness, free will, meaning, and everything of value (moral, aesthetic, institutional) – is to be scooped up from the physical universe and tucked inside our minds, wholly distinct from the material world although associated with, and perhaps in two-way interaction with, living human brains.

As we have seen in previous chapters, many of Descartes's near contemporaries – Galileo, Newton, and others – saw things in somewhat similar ways.

Cartesian dualism is, nevertheless, beset with problems.

There is the wild implausibility of the idea that there are ghostly Cartesian "minds," burdened with the rich content of all our experiences, feelings, desires, and thoughts, distinct from our brains, and yet wholly invisible to everyone other than the person whose mind it is. Why should brains have these mysterious, invisible, ghostly counterparts? What physical processes occurring in brains could conceivably generate such ghostly entities?

There is the problem of how mind and brain can interact. The brain must interact with the mind – if we are to have any contact with, and know anything about, the physical world. The mind must interact with the brain – if we are to have any free will. The latter interaction means that some physical events in the brain are caused, at least in part, by the mind. Given Cartesian dualism, there can only be free will if physical laws are violated in the brain. Poltergeist-like physical events must occur in our brains whenever we exercise our free will, so that our conscious mind influences what our bodies do. Cartesian dualism can only reconcile physicalism and the world as we experience it by denying that physicalism holds as far as conscious brains are concerned – or by denying that we have any free will at all.

There is the problem of how perception can deliver knowledge of the world external to us. If everything we experience is mental in character, inside our minds, including all our perceptual experiences

of touch, shape, colour, sound, smell, taste, how can we know anything at all about the world around us via experience? Does not
Cartesian dualism tell us that our experiences of the world are no
more than a vast delusion? Physical reality is quite other from the
way we experience it to be.

And there is a more general problem about how we can acquire
any knowledge at all about the universe around us. Descartes thought
this latter problem could be solved by recourse to "clear and distinct
ideas." God, being benign, would not deceive us. He would have created a universe capable of being known by us. All we have to do is to
make sure our ideas about it are clear and distinct. But this line of
thought became less than convincing once the immense predictive
and explanatory success of Newtonian mechanics became apparent.
Newton's law of gravitation may be, in some sense, clear and distinct,
but it was also widely regarded as incomprehensible by Newton's
contemporaries and successors – and even by Newton himself. If
Newton's law is regarded as clear and distinct then it is at once clear
that there are endlessly many rival possible laws just as clear and
distinct. Clarity and distinctness is no longer an unambiguous,
assured guide to truth. Instead, one has to appeal to evidence, to
experience. But it is just here that Cartesian dualism creates an insu-
perable problem. How can experience deliver knowledge about the
real world around us?

One of the extraordinary features of philosophy after Descartes is
that Cartesian dualism comes to be quite widely rejected but the
problems generated by Cartesian dualism, those just indicated, come
to occupy a central place within philosophy. The problem of the relationship between the mind and the brain – the "mind/body problem"
as it came to be called – along with the problem of free will and determinism, and the problem of how knowledge can be acquired by
means of perception: these key problems that confront one the
moment Cartesian dualism is accepted are central to the whole tradition of philosophy after Descartes – even though Cartesian dualism
itself is rejected. Instead of rejecting Cartesian dualism and focusing
attention on the problem Cartesian dualism sought to solve – our
fundamental problem, indicated above, the human world/physical
universe problem – philosophy rather preoccupied itself with the
problems Cartesian dualism generates *even though Cartesian dualism itself is rejected.* This is perhaps the fundamental failure of philosophy after Descartes: the failure to put at the heart of the discipline

our fundamental problem, the human world/physical universe problem, which Cartesian dualism tries, and fails, to solve.[2] It is bad enough to go on trying to solve problems generated by a doctrine one has rejected. It is even worse to ignore the basic unsolved problem the rejected doctrine sought, and failed, to solve in the first place.

This fundamental failure then led to others which served to widen the gulf between science and philosophy, and led philosophers to adopt doctrines which made it impossible even to *formulate* the fundamental problem of philosophy, let alone set about improving our attempted solutions to it. As science forged ahead, philosophy became increasingly alienated from its proper basic task.

It began with John Locke. In his *Essay concerning Human Understanding*, Locke begins with a tirade against "innate ideas" – ideas we are born with, independent of experience. The intended target is Descartes's claim that we can acquire some knowledge about the world by reason alone independent of experience. But to argue that we do not have innate ideas is rather beside the point. We might well have such ideas, and yet be incapable of acquiring any knowledge about the world by reason alone (and vice versa, of course).

In any case, having convinced himself that all ideas come from experience, Locke goes on to spell out how, in his view, sensory experience leads to ideas, and to knowledge. The whole discussion implicitly presupposes something like Descartes's dualist view. We only ever experience our own sense impressions – visual, auditory, tactile, etc. Everything else is inferred. The real world differs profoundly from the way we experience it to be. Colours, sounds, smells, tactile qualities, that we experience, are in us. They are not real properties of things external to our minds.

At once Locke is confronted by the problem that confronts all those who conceive of our relationship with the world in quasi-Cartesian terms and reject the idea that reason alone can deliver knowledge about the world: if we only ever experience our own sense impressions, how can we acquire any knowledge at all about the world external to our minds? How can we acquire any knowledge of *matter* if we are permanently locked up inside our *minds*?

Locke's proposed solution to this problem is to distinguish between what he calls *primary* and *secondary* qualities. Primary qualities are properties that things external to us really do possess – such as extension and shape – which produce in us ideas (or sense impressions) which resemble their external cause. We see an object as spatially extended, and it really is spatially extended. Secondary qualities, on the other hand, are some concatenation of primary qualities which produce in us ideas (or sense impressions) very different from their external cause. Thus when we see a red rose, secondary qualities of the rose – real physical properties – produce in us the visual sensation of redness that is, according to Locke, quite different from any real physical property possessed by the rose. Secondary qualities are, for Locke, real physical properties of things external to us which produce in us ideas, such as sensations of colour, sound, smell, and tactile qualities, that do not represent anything that actually exists external to us.[3] Today, many would say that it is the structure of molecules that make up the rose that absorb and reflect light of such and such wavelengths that leads us to see the rose as red – even though redness as we experience it is not out there in the world around us.

Bishop Berkeley (1685–1753) was quick to highlight a devastating objection to Locke's proposed solution to the problem. What entitles us to hold that our ideas of primary qualities accurately represent their external cause, whereas our ideas of secondary qualities do not? If all we ever experience is our own inner sensations, then we can have no basis whatsoever for holding that some inner sensations resemble what is external to us, whereas others do not. We can never hold an inner experience in one hand, as it were, and its external cause in the other hand, and compare the two to see whether or not the first resembles or accurately represents the second. Indeed, concluded Berkeley, we have no grounds for holding that anything exists other than our sense impressions. "To be is to be perceived," he proclaimed. That which cannot be perceived – the material world – does not exist.[4]

Given Berkeley's position, then, it becomes quite impossible even to formulate our fundamental problem. The physical universe, that which gives rise to the problem in its modern form, has simply ceased to exist.

With David Hume, the next philosopher to be considered, matters become even more serious. Hume argued that all our ideas are faint copies of prior sense impressions. There can be no idea that is not derived from prior sense impressions.[5] But this immediately implies that we can have no idea of a universe that is unobservable. The very idea of an unobservable universe is meaningless.

This is even worse than Berkeley's position. Berkeley held that we can have no reason to suppose that unobservable matter exists, and argued that it does not exist. Hume goes further, and argues that the very idea of unobservable matter is meaningless. We can have no such idea at all. Natural philosophy – or science – is devoted to improving our knowledge about not just that which does not exist, but that about which nothing meaningful can be said. We are moving further and further away from being able to formulate our fundamental problem. Philosophy is becoming increasingly at odds with science.

Hume's thesis that all our ideas are copies of prior sense impressions is one form of a disreputable mode of argument that crops up again and again in philosophy, from Plato to Wittgenstein. First, a theory of meaning is put forward. Meanings, concepts, are *Forms*, eternal intellectual entities that exist independently of humanity, but which philosophers may see clearly, thus deciding for the rest of humanity how they should live – namely in servitude to philosophers (Plato). Meaningful ideas are all copies of prior sense impressions (Hume). The meaning of a proposition is its method of verification (logical positivism). The meaning of a word is its *use* (Wittgenstein). The proposed theory of meaning may seem innocent enough at first, but then, by means of a subtle, scarcely noticed intellectual conjuring trick, the *theory* becomes a *criterion* of meaningfulness. Anything which might tell against the "theory" is simply declared to be meaningless – and so nothing can count against the theory! Armed with this weapon, the philosopher then proceeds to deploy it to solve the problems of philosophy, all opposition annihilated by means of the devastating charge of "meaningless!"

All attempts to solve philosophical problems by means of analysis of meaning, an appeal to some theory or criterion of meaning, are inherently intellectually disreputable, and deserve to be treated accordingly.

There is one use that Hume made of his theory or criterion of meaning that deserves to be mentioned in passing, because of the significant role that it plays in our understanding of the nature of the physical universe. Hume considered whether there can be a necessary connection between cause and effect, and concluded that we can have no (meaningful) idea of such a necessary connection, because no sense impressions can give rise to such an idea. All we ever perceive is one state of affairs being followed by another state of affairs, perhaps in a regular fashion. A foot kicks a ball, and the ball shoots away but, however many times we may observe this, nothing we perceive corresponds to *necessity*, except, perhaps, our unshaken conviction that the ball will shoot off when kicked. The idea that physics can capture that which determines *necessarily* why one event is followed by another must, according to Hume, be abandoned. But here, as elsewhere, Hume is wrong, as we shall see in chapter 5.

Hume led to Kant. And Kant endorsed and intensified Hume's ferociously skeptical attitudes towards the material world, the entire domain of natural science. Kant thought that the material world – or the *noumenal* world as he called it – does exist, but he held firmly that nothing whatsoever can be said about it, except that it exists. The subject of science, in so far as it is the material world, has been removed entirely from human reach.[6]

Kant is a paradoxical character. He took science very seriously, and even contributed to it.[7] Nevertheless, according to Kant, science is about the phenomenal world, the world of experience, not the real world, the material world, which is, for Kant, unknowable, and such that nothing meaningful can be said about it except that it exists.

The outcome of this progression in philosophy, from Locke to Kant, is that the fundamental problem of philosophy cannot be formulated. That which sets the problem, the physical universe, has been intellectually annihilated, or at least cast into the realm of the utterly unknowable. Instead of Cartesian dualism and its implications being firmly rejected, the implication concerning the impossibility of knowing anything about the physical world by means of experience is firmly adopted, and as a result it becomes impossible even to formulate our fundamental problem.

PHILOSOPHY AFTER KANT

Kant's philosophy, famous for its obscurity, led to a great upsurge of obscure work in metaphysics, often idealist, anti-rationalist, and indifferent if not hostile to natural science. Kant led on, unwittingly, to Fichte (1762–1814), Schelling (1775–1854), Schleiermacher (1768–1834), Hegel (1770–1831), Schopenhauer (1788–1860), Husserl (1859–1938), and Heidegger (1889–1976). Bombastic metaphysics became all the rage, spreading even to Britain with the work of T.H. Green (1836–1882), F.H. Bradley (1846–1924), and J. McTaggart (1866–1925), and to France with existentialism and the work of Sartre (1905–1980) and Merleau-Ponty (1908–1961). The anti-scientific and idealist character of this body of post-Kantian work again made it impossible even to formulate the basic problem of philosophy, our fundamental problem of all of thought and life.

Inevitably, a reaction set in. G.E Moore (1873–1958) did much to initiate it by criticizing some of the outlandish assertions of the metaphysicians in the name of common sense.[8] Bertrand Russell (1872–1970), along with his one-time student Ludwig Wittgenstein (1889–1951), contributed to the reaction by emphasizing that the world is made up of *facts*. They propounded a doctrine called *logical atomism*. There is an element of irony in this being a part of a movement against metaphysics in that the doctrine has itself a distinctly metaphysical air about it, especially in the hands of Wittgenstein. Logical atomism holds that the world is made up of *atomic facts* – facts that are logically independent of one another.[9] One problem this doctrine faced was that no one could come up with a single convincing example of an atomic fact. There are good grounds for holding that there are none – as a glance at Maxwell (1968a) might convince one. Facts in the real world tend to be logically related to one another. This is especially true of facts about the physical universe.

Russell also contributed to the anti-metaphysical movement by helping to establish the view that the proper job of philosophy is *analysis* – logical, philosophical, or conceptual. And Russell produced what was later taken to be a paradigmatic case of philosophical analysis. This holds that "The King of France is bald" is to be analyzed to assert, "There is a man who is at present King of France; there is only one such man; and he is bald."[10]

Vienna in the 1930s then spawned a movement dedicated to the celebration of science and the annihilation of metaphysics once and for all. This movement is called *logical positivism*, and its members included Moritz Schlick (1882–1936), Rudolf Carnap (1891–1970), Carl Hempel (1905–1997), Otto Neurath (1882–1945), Hans Reichenbach (1891–1953), Friedrich Waismann (1896–1959), Herbert Feigl (1902–1988), and Philipp Frank (1884–1966). Wittgenstein was a sort of aloof figurehead. According to logical positivism, the meaning of a proposition is given by the method of its verification. All meaningful propositions fall into two classes, empirical and analytic. Empirical propositions are verified by an appeal to evidence, analytic ones by an appeal to the meaning of constituent terms, as when we convince ourselves that "All bachelors are unmarried" is true in virtue of the meaning of "bachelor" and "unmarried." Analytic propositions can be established with certainty but assert nothing about the world. Only propositions verified empirically make assertions about the world.

Metaphysical propositions, however, are put forward as being about the world and proved by reason alone. But this is not possible. Such propositions are neither empirical nor analytic. Hence they are all meaningless.[11]

Logical positivism faced the dreadful problem, however, that scientific laws and theories cannot be conclusively verified either, and thus are all meaningless too. The logical positivists struggled to formulate a version of the verification principle that included as meaningful only that which they wanted to regard as meaningful, and excluded everything else, but they failed.

It might seem that this anti-metaphysical movement, initiated by Moore and Russell and developed by the logical positivists, would be better able to give centre stage to our fundamental problem – the human world/physical universe problem – in view especially of the central role given to science. But this did not happen, for several reasons. The analytic view of philosophy rendered the fundamental problem – a problem concerning the real world – beyond the scope of philosophy. In order to formulate it, one needs to appeal to metaphysics, the metaphysics of physics, namely physicalism; but logical positivism held metaphysics to be meaningless. Again, the central doctrine of logical positivism – the verification principle – led to the view that factual scientific statements are about actual and possible sense data; but this amounts to a form of idealism, to the denial of the existence of the physical universe independent of human experience. Once again, our fundamental problem cannot even be formulated because the physical universe, that which poses the problem, is removed from view.

Logical positivism had an immense impact on much subsequent philosophy, especially in the English speaking world, long after its demise. Somewhat like Cartesian dualism, implications of the doctrine continued to be influential even though the doctrine itself had been rejected. It lent support to the view that philosophy could not be about real problems in the real world – since philosophy is not empirical – and must therefore confine itself to *analysis*, and to producing analytic propositions, as mathematics and logic do.

After World War II it was clear that philosophy had split into two mutually hostile camps. On the one hand there is continental philosophy, stemming from the idealist metaphysicians indicated above, against or indifferent to natural science, anti-rationalist, often obscure to the point of incoherence, and including such doctrines as phenomenology, existentialism, critical theory, structuralism, post-structuralism, and postmodernism. On the other hand there is analytic philosophy, stemming from Moore, Russell, logical positivism, and Wittgenstein, committed to the idea that the task of philosophy is analysis, lucid about not very much.

Analytic philosophy has never recovered from the disastrous idea that the proper basic task of philosophy is to analyze concepts. This is a recipe for intellectual sterility at best, intellectual dishonesty at worst.[12] Built into the meaning of the kind of words philosophers are interested in – mind, knowledge, consciousness, justice, freedom, explanation, reason, and so on – there are various kinds of often highly problematic *assumptions*, factual, theoretical, metaphysical, evaluative. Instead of imaginatively articulating and critically assessing such assumptions directly, philosophical analysis seeks to arrive at definitive meanings for these concepts as if this can be done in a way which is free of problematic factual and evaluative doctrines. This is a recipe for sterility and dishonesty for, in arriving at such definitive meanings, problematic factual and evaluative doctrines are implicitly decided, but without explicit discussion of these doctrines, and without consideration and critical assessment of alternatives. The whole process is, in other words, profoundly irrational. The classic example of all this is Gilbert Ryle's *Concept of Mind*, which claims merely to analyze the meaning of mental concepts but which thereby, implicitly, espouses behaviourism even though this is explicitly denied.[13]

It may be objected that analytic philosophy has long moved on from this Rylean conception of its task, and no longer confines itself to conceptual analysis. Maybe so; nevertheless, contemporary philosophy has not repudiated fully its analytic past, and is still crippled by it. As a result, it still engages in "puzzle solving," and fails to take up its proper task.[14]

Neither wing of philosophy has been able to give centre stage to our fundamental problem – the human world/physical universe problem. Neither wing takes its basic task to be to keep alive awareness of what our most fundamental problems are, what our best attempts are at solving them, and what the relative merits and demerits of these attempts are. Neither wing reveals an awareness that this is what philosophy ought to do. Neither wing attempts to get schools and universities to grapple, imaginatively and critically, with

fundamental problems in a sustained way, and in a way which interacts with the more specialized problem-solving of all the other disciplines of academic inquiry. I know of no academic philosophers who
strive actively to pursue philosophy in such a way, or even conceive
of philosophy such a manner.

Perhaps I overstate things a bit here. Certainly Karl Popper did
just what I have said a philosopher should do, and thereby made
immensely significant contributions to thought, especially in his first
four books.[15] Bertrand Russell tackled fundamental problems, especially in some of his later, more popular books. J.J.C. Smart, Thomas
Nagel, Daniel Dennett, Peter Singer, David Chalmers, and Tim
Maudlin have also sought to contribute to thought about fundamental problems.[16] But even here, what is lacking is an awareness of the
urgent need to transform academia so that it comes to tackle global
problems – global intellectually, and global in the sense of being
about the welfare of the planet and humanity – in a lively, imaginative, and critical way, and in a way which both influences and is influenced by specialized problem-solving, so that all four elementary
rules of reason may be implemented instead of just one.[17] My forty-
year-long effort to get this message across to my fellow philosophers
has not, so far, met with much success.[18]

All this is absolutely outrageous, philosophers may object. Academic philosophy has long ago abandoned conceptual analysis. For
decades, it has been a standard task of philosophy to discuss diverse
aspects of the problem of how the world as we experience it can
exist if the universe really is more or less as physics tells us it is. Philosophy already does just what I have argued it does not do, but
ought to do.

There is, I admit, an element of truth in this objection. I will discuss
the matter in a bit more detail below, in the last section of this chapter. It is, nevertheless, my view that, over the centuries, academic philosophy lost its way. What began so promisingly with René Descartes
in the seventeenth century has dwindled either into anti-rationalist,
anti-scientific metaphysical nonsense, or into sterile analytic puzzle-
solving, as far as the mainstreams of philosophy are concerned,
ignoring important exceptions.

Whitehead once said that modern philosophy is a series of footnotes to Plato. It would be more accurate to say that it is a series of
footnotes to Descartes. Cartesian dualism is rejected, but problematic implications of the doctrine dominate subsequent philosophy

down to today. As I have tried to show, Descartes led to Locke, Berkeley, Hume, Kant, and to the anti-rationalist, anti-scientific nonsense of continental philosophy. The reaction against this led to the esoteric emptiness of analytic puzzle-solving.

Instead of living in Descartes's shadow – and in the shadow of a long series of intellectual blunders made over the centuries – what we philosophers need to do is to return to the fundamental problem which Descartes tried, and failed, to solve – the human world/physical universe problem I articulated at the outset:

How can our human world, and the world of sentient life more generally, imbued as it is with the experiential, consciousness, free will, meaning, and value, exist and best flourish embedded as it is in the physical universe?

REMARKS ON HOW TO SOLVE OUR FUNDAMENTAL PROBLEM

What is the solution to the problem, granted that Cartesian dualism is untenable? Elsewhere I have written extensively on the subject,[19] so here I confine myself to a few brief remarks.

The person who has made a greater contribution towards solving the problem than any other is not a philosopher at all. He is a scientist: Charles Darwin (1809–1882). Darwinism helps explain how and why purposeful living things can evolve – have evolved – in a physicalistic universe. We need, however, to adopt a version of Darwinism which recognizes that the mechanisms of evolution themselves evolve as life evolves, purposive action playing an increasingly important role, especially when evolution by cultural means comes into play as a result of learning and imitation.[20] We human beings are, above all, the products of evolution by cultural means. Such a version of Darwinism enables us to see that Darwinian evolution merges seamlessly with human history.

Cartesian dualism blunders right from the outset, when it assumes that physics could be in principle comprehensive and complete about the world around us. Actually, physics, and that part of science in principle reducible to physics, seeks to depict only a highly selected *aspect* of all that there is – the causally efficacious aspect, as it might be called, which determines how events unfold. Theoretical physics seeks to depict that which everything has in common with everything else, and that which needs to be specified in order that a description of a state of affairs at one instant can imply descriptions of states of affairs at subsequent instants – descriptions couched in exactly the same terms.[21] This does not mean that a complete physics would tell us everything factual about the world around us. It would not necessarily tell us about what things look like, sound like, feel like, or what is like to *be* a certain kind of physical system (such as a living person). Colours, sounds, tactile qualities will be ignored by physics if they play no role in the predictive and explanatory task of physics.

An elementary argument establishes that physics cannot predict and explain experiential qualities. We can only know what redness as we see it is, if we have at some stage in our life experienced the visual sensation of redness. A person blind from birth does not know what redness is. Such a person is not, however, debarred thereby from understanding all physics, including optics and the theory of colour perception. He or she is not debarred from understanding all implications of physics. That means physics cannot predict something like "This rose is red" (where "red" is to be understood as the colour we see), however complete the physical description of the rose and its environment may be.[22]

But this built-in incompleteness in principle of physics does not matter. Redness and other such experiential qualities do not need to be depicted for physics to perform successfully its predictive and explanatory tasks.

Furthermore, physics must omit these experiential qualities. If it included them, the beautifully unified, explanatory theories of physics would become horrendously disunified and non-explanatory, because endlessly many complex postulates linking physical conditions and experiential qualities would be added to physical theory. This would destroy the unity and explanatory power of physical theory. Thus omitting the experiential is the price that physics pays to be able to develop the marvellously unified and explanatory theories it has developed.[23]

What all this means is that the silence of physics about colours and sounds as we experience them provides no grounds whatsoever for holding that they do not exist out there in the world. Physics is designed by us specifically to avoid any mention of such qualities or properties. We should take it that the world is, in part, as we experience it to be (except when we are suffering from illusions or hallucinations).

This view that things have two aspects, the *physical* and the *experiential* (or mental), can be traced back to Baruch Spinoza (1632–1677).[24] The version sketched here explains why physics does not, and cannot, predict and explain the experiential.

It also has a major bearing on the problem of perception and the problem of our knowledge of the external world – two problems that figure prominently in the history of philosophy after Descartes. Two views can be distinguished about what it is that we really see – what we most basically experience: *internalism*, which holds that we most basically experience our own inner experiences, and everything else is "inferred" from that, and *externalism*, which holds that we most basically experience the world around us, and only "infer" knowledge about what goes on inside us via our perceptual knowledge of things external to us. Cartesian dualism, of course, implies internalism. Probably a majority of philosophers, and scientists too, who come after Descartes, take internalism for granted. If one holds the view that colours, sounds, smells, tactile qualities, as we experience them, do not exist out there in the world around us, one is all but obliged to accept internalism, because this viewpoint holds that things external to us differ profoundly from the way we ordinarily experience them to be, our ordinary perceptions being deceptive about the world around us in a wholesale, systematic way. But if we hold the view indicated above, namely that physics is specifically designed to say nothing about experiential qualities, and therefore its silence about them provides no grounds whatsoever for holding that they do not, objectively, exist in the world around us, then we may hold that things around us are as they appear to us, in that they do indeed possess the experiential qualities we experience them as having. We may adopt externalism as our view about what we most directly know about in perception. We see what we ordinarily take ourselves to see, aspects of the world around us.[25] This is, of course, just what Darwinian evolution would arrange for us to be able to see. Animals which could not see aspects of their environment, but only the contents of their own minds, would not last long in the real world.

The version of the two-aspect view sketched above also has major implications for the philosophical part of the mind/brain problem. It implies that this problem is analogous to, for example, the green grass/molecular structure problem. That brain processes can be conscious sensations, feelings, thoughts, ought perhaps to be no more mysterious than that a leaf (with a certain molecular structure) can be green.[26]

The view I have sketched provides the proper framework, I claim, within which all our more specific, specialized problems may be tackled: scientific problems, technological problems, historical problems, problems about the nature of our human world, and practical problems of living, personal, social, and global. In particular, the above provides the proper framework within which to tackle the largely unsolved problem of how to interconnect what goes on in the brain with what happens to the person when that person thinks, sees, imagines, decides, and acts – the problem of interconnecting how the brain controls action with how the person does. This is both a very difficult factual, empirical problem, and a conceptual one.[27]

Descartes, Locke, Berkeley, Hume, Kant, and many philosophers who followed made a bad mistake in accepting what Cartesian dualism would seem to imply: we really, most directly see, not aspects of things in the environment around us, but rather the contents of our minds. This blunder, perhaps more than any other, has condemned so much philosophy to irrelevance, and triviality.[28]

Chapter 3 began with a story philosophers sometimes tell about the way the territory of philosophy has become dreadfully depleted over the centuries as component parts have broken away and established themselves as independent disciplines: first the natural sciences, then the social sciences, then logic and linguistics. The actual story philosophers ought to tell is quite different. The proper task of philosophy is to keep alive awareness of our fundamental problems, above all our most fundamental problem, formulated above. It is to sustain, or create, awareness of what our best attempted answers to these basic questions are, and why these answers are more or less inadequate. Philosophy needs to promote and, if it can, contribute to, our best efforts to improve our attempted solutions to our fundamental problems. It needs, too, to highlight the way in which answers to these fundamental problems tend to be implicit in much that we think and do in all areas of human life, the inadequacy of these answers having adverse consequences for much that we think and do. It is important to engage in some serious thinking about our fundamental problems and how they are to be solved both for its own sake, and for the sake of everything else!

The success and progress of philosophy are to be judged in terms of the extent to which these tasks have been and are being fulfilled. By and large, philosophy after Descartes down to today has not been too successful, as we have seen in this chapter and the last one. The initial blunder, sustained through the centuries, was the failure to appreciate that science cannot proceed without some kind of metaphysical conjecture about the ultimate nature of the universe, almost bound to be false, and hence the need for something like natural philosophy and aim-oriented empiricism. It was this philosophical blunder which led to the disintegration of natural philosophy into science and philosophy, and to an ever-widening gulf between the two. In addition, the failure of philosophers after Descartes to develop more adequate attempts at solving our fundamental problem than Cartesian dualism led to the adoption of philosophical doctrines which made it impossible even to *formulate* our fundamental problem, let alone set about trying to help solve it. Doctrines developed by Locke, Berkeley, Hume, Kant, and those who followed rendered any metaphysical conjecture about the ultimate nature of the universe either inherently false or meaningless. Instead of doing what most needs to be done, philosophy turned this into something it is impossible to do! The dwindling significance of philosophy over the centuries is the outcome, not of the breakaway success of science, but of the long-standing failures of philosophy itself.

PHILOSOPHY TODAY DOES TACKLE FUNDAMENTAL PROBLEMS!

It may be objected that the attack on philosophy of this chapter and the last vastly overstates the case. Even if the history of philosophy does reveal a failure to formulate and tackle the fundamental problem as formulated above, this is no longer the case. Philosophers no longer fear metaphysics, or dismiss all metaphysics as meaningless. Philosophy as conceptual analysis was abandoned decades ago. Contemporary philosophy takes science seriously, takes the view of the world that emerges from science seriously, and seeks to solve the problems that arise as a result. For decades, philosophers have tussled with the problems of how there can be sentience, consciousness, free will, meaning, and value if the world really is as science tells us it is. Again, the question of what it is that science tells us about the world has been subjected to sustained scrutiny. Even if some of the strictures against philosophy once applied, they no longer do. Academic philosophy already does what this chapter says it ought to do.

I have some sympathy with this objection. Academic philosophy has improved in recent decades. Indeed, I have already suggested that this is the case, and I have cited the work of Karl Popper as a noteworthy example. Not only did Popper tackle urgent, fundamental problems about science, politics, liberalism, and social problems with exemplary clarity and originality; he argued that philosophy has its roots in problems of the real world, "*problems which arise outside philosophy* – in mathematics, for example, or in cosmology, or in politics, or in religion, or in social life."[29] And again, "*We are not students of some subject matter but students of problems.* And problems may cut right across the borders of any subject matter or discipline."[30]

I am inclined to think, however, that J.J.C. Smart's *Philosophy and Scientific Realism*, published in 1963, had a much bigger impact in prompting some philosophers, at any rate, to abandon the sterilities of conceptual analysis, and grapple with the serious problems posed by modern science. Smart defended the view that everything is just physics. The world is made up exclusively of fundamental physical entities. The mind is the brain. Everything else that seems to exist is just illusory. (This is of course just Cartesian dualism brought up to date scientifically, without the Cartesian Mind.)

Smart's book provoked a tremendous burst of philosophical discussion about "the identity thesis" as it came to be called, the thesis that the mind just is the brain. Neuroscience became a hot topic within philosophy. Some philosophers, grappling with the problem of free will, have argued that probabilistic quantum theory makes free will possible.[31] Others have argued against physicalism as defended by Smart – the doctrine that everything is made up of fundamental physical entities. They have argued that, as complex physical systems come into existence, emergent properties arise that cannot be reduced to physics.[32] Philosophers of science have debated the question of what it is that science tells us about the world. Many have argued for scientific realism: fundamental physical entities, postulated by accepted theory, electrons, photons, quarks, gluons, and neutrinos, really do exist. Others have contested this view, arguing that physics provides knowledge only about that which is in principle observable, unobservable fundamental physical entities thus lying beyond the scope of scientific knowledge.[33] There is a vast literature on the problem of understanding *qualia* – inner experiences – if the world is as science seems to tell us it is. Philosophical controversy has raged in recent decades as to whether qualia do indeed exist, or whether their apparent existence, based on personal experience, is just an illusion.

All this would seem to indicate that problems created by the scientific conception of the universe for the way we ordinarily understand our world have become central to academic philosophy in recent decades. Does this not make nonsense of my claim that philosophy has failed to keep alive awareness of these problems?

It does not. In the first place, my claim that philosophy, for much of its history, since Descartes, and until recent times, has developed doctrines that have made it impossible even to formulate, let alone discuss, our fundamental problem as I have stated it above, remains unaffected.

Secondly, conceptual analysis still lingers on, as a glance at any recent issue of *Mind*, a leading philosophy journal, will attest.

Third, in this chapter I have criticized philosophy for rejecting Cartesian dualism but continuing to tussle with problems generated by the rejected doctrine, instead of returning to the original problem that Cartesian dualism can be regarded as attempting to solve – the fundamental human world/physical universe problem. This criticism is not rebutted by the observation that philosophers today grapple with the problem of how we can be conscious and have free will if the universe is more or less as modern science tells us it is. These are just the problems that Cartesian dualism creates. The crucial question is: Are these problems set into the broader context of the human world/physical universe problem? It is here that contemporary philosophy fails.

The human world/physical universe problem includes, of course, the problems of how there can be sentience, consciousness, and free will in the physical universe; but it concerns much more than that as well. It includes the problem of how things around us can objectively[34] possess colours, sounds, smells, and tactile qualities as we experience them. It includes problems of how things around us can possess aesthetic qualities, and human actions and institutions can possess moral and intellectual qualities. And it includes problems of living – problems about what we need to do, how we need to live, to achieve what is of value. What contemporary philosophy fails to do is set the problems it discusses into the broader context of the fundamental human world/physical universe problem. This failing is especially serious when it comes to the problem of consciousness – the problem of the existence of qualia – in the physical universe. It is vital to begin with the possibility that extra-physical, experiential qualities are not only associated with living brains, but are also, as perceptual qualities, possessed by such things as green leaves and yellow sand. We need to do this simply in order to formulate the initial problem properly. But we also need to do it in order to *solve* the problem, as I have argued at some length.[35] We need to set the mind/brain problem into the context of the broader, more fundamental human world/physical universe problem in part in order to bring to the fore the crucial question: What is it that physics seeks to tell us about the universe? Physics is, as it were, explicitly designed not to say anything about the experiential; if it did, it would cease to be explanatory. Thus the silence of physics about colours and sounds, as we perceive them, provides no reason whatsoever for holding that colours and sounds do not exist in the world around us. There is a *reason* why physics says nothing about the experiential, whether physics is applied to leaves and sand external to us, or neurons and synaptic junctions inside our heads. The silence of physics about the greenness of leaves, the yellowness of sand, is as mysterious, or as unmysterious, as its silence about the inner experiences associated with the activity of neurons and synaptic junctions inside someone's head. Restrict qualia to processes going on inside our heads, and it does indeed become inexplicable that, of all that exists and occurs in the universe, it is just these neurological, or ultimately physical, processes that have experiential qualia associated with them. The insoluble consciousness/brain problem is created by the failure to formulate it properly in the first place. In other words, in failing to set the problem of consciousness into the broader context of the human world/physical universe problem, much contemporary philosophy not only fails to formulate the problem properly. More seriously, it deprives itself of the solution – the solution to the philosophical part of the problem, that is.[36]

Sometimes, it is true, philosophers do consider the broader problem. Thus, Wilfrid Sellars wrote of "the manifest image" and "the scientific image":[37] these correspond, roughly, to what I mean by "the human world" and "the physical universe." Sellars makes clear that resolving the conflict between the manifest and scientific images is a fundamental problem. For Sellars, indeed, "The aim of philosophy ... is to understand how things ... hang together."[38] And again, "What is characteristic of philosophy is not a special subject-matter, but the aim of knowing one's way around with respect to the subject-matters of all the special disciplines."[39] A hint of a similar contrast between "the world of science" and "the world of human life and experience" is to be found in Whitehead.[40] In the main, however, philosophers fail to put problems of sentience, consciousness, and free will into the broader, more fundamental context of the human world/physical universe problem.

Fourth, it can hardly be said that the rest of philosophy – moral philosophy, political philosophy, aesthetics, epistemology, philosophy of meaning and language – is put into the context of, and takes as fundamental, the human world/physical universe problem.

These four failings scarcely touch, however, my main criticism: philosophy fails to take its basic task to be to keep alive general awareness of the human world/physical universe problem as our fundamental problem of thought and life. It fails to try to establish this problem as one that all academics ought to be aware of and ponder, from time to time. It fails even to try to establish, in all universities, a symposium, open to everyone, devoted to the imaginative and critical exploration of the problem and devoted, too, to the exploration of how attempts at solving the problem may influence, and be influenced by, more specialized research conducted in disciplines from physical science to the social sciences and humanities. Philosophers do not seem to appreciate that such a symposium is needed if academic inquiry is to meet elementary requirements of rationality spelled out in the four rules of rational problem solving on page 64.[41] If academic inquiry does not include sustained discussion of our fundamental problems conducted in such a way that it can influence, and be influenced by, more specialized research of all disciplines, then not only is academic inquiry irrational in a wholesale, structural way; it is also unlikely to do justice to the fundamental problems, intellectual and practical, that confront humanity. Academia restricted to specialized research is ill-equipped to help humanity resolve problems of the real world. Humanity suffers from the failings of modern philosophy – failings most philosophers, even today, seem entirely unaware of.[42]

To sum up: academic philosophy has improved in recent decades but still needs further radical improvement if it is to become fit to join with natural science in recreating natural philosophy in its modern form.

5

Why Science Needs Philosophy, Part I: Physics

Today the scientific community takes for granted and seeks to implement standard empiricism (s e). This asserts, as Karl Popper has put it, that "in science, only observation and experiment may decide upon the *acceptance or rejection* of scientific statements, including laws and theories."[1] The simplicity, unity, or explanatory character of a theory may influence its adoption for a time, but not in such a way that nature herself, or the phenomena, are assumed to be simple, unified, or comprehensible. *In science, no thesis about the world can be accepted as a part of scientific knowledge independent of empirical considerations.*

But s e, as we have seen in chapter 3, is untenable. Persistent acceptance of *unified* theories only, when endlessly many empirically more successful disunified rivals are always available, means that physics does accept, as a part of scientific knowledge, a thesis about the world independent of evidence – even, in a sense, in violation of evidence – namely, that some kind of underlying unity exists in nature.

Science needs to reject s e, and accept and implement, in its stead, a new, more rigorous conception of science which acknowledges, and seeks to improve, highly problematic, untestable, metaphysical theses concerning the knowability and comprehensibility of the universe, inherent in the scientific enterprise. According to this view, which I have called aim-oriented empiricism (a o e), physics accepts, as a part of theoretical knowledge, a hierarchy of five metaphysical theses: see figure 2 on page 85. These assert less and less, and thus become more and more likely to be true, as one ascends the hierarchy. Furthermore, as one ascends, the theses become more nearly such that their truth is required for science, or the pursuit of knowledge, to be possible at all.

This is the case as far as the top two theses are concerned. They are such that we will never, in any circumstances whatsoever, need or want to reject them. The three theses lower down in the hierarchy are revised (1) so as to be compatible with what is above in the hierarchy, (2) so as to accord best with the most empirically progressive developments in theoretical physics, and (3) so as to hold out the greatest hope of leading to such empirically progressive developments. Associated with each metaphysical thesis, M, there is a methodological rule: accept that thesis or theory, one down in the hierarchy, which accords best with M. Thus, as metaphysical theses at levels 3, 4, and even possibly 5 are revised, methods are revised as well. As we improve our scientific knowledge about the universe we improve metaphysical assumptions and associated methods. We improve our knowledge about how to improve knowledge. There is something like positive feedback between improving knowledge and improving knowledge-about-how-to-improve-knowledge, the nub of scientific rationality, and a key reason for the extraordinary progressive success of natural science.

Standard empiricism (SE) demands that metaphysics and philosophy be excluded from science. Aim-oriented empiricism (AOE), by contrast, demands that metaphysics, methodology, and thus, in a sense, philosophy, are vital, integral parts of natural science. In the interests of rigour and success, AOE demands that we put science and philosophy together again, and recreate natural philosophy.

But does this amount to anything more than window dressing? Would science really be substantially affected and *improved* by the rejection of SE, and the acceptance and implementation of AOE in its stead? If so, how, and why?

It is important to appreciate what is at issue here. The task is not to compare science pursued in accordance with SE, with science pursued in accordance with AOE. Science *cannot* be pursued in accordance with SE! What we need to compare are the following:

(a)　Science pursued by a scientific community that accepts, and attempts to implement, SE.

(b)　Science pursued by a scientific community that accepts and implements AOE.

As I have already remarked, from the time of Kepler and Galileo onwards, science has in fact put something like AOE into practice. If it had not, we would still be stuck with Aristotelian science. But AOE has been put into scientific practice in an inept, hypocritical way, because the scientific community has believed it ought to be implementing SE. Important elements of AOE have been constrained and stifled by the attempt to put SE into practice. So, we need to compare (a) implementation of AOE constrained, stifled, and rendered implicit by the attempt to implement SE, and (b) explicit acceptance and implementation of AOE. Would the overthrow of the rhetoric of SE, permitting explicit and thoroughgoing implementation of AOE, really make much of a difference – really lead to the improvement of science, to its transformation into natural philosophy?

I now consider a number of ways in which throwing off the yoke of SE, and adopting and explicitly implementing AOE in its stead, really would change and improve science.[2] In this chapter, I consider implications for theoretical physics. In the next chapter I consider implications for other branches of natural science, such as evolutionary biology and neuroscience, and, briefly, social science, such as psychology. Issues concerning the human value of science, whether cultural or practical, will also be taken into account, as well as broader implications for rationality and problems of civilization.

In what follows I show that implementing AOE explicitly in physics would: (1) enhance rigour; (2) and (3) extend the scope of scientific knowledge; (4) clarify non-empirical requirements for the acceptability of physical theories; (5) facilitate improvement of metaphysical assumptions of physics so that they lead the way in the development of new theories; (6) improve non-empirical criteria for the acceptance of physical theories; (7) help the development of correct interpretation of new theories in physics; (8) provide physics with a rational if fallible and non-mechanical method for the discovery of new fundamental theories in physics; (9) enable physics to do better justice to the search for explanation and understanding; (10) assist the discovery of viable alternatives to physicalism; (11) do better justice to scientific progress; and (12) throw light on the scientific status of string theory.

I ENHANCED RIGOUR

Many scientists will be appalled at the idea that science should be modified to include metaphysics, philosophy, epistemology, and methodology. They will see such a proposal as a threat to the intellectual integrity of science, its intellectual rigour. But the actual situation is just the opposite. As I explained in chapter 3, in moving from SE science[3] to AOE science we do not degrade intellectual rigour; we enhance it. SE science lacks rigour in that it has a contradiction built into it: SE holds that in science all claims to knowledge are based on evidence whereas actually science accepts implicitly a substantial metaphysical thesis concerning the unity of nature which is, if anything, accepted *against* the evidence, in that unified theories are persistently favoured over empirically more successful disunified rivals. AOE science is free of this contradiction. Furthermore, AOE science has enhanced rigour in that it is designed to subject substantial, influential, and problematic metaphysical assumptions (concerning the unity, comprehensibility, or knowability of the universe) to sustained imaginative and critical scrutiny in such a way as to offer the best hope of improving these assumptions. SE science cannot do this as the relevant assumptions cannot be explicitly acknowledged.

This enhanced intellectual rigour of AOE is no mere formal matter. All the other advantages of AOE science over SE science stem from it.

2 INCREASE IN SCOPE OF KNOWLEDGE

In moving from SE science to AOE science, there is a very substantial increase in the *scope* of theoretical knowledge in physics. Granted SE, theoretical knowledge in physics is confined to empirically corroborated laws and theories. Accept AOE and, in addition, theoretical knowledge includes physicalism, the thesis that the universe is such that, inherent in all phenomena everywhere there is a physical entity, precisely the same everywhere at all times and places, which, together with varying states of affairs, determines (perhaps probabilistically) how events unfold in space and time. The universe is such that, in other words, a yet-to-be-discovered physical theory exists which is (a) unified, (b) true, and (c) capable in principle of predicting and explaining all physical phenomena. In one way, from the standpoint of physics, this thesis may seem disappointing: it is a *metaphysical* thesis, incapable of predicting any empirical phenomena whatsoever. In other respects, however, it is far from disappointing. It is a thesis about the ultimate nature of reality. Even though it is a *conjecture*, nevertheless it has a very secure place within physics. As we have seen, physical theories which clash with it too severely, whatever their empirical success may be, are rejected out of hand, not even considered indeed. The thesis has such a secure place in physics that it persists throughout theoretical revolutions. It is thus a far more secure item of theoretical knowledge than any theory of physics, however securely established empirically. All such theories, sooner or later, turn out to be false, as we saw in chapter 3. (And AOE tells us that all physical theories about a limited range of phenomena, that cannot be immediately generalized to apply to all physical phenomena, are false, even though incredibly successful empirically.)

3 INCREASE IN KNOWLEDGE OF PROFOUND HUMAN SIGNIFICANCE

Not only is there a substantial increase in theoretical knowledge. This increase is about a matter of profound significance for humanity. For physicalism, as we have seen, has dramatic implications for our human world, our understanding of the meaning and value of human life. Fundamental questions arise about how there can be consciousness, free will, meaning, and value – the world as we experience it – if physicalism is true. Whereas SE science holds all this at arm's length, AOE science brings these fundamental questions into sharp focus. And, from the standpoint of its human significance, what matters is physicalism itself, rather than the specific version of physicalism we may one day capture by means of the true physical theory of everything.

4 CLARIFICATION OF CRITERIA FOR THEORY ACCEPTANCE GENERALLY HELD TO BE NON-EMPIRICAL

Almost all physicists, and most philosophers of science, acknowledge that a physical theory, in order to be accepted, must be (a) sufficiently empirically successful, and (b) sufficiently *simple* and *unified*, or *explanatory*, *intelligible*, *elegant*, or *beautiful* – various terms are used in this context. Paul Dirac went so far as to declare that "it is more important to have beauty in one's equations than to have them fit experiment."[4] It is also rather generally acknowledged, however, that it is not at all clear as to *what* these non-empirical criteria for theory acceptance amount to, or *why* it can be justifiable to employ them in physics. What is it for a theory to be unified (or explanatory, or beautiful, etc.)? How can it be justifiable to prefer a unified theory

to a disunified one, even when the latter is more empirically successful? Even Einstein confessed that he was baffled.[5]

SE fails to solve these two problems. Both are solved, however,
within the framework of AOE. AOE brings absolute clarity to the
questions of *what* it is exactly that a physical theory must possess to
be acceptable from a non-empirical standpoint, and *why* this justifies
acceptance of the theory in question as long as empirical requirements are sufficiently well satisfied in addition. The solution to these
two problems has already been indicated in chapter 3 in the argument leading up to AOE. In order to be unified, a physical theory, T,
must make precisely the same theoretical assertion about all the possible phenomena to which it applies. The *content* of the theory must
be the same. If the theory specifies N distinct contents, the theory is
disunified to degree N. For unity, we require that N = 1.

There is a refinement. As we saw in chapter 3, there are *different*
ways in which the distinct contents of disunified theories can differ,
one from another. A disunified theory may assert that there are different laws *at different times*, or *at different places*. Or laws may vary
as mass, distance, relative velocity, or some other physical variable
changes. Or a theory may postulate two distinct forces, one operating in one range of possible phenomena, the other operating in
another range. Or, less radically, a theory may postulate one force but
more than one kind of particle, each kind having its own distinctive
mass or charge. In appendix 1, I point out that there are eight different kinds of disunity, all, however, exemplifying the same basic idea.

It is very important to appreciate that what are generally called
"non-empirical" criteria of theory acceptance are actually partially
empirical in character. In demanding that a theory be unified we are
demanding, in effect, that it exemplifies the level 4 thesis of physicalism, P. In practice, in physics more is required: an acceptable theory
needs to exemplify the currently accepted level 3 metaphysical blueprint, B – ideally, a special case of physicalism.[6] What P and B are, at
any given moment in the development of physics, will be influenced
(more or less effectively) by the character of the most empirically
successful theories up to that moment – by the whole way in which
theoretical physics has progressed up to that moment. Long-term
empirical considerations, in short, influence which versions of P and
B are accepted at any given stage.[7] (If Aristotle's view of the cosmos
had led to a much more empirically successful research programme
for physics than Galileo's, Aristotle's view would be today accepted

at level 4, instead of physicalism.) Metaphysical theses, though not empirically testable, can nevertheless be assessed in a quasi-empirical way in that they can be more, or less, empirically *fruitful*. A metaphysical thesis, B, is empirically fruitful if a series of theories, T_1, T_2 ... T_n, each more empirically successful than its predecessor, can be regarded as drawing ever closer to capturing B in the form of a testable theory (or, in other words, if T_1, T_2 ... T_n become increasingly B-unified: see appendix 1). The demand that a theory must be unified to be acceptable is thus a quasi-empirical demand. It commits physics to accepting the hierarchy of theses, from level 3 to 5, all of which could be false, and could, in increasingly extreme circumstances, require revision – in which case quasi-empirical criteria for theory acceptance would need to be revised as well. AOE facilitates such revision when and where it is most likely to be needed, at level 3, whereas SE does not. That, indeed, is the basic rationale for AOE, the reason why AOE is superior to SE.

5 BLUEPRINT ARTICULATION WITHIN AOE PHYSICS

According to the version of AOE expounded in chapter 3 and figure 2 on page 85, knowledge in physics is to be represented at seven levels. But only the four lowest levels have an active role to play in theoretical physics.[8] SE and AOE physics differ in that SE recognizes knowledge only at levels 1 and 2, whereas AOE adds to this knowledge at levels 3 and 4. But even though SE physics fails to acknowledge theses at levels 3 and 4, these theses have nevertheless played a substantial role in the history of physics, in influencing, for better or worse, *discovery*, *acceptance*, and *interpretation* of physical theories. The important difference between SE and AOE physics is that the former, because it does not explicitly recognize knowledge at level 3, tends, at any given stage in the development of physics, to accept that level 3 metaphysical blueprint which relates to a past theory, and not to the most recent theory. As a result, within SE physics, implicitly accepted level 3 metaphysical blueprints tend to impede the discovery, acceptance, and correct interpretation of new theories. Metaphysics is always one step behind new theory. By contrast, AOE physics, as a result of making explicit and subjecting to sustained criticism and attempted improvement theses at level 3 (and, if required, at level 4), is able to develop level 3 metaphysical blueprints which aid the discovery, acceptance, and interpretation of new theory. In brief, AOE physics promotes what may be called "blueprint articulation" which promises to aid progress, whereas SE physics, in disavowing knowledge at levels 3 and 4, falls victim to the acceptance of out-of-date metaphysical blueprints, and thus impedes progress. Below, I shall discuss this difference in connection with the discovery, acceptance, and interpretation of five fundamental theories: Newtonian theory, classical electrodynamics, special relativity, general relativity, and quantum theory.

But first, I attempt to indicate how "blueprint articulation" might have been done in the past and, to some extent, how it has been done. I hope to show that blueprint articulation can indeed have fruitful consequences for theoretical physics (and therefore that something similar may be fruitful for other branches of natural science as well).

In what follows, I shall engage in blueprint articulation with one hand tied behind my back. I begin with the corpuscular blueprint, as it was understood in the seventeenth century, and I set about *improving* it, ignoring all input from evidence, from empirically successful theories. I do this in an attempt to highlight just how fruitful blueprint articulation can be, and in an attempt to counter the obvious criticism that what I do is informed by hindsight. The idea is to see what Newton, Huygens, Leibniz, Johann Bernoulli, Maupertuis, Emilie du Châtelet, and d'Alembert[9] might have done had they become passionately convinced of AOE, physicalism, and the vital role blueprint articulation has for natural philosophy![10]

We begin, then, with the corpuscular hypothesis of the seventeenth century, held in various versions by such figures as Galileo, Descartes, Huygens, Locke, Gassendi, and Boyle.[11] This vividly depicts how it might be possible to reduce the vast diversity of substances and processes in the world to just one kind of entity, and one process: atoms variously arranged, and in various kinds of relative motion.

One crucial issue must be decided before we begin. What notion of force can legitimately be associated with the corpuscular hypothesis? A basic idea of the hypothesis, I take it, is that corpuscles are in uniform motion with respect to each other unless in collision with one another. When two corpuscles collide, each experiences an instantaneous and infinite repulsive force, there is an instantaneous change of motion, and the two corpuscles fly apart, once again moving with constant velocity. We may take it, then, that the corpuscular hypothesis holds that bodies move with constant relative velocity when free of force, a force impressed on a body having the effect of changing the velocity of the body. This is, roughly, the Newtonian notion of force (or a generalization of it).

Four considerations only will now be permitted to motivate modification of the corpuscular and other blueprints: (a) incompatibility with the level 4 thesis of physicalism; (b) internal inconsistency; (c) lack of generality; and (d) presence of some feature that has nothing to do with exemplifying physicalism. That blueprint is to be preferred which removes any one, or all, of these potential defects. (b) needs no justification, and nor does (a) or (d), given AOE. The rationale for adopting (c) can be put like this. We seem to live in a highly uncharacteristic corner of the universe: the Earth. Our experience of the universe, and all the phenomena it contains, is likely to be limited. Therefore, it is not unreasonable to suppose that even our best ideas about how the universe may be physically comprehensible are likely to be tied much too restrictively to the very special conditions of our local circumstances – conditions on Earth. It is thus reasonable to hold that our initial best blueprint ideas need to be generalized, perhaps repeatedly, if they are to stand much chance of capturing the actual nature of the universe.

In connection with (d), we need to appreciate that each blueprint constitutes a possible ideal for a theory to be *explanatory*. According to AOE, the ideal explanatory theory exemplifies physicalism. In physics, familiar phenomena around us are explained by being reduced to something highly unfamiliar – ideally, some version of physicalism. But associated with common sense ideas of explanation there is the opposite idea: an explanation reduces the *unfamiliar* to the familiar. It may well be that this customary idea of explanation introduces ideas into physics that are extraneous and spurious. If so, they need to be eliminated, in accordance with (d) above.

Let us now see whether the above four considerations, brought to bear on the corpuscular blueprint, ignoring all input from empirical considerations, can lead to the development of blueprints that would have been helpful for the discovery of new theories in physics.

Perhaps the most obvious defect of the corpuscular blueprint, B_I, is that it does not accord well with physicalism.

Physicalism asserts, in effect, that the physical universe is such that that which exists at any instant divides into two parts, V and U. V varies from place to place and time to time. U is the same everywhere, at all places and times, throughout all physical phenomena: it determines, together with V, at any instant, how V changes with time. U corresponds to the true physical "theory of everything." V corresponds to so-called initial conditions, the variable instantaneous relative positions and motions of particles, for example.

B_1 does not accord well with physicalism because it holds that U is made up of two very different elements: the physical properties of corpuscles on the one hand (which determine the way they move and interact), and the properties of empty space, on the other hand.

A more serious defect of B_1, perhaps, is that it cannot do justice to collisions between corpuscles. The corpuscles are infinitely rigid: they do not change their shape. This means that when two corpuscles collide, they instantaneously experience an infinite repulsive force. There is a discontinuity. It is by no means clear what the outcome of experiencing an infinite force for an instant would be.

Viewed from the perspective of physicalism, B_1 makes an illegitimate appeal to sensory experience – to our familiarity with the tactile properties of solid objects such as billiard balls. If we strip this away, and consider corpuscles merely as exemplifying (more or less adequately) the basic idea of physicalism, then corpuscles should be specified as follows. Associated with each corpuscle there is a closed surface of some definite invariant shape and size, which is such that the instant two such surfaces touch, the two corpuscles experience an infinitely repulsive force. Let us call this modified version of the corpuscular blueprint B_2: see figure 3 below.

Reformulated in this way as B_2, it is at once clear that the corpuscular blueprint is nothing more than an extremely arbitrary special case of a much more general blueprint, B_3, expounded by Boscovich in 1758,[12] and also by Kant in 1756 and 1786.[13] Instead of conceiving of a corpuscle as a closed surface upon which there is an infinitely repulsive force that is zero everywhere else (extreme discontinuity), we conceive of it as a point-particle with mass surrounded by a rigid, spherically symmetric, centrally directed field of force which varies *continuously* with distance, only being infinitely repulsive where the point-particle is. The corpuscle is an arbitrary, discontinuous special case of Boscovich's point-atom (only favoured on the entirely spurious grounds that the corpuscle reminds us of the billiard ball). The force, which for the corpuscle is infinite on a rigid closed surface, becomes, for Boscovich, finite everywhere, and continuously varying with distance, being infinitely repulsive at one point only, namely where the particle is.

This Boscovichean blueprint, B_3, is much more general than the corpuscular blueprint, B_2, and is therefore to be preferred.

B_3 possesses two other advantages as well over B_2 (and B_1). First, the infinitely repulsive force, the point of discontinuity, of B_1 and B_2 has become harmless: it just means that no two point-particles ever occupy the same spatial point.[14] Second, attractive and cohesive forces can be accounted for by the blueprint in a simple, non-ad hoc fashion, without any departure from spherical symmetry, by attributing to point-atoms alternating regions of attractive and repulsive forces. It is conceivable that many point-particles might cohere together to form stable solid objects.

There is another way in which B_2 can be generalized. We can suppose that there are different kinds of point-particle, each kind having associated with it a rigid, spherically symmetric force, varying with distance in a fixed way, that is entirely attractive, or entirely repulsive, there being none of the apparently arbitrary changes from attractive to repulsive, associated with the Boscovichean B_3. Let us call this blueprint B_4. This blueprint, on the face of it, makes available various possibilities. It could be that point-particles divide up into two categories, those that attract similar particles, and those that repulse them. Or it could be that there are similar particles that are either positively or negatively charged, like charges repelling one another, unlike charges attracting. This could be generalized further, there being N different kinds of particle having the same force law, of the same strength, where N is some small, positive integer, like particles repelling, unlike particles attracting.

How do B_3 and B_4 compare? In their simplest forms, B_3 postulates just one kind of point-particle, whereas B_4 postulates two. Both would seem to be able to do what B_1 cannot do without serious complications (corpuscles with hooks), namely imply the existence of attractive and cohesive forces, and stable macro objects. (In the case of B_4, this is less certain. One can conceive of a B_4 theory predicting atoms, made up of two particles, one positive, the other negative, in rotation around each other. But what is the explanation for such atoms grouping together to form cohesive blocks of matter?) B_3 suffers from the defect that force-fields surrounding point-particles vary, in an apparently arbitrary fashion, in both strength and direction as one moves away from the central point-particle; B_4 may avail itself of the non-arbitrary law that forces fall away as $1/d^2$ as one moves away from the central point-particle, in just the same way as the area of the surface of a sphere of the same radius increases. This law is not arbitrary, it may be maintained, because it emerges from the geometric properties of space. B_4, unlike B_3, permits two particles, one positive, the other negative, to occupy the same point in space, with no clear idea as to what would be the outcome. Perhaps this can be declared to be an infinitely improbable event, and hence one that will not occur.

That there are at least two different ways of generalizing B_2 serves to remind us that blueprint articulation does not produce a single series of potentially better and better blueprints: it is reasonable to suppose that, at any stage, it will produce a number (a small number, it is to be hoped) of viable alternatives.

The point-particle blueprints, B_3 and B_4, assume that the force-field surrounding each point-particle is *rigid* (a feature inherited from the corpuscular blueprint), so that the point-particle always remains at the centre of its force-field, however it may move. This means changes in the force-field, due to the motion of the point-particle, are transmitted instantaneously, throughout space. A more general blueprint, B_5, removing defect (c), would postulate that changes in the force-field, due to changes in the motion of the point-particle, are transmitted at some finite, fixed velocity – infinite velocity being a special case. (Michael Faraday understood clearly that it is the introduction of the idea that changes in the electromagnetic field of force travel at finite velocity that transforms Boscovich's theory so that the field of force acquires an independent reality. Einstein once said that there are two ideas in physics: the particle and the field. One of them was created by Faraday.)

This generalized blueprint, B_5, introduces, however, a new complexity. We can no longer specify initial conditions solely in terms of the relative positions and velocities of point-particles; we must in addition specify the force-field associated with each point-particle at each point in space (its spatial character depending on the past motions of the point-atom).

This new complexity can, it would seem, be simplified if we adopt one further modification. Instead of postulating a number of distinct force-fields, one to each point-particle, we may instead postulate just one, single, unified field, created by point-particles, and in turn acting on point-particles. We have arrived at a new blueprint, B_6: the particle/field blueprint (a simplified version of the blueprint which may be associated with James Clerk Maxwell's theory of the electromagnetic field).

The two steps just indicated, from B_4 to B_5 (finite velocity of changes in the field of force) to B_6 (fields of force of all particles coalescing into one field), have a dramatic outcome: it creates a new kind of fundamental entity for physics, the field, with its own existence independent of the particles that create, and are acted on by, the field.

But can we really make sense of the idea of a field that has no underlying material or mechanical substratum or aether? What the above line of argument has shown is that the idea of a field with no underlying aether is simpler, more intelligible and acceptable than the idea of a field with an underlying aether. Granted the account of necessitating physical properties I have spelled out elsewhere[15] (and to be indicated in point 7 below), we can say, simply, that the aetherless field is a physical entity whose variable properties are such that they determine, at each spatial point, the way a charged test particle would accelerate were it to be placed at that point. The unchanging property of the field is the same everywhere, at all times and places, and determines the way the variable properties change. All this beautifully exemplifies the basic idea of physicalism. Such a physical entity, spread out continuously in space and varying in intensity in space and with time, may well seem unfamiliar and strange granted that we are primarily familiar with solid objects located in definite spatial regions; such considerations have nothing to do with comprehensibility and acceptability as this arises within the context of theoretical physics.

If, now, we postulate that such a field possesses an underlying material aether, we will be obliged to develop a further theory specifying the manner in which the particles of the aether interact with one another; we will need to postulate a Boscovichean force, which we may in turn need to interpret in terms of a force-field, a step which threatens to lead to an infinite regress. Even if the aether is continuous, we still need some infinitesimal analogue of force to account for the properties of the aether. A blueprint that postulates a field without an aether is, in short, a far more acceptable and comprehensible than one which postulates a field with an aether.

Two serious problems do, however, arise in connection with this new particle/field blueprint, B_6.

First, a major problem arises in connection with the interaction between charged point-particle and field: the point-particle creates an infinitely intense field at the point where it is located in space, which means, in turn, that the field produces infinitely strong forces

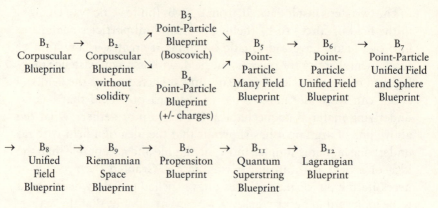

Figure 3 Blueprint articulation

on the particle. No such problem arises within the Boscovichean blueprint, B_3, or B_4 or B_5, because each point-particle is only acted on by the force-fields of other point-particles. The problem arises when the distinct force-fields of the distinct particles are unified to form *one* field, so that each particle both creates and is acted on by one and the same field. It is this step of unification, in the transition from Boscovichian to particle/field blueprint, that creates the problem.

It might be possible to solve this problem, in principle, by qualifying the transition from many fields to one, brought about by the step from B_5 to B_6 – the step that creates the self-interaction problem. One might try placing each point-particle at the centre of a small, rigid sphere of fixed radius, r, the field produced by each point-particle inside each sphere having an effect only on other point-particles. (A ghost of the original corpuscle returns!) Let us call this B_7. Since the field generated by the point-particle is only infinite inside the sphere, this infinity is harmless. Interactions between point-particles are unaffected as they enter each other's spheres: each point-particle continues to respond to the field at the point it occupies – the strength of the field at this point, as far as that point-particle is concerned, being due only to all the other (relevant) point-particles in the universe. There is a permanent surface of discontinuity in the field on the surface of the sphere surrounding each point-particle: but this discontinuity is, it seems, harmless, as it could only affect the point-particle at the centre of the sphere, and that point-particle can never pass through the surface of the sphere that surrounds it. On the surface of the sphere there is a discontinuous change, not in the strength of the field, but rather in the *interpretation* of that part of it due to the point-particle inside the sphere: that part of the field, inside the sphere, does not act on the point-particle inside the sphere. The laws which determine the way changes in the field propagate through space are otherwise the same inside and outside the spheres.

Is B_7 consistent, in the sense that a physical theory, compatible with it, could be formulated that would be consistent? I am not sure.

Einstein hoped to overcome this problem by developing a self-interacting, non-linear unified field theory according to which "particles" would be no more than especially intense regions of the field. This Einsteinian "unified field" blueprint, B_8, has not (so far) produced a successful physical theory.

The second major problem that arises in connection with the particle/unified field blueprint, B_6, has to do with the *finite velocity* of transmission of influences through the field. In moving from the Boscovichean to the particle/field blueprint, we have not changed the key notion of force, given by the equation $F = ma$ (where m is mass, and a is acceleration). The strength of a force is an absolute quantity; hence acceleration too is an absolute quantity (and not merely a question of choice of reference frame). Velocity, however, can be regarded as something which depends merely on choice of reference frame. With respect to what, then, is the velocity of transmission of influences through the field to be measured?[16] This question goes to the heart of the particle/field blueprint, since the idea that influences in the force-field take time to travel, and therefore have some finite velocity, is the key distinction between the particle/field and Boscovichean blueprints. Let the velocity of transmission of the particle-field blueprint tend to infinity, and the blueprint reduces to some version of the Boscovichean blueprint. One possibility is to let the velocity of transmission be a constant relative to an underlying aether, but this, as we have seen, only introduces further complications, and destroys the field as a fundamental physical entity. Another possibility is to let the velocity of transmission be a constant relative to the *source particle*. This, however, violates the *unification* of the distinct force-fields of the Boscovichean blueprint, the second crucial step in moving from the Boscovichean to the particle/field blueprint. The existence of different *velocities* of changes in the field, associated with the different velocities of source particles, would be close to associating a different *field* with each source particle. The *unified* particle/field blueprint postulates that, within the unified field, changes in intensity and/or direction of the field travel at some *finite* velocity, and thereby creates the profound dilemma as to *what it is* that this velocity is lawfully related to.

Einstein solved this second problem by means of the extraordinary proposal that changes in the field travel at one and the same velocity with respect to *all* inertial reference frames, however they may be moving (with constant velocity) with respect to each other. Our ideas about space and time need to be modified just sufficiently to transform this apparently absurdly contradictory idea into a self-consistent theory. As we shall see below in point 8, this is the nub of the special theory of relativity.

It is, I think, a bit excessive to think that Huygens, Maupertuis, or d'Alembert might have come up with special relativity as a result of subjecting the corpuscular hypothesis to sustained blueprint articulation, of the kind I have just illustrated. It is significant, however, that this process of blueprint articulation, taking the corpuscular hypothesis as its starting point, and without any input from evidence, has come up with blueprint ideas and problems that lie at the heart of modern physics: the idea of the field; the problem of self-interaction of the point-particle embedded in the field; and the problem of how a fundamental physical theory can specify a finite *velocity*. The first problem plagued the precise formulation of classical electrodynamics, arose again in connection with quantum electrodynamics and other quantum field theories, and has only been solved, perhaps somewhat dubiously, by means of a mathematical procedure known as "renormalization." The second problem was solved brilliantly by Einstein, as I have indicated.

There are one or two further blueprint generalizations that I would like to mention. First, one might seek to generalize the notion of "force," so that it depends, not just on the strength of the field, but also on the velocity of the particle. The field might be such that the forces between particles are no longer centrally directed but are, perhaps, at right angles to the line joining two stationary particles.

Very much more significantly, the conception of space, so far taken for granted, might be generalized to take into account "curved" space. A two-dimensional flat Euclidean plane can be distorted to form the curved space of a sphere (uniform positive curvature), or of a saddle (uniform negative curvature). These curved surfaces can be conceived of as geometric objects that exist within three-dimensional flat Euclidean space. But there is also the possibility of specifying the curvature of a two-dimensional surface in terms of measurements made entirely on the surface itself. Curvature can be characterized, not in terms of the radius of the sphere that best fits the surface at the point in question, but rather in terms of the angles of a minute triangle drawn on the surface around the point in question. If the angles add up to more than 180 degrees, the curvature is positive (like a sphere); if equal to 180 degrees, the curvature is zero, like a flat plane; and if less than 180 degrees, the curvature is negative, like a saddle. Once this step has been taken, it becomes possible to generalize two-dimensional curved surfaces to take into account the possibility of three-dimensional curved physical space – and indeed curved spaces of any number of dimensions.

A much more profound generalization is to consider that space might have variable curvature, from place to place. First, we can imagine a surface with hills and valleys, curvature varying from place to place, the variable curvature being specified solely in terms of measurements made on the surface itself. Then we can imagine generalizing this to take into account variable curvature of three-dimensional physical space – or, more generally still, variable curvature of a space of any dimensions. These profound generalizations of the whole conception of space were made by Carl Friedrich Gauss and Bernhard Riemann in the nineteenth century. These Gaussian, Riemannian contributions to thought are customarily put into mathematics, but they deserve also to be given a prominent place in the history of blueprint articulation of physics.[17]

There is just one further blueprint generalization that I wish to consider here, very briefly. So far it has been assumed throughout that determinism dominates the universe. This can be generalized. The universe might be probabilistic. That which exists at one instant might only determine what exists at subsequent instants probabilistically. There are at least two possibilities: probabilistic events occur (a) continuously, or (b) intermittently, in time. Below, I will consider how this probabilistic blueprint, B_{10}, can be developed when I come to discuss quantum theory.

Boscovich, Faraday, Gauss, Riemann, Einstein, and others have, over the centuries, made important contributions to blueprint articulation, as I have indicated above, despite the prevalence of SE. How, then, would general acceptance of AOE help?

AOE helps in a number of ways. As I have tried to show, it provides a framework for the development and assessment of blueprint ideas. SE, by contrast, does not. AOE stresses the importance of developing and assessing blueprint ideas within physics; SE does not. AOE, if implemented, would create a tradition of blueprint articulation: there would be physics journals devoted to it, and it would figure in textbooks and education. SE, by contrast, suppresses all this. AOE stresses the vital need to develop a good, acceptable blueprint that does justice to the current theoretical situation in physics: SE serves to obscure the need for a good blueprint, and may even conceal the fact that no such blueprint exists. The outcome, as I have already mentioned, is that physics, dominated by acceptance of SE, tends dogmatically to accept blueprints relevant to past theories, and this has adverse consequences for the discovery, acceptance and interpretation of new theories, as I hope now to show. Progress in theoretical physics is impeded.

But does not theoretical physics today repudiate SE, and accept something like AOE, in that, during the last three decades or so, a vast amount of work has been devoted to string theory (or M-theory), even though the theory – or blueprint as it should perhaps be called – has not produced a single successful new prediction? Is not this blueprint articulation *par excellence*? My answer is: No. In one vital respect, string theory does not constitute an acceptable blueprint. At present, no such blueprint exists – a crisis in physics that general acceptance of SE serves to obscure. I shall return to this issue below in point 12.

I now discuss how acceptance of SE tends to obstruct the *acceptance, correct interpretation*, and *discovery* of fundamental new theories in physics.

6 THEORY ACCEPTANCE

In chapter 2 we saw how failure to engage in blueprint articulation can impede acceptance of a new, empirically successful theory. French natural philosophers, as a result of taking Cartesianism for granted, were incapable of taking Newton's law of gravitation seriously for decades, despite its immense empirical success. In a sense, even Newton could not accept his own law, interpreted as the statement that gravitation is a force that acts at a distance across empty space, because it did violence to the Cartesian idea that all action must be by contact. Only gradually did it dawn on some natural philosophers that something like the metaphysical blueprint expounded by Boscovich in 1758 might be inherently more acceptable than Cartesianism, there thus being nothing inherently unintelligible about the force of gravity acting at a distance through empty space. AOE science, in encouraging and facilitating blueprint articulation, the improvement of accepted blueprints, increases the chances that when a good, new, fundamental theory emerges, an appropriate metaphysical blueprint will already have been developed; it decreases the chances that acceptance of such a theory will be impeded, perhaps for decades, by widespread acceptance of a blueprint that is associated with earlier theoretical ideas, and which is, in any case, itself inherently unsatisfactory.

Something somewhat similar occurred in connection with the next great contribution to fundamental physical theory – James Clerk Maxwell's theory of the electromagnetic field which unifies electricity, magnetism, and optics. Maxwell's theory, like Newton's, went through a long process of development after its author's death. Maxwell put his theory forward in two papers, *On Physical Lines of Force*, published in 1861 and 1862, and *A Dynamical Theory of the Electromagnetic Field*, published in 1865. But what we now know as Maxwell's equations were first formulated by Oliver Heaviside in 1884: these were equivalent to, but a great simplification of, Maxwell's original equations (although Maxwell had himself formulated something similar, in words, in a brief paper published in 1868).[18] Maxwell had nothing to say about the production of electromagnetic waves, and may not even have realized that an oscillating electric current would generate such waves. He may have thought that light was produced as a result of a non-electromagnetic interaction between matter and the aether.[19] G.F. FitzGerald, who contributed much to the development of the theory, at one stage around 1879 thought he had *proved* that an oscillating current could not produce electromagnetic waves – although before long he realized he was mistaken.[20] Electromagnetic radiation, in the form of radio waves, was finally produced and detected by Heinrich Hertz in 1888. Throughout the final two decades of the nineteenth century and the first decade or so of the twentieth, Maxwell's theory continued to be developed until it reached something like the form accepted today: a theory of the electromagnetic field, construed to be composed of two interacting elements, the electric and magnetic components, at right angles to each other in direction, changes in one producing changes in the other, such changes being transmitted through space at the velocity of light, the electric component being produced by electric charge, magnetism being the product of charge in motion (for example in an electric current down a wire).[21]

If we take Maxwell's theory of the electromagnetic field to be his (or Heaviside's) equations interpreted in the way I have just indicated, then it has to be said that general acceptance of *this* theory only came about in the early twentieth century, after general acceptance of Einstein's special theory of relativity, some years after it was put forward in 1905.

Almost all those who did so much to develop Maxwell's theory after his death – men like G.F. FitzGerald, Oliver Lodge, William Thomson, Joseph Larmour, H.A. Lorentz, and others – were firmly of the view that the theory had to be understood in terms of the aether, a mysterious substance, a "jelly" or "vortex sponge," that filled all of space. Much effort was put into developing theories of the aether which would succeed in doing justice to the successful experimental predictions of Maxwell's theory.[22] Some of these accounts of the aether, built up in terms of cog wheels, elastic bands, fluids, and other mechanical devices, were only intended to be used for teaching and research purposes, and were not meant to be taken seriously, as depicting the real nature of the aether. They did however provoke Pierre Duhem, the famous French historian and philosopher of physics, to comment around 1900 as follows on a book by Lodge:

> Here is a book intended to expound the modern theories of electricity and to expound a new theory. In it there are nothing but strings which move around pulleys, which roll around drums, which go through pearl beads, which carry weights; and tubes which pump water while others swell and contract; toothed wheels which are geared to one another and engage hooks. We thought we were entering the tranquil and neatly ordered abode of reason, but we find ourselves in a factory.[23]

Much effort was, however, expended in attempting to develop a realistic theory of the aether – the aether seen as necessary in order to make sense of Maxwell's theory. Maxwell himself seems to have believed in the existence of the aether, even if he may have had doubts about discovering its real nature.[24] As late as 1931, Lodge said of the aether theories of earlier decades that he expected "posterity will recognize some inklings of truth in these hydrodynamical speculations."[25]

In short, FitzGerald, Lodge, and the others, in demanding that Maxwell's theory be understood in terms of some kind of material aether, did not accept the theory as it ultimately came to be understood. Failure to engage in blueprint articulation, of the kind indicated above in section 5, led these physicists to demand that Maxwell's theory be understood in terms of a wholly inappropriate metaphysical blueprint. Acceptance of Maxwell's theory as it ultimately came to be understood was delayed for several decades as a result.[26]

It is not even anachronistic to hold that the theory might have been interpreted and accepted as a fundamental field theory, devoid of the aether, in the nineteenth century. Michael Faraday understood clearly that, instead of trying to understand the electromagnetic field in terms of an underlying material aether, it would make better sense to try to understand *matter* in terms of the electromagnetic field.

It must be admitted that there were those who were less enamoured of speculations about the nature of the aether, for example J.H. Poynting,[27] who made an important contribution concerning the flow of energy in the electromagnetic field, and Heaviside.[28] Hertz famously said that "Maxwell's theory is his system of equations,"[29] but seems to have come to believe in the aether nevertheless.[30]

I have argued, so far, that general acceptance of Newton's and Maxwell's theories was retarded by the failure to put AOE explicitly into practice. I have not, yet, argued that acceptance of SE is to blame. SE *is* to blame, however, in connection with the next theory to be considered: quantum theory. But SE does not *delay* acceptance of quantum theory. It does the opposite: it renders acceptance of the theory too *rapid*. It leads to the acceptance of a version of the theory that ought not to have been accepted (and, as a result, has delayed, perhaps, formulation and acceptance of an acceptable version of the theory).

A fundamental problem confronted by those associated with the discovery and development of quantum theory – Planck, Einstein, Bohr, de Broglie, Heisenberg, Schrödinger, Born, Dirac, and many others – is the following: What is the nature of quantum entities, electrons, photons, atoms, and the rest, in view of their apparently contradictory wave and particle aspects? Direct a beam of electrons, all with the same momentum, at a screen with two slits in it, and behind the screen by means of a photographic plate, say, individual electrons will be detected as particles, each detection a dot with a precise location in the photographic plate. But, as more and more electrons arrive, the dots register as a series of dark bands, where many electrons are detected, interleaved with light bands where hardly any are detected. These bands disappear if first one slit is blocked, and then opened again and the other blocked. The bands only appear if both slits are open together. If it is assumed that each electron when it encounters the two-slitted screen is not a particle but a *wave* that goes through both slits, the pattern of dark and light bands can be explained. Where there is a dark band, waves emerging from the two slits reinforce each other, a crest from one slit reinforcing a crest from the other slit. But where there is a light band, waves from the two slits cancel each other out, so that a crest from one slit is cancelled by a trough from the other slit. This experiment, incidentally, can be done with photons and other elementary particles, and even with atoms and molecules. The "interference" bands, as they are called, are characteristic quite generally of waves. One can perform the two-slit experiment with water waves in the bath.

How can an electron – or photon, atom, or molecule – be a wave-like entity when it encounters and passes through the two-slitted screen, and yet abruptly become a particle-like entity when it encounters the photographic plate?

Bohr, Heisenberg, Born, and most other physicists working on quantum theory (QT) around the time it received a definite formulation, in 1925 and 1926 with the work of Heisenberg and Schrödinger, decided that the above problem about the ultimate nature of quantum entities could not be solved. They decided to interpret QT as being about, not electrons, protons, atoms, and molecules, but rather *the results of performing measurements on these quantum entities.* At a stroke, it did not matter that the new QT of 1926 does not specify consistently what an electron or atom is. The theory evades the issue in being about *measurement*, not *quantum entities*, and as a result does everything (from the standpoint of SE) that a physical theory should do, namely successfully predict experimental results.

This version of QT, the Copenhagen or orthodox interpretation of the theory (OQT), has become one of the most empirically successful theories of all time. No other theory successfully predicts such an astonishing range and diversity of phenomena with such accuracy. At the time of writing, there is still no known phenomenon which goes against the theory.[31]

Given SE, there seem to be no valid *scientific* grounds for objecting to OQT whatsoever. Nevertheless, some physicists did object: Einstein, Schrödinger, de Broglie, and others. However, even they were obliged to admit that OQT satisfied all objective criteria for acceptability, in that it met with extraordinary empirical success.

Granted AOE, however, all this changes dramatically. OQT becomes all but unacceptable.

The point is this. As a result of being about measurement only, OQT is obliged to call upon some part of classical physics for a treatment of the measuring instrument. OQT is made up of two very different parts: a component that deals with the quantum system (electron or atom, etc.), and a component, taken from classical physics, that applies to the measuring apparatus. This means that OQT is an appallingly, unacceptably *disunified* theory. It is what I have called a "patchwork quilt" theory: one law for quantum systems, Schrödinger's equation, and another, quite different set of laws for the measuring apparatus, some part of classical physics. A patchwork quilt theory as disunified as this is unacceptable *despite its great empirical success*.

It might be thought that in principle, even if not in practice, OQT could dispense with (some part of) classical physics, and apply QT to the whole proceedings, quantum system *and* measuring process. But this cannot be done, for two reasons. First, OQT, as a result of failing to solve the fundamental wave/particle problem, lacks its own quantum ontology. It cannot be interpreted as being about anything that actually exists, in physical space, evolving in time. So it cannot be interpreted as being about measuring instruments described in quantum mechanical terms. Second, if OQT is applied to the measuring process, it gives what appear to be spectacularly *wrong* answers. In the case of the two-slit experiment described above, when just one electron interacts with the photographic plate, OQT predicts that the plate goes into what is called a *superposition* of all possible outcomes – the electron arriving at all possible positions on the photographic plate until a *further* measurement is made on the plate by an additional measuring device that is, itself, described in classical terms.

OQT is thus an unacceptable theory. As Einstein said of Bohr, Heisenberg, and the others, "they do not see what sort of risky game they are playing with reality – reality as something independent of what is experimentally established."[32]

Here, then, is a case where general acceptance of SE has had profound and long-term damaging consequences for physics. It has resulted in acceptance of a theory, OQT, that has dominated physics in the twentieth and twenty-first centuries, that ought not to have been accepted.

Disunity is by no means the only defect that OQT suffers from. OQT also (a) lacks precision; (b) lacks explanatory power; (c) is ambiguous as to whether the quantum domain is deterministic or probabilistic; (d) is such that it is inherently unsuited for unification with general relativity; and (e) is limited in scope in that it cannot be applied to the early universe or the cosmos as a whole. All these defects stem from the key defect: the failure to solve the quantum wave/particle problem and provide a consistent conjecture as to what quantum entities are when not subject to observation. It is this key defect that compels OQT to be a theory about the results of measurement, which in turn leads to disunity, and the other defects, as we shall now see.

(a) OQT is imprecise because the notion of measurement is imprecise. (b) The theory lacks explanatory power, despite its great empirical success, in part because of its failure to explain phenomena in terms of the interactions of quantum entities, in part because of the disunity of the theory (only unified theories are explanatory). In addition, OQT cannot explain fully how classical phenomena emerge from quantum phenomena because some part of classical physics must be presupposed for measurement. (c) The basic dynamic equation of OQT, Schrödinger's time-dependent equation, is *deterministic*; quantum systems thus evolve deterministically, according to OQT. But the experimental predictions of OQT are, in general, *probabilistic*. Does this mean probabilistic events occur objectively in nature, the laws of the quantum domain being fundamentally probabilistic in character? Or are the probabilistic predictions of OQT somehow the outcome of our intervention or perspective, and not in physical processes themselves? OQT provides no unambiguous answer to this crucial question.[33] (d) OQT is unsuited for unification with general relativity just because it is a theory about the results of performing measurements on systems. A unification of OQT and general relativity which preserves this feature of OQT would be a theory that predicts the outcome of performing measurements on space-time from outside space-time: clearly impossible. (General relativity is a theory about the nature of space-time, how its curvature is affected by the presence of matter, or energy more generally.) (e) Essentially for the same reason, OQT cannot be applied to the early universe, or the cosmos as a whole. There were no measuring devices around in the early universe; and measurements cannot be made on the cosmos as a whole from outside the cosmos![34]

These further defects reinforce the basic point: because of its failure to solve the quantum wave/particle problem, OQT suffers from multiple defects to such an extent as to render it unacceptable.

What, then, ought to have been done, given that OQT is unacceptable? The view, around 1930, ought to have been along the following lines. The immense predictive success of OQT must, of course, be acknowledged. OQT deserves to be accepted as a working tool to predict phenomena, until something better turns up, but it cannot be regarded as an acceptable fundamental explanatory theory, in view of its multiple defects (especially disunity). It is vital to recognize that the fundamental defect is the failure to solve the quantum wave/particle problem, as all the other defects stem from this key defect. A basic problem for theoretical physics must be to develop a version of QT which specifies precisely what electrons, atoms, molecules may be when not undergoing observation – a version of QT which does even better empirically than OQT.[35] This is what AOE would suggest.

What actually occurred, from 1930 onwards, was very different. Bohr, Heisenberg, Born, and most other physicists at the time argued that OQT had to be accepted, opposition amounting to no more than a failure to adjust to unfamiliar ideas. Bohr's defence of OQT, in particular, was not just dogmatic; it was confused in that it was couched in terms of the idea that "wave" and "particle" are "complementary" ideas that never apply to the same experiment (which is wrong, as both apply to the two-slit experiment, as we have seen, and to many other experiments too; one should not invoke the mistaken idea of complementarity to defend OQT). Some physicists did protest, as I have indicated, but they were ignored. A vast literature grew up on the interpretative problems of QT, but it mostly ignored the key defect of OQT, and often the other defects as well.[36] Much of it was devoted to solving what was called "the measurement problem" – the problem, that is, of showing that what goes on during measurement conforms to the Schrödinger equation. But this is an absurdity: Schrödinger's equation is *deterministic*, and the outcome of measurement is, in general, *probabilistic*, so measurement cannot conform to Schrödinger's equation.[37]

Dramatic theoretical developments occurred: Dirac's relativistic QT of the electron, quantum electrodynamics, quantum electroweak theory (which partially unifies electromagnetism and the weak force), quark theory, quantum chromodynamics (the quantum field theory of the force between quarks inside protons, neutrons, and other "particles"), the standard model (a quasi-synthesis of electroweak theory and chromodynamics) and, most recently, string theory which depicts "particles" as tiny closed strings and seeks to unify the standard model and general relativity (thus being a candidate "theory of everything").

All these theories suffer from the defects that plague OQT. They are *all* unacceptably disunified, non-explanatory, ambivalent about determinism or probabilism, etc., etc., because of the failure to solve the basic wave/particle problem inherited from OQT. And yet, theoretical physics goes on its heroic way, blindly ignoring this fundamental problem.[38] And SE strongly reinforces this attitude. All the quantum theories mentioned are spectacularly successful empirically – apart from string theory which so far has made no correct experimental predictions at all.

How, then, is the basic quantum wave/particle problem to be solved? There are two possibilities to consider: probabilism and determinism. I first consider probabilism, briefly considered above in section 5 on blueprint articulation (B_{10}), and then determinism.

Perhaps QT is trying to tell us that nature is fundamentally probabilistic. Even though the basic dynamic law of QT – Schrödinger's equation – is deterministic, the predictions of the theory are, in general, probabilistic. Let us conjecture, then, that the basic laws of the quantum domain are probabilistic. The physical entities of the quantum domain, electrons, protons, and the rest, interact with one another *probabilistically*.

At once a possible solution to the quantum wave/particle problem leaps into view. The particle and wave are entities of classical, *deterministic* physics – the physics of Newton and James Clerk Maxwell. If entities of the quantum domain interact with one another probabilistically, then they will differ in character quite fundamentally from the classical particle and wave. Given probabilism, it would be a disaster, wholly incomprehensible, if quantum entities were either a classical, deterministic wave or particle. The traditional quantum wave/particle problem is, in other words, the *wrong* problem. Instead of asking "Is the quantum entity a particle or wave?," we need to ask:

1   What kind of unproblematic, fundamentally probabilistic physical entities are there, as possibilities?
2   Can quantum entities be construed to be some variety of unproblematic probabilistic entity?

There are two possibilities. Probabilistic events might occur continuously in time, or only intermittently, when specific physical conditions arise. QT suggests the latter. The theory asserts that quantum states evolve deterministically until a measurement is made. Conceivably, then, measurement is a *sufficient condition* for a probabilistic event to occur, but not a necessary condition. OQT has not been correctly formulated because *precise, physical, quantum mechanical conditions* for probabilistic events to occur have not been specified. The physical states of quantum entities evolve deterministically until, intermittently in time, the conditions for probabilistic events to occur arise: then, instantaneously, Schrödinger's equation is suspended, and a probabilistic event occurs. One physical state is "actualized" probabilistically from many, possibly infinitely many, possible states.

Let us call physical entities that interact with one another probabilistically *propensitons*, and let us call them *intermittent propensitons* if they interact with one another probabilistically intermittently in time.

Here is a simple-minded model of an intermittent propensiton. The universe consists of spheres, which expand steadily, in a deterministic fashion, until two (or more) touch. That is the condition for probabilistic collapse. Instantly each sphere collapses into a minute sphere of some definite, common radius, each sphere somewhere inside the volume of the larger sphere, the precise position only probabilistically determined. Each minute sphere then expands as before, until two spheres touch once more.

Viewed from the standpoint of determinism, this fundamentally probabilistic object seems thoroughly odd, if not downright unintelligible. But viewed from the standpoint of probabilism (a blueprint generalization of determinism), the intermittently collapsing sphere is just about the simplest, most intelligible object one can imagine. It is to probabilism what the particle or the wave is to determinism. It is thus highly significant that all one needs to do is add one or two further, wholly comprehensible details, and one ends up with objects just like those depicted by quantum theory!

The above model can be made a bit more interesting by supposing each sphere is made up of a "stuff" which varies in intensity in a wave-like way. The intensity of the stuff determines the probability of where the sphere will be localized when it undergoes probabilistic collapse. It has high probability of being localized where the stuff is intense, low probability where the stuff is tenuous.[39]

Let us suppose, now, that each propensiton can have any shape in space, and that its deterministic evolution occurs in accordance with Schrödinger's equation. Imagine, now that such a propensiton is sent towards a two-slitted screen. Most of the propensiton is reflected by the screen, but some passes through both slits, the wave-like stuff of the propensiton forming interference bands of varying intensity on the photographic plate. But this interaction of the spatially smeared-out propensiton with the photographic plate is, let us suppose, just the condition for an intermittent probabilistic interaction to occur. The spatially smeared-out propensiton collapses instantaneously and probabilistically into a tiny spatial region. Instantaneously, the propensiton registers itself as a tiny dot on the photographic plate, but most probably in a region of high density of the stuff of the propensiton before collapse. Repeat the experiment many times, and gradually an interference pattern, made up of dots, will be built up on the photographic plate.

We can, in short, interpret QT to be about intermittent propensitons. Electrons, protons, atoms, and molecules are a new kind of fundamentally probabilistic entity: the intermittent propensiton. The electron or proton, as depicted by QT, can be construed to be a thoroughly *intelligible* version of the simplest, most intelligible intermittent propensiton conceivable – the spontaneously collapsing sphere, considered above. The quantum wave/particle problem is, in essence, solved.[40] And the version of QT that emerges can be called *propensiton quantum theory* (PQT).[41] The quantum domain has only continued to seem baffling and unintelligible to so many because of the general failure to engage in blueprint articulation and view QT from the perspective of probabilism. That, in turn, is a consequence of the dominance of SE, and the failure to implement AOE.

But one crucial question remains: what is the precise physical condition for intermittent probabilistic events to occur – for the spatially smeared-out propensiton to collapse instantaneously and probabilistically into a tiny dot somewhere on the photographic plate?

My proposal is that probabilistic events occur when new "particles" are created, new bound systems or stationary states.[42] Such events occur, in other words, when, as a result of a collision, an atom loses an electron, a molecule is broken up into two distinct parts, or an electron and a positron collide, annihilate each other, and create photons.[43] We require energy in the form of mass to be transformed into energy in some other form, or vice versa.

The general idea can be illustrated by means of the following specific case. An electron collides with a hydrogen atom (which consists of an electron in orbit around a proton). There are, let us suppose for simplicity, just two possible outcomes: (1) there is what is called an *elastic* collision, the outcome being an electron and an atom; (2) there is an *inelastic* collision, so that energy in the form of mass is converted into, or created out of, energy due to motion (kinetic energy), and in this case the outcome is that the hydrogen atom is dissociated, and two electrons and a proton emerge. Both these outcomes emerge, as a superposition, each having a quantum mechanical potential existence. Everything, so far, occurs in accordance with the Schrödinger equation. OQT predicts that the superposition of (1) and (2) continues until a measurement is made, in which case either (1) or (2) will be detected, probabilistically determined by OQT. By contrast, PQT predicts that the superposition of (1) and (2) collapses spontaneously and probabilistically, in the absence of measurement, when the initial interaction between the electron and the hydrogen atom is at an end.[44]

As I have shown elsewhere, this version of PQT can recover all the empirical success of OQT. It is of decisive importance to appreciate that all quantum measurements that actually *detect* quantum systems (electrons, photons, etc.) invariably involve *inelastic* interactions – precisely the kind of interaction which, according to PQT, leads to a probabilistic occurrence.[45] But PQT also predicts that probabilistic events occur when OQT predicts that they do not, because no measurement has been made. This difference means that, in certain conditions, PQT and OQT make *different* experimental predictions. Crucial experiments to decide between OQT and PQT are possible. But they are difficult to perform, and have not, as far as I know, yet been performed. In the case of the collision between the electron and hydrogen atom, considered above, one would need to allow the outcome of the collision, (1) and (2), to evolve until PQT predicts that a probabilistic collapse occurs into *either* (1) *or* (2), and one would then need to subject the system to forces which have the effect of returning the outcome to the original state, the electron and the hydrogen atom, a measurement then, finally, being made. OQT predicts interference effects. The experiment is conceptually analogous to the two-slit experiment, the final outcome evolving along two indistinguishable paths, (1) and (2), comparable to the two slits. PQT, by contrast, predicts no interference effects since, according to this theory, the superposition of (1) and (2) collapses probabilistically into either (1) or (2) before the measurement is made.

This particular crucial experiment is impossibly difficult to perform. But, as I have indicated, there are other crucial experiments which might be performed, especially having to do with decaying systems.[46]

AOE physics would actively seek to put PQT and OQT to the test of experiment, and would endeavour to develop alternative versions of PQT, all as a matter of the utmost priority. SE physics has done nothing of the kind. I have myself experienced personally the way in which SE physics discourages criticisms of OQT, and discourages attempts to develop a better version of quantum theory. I first proposed that the problems of QT could be solved by specifying a precise quantum mechanical condition for probabilistic collapse to occur in 1972.[47] I was resoundingly scolded by two well-known American physicists, William Band and James Park, for having the temerity to speak about matters I, as a philosopher of science, knew nothing about.[48] As a matter of fact, it was the two physicists who got things wrong, as I pointed out in a subsequent article.[49] Unfortunately, my original paper was published without the final two sections, which contained my more specific proposals. These were finally published, after long delays, in my (1976b). The conjecture that probabilistic events occur when new particles are created appeared in a paper published in 1982, and again in a long paper published 1988.[50] (An earlier paper published in 1985 tackled the problem of instantaneous collapse being incompatible with special relativity.[51]) Then, finally, a well-known theoretical physicist took note of my efforts. Euan Squires welcomed my idea but suggested that it had not yet been formulated with sufficient precision.[52] I managed to meet this request for precision in a paper published in 1994 – and in subsequent work.[53]

Physicists have shown almost no interest in this work whatsoever. I did, on one occasion, receive a note from Louis de Broglie expressing interest in one of my papers. Paul Dirac, shown a sketch of my work, remarked, "Ah yes, but where are the equations?" More recently, in 2013 Rudolf Haag expressed interest in my approach.[54] And Euan Squires was critically sympathetic. But aside from that, nothing.

This lack of interest is astonishing. The quantum wave/particle problem goes to the heart of modern theoretical physics, as I have tried to show. One might have thought that a proposal to solve the problem would have provoked more interest. Everyone commenting on QT emphasizes just how mysterious, how inexplicable, the quantum world appears to be. Probabilism, perhaps uniquely, promises to make the quantum world thoroughly intelligible. Electrons, atoms, and other quantum entities behave in just the way one would expect intermittent propensitons to behave, as I have tried to make clear. Behaviour that seems baffling and inexplicable when viewed from the standpoint of common sense, classical physics, or determinism, becomes thoroughly comprehensible when viewed from the standpoint of intermittent probabilism. Quantum entities may be *unfamiliar* because we ordinarily have no familiarity with fundamentally probabilistic objects; but they are thoroughly comprehensible nevertheless, when viewed as intermittent propensitons. It is inconceivable that AOE physics would betray such indifference to a proposal as to how such a fundamental problem can be solved, and a better theory developed.

I attribute this lack of interest to the fact that SE still dominates physics. As a result, the serious problems of QT tend to be rendered invisible; they are ignored, or downplayed in importance. What matters, for SE physics, is predicting more and more phenomena more and more accurately: that the theory that does this should, in addition, *explain* and *promote understanding* is unnecessary. Failure to provide explanations and understanding is thus not a serious failing at all. Furthermore, given that SE dominates, the crucial metaphysical idea that nature might be fundamentally probabilistic cannot receive the attention it deserves, and it may not even be possible to publish discussion of it in a physics journal, because it is not a testable theory (or a piece of mathematics). Elementary blueprint articulation which, given AOE physics, would rapidly come up with the possibility of probabilism, does not take place explicitly within SE physics at all – even if individuals may ponder these issues. As a result of the dominance of SE, there is a long-standing failure to appreciate just how important and fundamental the quantum wave-particle problem is for the future of theoretical physics, and thus a failure to appreciate the importance of a proposal for its solution. Finally, as far as my own work is concerned, it has not helped at all that I am a philosopher of science, not a physicist; SE physics does not take kindly to the idea that a philosopher of science might have something of value to contribute to physics.

Here, then, is a very dramatic way in which general acceptance and attempted implementation of SE has harmed science. It has led to the acceptance of a theory, OQT, that ought not to have been accepted, and it has led to a general blindness to, and indifference to, an approach which might well turn out to solve a fundamental problem of physics, and thus lead to a theory, some version of PQT, which meets with predictive success *and* provides genuine explanations and understanding.

Probabilism is just a possibility – a generalization of determinism. But given that it promises to resolve the long standing problems of QT, it is a possibility that deserves to be taken more seriously than it has been so far.

I must now, much too briefly, qualify what I have said so far, in various ways.

To begin with, PQT has not been quite as resoundingly neglected as I have so far suggested. In 1986, fourteen years after I began my advocacy of the approach, three Italian physicists, entirely independently of my work, put forward a version of PQT (see Ghirardi, Rimini, and Weber 1986). They proposed that an individual quantum entity, perhaps in a highly unlocalized state, has a minute probability of becoming spontaneously localized – such a minute probability that it is only likely to occur after the passage of thousands, perhaps millions, of years. This means that a single quantum entity will never be observed to undergo such a spontaneous localization in the laboratory. During the process of measurement, however, millions of quantum entities, electrons, protons, atoms, molecules, interact with one another and become "quantum entangled" – that is, all a part of the same quantum state. All it requires is for *one* of the entangled quantum entities to become spontaneously localized, and at once all the others will be localized as well. But as the quantum-entangled state consists of millions of such entities, it is overwhelmingly probable that this will occur in a fraction of a second. Thus can one explain why measurement leads to definite, probabilistic results, and not to a super-position of such results (as the Schrödinger equation predicts).[55]

Ten years later, in 1996, Roger Penrose put forward another version of PQT. His idea is that, whereas quantum systems evolve into superpositions of states, space (or space-time) does not. Suppose now that a quantum object with mass goes into a superposition of being located at two positions in space. General relativity would seem to imply that space itself would evolve into something like a superposition of two distinct curvatures, one associated with the object being in one location, the other with the object in the other location. If the mass is sufficiently large, and the locations are sufficiently distant from one another, space cannot tolerate – as it were – the possibility of there being a superposition of distinct curvatures and, as a result, a probabilistic event occurs, and the quantum object becomes localized in one or other position in space. It is the interaction of QT with general relativity that provokes probabilistic transitions.[56]

Penrose's idea has received far more attention than mine. This is perhaps deserved. The idea is easier to test experimentally. And, if correct, it makes a profound additional contribution to physics in that it links up, in an entirely new way, QT and general relativity.

There is a tendency to view all such "collapse" versions of QT (as they are called), not as exemplifying probabilism and thus providing a possible solution to the fundamental wave/particle problem, but rather as attempted solutions to the measurement problem.[57] Viewed in this latter way, collapse theories seem ad hoc, and somewhat implausible, and that may account for general lack of interest in this whole approach. Furthermore, neither Ghirardi and company, nor Penrose, has stressed that probabilism promises to solve the wave/particle problem, thus rendering the quantum domain intelligible.

Probabilism is just one possibility. The other is determinism. A deterministic approach to solving the wave/particle problem goes back to the early times of QT. It is due to Louis de Broglie[58] and David Bohm,[59] and holds that the electron is *both* wave *and* particle. Each electron is a particle, but has associated with it a guiding wave which goes through both slits of the two-slitted screen, and guides the electron onto the photographic plate where it is detected as a dot. The whole process is deterministic; the probabilistic outcomes are due to the probabilistic distribution of initial positions of the electrons in the ensemble of electrons. Measurement provokes no collapse: empty quantum waves persist for ever.

Bohmian mechanics (B M), as it is sometimes called, does however face problems. B M asserts that the quantum state, associated with the particle, can be precisely the same for many particles even though these have different initial locations. As the quantum state is associated with the particle, one would expect particles with different locations to have somewhat different quantum states – which would lead to predictions somewhat different from O Q T. Such a version of B M has not, to my knowledge, been formulated, let alone tested.

A second problem is that B M predicts that particles can travel faster than light. It may be argued that this does not matter in a non-relativistic theory. The suspicion must be, however, that such faster-than-light velocity must pose a problem when it comes to developing a relativistic version of the theory – and, tellingly, no such theory has been developed.

Many physicists today would probably claim that O Q T has been superseded by *decoherence*.[60] Decoherence is the view that quantum systems interact with their environment before measurement results emerge, and it is this which ensures that systems are found to have a definite value of that which is measured – position, momentum, energy, or whatever – and not some superposition of such values. On this view, Q T can be interpreted as a theory about how quantum systems interact with their environment, quantum mechanically described: the recourse to classical physics for measurement is thus no more than a practical convenience, not a matter of conceptual necessity.

But, needless to say, decoherence does not, in itself, solve the problem. Is probabilism or determinism supposed to hold sway? If probabilism, then probabilistic decoherent Q T is unacceptably imprecise: no *precise* quantum mechanical conditions for probabilistic collapse are specified. If determinism, then decoherence leads to the view that *all* outcomes occur. Whenever O Q T predicts that any one of an immense number of outcomes are possible, perhaps even *infinitely* many (an electron detected in different places, or with different momenta), deterministic decoherence predicts that *all* these outcomes occur. We observe just one outcome; and endlessly many, possibly even infinitely many, different versions of ourselves observe different outcomes. This is Everett's interpretation of Q T, first put forward in 1957.[61] If these endlessly growing alternative outcomes all coexist, how come we have no experience of them? Deterministic decoherence claims to provide the answer. Q T itself predicts that what exists in one outcome can have no effect on what exists in another outcome – as long as interactions with the environment have become sufficiently complex to exclude the possibility of interference effects arising.

The Everett interpretation of QT (or what I have called "deterministic decoherence") faces four problems. First, there is the wild implausibility of supposing that *all possible outcomes* occur. Where you are now, as you read these lines, contains not just you, but billions upon billions upon billions of alternative realities as well, created ever since the universe began with the big bang. These extra realities may well include empty space, the centre of stars, even black holes. Taken all together, the density of matter is almost infinite. Is this plausible? (This is the implausibility that one incurs as the cost of refusing to contemplate probabilism.) Second, this interpretation of QT fails to solve the fundamental quantum wave/particle problem. It does not tell us what quantum entities are, and how they can give rise to the macroscopic world we experience around us. The response of supporters of Everett to this objection tends to be: "Just as the nature of the classical electromagnetic field is given by Maxwell's equations, so too the nature of the quantum domain is given by Schrödinger's equation." But Maxwell's equations only specify the nature of the electromagnetic field when given a specific physical interpretation: what is the physical interpretation of QT, according to Everett? QT specifies the quantum state of a quantum system by attributing a complex number to each point in space. OQT gives this a definite physical interpretation: mathematical operations performed on the complex numbers specify the probabilities of obtaining such and such a result if a measurement is made. Thus, if $\Psi(x,y,z,t)$ represents the complex number to be associated with each point $(x,y,z,)$ at time t, thus representing the quantum state of a quantum system, then $|\Psi(x,y,z,t)|^2.dV$ represents the probability of finding the particle in volume element dV, if a position measurement is made. PQT interprets Ψ in such a way that it attributes values of *propensities*, probabilistic generalizations of dispositional properties such as mass and charge, to the quantum system: these *propensities* determine probabilistically the outcome of probabilistic interactions, should the conditions for them to occur arise. Macroscopic objects that we experience are the outcome of billions of quantum probabilistic occurrences. But Everett QT cannot avail itself of such physical interpretations: it is restricted to attributing complex numbers to points in space, and it remains wholly unclear how our world can emerge from a barrage of such complex numbers.[62]

A third problem arises in connection with the evolution of many worlds from one. Suppose we conduct an experiment with one electron, detected by means of a photographic plate, there being 10,000 possible outcomes, all of which occur (according to Everett). If everything occurs in accordance with the Schrödinger equation, then the one electron must be shared between 10,000 "worlds," which cannot do justice to the fact that there is definitely one detected electron in "our" world. Everett needs an extra postulate which specifies precisely when one electron becomes 10,000 electrons, one for each world. But this means the one world cannot split into 10,000 worlds continuously, in accordance with Schrödinger's equation, as required by decoherence. It must occur at some precise instant, at the moment when the one electron becomes 10,000. But it is just this extra postulate, specifying precisely when, under what conditions, splitting of worlds occurs, that the modern decoherence version of Everett does not provide.

Fourth, there would seem to be a problem as to how the many worlds view can do justice to the empirically successful probabilistic predictions of OQT in all circumstances. If probabilistic predictions are matched by number of outcomes – the higher the probability of an outcome, so the larger the number of outcomes associated with it – one can begin to see how the many worlds view could do justice to the probabilistic predictions of OQT. But this correlation of probabilistic predictions and number of outcomes may not always hold. Suppose the quantum state of an electron is such that there is a probability of .99999 that the electron will be detected in the spatial region R_1, and a probability of .00001 that it will be detected in R_2. Furthermore, we may suppose that there is just one outcome that constitutes detection in R_1, but 1,000 distinct outcomes that constitute detection in R_2. How can the many worlds interpretation of quantum theory do justice to these probabilistic predictions in these circumstances? Repeat the experiment many times, and almost all experiments (in almost all branching universes) will repeatedly detect the electron in region R_2, which has a probability of .00001 (or a probability of $(.00001)^{10,000}$ if the experiment is repeated 10,000 times). In almost all the branching universes, in other words, the probabilistic predictions of OQT are horribly violated. Everett QT, in order merely to be a candidate for consideration, must be able to predict the successful *probabilistic* predictions of OQT, and yet it seems Everett fails dreadfully to meet this elementary requirement (for almost everyone).

I assume versions of the experiment I indicate have been performed many times, and they have all verified OQT and refuted Everett QT. Everett QT is, it seems, not just highly falsifiable; it has already been falsified. But if no version of the experiment I indicate has been performed, then it should be performed, and Everett should be put the test of experiment!

I have not argued that probabilism and some version of PQT are *true*. Rather, I have argued that probabilism is a plausible possibility, given the immense empirical success of QT. Probabilism deserves serious attention.[63] It may well be possible to formulate a version of PQT which triumphs empirically over OQT. Theoretical and experimental work ought to explore this possibility as a priority within theoretical physics. But this option has been, by and large, ignored because of the dominance of SE, and the failure of physics to implement AOE. Dogmatic acceptance of OQT for some sixty years after its first formulation has degraded, and still degrades, the endeavour to improve our understanding of the physical universe, just as Einstein upheld.

7 CORRECT INTERPRETATION

Within SE physics, theories are regarded as specifying laws, or regularities, which physical phenomena obey. This makes sense if God is in charge, but otherwise it does not. It would seem that there must actually *exist* something in the physical universe which *determines* that phenomena continue to conform to physical law, from moment to moment. It is not enough, it would seem, for physics just to *specify* regularities; for genuine explanation and understanding, physics must specify, surely, what it is in the physical universe that ensures, that makes it necessary, that phenomena observe regularities. Otherwise, the more universal and precise the regularities are that physics discovers, the more baffling, the more incomprehensible, it becomes that these regularities should invariably be observed.

This issue, fundamental to the quest to understand the cosmos, cannot really be discussed within SE physics, because it concerns metaphysics and the interpretation of physical theory, which lie beyond the scope of what is empirically testable. The issue is not, however, excluded from AOE physics.

Long ago in 1738, when the lines between science and philosophy were not so sharply delineated as they are today, David Hume argued that we cannot make sense of the idea that what exists at one instant *necessarily determines* what exists at the next instant.[64] Hume's conclusion seems to have filtered into physics, where it has remained a fixture ever since.

Hume argued, in essence, that from a specification of what exists at one instant we cannot logically derive anything about what exists at the next instant. But Hume is wrong. We need to be epistemologically more modest than Hume. We cannot *know* that necessary connections between successive states of affairs do not exist. Perhaps, for all we can know for certain, a specification of what exists at one instant does necessarily determine what exists at the next instant.[65]

Ordinary dispositional properties that we attribute to objects around us – properties like solidity, opacity, inflammability, rigidity, stickiness, and so on – do carry implications about how the objects that possess these properties will change, in certain circumstances. An inflammable object, exposed to a naked flame, will burst into flames, and if it does not, then it is not inflammable. We can interpret physical theories as attributing such dispositional, or necessitating, properties to physical entities: properties like mass, electric charge, and gravitational charge. An object that is electrically charged of necessity accelerates when exposed to an electric field, and if it does not, it is not charged in the first place. These fundamental physical necessitating properties are just like common sense dispositional properties except that they are much more *precise*, and much more *universally possessed* by physical entities. Furthermore, these physical necessitating properties may be *propensities* and only determine what occurs *probabilistically* (as discussed in the last section).

The idea is that the true physical theory of everything would provide the means to describe instantaneous physical states of affairs in terms of such necessitating properties: such a description, together with initial conditions, would logically imply what exists subsequently. What is required for necessary connections to exist between successive instantaneous states of affairs, E_1 and E_2, is that no more than a description, D_1, of what exists at the time of occurrence of E_1 logically implies what exists at the time of occurrence of E_2. D_1 does no more than specify what exists at the time of occurrence of E_1 in the sense that if anything is removed from D_1, something that exists at the time of occurrence of E_1 is no longer described.

In order to specify such necessitating properties, a physical theory must be interpreted *essentialistically*. Consider Newton's law of motion, F = ma (a is acceleration), and his law of gravitation $F = Gm_1m_2/d^2$. Mass here plays a double role. In the law of motion, it is inertial mass, here to be interpreted as a dispositional or necessitating property that determines precisely how an object with mass changes its motion in response to an impressed force. It does so, so that F = ma. In the law of gravitation, m_1 and m_2 specify what may be called *Newtonian gravitational charge* (equal to inertial mass). If there are two objects with gravitational charges m_1 and m_2, distance d apart, then of necessity there is a force of attraction F between them such that $F = Gm_1m_2/d^2$. Newton's law of gravitation merely makes explicit what it means to say of two objects that they possess Newtonian gravitational charges of m_1 and m_2. From the statement that there are two objects with gravitational charges m_1 and m_2, distance d apart, in otherwise empty space, it can be deduced that there will be a force of attraction F between them such that $F = Gm_1m_2/d^2$, and each object will accelerate towards the other in accordance with F = ma. Both laws are to be interpreted as *analytic* propositions. They are true in virtue of the meaning of the constituent terms, just as "All bachelors are unmarried" is.

It might seem fatal to physical essentialism that fundamental laws, like Newton's, must be interpreted as *analytic* propositions, devoid of factual content. Not at all! All the *empirical content* of Newtonian theory, essentialistically interpreted, stems entirely from some such existential statement as "The universe is made up of particles with Newtonian mass (with inertial mass equal to gravitational mass)." When theories, essentialistically interpreted, are refuted and revised, ideas about what necessitating properties exist are refuted and revised and, as a result, some (analytic) law propositions are discarded as irrelevant, and others are adopted as relevant to properties conjectured to exist.

Transforming Newtonian theory from a theory that merely specifies regularities to one that asserts that the universe is made up of particles that possess the necessitating property of Newtonian mass (inertial and gravitational) does not make the theory more secure. If anything the reverse: it is possible (though wildly implausible) for Newtonian theory interpreted as merely specifying regularities to be true, and Newtonian theory interpreted essentialistically to be false (because Newtonian necessitating properties do not actually exist in the world). The crucial point is that Newtonian theory interpreted essentialistically postulates the existence of that which, if it really does exist, determines necessarily that phenomena observe Newton's laws. Newtonian theory interpreted essentialistically explains, and enables us to understand, potentially, in a way that the theory interpreted as specifying mere regularities cannot do.

All this has implications for the interpretation of the three theories discussed above: Newtonian theory, classical electrodynamics, and quantum theory. All three theories deserve to be interpreted essentialistically. The Newtonian particle needs to be interpreted as a localized object with Newtonian mass that has, as a result, a force-field associated with it spread throughout space which determines, necessarily, the force on any other Newtonian particle at any other position in space. The field of classical electrodynamics needs to be interpreted as an entity spread out continuously in space that determines (a) the force a unit charge would experience were it to be placed in the field at any point, and (b) the force a unit change would experience were it to have such and such a velocity. And quantum theory needs to be interpreted, perhaps, so as to attribute *propensities* – probabilistic necessitating properties – to quantum entities, such as electrons, protons, and atoms.[66]

In order for there to be a good chance of arriving at the correct physical interpretation of a new physical theory, it is important to engage in sustained blueprint articulation, of the kind indicated in section 5 above, so that, ideally, metaphysical ideas appropriate to the new theory arrive on the scene before the theory itself arrives. The discussion of section 6 above reveals that the correct interpretation of Newtonian theory, Maxwellian electodynamics and quantum theory have all been delayed, for several decades, because persistent attempts have been made to interpret these theories in terms of outdated metaphysics. In all three cases, correct interpretations have been long delayed by the failure to put AOE into practice, and so engage in blueprint articulation. And no theory in physics receives an essentialistic interpretation by the physics community. Physical essentialism cannot even be discussed as an option within SE physics, because such metaphysical and interpretative issues fall outside what SE holds to be "science." Once again, failure to implement AOE blocks the correct interpretation of physical theory.

8 THEORY DISCOVERY

A O E provides theoretical physics with a rational, if non-mechanical and fallible, method for the discovery of fundamental new theories.[67] S E provides no such thing, and nor can it.

Scientists and philosophers of science who take some version of S E for granted tend to agree that there is no rational method of discovery in physics – or even in science more generally. Thus Popper says that "the act of conceiving or inventing a theory, seems to me neither to call for logical analysis nor to be susceptible of it."[68] There is a very good reason why there can be no rational method for the discovery of new theories in physics granted S E. Insofar as S E provides guidelines for the discovery of new theories, these would have to be based on existing laws and theories – on ideas for new theories compatible with existing theories.[69] But these are just the wrong kind of ideas to consider. As we saw in chapter 3, page 86, new theories in physics *contradict* predecessor theories. Good ideas for new theories need to contradict existing theories. Theoretical physics pursued within the framework of S E directs attention towards exactly the *wrong* kind of ideas for new theories. From the standpoint of S E, it is all but inexplicable that new theories do get discovered in physics.

How, then, has this inexplicable act of discovering a new theory ever been performed, if S E has been widely accepted? The answer to this comes in three parts.

First, the above overstates things a bit. There is at least one obvious, limited method of discovery that can be implemented, granted S E. An existing law or theory may be taken as a model for a comparable new law or theory, applicable to a different range of phenomena. Thus Newton's inverse square law of gravitation may be taken as a model for laws governing the attraction and/or repulsion between electrically charged objects, and magnetic poles.[70] S E provides us, however, with no rationale for holding that this strategy will meet with success. Granted S E, it is not clear why a theory of one force should resemble the theory of another force. A O E, by contrast, is able *both* to exploit this strategy of discovery *and* provide a rationale for it. A O E holds that there is underlying unity of physical law in nature. Ultimately, there is just one force, with one equation depicting its character. Granted our present imperfect knowledge, which recognizes three or more distinct forces, approximate aspects of the one underlying force, it is not unreasonable to suppose that the law governing one force will resemble the laws governing the other forces.

Second, theoretical physicists today recognize that so-called symmetry principles play a vital role both in the discovery and acceptance of theories. I will have more to say about symmetry principles below.

Third, the main reason why new theories in physics have been discovered despite general acceptance of s e is that creative theoretical physicists have struggled, in private as it were, to articulate and develop metaphysical ideas relevant to the discovery of new theories – just that which s e excludes from the public face of science. Some creative physicists have pursued something approaching aspects of a o e physics in their personal thinking, even if public view of this is obscured by the prevalence of s e.

What the transition from s e to a o e physics does, then, is to make publicly explicit, and so criticizable and improvable, that which remains implicit granted s e. This transforms the whole process of theory discovery. At once a number of relevant ideas become publicly available, and a number of problems become publicly specifiable which, if tackled, may well lead to good candidates for new theories. The transition from s e to a o e adds to level 1 evidence, and to level 2 theories, T_1 and T_2 say, the vital additional items of theoretical knowledge: the level 3 thesis of the current best blueprint, B, and the level 4 thesis of physicalism, P. B and P, together with the process of blueprint articulation illustrated above, play a crucial role in the discovery of new theories.

The basic task is to modify T_1, T_2, B, and perhaps P, so as to remove, or at least decrease, the clashes between them. It is reasonable to hold that T_1 and T_2 clash with each other. At one time T_1 and T_2 would have been Newtonian theory and classical electrodynamics: as we shall see, these two theories clash. Nowadays, the two basic theories are quantum theory and general relativity – or perhaps the standard model (the quantum field theory of fundamental particles and fields) and general relativity: these notoriously clash as well. T_1 and T_2 individually are almost bound to clash with B. And B almost certainly clashes with itself – it is internally inconsistent. And B clashes with P. The basic task is to modify T_1, T_2, B, and perhaps P, so as to decrease these clashes in such a way that a candidate new theory emerges – or at least an idea for such a candidate.

AOE suggests two related strategies for the discovery of new theories.

The first involves attempting to get at the root of the clash between T_1 and T_2 by paring away from T_1 and T_2 everything not involved in the clash until two principles contradicting each other are arrived at, p_1 from T_1, p_2 from T_2, the idea being then to modify p_1, or p_2, or both, or some background assumption, so that a new unified idea, U, emerges, a synthesis of p_1 and p_2, and a possible core idea for a new theory, T_{1+2}, that unifies T_1 and T_2. Below I will suggest that this is how Einstein discovered special and general relativity.

The second strategy involves engaging in blueprint articulation. B is modified to form B*, say, which has no, or fewer, internal inconsistencies and, at the same time, better exemplifies the level 4 thesis of physicalism, or does better justice to the character of T_1 and T_2. The task then becomes to make B* precise, so that it becomes a new, empirically testable theory. Elements of this strategy can be found in Faraday's contribution to the discovery of classical electrodynamics, and Einstein's discovery of general relativity. However, general acceptance of SE has up till now discouraged this strategy, and prevented it from being successfully implemented.

To what extent has discovery of the great theories of physics accorded with either of these two strategies implied, or at least suggested, by AOE?

In one important respect, Newton's discovery of his theory of gravitation does seem to accord with the first strategy. As I remarked in chapter 1, Newton's *Principia* has a diagram of projectiles being hurled horizontally from the top of a mountain at greater and greater velocities until the rate of fall of the projectile matches the rate at which the surface of the earth falls away as the projectile travels, and as a result the projectile goes into orbit round the earth. The diagram strongly suggests that the physical laws that underpin Galileo's laws of terrestrial motion are the same as those that underpin Kepler's laws of planetary motion. But the key insight required to unify Galileo and Kepler needs to come from elsewhere. It is that both sets of laws are the outcome of a *force* – the force of gravitation. Objects free of force travel in straight lines with uniform velocity. Hence, stones thrown on earth fall as they do because they are subject to a force – the force of gravitation – directed downwards (towards the centre of the earth), and planets travel as they do because they are subjected to a force directed towards the sun. As I mentioned in chapter 2, Hooke may have been the first person to have the idea, but it was Newton who was able to derive the motions of stones, planets, moons, and comets from his laws of motion and his law of gravitation, $F = Gm_1m_2/d^2$.

In one other respect, Newtonian theory fits the general pattern of theoretical unification perfectly. In unifying Galileo and Kepler, Newtonian theory also *corrects* both Galileo and Kepler. A body falling near the earth's surface does not fall precisely with constant acceleration (as Galileo held) because, as the body falls, it gets closer to the centre of the earth, and so the force of gravitation increases very slightly, and so the acceleration too. And planets do not move precisely in ellipses (as Kepler held) because the planets attract each other, and the planets attract the sun, and this causes the planets to deviate slightly from precise elliptical paths (as Newton demonstrated in the *Principia*).

Newton's discovery of his law of gravitation received no help from the metaphysical blueprint prevalent at the time – the corpuscular hypothesis. The latter actually blocked acceptance of Newton's law for decades, especially in France, as we saw in chapter 2. Even Newton failed to accept his law, if interpreted as postulating a force acting at a distance across empty space, so wedded was he to the idea of action by contact, the key idea of the corpuscular hypotheses. There can be no doubt that Boscovich's blueprint would have helped – but it was only formulated decades after the publication of the *Principia*.[71]

What of the discovery of classical electrodynamics? Does this fit either of the two strategies of AOE indicated above? Despite the fact that classical electrodynamics is a theory that introduced a new fundamental entity into physics – the field – which was of profound significance for later theoretical developments, and brought about astonishing theoretical unity in that it unified electricity, magnetism, and optics (and subsequently gamma, x-, infrared, ultraviolet rays and radio waves), nevertheless discovery of the theory reveals a somewhat intermittent exploitation of the rational methods of discovery of AOE.

Some Newtonians after Newton guessed that the force between electrically charged objects and magnetic poles might vary with distance in accordance with an inverse square law, like Newton's law of gravitation. However, attempts to establish this experimentally at first produced results that contradicted these hypotheses, or produced no results at all, until Charles-Augustin Coulomb corroborated the conjectured laws experimentally in 1785.[72] It is significant that Coulomb was a Newtonian, vehemently opposed to Cartesianism: metaphysical convictions played a role in Coulomb's discovery.

In 1820 Hans Christian Oersted made what was then the extraordinary discovery that an electric current has an effect on a magnet. He discovered that a wire carrying an electric current has a circular magnetic field around it. Oersted had long believed in, and sought, a connection between electricity and magnetism, as a result of his conviction that all forces are, ultimately, diverse aspects of just one force, which was in turn the outcome of his interest in Kant and Germanic *Naturphilosophie*. Here, a potentially fruitful metaphysical conviction did play a role in a momentous experimental discovery.

André-Marie Ampère was quick to follow up Oersted's discovery. He realized, months after Oersted's discovery, that if an electric current produces a magnetic force then, quite possibly, all magnetic phenomena might be caused by electric currents. The magnetic properties of an iron magnet might be due to the summation of minute circular electric currents in the iron. Ampère went on to develop, and to some extent corroborate experimentally, a mathematical theory of the force between electric currents. Ampère again was predisposed to reduce magnetism to an aspect of electricity: he believed in an underlying unity of nature, and held that all forces should ultimately be aspects of just one underlying force.[73] Once again, a metaphysical view seems to have played a fruitful role in a scientific discovery.

This can be said, too, of Michael Faraday's all-important contributions to electrodynamics. It is to Faraday that we owe the crucial idea of the field – a physical entity spread out in space, varying in strength and direction in space and time, and exerting a force on a charged particle in the field. Faraday formed his idea of the field in response to a number of factors. There was, perhaps first of all, his experiences and experiments with magnets, electric currents, and electrolysis. Sprinkle iron filings on paper under which there is a magnet – as Faraday did – and there, in the way the iron fillings organize themselves in response to the magnet, is a graphic illustration of the magnetic field surrounding the magnet. There can be no doubt that Faraday's experimental discoveries and his metaphysical ideas concerning the electromagnetic field developed in tandem with one another, each suggesting developments in the other. Faraday was influenced by Boscovich. Crucially, Faraday appreciated that, if changes in the field travel through space at a finite speed, then the field would acquire an existence independent of the charges that produce the field, to an extent not present in Boscovich's theory. Faraday had reasons to believe changes in the field might travel at a finite velocity, for he held that light might well be vibrations in the electromagnetic field, and it was known, of course, that light travels with a finite velocity. Faraday announced that light might be waves in the electromagnetic field before Maxwell's theory produced grounds for holding that this might indeed be the case. Faraday went further. He proposed that charged particles might be no more than distinctive regions or points of the field – the place where his lines of force meet. Faraday's contemporaries and immediate successors held that the electromagnetic field, if it was to be physically comprehensible, had to be understood in terms of a more fundamental quasi-material aether. Faraday, alone at the time, appreciated that, quite to the contrary, physics should seek to understand matter, and forces between material objects, in terms of an underlying field, the fundamental physical entity. In this respect, Faraday anticipated Einstein.

Faraday's contributions to theoretical physics are astonishing. As I have already remarked, Einstein once said that there are only two ideas in physics: the particle, and the field. Faraday invented one of them. The field lies at the heart of all of modern physics. Faraday even grasped that there ought to be, ultimately, just one unified field, and he sought to find a connection between electromagnetism and gravity (in this, of course, he failed). He did succeed, however, in finding a connection between magnetism and light – namely that a magnetic field rotated the polarization of light. Faraday's field ideas emerged out of his experimental work, and helped direct that work, and led it to his great experimental discoveries: electromagnetic induction, the electric motor and dynamo, and the laws of electrolysis. And Faraday did all this without a knowledge of mathematics. Perhaps in part for that reason, in his lifetime, and even down to today, Faraday tends to be celebrated as a great experimentalist, but ignored as a great theoretical physicist. The main reason for this neglect, however, is undoubtedly that Faraday's theoretical work – leaving aside his laws of electrodynamics and electrolysis – does not fit into the framework of SE, because it is metaphysical in character, and does not amount to a testable theory. Viewed from the perspective of AOE, Faraday's theoretical contribution, at level 3, is immense; viewed from the perspective of SE, it disappears.

James Clerk Maxwell had no doubts about the profound significance of Faraday's theoretical ideas. He said of Faraday that he was
"in reality a mathematician of a very high order" in the sense that he
employed physical ideas much as mathematicians employ mathematical ideas "by means of which we form a mental representation of the
facts, sufficiently general ... to stand for any particular case, and sufficiently exact ... to warrant the deductions we may draw from them
by the application of mathematical reasoning."[74] Maxwell began his
journey towards formulating his equations of the electromagnetic
field by reading Faraday's *Experimental Researches in Electricity*.
In his first work on the subject, "On Faraday's Lines of Force,"[75]
Maxwell sought to capture Faraday's idea of the electromagnetic field
by means of mathematical equations, paying particular attention to
Faraday's notion of "lines of force" which indicated the direction and
strength of the field.[76] Maxwell was also influenced by earlier work by
William Thomson which also sought to capture Faraday's idea of the
field, Thomson in turn influenced by Joseph Fourier's work on heat
diffusion. In subsequent work, developing his mathematical description of the electromagnetic field, Maxwell employed analogies from
the flow of a fluid, and even, finally, employed a complex mechanical
model of the aether made up of rotating wheels, and wheels between
wheels to facilitate rotation.[77] Maxwell seems to have held that physical reality would be forever unknown and unknowable, there being
no such thing as the physically correct interpretation of a theory.
Instead, one should develop and make use of a variety of physical
interpretations or models, as an aid to understanding.

There can be no doubt that Faraday's metaphysical idea of the
field played a very substantial role in Maxwell's formulation of the
equations of electrodynamics. But other ideas played a role as well:
heat diffusion, the flow of a fluid, and even a complicated mechanical model.

It is only with Einstein's discovery of his special and general theories of relativity that the two strategies for discovery associated with
A O E, mentioned above, really come into their own. Einstein's discovery of special relativity illustrates dramatically the first of these two
strategies.[78] The two theories in conflict are Newtonian theory (NT)
and Maxwellian electrodynamics (MT). These conflict because, given
their most natural interpretation, NT is about forces at a distance
between point-particles with mass, whereas MT is about one entity,
the continuous electromagnetic field.

In 1905 Einstein made five profound contributions to physics, all of which, in one way or another, explored elements of the clash between NT and MT – the clash between the particle and field viewpoints. One contribution sought to determine the size of molecules. Another sought to establish the reality of atoms or molecules by demonstrating that Brownian motion (the random motion of a particle suspended in a fluid or gas) could be explained by the buffeting of the molecules of the fluid or gas. Another, one of the earliest contributions to quantum theory, proposed very dramatically that light, known to be a wave phenomenon, also has particles, or light quanta, associated with it. Einstein used this hypothesis to explain what the wave theory could not explain: the manner in which x-rays, when directed at a metal, emit electrons (the photo-electric effect). Yet another derived the most famous equation in physics: $E = mc^2$. This equation, in revealing that mass, characteristic of the particle, is a form of energy, has suggestive implications for the particle/field issue. Finally, there is Einstein's famous paper expounding special relativity.[79]

Special relativity emerges from consideration of a rather more specific clash between NT and MT. NT asserts that forces affect accelerations, not velocities. Dynamic laws (laws concerning forces and their effects), formulated within the framework of NT, do not pick out any special velocity any more than they pick out some special place or time. But MT does pick out a special velocity: the velocity of light, the velocity that, according to MT, vibrations in the field strengths of the electromagnetic field travel through space.

This conflict only arises if MT is interpreted in the way I have argued it ought to be interpreted, as a fundamental field theory. The conflict is avoided if MT is interpreted in terms of an underlying aether. In that case, the velocity of light can be held to be constant relative to the aether. In his paper Einstein argued against this interpretation on the basis of symmetry, and evidence.[80] And all along, Einstein seems to have favoured interpreting MT as a fundamental field theory.[81]

One might attempt to reconcile NT and MT by holding that the velocity of light is a constant relative to the source. Einstein tells us that he abandoned this approach because of the complications to which it led (see Shankland 1963). Evidence against this hypothesis only came in later, in 1913, with observations of double stars.

If the velocity of light is not constant relative to the aether (because there is no aether), and if it is not constant relative to the source, what is it constant relative to? And how can this paradoxical lawful constancy of a *velocity* be reconciled with the Newtonian requirement that, as far as fundamental laws are concerned, there are no special velocities, any more than there are special points in space?

Einstein set out to solve this problem, and resolve this specific conflict between NT and MT, as follows. From NT Einstein extracted the (restricted) principle of relativity: the laws of nature have the same form relative to a set of reference frames all moving with constant velocity with respect to each other (so-called inertial reference frames). From MT he extracted the principle (implied by MT, and basic to the field concept, as we have seen) that it is a law of nature that the velocity of light in the vacuum is a constant, c. These are the two basic postulates of special relativity.[82] These postulates, taken together, imply the apparent absurdity that one flash of light will have the *same* velocity c with respect to *all* inertial reference frames, whatever velocities they may have with respect to each other. How on earth can this out-and-out absurdity possibly be?

There is just one way in which it is possible, and Einstein found it. Suppose relative velocity changes measured lengths of rods, and rates of clocks, and hence measured velocities. In that case it is just about conceivable that light does have the same velocity c with respect to *all* inertial frames. It just might be the case that length of rods, rates of clocks, and so measurements of velocity, vary in precisely the right way, as we go from reference frame to reference frame, in relative motion. Given a few very natural assumptions about how measurements of length and time, made in different frames, are related to one another (such as the relationship is linear, symmetric and isotropic), it turns out that there is just *one* way to arrange for light to have the same velocity c in all reference frames: this is contained in the so-called Lorentz transformations, the physical nub of special relativity. They specify how measured length and time-intervals change, as we go from one frame to another, in uniform motion with respect to each other.[83]

Special relativity has a number of dramatic consequences. It implies that if two bodies, two rocket ships say, are in rapid relative motion, each measures the other as contracted in length, as having clocks that go slow, and as being of increased mass – length and time tending to zero, and mass to infinity, as relative velocity tends to the velocity of light, c. (This means that no body can attain the velocity of light.) Special relativity also implies $E = mc^2$. Mass is a form of energy.

From the standpoint of AOE, special relativity is profoundly significant in a number of ways.

First, its discovery is a dramatic illustration of one of the two methods of discovery of AOE.

Second, the theory brought greater unity to theoretical physics in a number of different ways. It did this by resolving the above clash between NT and MT. It did it by further unifying MT. How the electromagnetic field divides up into the electric field and the magnetic field depends on one's reference frame. It differs for reference frames moving with respect to each other. But, according to special relativity, nothing fundamental can depend on what reference frame one is in. Thus, one must think of the electromagnetic field as one unified entity, not two distinct entities, the electric field and the magnetic field. Special relativity also unifies via the equation $E = mc^2$, the implication being that mass is a form of energy. And special relativity partially unifies space and time to form a new entity, space-time, as Hermann Minkowski demonstrated in 1908.[84] Although the distance, d, between two spatial points, given by $d^2 = x^2 + y^2 + z^2$, varies from frame to frame, the space-time distance between two events, given by $d^2 = x^2 + y^2 + z^2 - c^2t^2$ (where t = time), is precisely the same in all reference frames.[85] Relativity theory has the disturbing implication that judgements about simultaneity of distant events depend on one's reference frame. There is no absolute, frame-independent way of determining what is "now" throughout space, and so no frame-independent way of dividing off past from future. The implication appears to be that we must think of the universe as a four-dimensional entity that just (timelessly) *is*, "now" having no more objective significance than "here."[86] But there is still a distinction between space and time. Given any two events, E_1 and E_2, the interval between them is "time-like" if it is possible for a body to travel from one to the other (at less than the speed of light), and "space-like" if even light cannot travel from one to the other. Two time-like separated events have the same temporal order in all reference frames, whereas two space-like separated events have different temporal orders in different reference frames and are simultaneous in one reference frame. If light travels from E_1 to E_2 then the space-time distance between the two events is zero. This means that when you see a distant star, the space-time distance between the event of the light being emitted from the star, and the event of it being absorbed by your eye, is zero. In some sense, your eyeball is pressed against the surface of the star!

Third, special relativity is of great significance for AOE because it is, at one and the same time, a *physical theory* that makes empirical predictions, a *methodological principle*, and a *metaphysical blue-print*. This tripartite aspect is hard to understand given standard empiricism, but makes perfect sense given A O E. It is of course funda-mental to A O E that methodological principles correspond to meta-physical blueprints: this is depicted in figure 2 on page 85. In the case of special relativity, the blueprint is Minkowski space-time, and the methodological principle is Lorentz invariance. It is noteworthy that Einstein always called special relativity "the relativity *principle*," and he intended it to guide the way to the discovery and acceptance of a new dynamical theory. It has amply fulfilled that role, in being incor-porated into quantum electrodynamics, quantum electroweak the-ory, quantum chromodynamics, the standard model, and, as a limiting case, into general relativity.

Fourth, special relativity has had one further important impact on subsequent physics: it has led to an appreciation of just how signifi-cant *symmetry principles* in general are for theoretical physics.[87] They play a decisive role in guiding physicists towards the discovery of new theories, and they play a vital role in the acceptance of theo-ries.[88] Again, hard to understand given s E, this vital role of symmetry principles makes perfect sense, and is all but required, given A O E. As I have made clear elsewhere, the demand that a theory should satisfy symmetry principles is an aspect of the demand that it should be *unified*.[89]

Special relativity all but demands that we transform our whole conception of physics in that we abandon s E and adopt A O E in its stead. One can hardly do justice to the character and implications of special relativity unless something close to A O E is accepted. As I have made clear elsewhere, Einstein himself did come to adopt a view close to A O E, especially after his discovery of general relativity.[90] Again and again Einstein expressed his view that the universe pos-sesses an underlying unity and is physically comprehensible, an arti-cle of faith without which he "could not have a strong and unshakeable conviction about the independent value of knowledge."[91] Most phys-icists have continued, however, to pay lip service at least to s E, even though special relativity calls so strongly for physics to be under-stood in terms of A O E.

Einstein's discovery of general relativity exploited both of the two strategies of discovery of A O E, indicated above. As before, there are two fundamental conflicting theories, namely: Newton's theory of gravitation, and special relativity. These conflict because whereas

Newton's theory implies that gravitational influences travel instantaneously through space, special relativity implies that such influences cannot travel faster than light. As before, Einstein searches for new principles which will guide him to a new unifying theory. He seizes upon a principle which goes back to Galileo, and is a key element in Newton's theory: all bodies, whatever their mass, fall at an equal rate in a gravitational field. This makes it possible to declare, as a general principle – the principle of equivalence – that the effects of uniform acceleration and a uniform gravitational field are precisely the same. If you are in a lift, no experiment performed in the lift can distinguish between (a) being at rest in a gravitational field, and (b) accelerating uniformly in the absence of any gravitational field.

Next, Einstein considered a rotating disk. A measuring rod at the edge of the disk is accelerating because of its persistent departure from uniform motion in a straight line. According to special relativity, the rod will be slightly shorter than when placed at the centre of the disk, because of its relative motion. This means the geometry of the disk, as measured by the rod, will be non-Euclidean. The surface of the disk will be measured to be curved, not flat. Acceleration affects geometry. Therefore, by the principle of equivalence, *gravitation* affects geometry – the geometry of space. Einstein then made a wild speculative leap: perhaps gravitation *is* the variable curvature of space – or rather, of space-time. Perhaps mass, or energy density more generally, causes space-time to curve, and bodies simply pursue the nearest things to straight lines – geodesics[92] – in curved space-time. Newton's force of gravitation disappears. There is only curved space-time, bodies moving along geodesics in curved space-time. We have here the metaphysical blueprint for general relativity. It took Einstein several years of hard labour, however, to turn this blueprint idea into the precise theory of general relativity, specifying precisely how mass, or energy density more generally, curves space-time.

Einstein's discovery of general relativity exploits *both* strategies of discovery of A O E. It stems from a clash between two theories, as we have seen. And, almost uniquely in the history of physics, the precise theory emerges from the prior development of a new, appropriate metaphysical blueprint.

General relativity is a great achievement of unification. As a result of generalizing Minkowskian space-time and Newton's first law of motion (every body continues in its state of rest or uniform motion if no force is impressed upon it), Einstein is able to dispense entirely with Newton's force of gravitation. Bodies move freely along geodesics in curved space-time. Minkowskian space-time and special relativity emerge when there is no mass or energy to curve space-time.

How astonishing it is that now, some 100 years after Einstein's profound contributions to physics, the *implications* of these contributions for methodology and the philosophy of science have still not been generally appreciated by the scientific community. Einstein's work makes AOE all but explicit: only dogmatic allegiance of scientists to SE has obscured the point.

It may be objected: But if Einstein really did invent and apply the rational methods of discovery of AOE in creating special and general relativity, how come that the last thirty years of his life, devoted to the attempt to discover a classical field theory unifying general relativity and classical electrodynamics, led nowhere? The answer is that Einstein misapplied his own rational method of discovery. If he had applied it correctly, he would have sought to unify the two fundamental theories that emerged after 1915 and 1926: general relativity and quantum theory. He did not do this because he found orthodox quantum theory (OQT) deeply unsatisfactory. But the unsatisfactory character of OQT does not provide grounds for ignoring the problem. Einstein himself criticized Newtonian theory, and even suggested that such criticism might help with the discovery of theories in the future.[93] Defects of Newtonian theory did not deter Einstein from seeking to unify it and Maxwellian electrodynamics: equally, the defects of OQT should not have deterred Einstein from seeking to unify it and general relativity. If Einstein had applied his own method of discovery properly he would, once again, have been way ahead of the rest of the physics community, and might well have come up with further significant discoveries.[94]

Another objection might be: If I really have identified two rational methods of discovery, why have I not used them to discover a new theory myself? My answer is twofold. First, as I have stressed, the method of discovery of AOE, though rational, is fallible and non-mechanical. Even if you do not need to be an Einstein, you do nevertheless need to be a brilliant physicist and mathematician to employ these methods successfully. I am neither. Second, my best attempt is contained in my proposed version of quantum theory.

9 EXPLANATION AND UNDERSTANDING

AOE does far better justice to the search for scientific explanation and understanding than does SE. As far as theory acceptance is concerned, SE puts all the emphasis on empirical success, ostensibly non-empirical considerations such as the simplicity, unity, intelligibility, or the explanatory character of a theory being left somewhat obscure. As a result, SE physics is in danger of degenerating into the instrumentalist task of developing theories that merely predict more and more phenomena more and more accurately, and do not explain or enable us to understand. The most striking example of this is the long-standing acceptance of OQT which, because it fails to solve the wave/particle problem and is, as a result, merely a theory about performing measurements on quantum systems, fails to explain quantum phenomena, fails to provide us with understanding of the quantum domain. And this failure has persisted in subsequent theoretical physics down to today. Quantum field theory, quantum electrodynamics, quantum chromodynamics, the standard model, string theory: all these subsequent theories suffer from the same fundamental defect inherited from OQT. None can be interpreted as conjectures about what really goes on in the quantum domain. None provides genuine explanation and understanding. None of these theories yield clear answers to the following two elementary questions: What sort of entities are electrons, atoms, quantum fields? Is nature deterministic or probabilistic?

AOE physics would hold all these theories to be profoundly defective precisely because of their lack of unity, their failure to be genuinely explanatory, to answer elementary questions of understanding. AOE clarifies what it is for a physical theory to be genuinely explanatory, and puts the search for explanation and understanding of this mysterious universe in which we find ourselves centre stage in natural philosophy.

Furthermore, as I argued in section 7 above, explanation and understanding are more likely to flourish within AOE physics in that it is more likely that essentialistically interpreted physical theories will be developed which depict (conjecturally) what it is that necessarily determines events to occur in accordance with physical laws. SE physics is more likely to restrict physics to specifying physical laws or regularities, there being no explanation, no understanding, of what it is in existence that ensures these regularities are observed.

10 COSMIC PHYSICALISM

The basic rationale for making explicit the hierarchy of metaphysical theses of AOE is to facilitate development and critical assessment of alternatives, especially at the lower levels of the hierarchy, thus facilitating acceptance of the most empirically fruitful possibilities, in turn providing theoretical physics with the best possible help with the discovery, acceptance, and correct interpretation of good, empirically successful new theories. At once it may be asked: Is there a viable alternative to physicalism at level 4 (see figure 2 on page 85)?

Physicalism asserts that the physical universe is made up of two aspects: U, which exists in an invariant form everywhere, throughout all phenomena; and V, which varies from place to place and time to time. U and V together, at any one instant, determine (perhaps probabilistically) subsequent states of the universe, given by U and variable values of V.

A very early idea as to how the universe might be physically comprehensible was put forward by Parmenides some two and a half thousand years ago. Parmenides held that the universe is an unchanging homogeneous sphere. All change and diversity is, according to Parmenides, an illusion. Parmenides seems to have held this extraordinary view because he thought that the very idea of change or motion involves a contradiction. An object can only move if there is an empty space, a region of nothingness, into which it can move. But this in turn requires that nothingness exists, which amounts to holding that the non-existent exists, a contradiction. Hence there can be no motion, no change.

Democritus rejected Parmenides's conclusion, but accepted his argument as valid. Change and diversity do exist. Therefore the nothingness must exist too. We can suppose that Parmenides's cosmic sphere is surrounded by nothingness. In this nothingness other Parmenidean spheres may exist which, when shrunk down to a minute size, became atoms – each atom a tiny, internally homogeneous and unchanging Parmenidean cosmos. Thus was born one of the most fruitful scientific theories ever conceived: atomism. Richard Feynman once declared "All things are made of atoms" to be the single most important sentence of modern science.[95] All of subsequent theoretical physics revises and elaborates Democritus's response to Parmenides, from Boscovich's point-atom to Faraday's and Einstein's idea of the field, to string theory. Physicalism as I have formulated it above emerges from Democritus's reply to Parmenides.

But another response to Parmenides is possible. We may declare that Parmenides's homogeneous sphere is a state of the entire universe, exhibiting unity, at a very special time, namely the moment at or just before the big bang. Before the big bang, the entire universe is in a state of extreme unity, all disunity being merely virtual, somewhat like the virtual particle creation and annihilation processes which go on in the vacuum according to quantum field theory (on one popular reading of the theory at least). Then the big bang occurs, an instant of spontaneous symmetry-breaking: the outcome is a multitude of virtual prior-to-big-bang states, virtual Parmenidean spheres, as it were. The subsequent history of the cosmos is the unfolding of the interactions between these multitudinous virtual prior-to-the-big-bang entities. All the change and diversity that exists in the world around us is the outcome of the diverse ways in which virtual Parmenidean "spheres" are inter-related with one another. The cosmos is composed of itself: it is composed of billions upon billions of fleeting *virtual* big-bang cosmic states of supreme Parmenidean unity.

We have here, then, two versions of physicalism. There is the version that has emerged from Democritus's response to Parmenides, hitherto called physicalism, and which in what follows I will call "atomistic physicalism." And there is the version which emerges from the response to Parmenides just indicated, which I shall call "cosmic physicalism."

Atomistic and cosmic physicalism give diametrically opposed answers to the question: What is the nature of the physically simple or elemental? The first declares this to be either empty space, or the interior of the atom (as far as Democritus's version of physicalism is concerned). The second declares this to be a special state of *everything*!

Atomistic physicalism, as I have indicated, has been the dominant basic idea in the history of theoretical physics so far. It is possible, however, that it is *cosmic*, rather than atomistic, physicalism which is true. The following suggestive developments in theoretical physics during the twentieth century may well be interpreted as pointing towards cosmic physicalism.

1 A basic idea of atomistic physicalism is that the physically simplest, most elemental state of affairs that can exist is the vacuum: physical states of affairs become progressively more complex as one, or two, or … n atoms, or fundamental particles, are added to the vacuum. With the advent of field theory, however, this straightforward ordering of physical complexity begins to break down: here, presumably, we would have to say that the simplest state obtains when the value of the field is everywhere zero, a less simple state

arising when the value of the field is everywhere a constant value, more complicated states arising with increasingly complicated variable values of the field.

2 The idea that the vacuum is the simplest state, in that it is always present in an unchanging form, begins to break down with the advent of Einstein's general theory of relativity. According to this theory, as we have seen, the curvature of space-time varies with varying amounts of matter, mass or energy-density; and curved space-time itself possesses energy. Space is no longer a bland, unchanging arena within which more or less complex physical events unfold: the variable curvature of space, or of space-time, itself takes part in dynamical evolution.

3 With the advent of quantum field theory, empty space becomes even more complex in that it is full of so-called vacuum fluctuations. These may be pictured as follows. For very short times, there is an uncertainty of energy. Even in empty space, there may be enough energy, for a very short time, to create an electron/positron pair, or other particle pairs. But these "virtual" particles, as they are called, can exist only for a minute fraction of a second; then they annihilate each other and disappear, as the energy required for their existence is available only for a minute fraction of a second. The smaller the time interval, the tinier the region of space-time, so the greater the energy momentarily available, and the more massive the virtual particles may be. According to quantum field theory, each minute space-time region is full of virtual processes, involving the creation and annihilation of particle/anti-particle pairs. Indeed, all possible virtual processes occur that violate no other conservation law except that of energy (understood classically). The vacuum is a mass of seething activity, which averages out to nothing over sufficiently large space-time regions. One may, indeed, interpret quantum field theory as a theory of the vacuum, all possible physical processes going on, within minute space-time regions, as *virtual* processes. In supplying discrete units of energy, ΔE_1, ΔE_2, ... ΔE_n, we merely change some of the *virtual* processes into *actual* processes. There is a sense in which the most complex physical state imaginable is no more complex than the vacuum: it is just an energetic state of the vacuum such that some virtual processes are actual processes.[96]

In brief, quantum field theory transforms the simple, elemental, unchanging vacuum of nineteenth-century physics into a seething mass of complex, virtual processes – mirroring, in a ghost-like way, all the complexity of the most complex actual physical processes that exist when there is matter.

It might be supposed that quantum vacuum fluctuations are not real physical phenomena, but only artefacts of the formalism of quantum field theory given a certain (questionable) interpretation. But this does not take into account that vacuum fluctuations have been detected! This was done decades ago by means of the Casimir effect. According to quantum field theory, if two metal plates are held a small distance apart, virtual processes that involve the creation and annihilation of electron/positron pairs will tend to be *suppressed* in the space between the plates. This results in there being a small pressure tending to push the plates together, due to the *unsuppressed* virtual processes taking place in the space surrounding the two plates. This minute force, due to vacuum fluctuations – the Casimir effect – has been detected and measured.

4 Cosmic physicalism requires that there is a special state of the entire cosmos which is such that all diversity and change disappears: the very distinction between space and matter, we may presume, disappears, there being just *one* homogeneous, instantaneously unchanging *something*, which is also *everything*. This is made possible by big bang cosmology. It is conceivable that the big bang state of the universe, when all of space and matter was packed into a tiny region, was the Parmenidean state of instantaneous unity and homogeneity.

5 According to general relativity, the force of gravity is not a force at all; it is rather the tendency of the curvature of space-time to be affected by the presence of matter, or energy-density. With general relativity, one apparent force, gravity, becomes a feature of physical geometry. This suggests that it may be possible to carry this process of "geometricizing" physics further, the eventual outcome being the unification of space-time, on the one hand, and matter or energy on the other hand. Just this is required by cosmic physicalism.

6 According to the Salam-Weinberg theory of the electroweak force, at high energies the distinction between the electromagnetic force on the one hand, and the weak force on the other, disappears. As we go backwards in time towards the big bang, towards a time when the energy-density of the universe was sufficiently high, there existed just one unified force, the electroweak force. As the universe expanded, and the energy-density went down, the unity of the electroweak force was broken: the currently observed disunity of two forces with very different properties emerged. This is strikingly in

accord with the basic idea of cosmic physicalism: as we move backwards to the original big bang state, so we move towards a state of affairs of greater unity, simplicity, symmetry, or homogeneity. The potentially immensely important idea of cosmic spontaneous symmetry-breaking, which the Salam-Weinberg theory introduces at the level of fundamental theoretical physics, is precisely what is required to make cosmic physicalism a possibility. It is this development in theoretical physics, above all, which makes cosmic physicalism a viable possibility.

7 The idea of an initial state of high symmetry or unity evolving into something asymmetrical and disunified is further supported by superstring theory. According to this theory, space-time has ten or eleven dimensions. The dimensions that we do not observe are curled up into such a minute multi-dimensional "ball" that we do not ordinarily notice their existence. The idea here is that at the big bang state all the spatial dimensions were curled up in this fashion; the subsequent evolution of the universe consists of just three spatial dimensions growing in size to become, eventually, the space in which we find ourselves. Here, an original Parmenidean unity becomes disunity as three dimensions of space become dramatically different from the rest.

Here, then, are seven developments in theoretical physics and cosmology which took place during the twentieth century which may be taken to be steps towards cosmic physicalism, indications that it is in this direction that theoretical physics is progressively developing.

What would a theory of everything, T_C, that accords with cosmic physicalism look like? How would it differ from a theory of everything, T_A, that accords with atomic physicalism?

The major difference between any T_A and any T_C would be that they specify diametrically opposed conditions for the simple, elemental, unified, or homogeneous to exist. For T_A this is the vacuum, the state with as little as possible; for T_C this is a special state of *everything*, of the entire cosmos.

Another important difference is that, for any T_A, there is a fundamental difference between theory and initial conditions, even when the theory is applied to the cosmos as a whole. For all such applications, initial conditions must be specified in addition to the theory, and are not supplied by the theory itself. According to any T_C, however, the theory itself specifies a cosmic state of extreme unity. The initial state is, in a sense, given by the theory itself. It might even be the case that the theory is *only* applicable if the unique cosmic state of unity exists; universes for which this is not the case are, according to the theory, not possible. In this case the theory would specify, and assert the existence of, the initial cosmic state in a very strong sense.

Another important difference stems from the fact that, whereas T_A is not obliged to postulate an actual cosmic state of unique unity, T_C *is* obliged to postulate such a state. If we take this state to be in the past, then T_C is, in part, a theory about how disunity *develops* in time. T_C must imply that the cosmos evolves from an initial state of unity into states of increasing disunity, as a result of episodes of *spontaneous symmetry-breaking*. First principles do not require of any T_A that it provide such a cosmic history of increasing disunity. T_C, unlike T_A, is an inherently cosmological and historical theory.

Any T_C will only be able to predict a cosmic evolution of increasing disunity if it is fundamentally *probabilistic* in character. A deterministic T_C could only specify how an initial minute, or implicit, disunity becomes large or explicit with the passage of time, since the eventual cosmic diversity that we experience today would be precisely determined from the outset. Spontaneous symmetry-breaking, in other words, is an inherently *probabilistic* event (one asymmetrical state of affairs being selected probabilistically from a number of other asymmetrical possibilities). Any T_C must, then, be a fundamentally probabilistic theory, something that is not required, *a priori* as it were, from any T_A.

In the light of this argument, we may hold that the fundamentally probabilistic character of quantum theory (QT) provides an eighth suggestive pointer towards cosmic physicalism. (This requires of course that we interpret QT as being fundamentally probabilistic, in the first place. It also requires that QT can be interpreted in such a way as to associate fundamentally probabilistic events with spontaneous, cosmic symmetry-breaking.)

The considerations developed so far suggest that the universe might be physically comprehensible in the following manner. Initially, at or before the big bang, there is the Parmenidean state of supreme unity. All disunity is purely *virtual*. Then the initial spontaneous symmetry-breaking – or unity-breaking – event occurs (the big bang), and disunity becomes actual, being made up of billions of fleeting *virtual* Parmenidean states of supreme unity in each tiny region of space-time. Whereas before the big bang, unity is *actual* and all disunity is *virtual*, after the big bang it is disunity that is *actual* and unity that is *virtual*. Actual phenomena are the outcome of diverse inter-relations between virtual unified states of the entire cosmos confined to miniscule space-time regions. Each miniscule space-time element *is* the entire virtual cosmos in its supremely unified, prior-to-big-bang state. The cosmos is composed of itself.[97]

11 SCIENTIFIC PROGRESS

Viewed from the standpoint of SE, the prospects of science making real progress in knowledge and understanding look rather bleak. It is not just that there is no solution to the problem of induction. Worse, physics seems to advance from one *false* theory to another. As we have seen, again and again in the history of physics, theories that meet with astonishing empirical success turn out, sooner or later, to be false: Newtonian theory, Maxwellian electrodynamics, the whole of classical physics, quantum theory, general relativity, and almost certainly quantum electrodynamics, quantum electroweak theory, chromodynamics, and the standard model. As we saw in chapter 3, that successive theories turn out to be false in this way has been called by one philosopher of science "the pessimistic induction." There is even a serious problem as to what it could *mean* to say of a succession of false theories that they are getting closer and closer to the truth.[98] Philosophers of science have denied that there is any progress in knowledge through scientific revolutions.[99]

View all this from the perspective of AOE, however, and the prospects for real progress in scientific knowledge and understanding change dramatically. If the universe really is physically comprehensible (so that physicalism is true), then it follows at once that all dynamical theories that are about a restricted range of phenomena, and cannot be immediately generalized to apply to all phenomena, must be false. For physicalism asserts that that which determines (perhaps probabilistically) how events evolve, specified by theory, *is precisely the same everywhere, throughout all phenomena*. In order to be absolutely correct about what determines the evolution of any specific phenomenon, you must be able to specify what determines the evolution of *all* phenomena. At once it follows that physical theories that are about a restricted range of phenomena only cannot be precisely correct about what determines these phenomena. They must all be false. Hence, if physics advances by developing successive theories that apply to ever-wider ranges of phenomena, but not to *all* phenomena, then, granted the truth of physicalism, all these theories must be false. Physics is advancing in precisely the way it would need to advance if physicalism is true, and successive theories are getting closer and closer to specifying physicalism correctly in the form of a true, unified, testable theory of everything.

Furthermore, AOE provides the means to solve the problem of induction (see appendix 2). And it provides the means to solve the problem of verisimilitude – the problem of what it means to say of a succession of theories that they are approaching the truth.[100] Physicalism persists through theoretical revolutions in physics; successive theories and blueprints are, progressively, delineating the character of physicalism with increasing accuracy. The idea that theoretical knowledge does not persist through revolutions can only be held by those wedded to some version of SE.

12 STRING THEORY

String theory holds that fundamental particles, electrons, quarks, photons, and so on, are not particles at all but tiny closed strings, in ten or eleven dimensions of space-time. As I have already remarked, we do not see the extra spatial dimensions (six or seven) because these are curled up into a tiny ball, present everywhere, at every space-time point. There is just one kind of string, but strings differ in the way they vibrate, and it is this which gives rise to what appear to be different particles: electrons, quarks, and so on.[101]

For decades, theoretical physicists have invested a massive amount of work in developing string theory or M-theory. And yet, so far, no successful predictions have been forthcoming. This is, on the face of it, starkly at odds with SE. Does it not mean that most theoretical physicists have, in practice, rejected SE – and perhaps already accepted AOE instead?

There can be no doubt whatsoever that the manner in which string theory has been, and is, treated by physicists powerfully substantiates a basic point of the argument of this book, namely that *unity* is a vital requirement that an acceptable theory must satisfy, in addition to empirical success. String theory is taken so seriously by so many physicists because it promises to bring theoretical unification to all of physics. In the first place, that particles are really tiny strings has important implications for the unification of quantum theory and general relativity. Point-like particles trace out one-dimensional lines in space-time. When particles collide, they do so at a point, and this creates impossible infinities when attempts are made to calculate how such collisions occur within quantum gravity. Strings trace out tubes in space-time, and when strings collide they form trouser shapes in space-time. The collision is smooth; there is no unique point where it occurs. This difference makes it possible to calculate the collision of strings in quantum gravity. Furthermore, string theory holds out the hope of unifying all the diverse fundamental particles that appear to exist. They are all just one kind of string, diversity being due to diverse vibrational modes. Despite its lack of empirical success, string theory is taken so seriously by so many physicists because it promises to be the unified "theory of everything."

Does this mean that sᴇ is generally rejected by physicists today? No! In the first place, string theory has been resoundingly criticized by many on the grounds that no theory should be taken so seriously when it has failed to yield a single correct prediction.[102] These physicists have not rejected sᴇ. But secondly, even those who do take string theory seriously may not have rejected sᴇ. String theory is often defended as "work in progress." It should not be regarded as an accepted theory, like quantum theory or general relativity. It is a conjecture being worked on which one day, it is hoped, will produce successful predictions. It so happens that, in the past, all great theories have emerged in two ways. Either they have been developed over years by one individual (Newton and Newtonian theory, Einstein and general relativity), or they have been developed by many individuals over years or decades in a number of steps, each step meeting with empirical success along the way, and so being a contribution to physics in its own right (classical electrodynamics, quantum theory). String theory differs *only* in being the outcome of the work of many physicists *without* individual contributions making successful empirical predictions along the way. In this respect, string theory can be compared to general relativity before the latter was completed and made its first successful prediction, the big difference being that general relativity was the work of one physicist (Einstein), whereas string theory is the work of many. It is possible, in short, to argue along these lines that attitudes towards string theory are as compatible with acceptance of sᴇ as attitudes towards other theories (although persistent acceptance of unified theories *even when empirically successful* is in reality incompatible with SE, as we have seen.)

Even though string theory has not yet made any predictions that have been experimentally confirmed, the theory does, nevertheless, make predictions. String theory requires a symmetry to be true called *supersymmetry* (the theory is indeed called *superstring* theory). Supersymmetry postulates a connection between particles with integer spin like photons, called bosons, and those with half-integral spin like electrons, called fermions. Supersymmetry requires every known boson and fermion to have an as-yet-undetected supersymmetry partner. Experimental detection of these partners would corroborate supersymmetry, and constitute evidence for superstring theory. Failure to detect these particles would constitute evidence against superstring theory. In addition, the extra dimensions required by string theory have consequences that may be detectable experimentally.

String theory predicts that the extra spatial dimensions of the theory can be curled up in many different ways, leading to very many different universes more or less like ours. The theory predicts something like 10^{520} different universes. How is ours to be found among this vast array of possibilities? If it can be found, is this anything more than an accident, given the plethora of possibilities that the theory predicts? Or should all these possibilities be regarded as potential realities, realized, perhaps, in different epochs of the cosmos before the big bang? Can the theory really be held to be empirically falsifiable, if we have to trawl through 10^{520} possibilities to falsify it?

Can string theory be regarded as an acceptable blueprint for physics today? Do attitudes towards string theory suggest that physicists increasingly incline towards accepting AOE?

The basic idea of string theory, shorn of its mathematical details, might indeed be held to be a metaphysical blueprint for physics. Both blueprint and theory suffer, however, from one very serious defect. They inherit the defects of orthodox quantum theory. They are not about strings as such, but about the results of performing measurements on strings (even if no measurements are forthcoming). Like quantum theory, string theory does not declare unambiguously whether nature is deterministic or probabilistic. If probabilistic, no precise physical conditions are specified for probabilistic transitions to occur that make no mention of measurement. String theory is seriously defective on these grounds, whether regarded as a theory or a blueprint.

There are two further points to note in connection with the question of whether string theory constitutes a move away from SE towards AOE.

The first has to be with the way the theory was discovered and developed. It began life when a theoretical physicist, Gabriele Veneziano, discovered in 1968 a mathematical technique for predicting the results of collisions between hadrons – particles like protons and neutrons (which go to make up the nuclei of atoms). Two years later it was realized, by Yoichiro Nambu and others, that the new mathematical technique could be interpreted as asserting that protons and neutrons (and other hadrons), instead of being point-particles, are tiny strings. But, after its initial success, this new theory of strings was found to have serious empirical problems. And in the meantime, a much more successful rival theory had been developed. This built on an idea proposed in 1964 by Murray Gell-Mann, and independently by George Zweig, according to which protons and neutrons are made up of new kinds of particle called quarks. By the mid-1970s a quantum theory of the force between quarks had been developed, namely chromodynamics. This theory met with empirical success, and string theory was forgotten by everyone, except for two physicists, John Schwartz and Joel Scherk, who reinterpreted string theory as a theory about all fundamental particles, a theory which, to them, seemed to promise to unify quantum theory and general relativity. Eventually, in 1984, Schwartz and Michael Green showed that this new string theory of quantum gravity could be used to make sensible calculations, when all rival approaches to quantum gravity yielded absurd infinite results. String theory abruptly hit the headlines. Theoretical physicists started to work furiously to develop the new string theory.

Even this highly condensed early history of string theory reveals that the way the theory was discovered and developed differs strikingly from the method of discovery of AOE.

The second point is this: because SE is still the official philosophy of science among physicists, there is a persistent lack of understanding as to how untestable metaphysical ideas are to be rationally developed and assessed. There is a certain failure among string theorists, in particular, to appreciate the importance of trying to develop a number of rival level 3 ideas;[103] and there is a widespread failure to appreciate that such work can be *rationally* (if fallibly) assessed even before it issues in empirical predictions. Because of the failure to appreciate that work of this type can be assessed rationally, in practice what tends to influence this work is mere *fashion*. The vast majority of theoretical physicists working in this field of quantum gravity work on string theory (or M-theory), the fashionable thing to do; relatively few physicists explore other lines of inquiry. Few indeed are the physicists attempting to assess rationally the relative merits, the relative successes and failures, of the rival research programmes.[104] Thus, even though SE would seem to be blatantly violated in scientific practice, its influence still lingers on and prevents AOE from being put explicitly and fully into practice.

There is no agreed, acceptable, unproblematic metaphysical blueprint for physics today. That this lack constitutes a crisis in theoretical physics is obvious granted AOE, but is thoroughly obscured granted SE (which banishes metaphysics from physics). There are four fundamental problems. Is nature deterministic or probabilistic? How is justice to be done to the quantum domain *without any appeal being made to measurement*? How, in outline, are general relativity and quantum theory to be unified? How, and to what extent, is matter-and-force on the one hand, and space-time on the other, to be unified? There are other problems that need to be taken into account as well, such as the manner in which the standard model is to be unified, how the big bang, and inflation, are to be explained, the nature of so-called "dark matter," and the nature of "dark energy," which is believed to be responsible for the current speeding up of the expansion of the universe.[105]

Perhaps we need to see matter and forces absorbed into a richer kind of space, which evolves into something like a superposition of spaces with diverse geometries, even diverse topologies, until suffering instantaneous probabilistic collapse into just one. Or perhaps, more radically, we need to adopt cosmic physicalism.

6

Why Science Needs Philosophy, Part II: Natural Science

So far we have considered why theoretical physics needs philosophy: that is, metaphysics and methodology. I turn now to the question of why natural science as a whole needs philosophy. It is philosophy transformed in the ways argued for in chapters 3 and 4 that science needs, not philosophy as it is mostly practised today.

Physics is, of course, the fundamental natural science. All other branches of natural science either presuppose some part of physics, or presuppose some part of natural science that in turn presupposes physics. All the natural sciences are, in this way, interconnected. Thus, the fact that physics needs philosophy means that all of natural science does as well. But there are many much more significant ways in which natural science needs philosophy.

An important preliminary point to note is that aim-oriented empiricism (AOE) can be, and needs to be, generalized so that it becomes applicable to *all* branches of natural science, and not just to physics. All branches of natural science have more or less problematic aims – like physics. Unlike physics, the aims of other branches of natural science, in addition doubtless to making metaphysical assumptions, make assumptions about the findings of other, more fundamental sciences. Thus the aims of astronomy, astrophysics, and chemistry make assumptions about relevant parts of physics; the aims of geology make assumptions about relevant parts of physics and astronomy; biology makes assumptions about relevant parts of chemistry and geology; and so on. And each branch (and sub-discipline) of natural science makes assumptions about what there is for that discipline to discover that it would be of value to discover, for one reason or another. The aims of all branches of natural science are, in other words, more or less problematic: thus these disciplines, like physics, need to represent their aims in the form of a hierarchy, so that aims, and associated methods, may be improved as scientific knowledge and understanding improve.

Each discipline of natural science needs to articulate and implement its own version of AOE. Let us call the collection of these versions of AOE, each version more or less specific to a specific discipline of natural science, *generalized AOE (GAOE)*.

GAOE is able to do justice to three vital features of scientific method throughout all of natural science. First, it does justice to the way methods vary, from one discipline to another, and even within one discipline from one time to another. Aims change as we move from discipline to discipline, and within any one discipline as time passes, so methods change as well. Second, GAOE does justice to what is common to all scientific disciplines, the hierarchical structure of aims and methods. It also makes explicit the interconnected character of natural science – one discipline presupposing in its aims the findings of another. Third – and most important – GAOE facilitates positive feedback between improving scientific knowledge and improving aims and methods (improving knowledge about how to improve knowledge). This positive feedback feature is made possible by the hierarchical, meta-methodological character of GAOE. Aims and methods, high up in the hierarchy, help regulate how aims and methods, low down in the hierarchy, can be modified in the light of empirical success and failure. This positive feedback feature is, in my view, the nub of scientific rationality, and a major part of the reason for the explosive growth of scientific knowledge – much helped, of course, by the development of experimental methods (instruments and techniques). As I have already indicated, explicit allegiance to standard empiricism (SE) by the scientific community has not prevented scientists from putting something close to AOE – or GAOE – into scientific practice.

It may not be necessary for all scientific disciplines to articulate the whole hierarchical paraphernalia of GAOE. What is essential, however, is that each discipline recognizes *three* domains to which contributions can be made, three domains of discussion: (1) evidence, (2) theory, and (3) aims. This stands in sharp contrast to SE science, which recognizes only the first two.

One outcome of transforming SE science into AOE science is that the philosophy of science – the study of what the aims and methods of science ought to be – becomes a vital, integral part of science itself, as I mentioned in chapter 3 (note 51). Here, then, is one way in which science needs philosophy!

I now indicate several more ways in which including some discussion of problematic aims and philosophical ideas within natural science would serve both to *improve* science, and take it further down the path towards becoming natural philosophy.

I VALUES

The basic intellectual aim of science, as we have seen, is not truth per se; it is rather *explanatory* truth – truth presupposed to be explanatory. But explanatory truth is a special case of a more general aim – that of seeking *valuable* truth. Quite generally, all branches of natural science seek truth that is of value, either intrinsically or intellectually because of its inherent interest to us, or in a more utilitarian way in that it can be used to obtain other things of value – health, prosperity, travel, entertainment, that is, the whole technological panoply of the modern world. It is inevitable that values, of one kind or another, will be inherent in science in influencing scientists to pursue some lines of research and ignore others. And it is desirable that values should influence research. We want science to discover that which is significant or of value. A science that steadily accumulated a vast store of factual truths of irredeemable triviality and uselessness would not be regarded as making progress. The discovery of truth that is either of intrinsic interest or of use is essential for scientific progress. Simply to be published in a scientific journal as a potential contribution to scientific knowledge, it is not enough that the result be sufficiently well-established truth; in addition, it must reach some minimal level of value or potential use. Values, of one kind or another, in short, pervade all of science.

This is not to say, of course, that considerations of value can be permitted to influence judgements of truth. That it would be desirable or of value for something to be true does not, in itself, make it more likely to be true. Insofar as values do influence judgements of truth, they should do so *negatively*. The more important it is for something to be true, the more we need or want it to be true, the more severely critical we should be of it. If lives depend on scientific claims being correct (because otherwise aeroplanes will crash, bridges will collapse, or medicines will kill), the claims need to be subjected to experimental and critical scrutiny that is all the more searching and ruthless.

Judgements of value do, however, quite properly influence what is accepted, and rejected, to become a part of scientific knowledge in influencing, not judgements concerning truth and falsity, but judgements concerning *significance* and *triviality*. That which is irredeemably trivial deserves to be excluded from the body of scientific knowledge however well-established it may be.[1] One does not contribute to scientific knowledge by, merely, counting leaves on trees, or grains of gravel on paths, even though the result is definitively established!

Questions of value are, however, profoundly problematic. Of value to whom? Of value when? Today? In fifty or a hundred years' time? Of value in what kind of way? How does one judge between the value of knowledge and understanding for its own sake, and knowledge or technological know-how that can save lives as a result of curing or preventing disease, alleviating poverty? What ought to be the basic values inherent in the aims of natural science? Ought science in the UK, for example, to be for humanity as a whole, or even for those whose needs are the greatest, the poor of the earth? Or is it acceptable that science in the UK is, primarily, for "the growth, prosperity and wellbeing of the UK," as UK's scientific research councils declare?[2]

The aims of scientific disciplines, and the aim of natural science as a whole, are thus doubly problematic. On the one hand, there is the problem of identifying what we do not know that is discoverable by current techniques; and on the other, there is the problem of identifying what it would be of value to discover. Both need to be explored rationally, that is imaginatively and critically, as an integral part of science, in order to facilitate the identification of the region of overlap: that which is both *discoverable* and of *value* to discover. Each scientific discipline, in short, needs to include some discussion of untestable, metaphysical ideas concerning the domain of our ignorance, and ideas about what is of value, in order to give the discipline the best hope of identifying its best research aims.

SE science prohibits all this, in demanding that metaphysical ideas, and ideas about what is of value, are excluded from the intellectual domain of science. In prohibiting in this way attempts to discover the best research aims rationally, SE obstructs efforts to identify the best research aims, and thus damages science. Aim-oriented empiricism, by contrast, all but insists that science includes some sustained imaginative and critical discussion concerning the problematic question of what the best research aims might be – discussion that includes ideas about metaphysics and what is of value.

Decisions about what research aims are to be pursued will inevitably be made by research scientists and by grant-giving bodies, influenced no doubt by a combination of government, industry, the military and, perhaps, public opinion. What matters is that such decision-making can avail itself of sustained explicit, public exploration of possibilities. Only then can there be available a body of rational discussion of possibilities from which research scientists and grant-giving bodies can learn. And only then is there a basis for the critical assessment of decisions that have been made, and are being made, about what research to *support* and *do*.[3]

Scientists are at present reluctant to discuss their research aims, partly because this violates S E, and partly because of the fear that their own research project will be taken up and completed by another research team, perhaps with better access to funds, somewhere else in the world. There is a tendency, as a result, for scientists to be reluctant to inform colleagues about research aims.

Implementation of A O E intellectual standards might well help to overcome this reluctance. Given S E, there is no reward for proposing a new research aim which, when actively pursued, leads to significant contributions to scientific knowledge. As far as individual scientists or research teams are concerned, there is only loss and no gain to be had from publishing research aims. A O E transforms this situation, for, given A O E, the act of publishing a new research aim which leads subsequently to successful science *is*, in itself, to make an important contribution to science (to the third domain of scientific discussion, namely aims). If A O E is ever taken up by the scientific community, it may become necessary to guard against the danger that everyone publishes ideas for research but no one actually does the research!

Once it is acknowledged that questions about what is of value play an important role in scientific discussion of problems concerning research aims, it is clear that this discussion cannot be confined to professional scientists. Scientists may well be experts about what there is to discover, but they are not uniquely qualified to decide about questions of value. Discussion about research aims needs to be open to non-scientists. It is above all in this domain of research aims that scientists and non-scientists alike need to collaborate in creating an informed body of scientific literature. Furthermore, discussion concerning what it might be of value to discover needs to call upon rational (imaginative and critical) discussion of social problems – problems of living at all levels (individual, institutional, global) – wherever this may be pursued. I will have more to say about these matters below.

As we have seen, contributions to science can be of value in two very different ways: intellectually, or for practical purposes. Sometimes, of course, a contribution is of value in both ways simultaneously. Faraday's invention of the electric motor and dynamo are examples. But often contributions are of value primarily, possibly even exclusively, in just one way. Contributions to cosmology and fundamental theoretical physics, potentially of great value intellectually, may have no practical use whatsoever; and of course vice versa, scientific contributions of great practical use may be of little intrinsic intellectual interest. It is important to distinguish clearly these two ways in which contributions can be of value; only then can explicit attention be given to the thorny question of what fraction of total funds should be devoted to each aspect of science. Failure to distinguish the different ways in which science can be of value may lead to research that is of value in neither way.[4]

It is also important for fund-giving bodies to appreciate that it is unreasonable to require that *both* kinds of value are always relevant to research projects. As I have indicated, a research project that is potentially highly significant intellectually may have no practical use whatsoever.

There is a long-standing tendency to think that only practical use is of social significance, but this is absurd. Contributions to science that are, exclusively, of intellectual value may well be such that they are, potentially or actually, of great interest to non-scientists, and make a major contribution to culture. Modern cosmology is an example. Both aspects of science can be of great social value.

Modern science tends to be expensive. Much science is funded by those who can afford to pay: wealthy nations, governments, the military, and industry of wealthy nations. Whoever funds science is bound to influence the direction of research. This means that there is an inherent and inevitable tendency for the research priorities of modern science to reflect the interests of the wealthy, rather than the interests of those whose needs are the greatest, the earth's poor. And indeed, medical research tends to respond to the health problems of people in wealthy countries rather than people in poor countries. A great deal of scientific research, world-wide, is funded by the military of wealthy countries, especially the USA and the UK.[5] Much scientific research serves the interests of manufacturing and the economies of wealthy countries.

In the seventeenth century, Robert Boyle, one of the founding fathers of modern science, said of what he called the Invisible College – a sort of forerunner of the Royal Society, and so of organized scientific research – "The 'Invisible College' [consists of] persons that endeavour to put narrow-mindedness out of countenance by the practice of so extensive a charity that it reaches unto everything called man, and nothing less than an universal good-will can content it. And indeed they are so apprehensive of the want of good employment that they take the whole body of mankind for their care."[6] Many scientists pursue research in that frame of mind, and organizations like Scientists for Global Responsibility seek to keep the spirit of what Boyle had to say alive today. But does modern science globally put Boyle's declaration into practice in its priorities of research? Hardly! Does UK science, devoted to "the growth, prosperity and wellbeing of the UK," successfully embody the aspirations of Boyle's Invisible College? Not really.

It is in fact inevitable that expensive modern science will tend to reflect the interests of the wealthy rather than the interests of those whose needs are the greatest, the poorest on earth. Only sustained discussion of problems concerning the values and priorities of scientific research, carried on within the framework of AOE, can hope to address and counter this tendency.

I conclude that AOE science, in supporting sustained discussion of problems associated with the aims, values and priorities of research, is more likely to be sensitively responsive to the real needs of humanity than SE science. AOE science is more likely to be science that is of real human value. And by including discussion of problems of value as an integral part of science, AOE moves science further along the path towards becoming natural philosophy.

2 SOCIAL USE

Science seeks knowledge of value so that it will be used by people, ideally to enhance the quality of human life. It is not enough that knowledge be acquired; it needs to be made available so that it can be used by people and organizations, either to enhance personal and public curiosity, knowledge and understanding of aspects of the world, or to facilitate attainment of other goals of value by means of technological applications and in other ways. Science is, in other words, a part of a broader endeavour to help promote human welfare, help humanity make progress towards a better world. Science has social, humanitarian, even *political* goals.

But these goals are, once again, deeply problematic. Science devoted to the needs of – and made available to – the military, industry, agriculture, medicine, security, and transport all have problematic aspects. Science devoted to the needs of the military has resulted in armaments, whether conventional, chemical, biological, or nuclear, that are ever more lethal. In part as a result, deaths in wars have escalated: something like 12 million in the nineteenth century, perhaps as many as 180 million in the twentieth century, and we are not doing too well so far in the twenty-first century. Science devoted to the interests of industry has had an impact in a multiplicity of ways, of great benefit. But it has also assisted the discovery, extraction, and use of oil and coal which, via the massive increase in emission of carbon dioxide into the atmosphere, has led to global warming and all the threats to humanity, now and in the future, that are the outcome. Science devoted to promoting health by means of antibiotics, hygiene, and in other ways is of priceless value for billions; at the same time, it has led to the severe problem of population growth. And the evolution of bacteria resistant to antibiotics is an increasingly serious problem. Commercialization of medical research in the last few decades has led to priority being given to the development of drugs that will be commercially successful, such as drugs for indigestion, rather than to the development of new antibiotics which, only used occasionally for brief periods by any one person, are inevitably much less successful commercially. And drug companies do not fully reveal the results of their drug trials, so that doctors are not in a position to know about hazardous side effects. Agricultural research helps enormously to increase the yields of crops but, at the same time, develops pesticides such as DDT and neonicotinoids which play havoc with living things in the natural world: birds, fish, and bees and other insects. And the spread of agriculture leads to the destruction of tropical rain forests and other natural habitats, and so to the extinction of species. Almost all our current global problems would not have arisen were it not for the astonishing intellectual success of modern science and technology.

There is a long-standing view, associated with standard empiricism (SE), that science is itself morally neutral, and cannot therefore be blamed for its misuse, when it is employed to harm and kill. Scientific facts may be morally neutral. But what may well not be morally neutral are decisions to pursue one set of research aims rather than another, and to make the results of research available to one set of people or organizations rather than another set. Decisions concerning the priorities of research, and the way the results of research become accessible to the public, may well be morally charged.

The aim of making the results of science available to the public so that these results may be used in ways that are genuinely of benefit to all, now and in the future, is clearly highly problematic. This social or humanitarian aim of science needs sustained rational discussion, as an integral part of the scientific enterprise.

Somewhat analogous considerations arise in connection with the cultural or intellectual aspects of science. Here, the proper task of science is to stimulate curiosity, wonder, and perhaps delight in aspects of world around us. It is to ensure that people can acquire relevant scientific knowledge and understanding when they need it, and scientific knowledge is available in a form that is accessible to non-scientists. It is to try to ensure that people have a good understanding of the overall scientific picture of the universe, and how we and other living things fit in and have come to be.

This aim of promoting public scientific understanding is problematic because scientific literature is vast, highly specialized and technical, and incomprehensible to most non-scientists. Indeed, scientists from different specialities often cannot understand each other – even scientists from different branches of the same science. Experimental physicists may find contributions of theoretical physicists incomprehensible. In addition, scientific results tend to be published in journals that are freely available to academics but expensive for members of the public. Popular science writing, a growth industry in recent years, is a step in the right direction, but by no means the whole answer. Too much popular science does not attempt the serious, difficult task of enhancing understanding of scientific ideas, discoveries, theories and problems at a non-technical level: instead, misleading ideas are conveyed on the basis of analogy and metaphor. Rare indeed is it for a scientist to communicate new work to colleagues and public simultaneously, as Galileo did in *The Starry Messenger* and *Dialogue concerning the Two Chief World Systems*, and Darwin did in *The*

Origin of Species. Rare, too, is it to find popular scientific writing devoted to a serious discussion of open, unsolved scientific *problems*. Those who write on science for the public are so anxious to convey some idea of all that has been achieved that they neglect to discuss what has not been achieved, what is not known, the domain of our ignorance, what remains a mystery. And yet, if the aim is to excite interest in science, it is exploration of open *problems* that is most likely to excite it.[7]

Modern science has not been especially successful in promoting public scientific understanding. If the aim of "improving human knowledge" is interpreted to mean "the knowledge of scientific experts," modern science must be judged to be astonishingly successful. But if the aim is interpreted to mean "the understanding of humanity of the basic scientific picture of the universe and our place in it," modern science must be judged to be very much less successful. And yet, insofar as science is not just for scientists, it is public scientific understanding that, in the end, really matters. As Einstein once said, "Knowledge exists in two forms – lifeless, stored in books, and alive in the consciousness of men. The second form of existence is after all the essential one; the first, indispensible as it may be, occupies only an inferior position."[8]

General acceptance of SE by the scientific community may, once again, be responsible, at least in part, for the failures of modern science to achieve aims of *social use*, practical and intellectual. SE decides what is to count as a contribution to science: it is a contribution that meets with empirical success, and thus contributes to knowledge, conceived of in intellectual or institutional terms – essentially, a paper published in a scientific journal. It is this that matters, as far as professional scientists are concerned. Developing scientific work to the point that it can be used by people in ways that are of value, informing the public about scientific discoveries: such work does not contribute to science itself, according to SE, and hence carries far less scientific kudos.

But contributions to scientific knowledge, conceived of in purely intellectual or institutional terms, are merely of potential value. It is only when such contributions are *used* by people, in one way or another, to enrich human life, that science comes to life and has *actual* value. Purely intellectual contributions to science, confined to the institutions of science, indispensible as they may be, to echo Einstein's words, occupy only an inferior position. Such contributions are a means to what really matters: science contributing to the enrichment of human life (in intellectual or practical ways).

We need, in short, to conceive of the basic aim of science in social or humanitarian terms. And we need to recognize just how problematic this basic aim is. Science needs to include sustained discussion of the problems associated with the social, humanitarian aims of science. And that, in turn, means that science needs to become natural philosophy; it needs to include sustained informal discussion of scientific aims, problems, discoveries, ideas and guesses, open to scientists and non-scientists alike.

These serious problems concerning the social uses of science will be taken up again in chapter 8.

3 OUR FUNDAMENTAL PROBLEM

In chapter 3, I argued that our fundamental problem of thought and life can be formulated like this:

How can our human world, and the world of sentient life more generally, imbued with perceptual qualities, consciousness, free will, meaning, and value, exist and best flourish embedded as it is in the physical universe?

Natural science has a major role in helping us to improve our ideas as to how this problem is to be solved.[9] The problem only arises in the first place, in this form, because of the view of the universe ushered in with modern science – or natural philosophy – in the sixteenth and seventeenth centuries. The physical sciences have the task of improving our knowledge and understanding of the nature of the physical universe – that which creates the problem for us. The biological sciences have the task of improving our knowledge and understanding of how life can exist in the physical universe – how the myriad forms of life that exist on our planet today have come to be. And it is to be hoped that evolutionary theory, neuroscience, and perhaps other branches of biology will contribute to our understanding of consciousness and free will, their existence and evolution.

The problem itself, however, is philosophical and cannot be regarded as exclusively scientific. Science cannot suffice to solve it. In the first place, the world of experience, colours, sounds, smells, tactile qualities as we experience them, our inner experiences, consciousness: none of this can be predicted or explained by physics, or any part of natural science that is in principle reducible to physics, as we saw in chapter 4 (pages 106–7). Second, science cannot come to grips with what is of value.[10] It cannot determine for us what is of value, and it cannot decide for us what our goals should be in seeking to realize what is of value. It cannot determine what is just, or good. It cannot determine such human, moral qualities as generosity, kindness, friendliness. Science cannot decide what kind of society we should strive to achieve, or what kind of ideal world order we should seek to attain in the long term. All these are, however, aspects of our fundamental problem.

In short, we need to interpret natural science as contributing to the solution of our fundamental problem which is in essence *philosophical*, rather than *scientific*. We need to see science, ultimately, as a part of, or as contributing to, philosophy, rather than see philosophy as something that needs to be excluded from science.

Science needs to include, or interact with, sustained thinking about our fundamental problem in order to counteract the sins of overspecialization. This may indeed be regarded as the primary service that philosophy, properly conducted, provides science. In keeping alive thinking about our most fundamental problems, philosophy counteracts specialization, and helps to ensure that science puts all four rules of rational problem solving into practice, formulated on page 64 of chapter 3. Science needs philosophy (properly conducted) in order to be rational!

4 EVOLUTION

Darwin's theory of evolution makes a profoundly important contribution towards resolving our fundamental problem. It does this by enabling us to understand how life on earth, especially human life of value, has come to be in the physical universe. But in order to make this contribution towards resolving our fundamental problem, it is vital that Darwinian theory is correctly interpreted.

There is a long-standing tendency among biologists to interpret Darwinian theory as *eliminating* purposiveness from nature, rather than as explaining how and why it has evolved in an ultimately purposeless universe. It is emphasized that the mechanisms of evolution, of random variations and natural selection of the fittest, are purely blind and purposeless in character. All is "chance and necessity," to quote the title of a book by Jacque Monot.[11] Purpose is banished from biology, and from nature – or not given anything like the highly significant, pervasive role that it actually plays in Darwinian evolution. A paradigmatic expression of this viewpoint is to be found in Richard Dawkins's *The Selfish Gene*.[12] And certainly Dawkins has held this purposeless view. At a conference at the London School of Economics a few years ago he showed us a still from the BBC TV sitcom *Fawlty Towers*, in which John Cleese beats his car with a branch in punishment because it refuses to start. The intended implication was clear. It is as misguided for us to attribute purposes to living things as it is for Fawlty to attribute a purpose (being objectionable) to his car.[13]

But all this is nonsense. All living things are purposive in character. They are all goal-pursuing. And Darwinian theory tells us what the basic goal of living things is: to survive and reproduce. All other goals pursued by living things contribute to this basic goal. Plants pursue goals in the main by means of growth. Darwin's theory only becomes applicable when there are entities that pursue the goals of survival and reproductive success. Without this, the Darwinian mechanism of natural selection does not make sense.

Sometimes biologists get into great difficulties trying to define "life." That they do is, in itself, indicative of a failure to appreciate that life is essentially purposive in character. Living things are, quite simply, things that are naturally occurring and purposive.[14]

It may be objected that most biologists would of course acknowledge that animals, in living, pursue goals. I think that is probably correct. My point, however, is that there has been a failure to do full justice to the ubiquitous, highly significant role that purposive action plays in evolution. We need a new version of Darwinian theory that does justice to this role.

The purposive character of all of life needs to be appreciated simply in order to get into perspective what the basic task of Darwinian theory is, and the task of biology more generally. It is to improve our knowledge and understanding of the great mystery of what may be called *double comprehensibility*. Our world is riddled with double comprehensibility. The actions of all living things are such that they are open, in principle, to being explained and understood simultaneously in two very different ways: *physically* and *purposively*. What is incomprehensible, what needs to be explained, is the double comprehensibility of living things. It is their dual comprehensibility that is incomprehensible! Darwinian theory has the task of helping to explain how and why a multiplicity of things have come into existence here on earth that are amenable to being explained and understood in these two very different kinds of ways simultaneously. That this is the basic task of Darwinian theory makes it a very different kind of theory from those of the physical sciences. In order to fulfil the task, it is necessary for Darwinism to call upon both kinds of explanation, as we shall see.[15]

What is it for a thing to be purposive? We require that it can attain its goal, some specific state of affairs, in a range of circumstances in the given environment. The thing must be able to respond appropriately to a variety of conditions or occurrences so that it performs just the appropriate actions required to achieve the goal. All this is made possible by control mechanisms responsive to changing circumstances, and able to initiate appropriate action, control made possible, ultimately, by feedback. The atom of purpose is the thermostat. Its goal is to keep the temperature of the room at a fixed level. As the temperature rises, something in the thermostat expands, and that cuts off the heater; it contracts when the temperature falls, and that starts the heater.

That a thing is purposive and pursues a goal, in this sense, does not mean that it is conscious, or knows what it is doing. Purposive explanations, as understood here, render intelligible the actions of a goal-pursing thing, whether plant, animal, human, thermostat, or robot, by explaining the actions as being designed to realize the overall goal in the given environment, but without appealing in any way to sentience or consciousness. But even though there is no reference to inner experience or consciousness, even when these exist, nevertheless purposive explanations may refer to a sort of degenerate, control or functionalist version of inner experiences and mental states, such as belief, decision, desire, perception, and so on. We can say that the thermostat "believes" that the temperature of the room is 23°C, the guided rocket is "attempting" to hit its target, or "perceives" an incoming rocket and "decides" to take evasive action. We can declare that the chess-playing computer is "aware" of the threat of mate, and is "thinking" about how to meet the threat. All that is being asserted here is that the control-system of the goal-pursuing thing has states and processes associated with it that have functional roles corresponding to the functional roles that real beliefs, decisions, desires, etc., have in us, or in other conscious beings.

Those purposive beings that are sentient or conscious are open to being explained and understood by means of an enriched form of purposive explanation, which I shall call *personalistic* explanation. We understand another personalistically when we imagine that we are that other, with the other's experiences, feelings, desires, thoughts, beliefs, perceptions, intentions, plans.[16] Personalistic explanations are purposive explanations enriched by imaginative identification with the person, or being, whose actions are being explained and understood.

All living things are purposive in character, but evolution itself is not. The two basic mechanisms of Darwinian evolution, random inherited variations and natural selection, are devoid of purpose. They are blind.

There is, however, an important qualification. As evolution proceeds, the mechanisms of evolution themselves evolve, gradually incorporating into their operations more and more elements of purposiveness. Eventually, with the advent of evolution by cultural means, something like Lamarckian evolution comes into existence: inheritance of acquired characteristics.

The proper basic task of Darwinian theory is to help explain how and why the miracle of double comprehensibility, such a striking feature of the living world, has come to be. But in order to do this adequately, Darwinian theory must itself make use of *both* kinds of explanation, physical and purposive – or, when sentient and conscious beings are involved, physical and personalistic.

But Darwinian theory also seeks to help us understand how purposive, and personalistic, life has come to be in an ultimately purposeless universe. In order to achieve this, it is essential that the theory observes the following principle:

Principle of Non-Circularity: *The theory must not presuppose what it seeks to explain. If, at some stage in evolution, Darwinian theory itself employs purposive explanations, the theory must explain how purposiveness of this type has come into existence at this stage of evolution without using the very notion of purposiveness that is being explained. And just the same applies to the personalistic.*

Thus, if parental care is employed to explain some evolutionary development, the existence of parental care must itself be explained without this explanation itself invoking parental care. Or, if an appeal is made to empathy in order to explain some evolutionary development, an explanation for the prior evolution of empathy must be given which does not itself employ empathy as an explanatory notion.

Here, now, are three increasingly substantial ways in which purposiveness is involved in the mechanisms of evolution.

1 Once it is acknowledged that all living things are purposive, or goal-pursuing in character, it is clear that purposive action, ways of life, and in particular *changes* in ways of life, may well play a crucial role in subsequent evolution. Whether a mutation has survival value or not may well depend on how the animal is living. Thus, a prior change in the way of life may substantially influence whether a subsequent mutation has survival value or not. But the prior change in way of life may be due to change of habitat, or climate change. It may be such that its explanation appeals to purposive action. Thus changes in ways of life that need to be understood in purposive terms, and have nothing to do with genetic changes, can have substantial consequences for subsequent evolution. For a dog-like creature running about on land, a mutation which turns legs into flippers would be a disaster. But if the creature is already swimming in rivers and catching fish (as a result of prior changes in purposive action that had nothing to do with genetic changes), this mutation would have immense survival value.

2 The purposive actions of animals can have a decisive impact on what has survival value for other animals, whether of the same or different species. Animals unconsciously *breed* other animals as an (unintended) consequence of their actions.

Sexual selection is an example. One sex – typically females – may prefer to mate with those who possess certain characteristic features, and as a result, those features will tend to become more prevalent and exaggerated in the population. Thus, peahens, choosing to mate with those peacocks with the most splendid tails, inadvertently partly cause peacocks to have absurdly splendid tails. In order to explain the peacock tails, it is necessary to refer to the purposive actions of peahens, amongst other factors.

Offspring selection is another example. Parents, in choosing preferentially to feed offspring with certain characteristics (allowing offspring who do not have these characteristics to die), may thereby be a part of the cause of these characteristics to become more prevalent in the population. Likewise, some offspring may be better at manipulating parents to feed them than others, thus increasing the likelihood of their survival, and the spread, through the population, of these genetically determined manipulative techniques.

Other examples are provided by the predator/prey relationship. The fox, in hunting rabbits, kills those rabbits not so good at evading capture and death. In this way the fox helps breed rabbits better and better at evading foxes. And likewise, rabbits, in escaping from those foxes not so good at hunting, help breed foxes better and better at hunting (since foxes not so good at hunting tend not to survive and reproduce). Similarly, birds breed caterpillars and butterflies good at camouflage, and the latter, in getting better and better at camouflage, may help breed more perceptive birds able to see through it. Yet again, plant-eating animals may help breed plants better able to resist the destructive attention of the animal in question. And the plant may help breed animals better able to eat the plant.

If we grant that plants engage in purposive action in the main by means of *growth*, then we may extend the idea that purposive action influences evolution from animals to plants. Plant growth creates soil, and creates shade, both of which have had consequences for subsequent evolution. Shade in tropical rain forests creates selective pressures for young plants, in a clearing where there is sunlight, to grow quickly so as not to fall into the shade of more quickly growing plants. It also creates selective pressures for plants that can do photosynthesis in shady conditions. Genes that generate these traits will be selected for. And of course those cells, early on in evolution, which, as a result of growth and photosynthesis, generated oxygen in the atmosphere, made possible all of animal life.

3 Once individual learning, and the capacity to imitate, have come into existence, evolution by cultural means[17] becomes possible – a kind of evolution that mimics Lamarckianism, in that acquired characteristics are (culturally) inherited. An individual learns to do something new, others imitate the action, and it becomes a persistent activity of the group, even though no genetic changes have taken place. Purposiveness has become a part of the mechanisms of evolution in a much more radical way. These mechanisms have themselves evolved in a much more substantial fashion.

Evolution by cultural means is best understood as the development of a new method of reproduction. The characteristic way of life is reproduced, in part by the standard genetic means of sex, embryological development, birth and growth, but also in part by means of imitation. Reproduction by imitation makes possible quasi-Lamarck-ian evolution. An acquired characteristic – a new kind of action conducive to survival, learnt by an individual – can be passed on, by imitative reproduction, to offspring (and of course to others and their offspring).

In order to construe evolution by cultural means as involving a new, or additional, method of reproduction, it is essential to interpret the theory of evolution as being about *life*, ways of living, and not as being just about bodies – let alone genes or DNA molecules. But this is, I maintain, the proper way to construe the theory in any case.

It is important to appreciate that evolution by cultural means, even though not itself involving genetic changes, may have an important impact on subsequent genetically determined changes. Consider again the dog-like creature hunting, on land. Suppose now that one individual, perhaps by accident, discovers that fish can be caught in a river, which are good to eat. Others learn by imitation. Many dogs spend time in the river hunting fish. Now a mutation appears making legs somewhat flipper-like. Given the new way of life, which has evolved culturally, flippers have great survival value, even though they would have been disastrous before the evolution by cultural means took place. The dog-like creature becomes a beaver-like creature, and evolution by cultural means led the way. It is a part of the reason for the evolution, from dog to beaver.

This kind of evolutionary sequence was first suggested by Conway Lloyd Morgan as long ago as 1896.[18] Unfortunately, James Mark Baldwin subsequently took credit for the idea, and at the same time distorted it, so that it became the view that new behaviour, brought about by evolution by cultural means, later becomes genetically determined – an invalid notion, quite different from the important original idea that changes in behaviour, brought about by learning and imitation, can transform what has survival value, and so have an impact on subsequent evolution.[19] Unfortunately, it is the distorted version of the idea, which degrades the crucial point that purposive action can play a crucial role in evolution, that has received all the attention, by Dennett and others, after it was dubbed "the Baldwin effect" by G.G. Simpson.[20] I have elsewhere given a more detailed account of the history of the idea, how it has been distorted to make nonsense of the vital role purposive action plays, and how the idea needs to be understood.[21]

Even though evolution by cultural means began long before human beings came into existence, it is above all with human beings that this form of evolution really comes into its own. As a species, we are very similar to others in all sorts of ways. We share 98.4 per cent of our genes with chimpanzees. But in one dramatic way we are utterly unique. We are the product of evolution by cultural means to an extent far, far beyond anything found in any other species. It is this which accounts for the multitude of differences between us and all other species. Above all, of course, language is a product of evolution by cultural means. And language then makes endless other things possible, inaccessible to all other species. Art, science, democracy, justice, elaborate technology, planned social progress, even wisdom: these only become possible once there is language.

Purposive action, and especially changes in purposive action (which need not be brought about by genetic changes), play a leading role in evolution. We need a new version of Darwinism which interprets the theory to be about *life*, not *genes*, which recognizes that all life is purposive in character, and which holds that the mechanisms of evolution themselves evolve so as to incorporate purposiveness in increasingly substantial ways until something like Lamarckian evolution emerges with the arrival of evolution by cultural means.

A part of the problem is that biologists have been so afraid of being tainted by Lamarckianism that they have failed to appreciate the vital role that purposive action plays in evolution. They have failed to appreciate that stretching to eat leaves high up in trees is a part of the reason for the giraffe's long neck, even though these actions did not *cause* necks to be longer in offspring. If giraffes had not been stretching to eat leaves, and there had not been leaves to eat, the mutations that brought about the long neck would have had no survival value, and offspring with longer necks would not have survived. What has survival value – what survives – may depend crucially on how the animal is living, and a change in the way of life, not caused by any genetic change, may have dramatic consequences for subsequent evolution.

This version of Darwinism leads to a profound shift in the whole way in which evolution needs to be understood. The actions of animals, our ancestors, for millions of years in the past, have had a crucial role to play in bringing about our existence. Evolution is not just blind chance and necessity. Our animal ancestors, striving to live, to eat, to avoid being eaten, to mate, to rear young, are a vital part of the reason for our existence. They did not, of course, intend us to exist. Nevertheless, without their striving, we would not be here. We owe them a debt of gratitude.

What bearing has all this on the basic theme of this chapter: natural science's need for philosophy?

I have sketched two approaches to Darwinian theory. On the one hand, there are versions of Darwinism which eliminate purpose from nature, or give it no significant role to play in evolution. On the other hand, there is the version of Darwinism indicated here, which interprets the theory to be about how and why purposive life has evolved in the natural world, and which holds that the mechanisms of evolution themselves evolve, giving an increasingly important role to purposiveness as they do so. From the standpoint of SE science, this difference may not seem to amount to much. Nothing of great empirical import seems to be at stake. But from the standpoint of how we see ourselves in the world, how we construe our relationship to other living things, the difference is profound. If evolutionary theory is to do justice to the problem of understanding how our human world is related to the rest of nature, and how we have come to be, it is essential that it includes some sustained discussion of philosophical issues of the kind I have indicated here.[22]

5 CONSCIOUSNESS

Consciousness poses one of the most profound and baffling mysteries of all. How can the brain create, or *be*, consciousness? How can neurological processes going on in our brain *be* our inner experiences, our awareness, our thoughts, perceptions, and feelings?

For a century or so, consciousness was banned from natural science. Deemed an unscientific, philosophical issue, it was judged to have no place in empirical science. Neuroscientists dared not mention consciousness for fear that it would be the death of their reputations. There can hardly be a more striking illustration of the absurdity of excluding philosophy from science.

Then, in 1984, Francis Crick, with a scientific reputation so exalted he could afford to risk its demise, published a speculative paper on the location of consciousness in the brain.[23] The dam broke.[24] Abruptly, the problem of consciousness became, not just a legitimate topic for neuroscience, but one which some neuroscientists began to think they might eventually succeed in solving without any need to call upon philosophy at all.

It is entirely reasonable to hold that neuroscience will contribute to the solution to the mystery of consciousness. But will it suffice to solve it, without recourse to philosophy?

The answer would seem to be: No. As long as we restrict ourselves to neuroscience, we will encounter neurons, synaptic junctions, glial cells, but never an inner experience, a feeling, a desire, a thought, a perception, as we experience these things. The argument we encountered in chapter 4 which shows that physics cannot predict experiential features applies to neuroscience as well. It is in principle impossible for neuroscience to predict, and therefore explain, experiential features of consciousness: what it is to have visual, auditory, olfactory, and tactile experiences, or experiences of pain, desire, happiness, misery, and so on.

Do we suppose, with Descartes, that consciousness is distinct from the brain, but in two-way interaction with it? Or do we suppose that consciousness is a non-physical aspect of brain processes which we can only get to know about by having the relevant brain processes occur in our own brain? Or do we suppose that consciousness is a kind of illusion, there being nothing in addition to the brain processes that occur in our brains? Is consciousness something that biological beings alone possess, or could robots be conscious as well? Are non-physical, experiential features exclusively associated with conscious brains, or do they exist in the world around us as well, as perceptual features: colours, sounds, smells, tactile qualities as we experience them? Is grass really green, as we see it; or is grass in reality devoid of any non-physical, perceptual quality of greenness, there being only the visual sensation of greenness in us when we look at grass; or is there not even that, the visual sensation of greenness being no more than a specific pattern of neurological processes that occur in our brain when we look at grass? In order to assess the relative merits and demerits of these views, it is necessary to take into account wide-ranging considerations and arguments of just the kind generally regarded as philosophical. Neuroscience cannot, of itself, decide these philosophical issues.[25]

We may, one day, be able to correlate neurological processes and inner experiences, so that we know precisely the kind of neurological processes that correlate with, or *are*, the inner experiences of different colours, different sounds, smells, tastes, and tactile qualities. We may know why we are able to make the discriminations that we do make, between different colours, different tones or pitches of sound. But there is still a mystery. Why should this specific pattern of neurological processes give rise to, or *be*, the visual experience of *greenness*, and that somewhat different pattern give rise to, or *be*, the visual experience of *redness*? Why specifically *greenness*, and not the sensation of some other colour, or of something else entirely: the sound of a trumpet, the sensation of being tickled with a feather? Why are colours, sounds, smells, tastes, tactile qualities, as we experience them, correlated with the specific neurological processes we may suppose they are correlated with, and not correlated in some other way? Here again, it seems impossible that neuroscience should be able, of itself, to solve this mystery – unless we adopt the view that these distinctive, non-physical inner sensations do not exist at all, there being nothing more than brain processes, and discriminatory responses. It may seem impossible, indeed, that there should be any solution to this mystery. Elsewhere I have suggested a possible solution. However, it is such that it takes us far beyond neuroscience, as traditionally conceived.[26]

Neuroscience will never, of course, do justice to the miraculous richness of consciousness, its individuality and variety, its capacity to encompass inner worlds of feeling, thought, memory, and imagination, and at the same time the outer universe around us and all that it contains. But then philosophy can hardly do justice to the richness of consciousness either. It can only be hinted at by poetry, literature, music, art.

In arguing that to do justice to the problem of consciousness we need to bring together science and philosophy, I am, to a considerable extent, pushing hard at an already-open door. Here is one major problem tackled by both scientists and philosophers, many of whom collaborate with one another. There are the Towards a Science of Consciousness conferences, attended by scientists, philosophers, and others, which have been held every other year since 1994 at the University of Arizona, and at some other site on alternate years. There is the Association for the Scientific Study of Consciousness, also formed in 1994, which organizes conferences and brings together scientists and philosophers. And there are journals that publish work by neuroscientists, philosophers, and others such as *The Journal of Consciousness Studies* and *Consciousness and Cognition*. Leading figures in the fields of neuroscience and philosophy discuss each other's work. For many, in this field of consciousness studies, natural philosophy already exists!

6 FREE WILL

A famous experiment conducted by Benjamin Libet has been taken by some to establish that free will is an illusion.[27] Subjects of the experiment were asked to move their hand at an arbitrary moment decided by them, and to say when they made the decision, determined by noticing the position of a dot going round a clock face. Monitoring of the electrical activity of the subjects' brains established that the Readiness Potential – a pattern of electrical activity known to precede voluntary action – occurred some tenths of a second *before* the conscious decision to move the hand. This has been taken to demonstrate the illusory nature of free will, since it is the brain that causes both the hand to move and the subsequent conscious "decision." For free will, we would require that the conscious decision causes the Readiness Potential to occur subsequently in the brain which in turn causes the hand to move.

But the conclusion does not follow. We may interpret what the subject of Libet's experiment does in the following way. As one takes part in the experiment, one decides, consciously and freely, to put one's brain into a very special state such that an arbitrary impulse to move one's hand – in effect arbitrary fluctuations in brain activity of a sufficient size – leads to one's hand moving. That the decision to move one's hand now, at this arbitrarily chosen moment, is not free does not undermine the reality of free will in general, nor the freedom of one's decision to take part in the experiment, and put one's brain into the special state required. The free act, in other words, is to put one's brain into a special state so that some future random fluctuation of brain activity grows sufficiently to lead to one's hand moving. That is the free act, not the act of moving one's hand at the instant at which it occurs.

Even if this objection is not valid, there are plenty of others that have been made to the claim that Libet has shown that free will is an illusion.[28] And even Libet himself did not hold that his experiment demonstrated the illusory character of free will![29] In order to understand in what sense, and to what extent, we have free will we need both neuroscience and philosophy. In this field, as in the related field of consciousness, many neuroscientists, psychologists, artificial intelligence experts, and philosophers engage with each other's work. Here too, for many, natural philosophy already exists.

Problems of consciousness and free will cannot be solved by science, or by philosophy – or by the two working in isolation from one another. In order to solve these problems, we need both working together; we need natural philosophy. Both problems, it should be noted, are key components of our fundamental problem, formulated in section 3 (page 191).

7 EDUCATION

Young mammals learn by means of play. Kittens and cubs engage in mock combat and hunting, and lambs and fawns leap and prance, thus learning how to escape predators when adult. We are mammals too. Children, out of school, play, and learn by means of play. Almost certainly, our ancestors learned how to become adults by means of playful imitation of adult activities during the hundreds of thousands of years we evolved into human beings. It is very likely that our psychological makeup is such that we are especially well-fitted to learn by means of playful activity.

This has implications for all education. It means that successful learning is most likely to occur in schools and universities when elements of playful activity can be brought into the classroom, the lecture hall, the seminar and laboratory.

As it happens, much science education is based on the idea that, in order to learn science, you need to *do* it. Those learning science do observational and experimental work in the laboratory, and tackle theoretical problems: in a sense, they play at doing science, although the delight of play may not always be present!

But there is another mammalian instinct that science education also needs to call upon and encourage: inquisitiveness. Young children display obsessive curiosity. Why? Why? Why? they endlessly ask. But then formal education begins, and instinctive childish curiosity, instead of being given every encouragement to develop and flourish, tends to be crushed by an avalanche of answers to questions never asked, never discussed. The provision of answers so vastly outstrips questions asked, that the impulse to ask questions begins to wither and die. But without curiosity, the fundamental impulse behind science has been lost.

On the other hand, there is so much to be learned. Giving children and students the opportunity to ask questions and attempt to find answers would, it may seem, take up much too much time – especially teacher and lecturer time. Before exploration of a problem can be fruitful, the student must first acquire relevant background knowledge. A PhD must be obtained. And so scientific results are doled out, to be learned up and regurgitated in examinations, bereft of any discussion of the *problems* the scientific results were developed to solve in the first place. Education, when conducted in such a fashion, not only kills curiosity; it degenerates into something close to indoctrination. The student is not in a position to assess the relevance, the acceptability, of what she is being taught.

What is needed is a *problem-oriented* approach to scientific education – an approach which includes courses which take a genuine, even unsolved scientific problem, and set about attempting to solve it. Of course students will not possess the necessary background knowledge, skills, and expertise required even to understand the nature of the problem, let along make a contribution towards solving it. It will be the task of the course to enable students to go some way towards acquiring such background knowledge, skills, and expertise, incidentally as it were, as they struggle to comprehend the problem, consider and assess possible approaches to the solution. Science education conducted as the exploration of problems, if possible in a passionately playful fashion, could engender real insight into the nature of scientific research, and at the same time cause curiosity to flourish and not die.

Science education also needs to be conducted in such a way that the student is given every encouragement to follow up her own questions – to transform feelings of stupidity and bafflement into articulated questions, which are then followed up as pieces of research, topics for essays. And it is especially at this point that science is likely to become natural philosophy. Questions that haunt students are not likely to be neatly confined to any specific scientific discipline. It would be surprising if students doing physics or chemistry did not wonder, at times, about the relationship between the physical universe, the material world, as depicted by science, and the world as we ordinarily perceive it to be. Students doing biology are likely to wonder about the implications of Darwinian evolution and genetics for free will, for the meaning and value of human life. A course in a natural science, conducted properly, ought at some point to make some kind of contact with our fundamental problem – the problem of all of thought and life. There ought to be some discussion of how the problems of the specific science are related to more fundamental problems, including the most fundamental problem of all.

Science education needs to be done within the framework of natural philosophy.

8 METHODOLOGICAL VALUE OF NATURAL SCIENCE

Natural science is generally recognized to be of value in two ways: *intellectually*, in enhancing our knowledge and understanding of the world around us, and *practically*, in enabling us to achieve other goals of value such as health and prosperity by means of the application of knowledge and technology. There is, however, a third way in which natural science is, potentially, of value, almost universally overlooked and ignored. Science has great potential *methodological* value.

Natural science stands out from most other human endeavours in that it has made extraordinary progress across generations. This has been made possible by the exploitation of scientific method – specifically aim-oriented empiricism. At once the question arises: can AOE be generalized so that it becomes fruitfully applicable to other human endeavours with problematic aims that seek to make progress? Can a generalized version of AOE be exploited fruitfully in such fields as politics, industry, agriculture, economics, the law, the media, medicine? Could it be exploited by the general human endeavour to make progress towards as good a world as possible? Could it even be exploited in personal life? Might we be able to get appropriately generalized versions of AOE into personal, social, and global life, so that, in life, we begin to make progress towards happier, more peaceful, just, and wiser ways of living in a way that is, at least to some extent, comparable to the intellectual progress achieved by science? Can we, in brief, learn from scientific progress how to achieve social progress towards a better world?

It is all too apparent that basic aims in life – personal, social, institutional, global – are indeed often profoundly problematic. All personal aims in life are rendered problematic by the elementary fact that life ends in death. We pursue industrial and economic progress and, without intending it, bring about global warming, a threat to our future. We pursue health, and engender explosive population growth. We develop modern agriculture and, as a consequence, destroy natural habitats and bring about the rapid extinction of species. We seek national security, and provoke war. We strive to create a better world and the outcome is untold suffering and death – so much so that the very idea of attempting to create a better world has become suspect. Basic aims in life are often problematic, and we seem to be incapable of improving such aims when their undesirable or unrealizable character becomes apparent.

We do urgently need to learn from aim-oriented empiricist science how to improve problematic aims in life, if it is at all possible. But is it possible? In chapter 8 I will argue that it is.

Even standard empiricist science has important methodological implications for personal and social life. But s e science offers no help with *improving* problematic aims. For that, we need a o e science. Aim-oriented empiricism can be generalized to form *aim-oriented rationality*, a hierarchical meta-methodology designed to help us improve the aims and methods of all worthwhile human endeavours with problematic aims: politics, industry, agriculture, economic activity, finance, medicine, the law, the media, international relations, education, even personal life. We urgently need to get into all these areas of social life the progress-achieving methods of aim-oriented rationality. If we succeed, the outcome would be a world in which we make progress towards that which is genuinely of value, a state of affairs as good as possible, with something of the progressive success across generations so far achieved almost exclusively by science. From scientific progress we would have learned how to make social progress towards a better, wiser world.

But if humanity is to learn how to put aim-oriented rationality into practice in life, so as to realize what is of value and make progress towards a wiser world, it is essential that we reform our institutions of learning, our schools and universities, so that they become devoted to the task. In chapter 8 I argue that we need to bring about a revolution in the social sciences and humanities, so that their basic task becomes, first, to promote cooperatively rational tackling of problems of living in the great world beyond the university and, second, to help humanity discover how to get aim-oriented rationality into the fabric of personal and social life – into industry, politics, economics, the law, the media, and so on. Social science emerges, not primarily as *science* devoted to improving knowledge about social phenomena, but rather as social *methodology*, or social *philosophy*, devoted to helping humanity learn from, and exploit, the methodological lessons of natural philosophy in order to make social progress towards as good a world as possible. More generally, we need a revolution in academic inquiry so that the basic intellectual aim becomes to seek and promote *wisdom* – wisdom being construed to be the capacity and active endeavour to realize (apprehend and create) what is of value in life, for oneself and others, wisdom thus including knowledge, understanding, and technological know-how, but much else besides.[30]

7

Why Philosophy Needs Science

DO ALL BRANCHES OF PHILOSOPHY
NEED SCIENCE?

The idea that science needs philosophy is bound to be controversial.
Most scientists (until they have read this book!) will reject it. But the
reverse idea that philosophy needs science is hardly controversial at
all. Scientists will agree, a few philosophers may disagree on the
grounds that their particular branch of philosophy has no need of
science, but most philosophers will probably agree. So, in this chapter I will be brief.

Philosophy, properly conceived, has two basic interrelated tasks.
The first is the one emphasized at the beginning of chapter 3: it is to
tackle, imaginatively and critically, our most urgent, fundamental
problems – especially our most fundamental problem of all:

*How can our human world, and the world of sentient life more
generally, imbued with perceptual qualities, consciousness, free
will, meaning, and value, exist and best flourish embedded as it
is in the physical universe?*

This problem only arises, in the form stated here, because of the
view of the world ushered in with modern science. It is modern science that provokes modern philosophy, from Descartes onwards.
Natural science creates the problems philosophy seeks to solve.[1]
Furthermore, in order to tackle the more detailed philosophical versions of this problem, having to do with perception, perceptual qualities, consciousness, and free will, one can hardly proceed without

taking the findings of science into account. Problems of epistemology, metaphysics, philosophy of science, philosophy of mind, philosophy of language: all need input from natural science – from physics, cosmology, chemistry, biology, evolutionary theory, neuroscience. Even the philosophy of language should be put into an evolutionary context so that human communication by means of language may be understood to be a development of animal communication.[2]

But what of questions about what is of value? What of political philosophy, moral philosophy, aesthetics? These branches of philosophy all concern questions of value. Science, it may seem, has major and very alarming implications for questions about what is of value. Suppose we take the view that ultimately there is just physics. The world is made up exclusively of fundamental physical entities – electrons, quarks, and so on – interacting in accordance with precise (possibly probabilistic) physical law. All branches of science other than physics can in principle (not in practice) be reduced to physics. All of human life, our entire world, art, music, literature, cathedrals, friendship, love, democracy, justice, is just physics. Free will is an illusion. Consciousness is an illusion – if it is construed to be anything more than physical processes going on in brains. The entire world as we experience it is a kind of illusion. There is just physics. If this is what science tells us about the world, the implications for questions about what is of value seem dire indeed. How can anything be of value if everything is just physics, and we are no more than soft robots moving about and making noises in accordance with the precise laws of physics? Without anything being of value, branches of philosophy concerned with questions of value hardly make sense.

Simply in order to exist, then, political philosophy, ethics, and aesthetics must combat the above physicalist view as to what it is that science tells us about the nature of the universe. At the very least, these branches of philosophy need to explain how that which is of value can exist even though everything is, ultimately, just physics. How are moral and aesthetic qualities possible if everything is physics? Do arguments concerning rival political systems make sense if everything is governed by physical law?[3]

Granted that the above extreme physicalist view is to be rejected, major questions arise about what is wrong with the view, and what is to replace it. Whatever view is adopted about what it is that science tells us about the world, branches of philosophy concerned with questions of value can hardly just turn their backs on science and ignore its findings. Our moral, political, and artistic life takes place in the real world, and it is science that tells us what sort of world this is. What it tells us cannot just be ignored. Does what science tells us imply that all values are purely subjective? If so, does not this imply a kind of value, or moral nihilism, any view about what is good and bad being as valid as any other view? Can a case be made out for especially prizing generosity, kindness, friendship, justice, democracy, peace, if all values are subjective? Or can we make sense of the idea that value qualities exist in the real world – some people objectively possessing moral qualities such as friendliness or courage, some works of art being objectively beautiful, graceful, passionate, profound? Is our world imbued with value features, or does science prohibit the existence of such features altogether?[4] These questions go to the heart of political philosophy, ethics, and aesthetics: even when science is not explicitly mentioned, the scientific outlook on the world is nevertheless powerfully present in the background.

So far I have considered the tendency of science to call into question the very possibility of there being anything of value, or to place severe constraints, of a rather general character, on views about the nature of what is of value. But in addition, there is always the possibility that science will make quite specific findings that have much more specific implications for political and moral philosophy. Genes may be discovered that predispose those who possess them to specific kinds of actions or character traits: violence, criminality, impulsiveness, psychopathic lack of empathy with others, schizophrenia, alcoholism. Can those who posses such genes be held responsible for crimes or immoral acts they may perform? Again, brain scans may reveal that some individuals are especially prone, because of the structure of their brains, to commit criminal acts of violence. Can such individuals be held responsible for what they do?

Implications of science for political philosophy, for ethics, and aesthetics may by no means always be negative in character. Do evolutionary, archaeological, and anthropological findings about the mode of life of hunting and gathering tribes for thousands of years in prehistory have implications for politics today? Do we need, for example, to take seriously the idea that we have an inbuilt disposition to live in small communities in which everyone knows everyone else, vast, impersonal societies of the kind most of us live in today doing a kind of violence to our instinctive needs?[5] Should we try to transform modern societies so that they manage somehow to respond to our inherent need to belong to a small community? Again, evolutionary theory may have positive things to teach us about the origins and nature of morality. Is parental care in mammals, for example, a major source of our human, moral concern for the welfare of others? Might mammalian dispositions for play and for curiosity have things to teach us about human learning and education (as I suggested in chapter 6)?

I conclude that, as far as the first task of philosophy is concerned, all branches of philosophy need to attend to science.

PHILOSOPHY AND AIM-ORIENTED RATIONALITY

That brings me to the second basic task of philosophy. This is to discover what the aims and methods of diverse worthwhile human endeavours ought to be: science, politics, economics, law, education, art, personal life. Or, put in a slightly broader way, the task is to articulate, and to try to solve, rather general problems that arise in connection with these diverse endeavours. It is philosophy in this sense that we appeal to when we ask, of a theatre director perhaps, "What is your philosophy of theatre?"; or when we ask of anyone, "What is your philosophy of life?"

Philosophy in these two senses, given these two basic tasks, are closely interrelated, as I sought to make clear at the beginning of chapter 3. The answer we give to the fundamental problem, whether implicit or explicit, will inevitably have implications for our personal and social aims and ideals in life; and in adopting basic aims and ideals in life we thereby implicitly answer, in practice, the question, "What is of value in the real world?" – an answer that will, of course, be constrained and conditioned in multiple ways by the particular circumstances of our life.

This second conception of philosophy – *the philosophy of life endeavours*, as we may call it – needs to pay attention to science too, for all the reasons given above. In seeking to discover what our aims and ideals ought to be in life it can hardly be sensible just to ignore what it is that science tells us about the world, ourselves, and our history.

There is, however, an additional way in which science, or natural philosophy rather, has important implications for the philosophy of life endeavours. It has important *methodological* implications. This is a point I made briefly in the last section of the last chapter.

In the twentieth century, analytic philosophy recognized that many human pursuits legitimately give rise to associated philosophical disciplines. Thus science has philosophy of science associated with it; politics has political philosophy, law has legal philosophy, the arts have aesthetics, education has the philosophy of education, personal and social life has moral philosophy. These associated philosophical disciplines were all construed rigorously to be *meta-disciplines* in a quite specific, non-interactive sense. The philosophical discipline studies and seeks to understand the associated human endeavour but *does not itself seek to modify, or contribute to, the endeavour itself in any way*. The arrow of influence goes in one direction only, from the endeavour itself to the philosophy of the endeavour. Nothing goes from the philosophy to the endeavour itself.[6] From the outset, philosophy embraces sterility, and renounces all social impact! Thus, philosophy of science seeks to depict the aims and methods of science; it seeks to justify the methods of science, and seeks to improve knowledge and understanding of science, but does not seek, in any way at all, to influence science itself or make a contribution to science. Indeed, how could it? Contributions to philosophy of science are not empirically testable (in any straightforward way) and so do not qualify as potential contributions to science – according to all versions of standard empiricism, at least. Again, a sharp distinction is made between morality and ethics or moral philosophy. Ethics seeks to improve understanding of moral ideas, concepts, and arguments but does not seek to contribute to morality itself. And likewise, political philosophy does not seek to contribute to politics, and aesthetics seeks to improve understanding of the arts but does not attempt to contribute to them.[7]

But this self-inflicted impotency is a disaster. It seemed necessary in order to preserve the objectivity, the intellectual integrity, the independence, of philosophy. How can political philosophy retain its objectivity, and contribute to knowledge, if it degenerates into merely contributing to politics itself, thus becoming a part of politics? How can moral philosophy contribute to knowledge if it seeks merely to get across moral ideas, rather than ideas about moral ideas? And so on.

What is wrong with this self-imposed impotency view becomes startlingly apparent when one considers philosophy of science. If standard empiricism (s e) were correct, and the basic intellectual aim of science is the fixed one of truth, the impotency view might just about be defensible. For then one could argue that science does indeed have a fixed aim, and fixed methods, and the task of philosophy of science is to explicate what these methods are, and how they are to be justified, without in any way affecting or contributing to science itself. But s e is untenable. In chapters 5 and 6, we have seen that the aims of natural science taken as a whole, and the aims of individual disciplines of natural science as well, are profoundly problematic for all sorts of reasons. In order to be pursued rigorously – in such a way as to give the best chances of success – science must put aim-oriented empiricism (a o e) into practice, thus actively seeking to improve aims and methods as an integral part of the scientific endeavour itself. Philosophy of science, in seeking to articulate and justify aims and methods, must be an integral part of science itself, contributing to science, with arrows of influence going from science to philosophy of science, and vice versa too. This is, of course, the central argument for the need to recreate natural philosophy. Intellectual rigour demands that philosophy of science be an integral part of science itself.

At once the stark irony of the orthodox, impotency view of the philosophy of science becomes all too apparent. Philosophy of science seeks to depict and understand the rationality of science. This is its basic task. But *in dissociating itself from science, and adopting the impotency view of itself, the philosophy of science thereby helps to undermine the very thing it seeks to understand.* Not only does the orthodox view condemn philosophy of science to impotency. It serves to undermine the rationality of science, the very thing the philosophy of science seeks to comprehend. Only when science and the philosophy of science join together in creating a o e science – thus recreating natural philosophy – can we have a genuinely rigorous kind of science.

But this argument is quite general, as I sought to indicate at the end of the last chapter, and as I shall argue in a bit more detail in the next chapter. Whenever any endeavour has problematic basic aims – as most worthwhile endeavours do – we need to try to improve aims and methods as we pursue the endeavour. At the very least, this means that, as an integral, influential part of the endeavour itself, some attention needs to be given to the tasks of articulating *problems* associated with existing aims, and imaginatively exploring and critically assessing possible modifications of existing aims in an attempt to discover improved aims free of current problems, and improved associated methods. We need to try to discover improved aims and methods (as an integral part of the endeavour itself) in order to give ourselves the best chances of success. We need, in other words, to engage in the *philosophy* of the endeavour, in such a way that it forms an integral, influential part of the endeavour itself. And we need to do this in order to be *rigorous* or *rational*, and in order to give ourselves the best chances of achieving that which is genuinely of value.

But it is just this that the orthodox, impotency view of the philosophy of this or that endeavour (politics, education, or whatever it may be) does not allow. According to this view, the *philosophy* of endeavour X must not itself influence X, or be a contribution to X. This orthodox conception of what the philosophy of X should be can only serve to sabotage the success of X in that it will tend to stifle just the kind of two-way interactive philosophy of X that those concerned with X need to do, to try to improve problematic aims and associated methods.

And as for the point that the orthodox, non-interactive view undermines rationality, this can be demonstrated quite simply as follows.

Rationality, as the term is being used here, assumes that there is some probably rather ill-defined set of methods, rules, or strategies which, if put into practice, give us our best chances, when we try to solve problems or realize problematic aims, of achieving success (other things being equal). Any set of methods which takes us systematically astray is defective, and cannot embody rationality.

Consider now rationality methods, M, which fail to help improve problematic aims. Whenever basic aims are a bad choice, because they are undesirable, unrealizable, or both, the more "rationally" we pursue these aims in terms of the conception of rationality embodied in M, the worse off we shall be. But basic aims often are bad choices. This means that any set of methods, such as M, which fail to help us improve problematic aims, will systematically lead us astray, and thus cannot embody rationality. Genuinely rational methods must be such that they help us improve problematic aims. For that, in turn, we need to put what I have called two-way interactive philosophy into practice. The orthodox, impotent view of "the philosophy of X" actually serves to undermine the rationality of X.

What bearing has all this on the question of whether philosophy needs science? Well, here is one way in which philosophy has something of profound importance to learn from science – or rather, from natural philosophy. Just as successful natural philosophy requires there to be two-way interaction between science and philosophy of

science so that problematic aims of science (and associated methods) may be *improved* as science proceeds (there being something
like positive feedback between improving knowledge and improving
knowledge about how to improve knowledge), so too does this kind
of two-way interaction need to take place between *any* worthwhile
endeavour with problematic aims, and its philosophy. It is just this
that aim-oriented rationality facilitates (aim-oriented rationality
being a generalization of aim-oriented empiricism).

HOW SCIENCE AND PHILOSOPHY
NEED TO CHANGE

I conclude this brief chapter with a brief comment about how science
and philosophy need to change if the two are to come together to
recreate natural philosophy. By far the most substantial change needs
to come from philosophy.

Science needs to change in order to put explicitly into practice
what is at present implicit: aim-oriented empiricism. This involves
acknowledging that the intellectual aims of science are profoundly
problematic, in that they have substantial, highly problematic metaphysical, value, and political assumptions inherent in them. The
aims of science need sustained, imaginative, and critical attention as
an integral part of science to give us the best hope that they can
thereby be *improved*. Instead of two, at least three domains of scientific discussion need to be recognized: (1) evidence; (2) theory; and
(3) aims – the latter being open to both scientists and non-scientists.
Putting aim-oriented empiricism explicitly into scientific practice
has substantial implications for the intellectual and institutional
character of science, having to do with research, publications, education, and the way science is related to society. Nevertheless, there
is a sense in which all this involves making explicit what is already
implicit in science.

Far more radical changes are required from philosophy. The whole
character of philosophy needs to change. Academic philosophy needs
to be and do what I indicated at the beginning of chapter 3. It must
cease to be a specialized discipline alongside other disciplines,
obsessed with its own esoteric, specialized puzzles. It must become
again what it once was, that endeavour which seeks to keep alive
awareness of our most urgent fundamental problems – above all, our
most fundamental problem of all, formulated at the beginning of this

chapter. Academic philosophy needs to take up the vital and neglected task of counteracting the evils of rampant specialization. Its task is to encourage everyone to engage in a bit of pondering, now and again, about our global problems – global intellectually, and global in the sense of concerning humanity as a whole and planet earth. We all need ponder, from time to time, how problems we encounter in our lives, intellectual and practical, connect up with fundamental global problems that confront us all. And, related to these tasks, philosophy also needs to try to help humanity discover how to put aim-oriented rationality into practice in our personal, social, and global lives, so that we may learn how to improve problematic aims as we live.

8

Implications of Natural Philosophy for the Problems of Civilization

In this final chapter I spell out what are, in my view, the immensely important but so far almost wholly overlooked *methodological* implications of natural philosophy for social, political, economic, and even personal life. I have already touched briefly on this matter in chapters 6 and 7. But much more needs to be said. The methodological implications of natural philosophy are profound and revolutionary. They lead, potentially, to a new kind of academic enterprise – *wisdom-inquiry* – capable of enabling us to learn how to make progress towards as good, wise, and civilized a world as possible.

TWO GREAT PROBLEMS OF LEARNING

Humanity faces two great problems of learning: learning about the nature of the universe and our place in it, and learning how to create as good, as wise, as civilized a world as possible.

We cracked the first problem in the seventeenth century, with the birth of modern science – the birth, that is, of natural philosophy. We discovered a *method* for progressively improving knowledge and understanding of the natural world, the famous empirical method of science – even if we have not succeeded, until now, in getting entirely clear as to what this method consists in. There is of course much that we still do not know and understand, three or four centuries after the birth of natural philosophy; nevertheless, during this time, science has immensely increased our knowledge and understanding, at an ever-accelerating rate. And with this unprecedented increase in scientific knowledge and understanding has come a cascade of technological discoveries and developments which have transformed the human condition. It is this that has made the modern world possible, so different in a multitude of ways from the world experienced by people in Europe or North America only one or two centuries ago.

But it is much less certain that the second great problem of learning has been cracked. Many, indeed, doubt that it can be solved at all. The record of the past hundred years or so is not exactly encouraging when one takes into account the millions slaughtered in countless wars, the millions killed in death camps, the all too many totalitarian regimes, the hundreds of millions living today in conditions of abject poverty in Africa, Asia, and South America, the annihilation of languages, cultures, and traditional ways of life, the destruction of natural habitats and the rapid extinction of species, the impending disasters of climate change.

One might conclude that we are growing, not more civilized, but more barbaric. This is, however, to draw the wrong conclusion from history. All our distinctively twentieth- and twenty-first-century disasters have one underlying cause: we have solved the first great problem of learning without *also* having solved the second problem. It is this that menaces the future of humanity.

With rapidly increasing scientific knowledge comes rapidly increasing technological know-how, which brings with it an immense increase in the power to act. In the absence of a solution to the second great problem of learning, the increase in the power to act may have good consequences, but will as often as not have all sorts of harmful consequences, whether intended or not.

Just this is an all too apparent feature of our world. Science and technology have been used in endless ways for human benefit, but have also been used to wreak havoc, whether intentionally, in war, or unintentionally, in long-term environmental damage – a consequence of growth of population, industry, and agriculture, made possible by growth of technology. As long as humanity's power to act was limited, lack of wisdom, of enlightenment, did not matter too much: humanity lacked the means to inflict too much damage on itself or the planet.[1] But with the immense increase in powers to act that some of us have achieved in the last century or so, our powers to destroy have become unprecedented and terrifying: *wisdom has become, not a personal luxury, but a global necessity*. All our distinctively twenty-first-century global problems, to repeat, have arisen because we have solved the first great problem of learning without also solving the second problem. Solving the first great problem of learning without also solving the second is bound to put humanity into a situation of great danger, and has in fact done just that.

Some see modern science and technology as the great hope for the future of humanity. Others see them as a menace, the root cause of our current global problems. Both customary attitudes fail to get matters sharply into focus. What we suffer from is our success in solving the first great problem of learning plus our failure to solve the second problem. It is the extraordinary intellectual success of modern science and technology combined with our failure to solve the second great problem of learning that puts us into a situation of unprecedented danger, and is responsible for the genesis of our global problems and our current incapacity to resolve them. Now that some of us possess the immense powers to act, bequeathed to us by science and technology, it has become a matter of supreme urgency that we learn how to make progress towards as good, as wise, a world as possible.

But is this possible? Can it be done? Moral and political philosophers have struggled with the problem for millennia, and have not come up with anything very helpful. Many hold it to be impossible.[2]

There is, however, one approach to the problem that is, these days, almost entirely overlooked. We need to learn from our solution to the first great problem of learning how to solve the second one. We need, that is, to generalize the progress-achieving methods of science – or of natural philosophy rather – so that they become fruitfully applicable to the immense task of making social progress towards a wiser, more civilized world. And then we need to apply these generalized, progress-achieving methods to social life – to the unending task of creating a better, wiser world.

THE ENLIGHTENMENT

The idea of learning from the solution to the first great problem of learning how to solve the second problem has not been entirely neglected. It goes back to the Enlightenment of the eighteenth century. Indeed, this was the basic idea of the *philosophes* of the Enlightenment – Voltaire, Diderot, Condorcet, et al. – to learn from progress in natural philosophy how to achieve social progress towards world enlightenment.[3]

The best of the *philosophes* did what they could to put this immensely important idea into practice, in their lives. They fought dictatorial power, superstition, and injustice with weapons no more lethal than those of argument and wit. They gave their support to the virtues of tolerance, openness to doubt, readiness to learn from criticism and from experience. Courageously and energetically they laboured to promote rationality in personal and social life.[4]

Unfortunately, in developing the Enlightenment idea, the *philosophes* made a monumental intellectual blunder. They developed the Enlightenment programme in a seriously defective form, and it is this immensely influential, defective version of the programme, inherited from the eighteenth century, which may be called the "traditional" Enlightenment, that is built into early twenty-first-century institutions of inquiry. Our current traditions and institutions of learning, when judged from the standpoint of helping us learn how to become more enlightened, are defective and irrational in a wholesale and structural way, and it is this which, in the long term, sabotages our efforts to create a more civilized world, and prevents us from avoiding the kind of horrors we have been exposed to during the last century and this one – wars, poverty, environmental degradation, global warming – horrors that threaten to become so much more devastating in the decades to come.

Academia as it exists today is, then, the outcome of a botched attempt to learn from the solution to the first great problem of learning how to go about solving the second problem. What we need to do today is put right the structural defects in academia that we have inherited from the Enlightenment, so that academia becomes what it was intended to be, a key part of the solution to the second great problem of learning – exploiting what can be learned from our solution to the first problem.

Our task is not to dream up, out of the blue, a miracle cure for the disasters that threaten to engulf our world. It is the quite different one of correcting blunders long built into the intellectual/institutional structure of our universities which, all along, were intended to help humanity learn how to make progress towards as good a world as possible. There is a clear, cogent recipe available as to what we need to do to get universities to become what they were intended to be: the institutions of learning of humanity, rationally designed and devoted to helping us create a better, wiser world, actively engaged in that task, and capable of enabling us to discover how to do it. What we need to do is correct Enlightenment blunders, so that the basic, profound idea of learning from scientific progress how to achieve social progress may at last come to fruition.

The *philosophes* of the eighteenth century assumed, understandably enough, that the proper way to implement the basic Enlightenment idea was to develop social science alongside natural science.

Francis Bacon had already stressed the importance of improving knowledge of the natural world in order to achieve social progress.[5] The *philosophes* generalized this, holding that it is just as important to improve knowledge of the social world. Thus the *philosophes* set about creating the social sciences: history, anthropology, political economy, psychology, sociology.

This had an immense impact. Throughout the nineteenth century the diverse social sciences were developed, often by non-academics, in accordance with the Enlightenment idea.[6] Gradually, universities took notice of these developments until, by the mid-twentieth century, all the diverse branches of the social sciences, as conceived of by the Enlightenment, were built into the institutional structure of universities as recognized academic disciplines.

But, from the standpoint of creating a kind of inquiry designed to help humanity learn how to become civilized, all this amounts to a series of monumental mistakes.

In order to implement properly the basic Enlightenment idea of learning from scientific progress how to achieve social progress towards a civilized world, it is essential to get the following three things right.

1   The progress-achieving methods of science need to be correctly identified.
2   These methods need to be correctly generalized so that they become fruitfully applicable to any human endeavour, whatever its aims may be, and not just applicable to the endeavour of improving knowledge.
3   The correctly generalized progress-achieving methods then need to be exploited correctly in the great human endeavour of trying to make social progress towards an enlightened, civilized world.

Unfortunately, the *philosophes* of the Enlightenment got all three points disastrously wrong. They failed to capture correctly the progress-achieving methods of natural philosophy; they failed to generalize these methods properly; and, most disastrously of all, they failed to apply them properly so that humanity might learn how to become civilized by rational means. That the *philosophes* made these blunders in the eighteenth century is forgivable; what is unforgivable is that these blunders still remain unrecognized and uncorrected today, over two centuries later. Instead of correcting the blunders, we have allowed our institutions of learning to be shaped by them as they have developed throughout the nineteenth and twentieth centuries, so that now the blunders are an all-pervasive feature of our world.

The Enlightenment, and what it led to, has long been criticized: by the Romantic movement, by what Isaiah Berlin has called "the counter-Enlightenment,"[7] and more recently by the Frankfurt School, by postmodernists, and others.[8] The objection to the traditional Enlightenment I am expressing here is substantially different. In particular, it is the very opposite of all those anti-rationalist, romantic, and postmodernist criticisms which object to the way the Enlightenment gives far too great an importance to natural science and to scientific rationality. What I claim to be wrong with the traditional Enlightenment, and the kind of academic inquiry we now possess derived from it, is not too much "scientific rationality," but, on the contrary, not enough. It is the glaring, wholesale *irrationality* of contemporary academic inquiry, when judged from the standpoint of helping humanity learn how to become more civilized, that is the problem.

The traditional Enlightenment leads to a kind of academic inquiry which takes *knowledge* to be the basic intellectual aim. First, knowledge (about the natural and social worlds) needs to be acquired; then it can be applied to help solve social problems. I shall call this kind of academic enterprise *knowledge-inquiry*. Standard empiricist natural science is at its core. But, even though knowledge-inquiry dominates today in all universities around the world, it is nevertheless damagingly irrational. Correct the rationality defects of knowledge-inquiry – the three blunders of the traditional Enlightenment – and a new, more rigorous and more humanly beneficial kind of academic enterprise emerges, which I shall call *wisdom-inquiry*. Wisdom-inquiry includes aim-oriented empiricist natural philosophy.

THE "NEW" ENLIGHTENMENT

What exactly are the three blunders of the traditional Enlightenment, as embodied in academic inquiry today, giving rise to knowledge-inquiry – and what needs to be done to put them right? Let us take the three blunders in turn.

The *first* blunder concerns the nature of the progress-achieving methods of science. It has been spelled out in great detail in this book. It has been generally assumed – by scientists, by historians and philosophers of science, by almost everyone from the eighteenth century on – that science makes progress because it accepts and rejects theories solely in the light of evidence. Science progresses because it puts standard empiricism into practice. But standard empiricism is untenable. Science – or natural philosophy – has made progress because something somewhat resembling aim-oriented empiricism has been put into practice despite the conviction of the scientific community that science should conform to the edicts of standard empiricism. It is the implementation of the hierarchical meta-methodology of aim-oriented empiricism which gives us the greatest hope of rapidly improving our scientific knowledge and understanding of the world.

But what of the *second* blunder? The task, here, is to generalize the progress-achieving methods of natural philosophy appropriately so that they become progress-achieving methods that are, potentially, fruitfully applicable to *any* problematic, worthwhile human endeavour. The task, in other words, is to generalize scientific rationality so that it becomes rationality per se, helping us to achieve what is of value whatever we may be doing.

Needless to say, scientists and philosophers, having failed to specify the methods of science properly, have also failed to arrive at the proper generalization of these methods. The best attempt known to me is that made by Karl Popper. According to Popper, as I have already remarked, science makes progress because it puts into practice the method of proposing theories as conjectures, which are then subjected to sustained attempted empirical refutation.[9] Popper argues that this can be generalized to form a conception of rationality according to which one seeks to solve problems quite generally by putting forward conjectures as to how a given problem is to be solved, these conjectures then being subjected to sustained *criticism* (criticism being a generalization of attempted empirical refutation in science).[10]

Popper's ideas about scientific method and how it is to be generalized are an improvement over eighteenth-century notions, but they are still defective. Popper's conception of scientific method is defective because it is a version of standard empiricism which, as we have seen, is untenable. It fails to identify the problematic aim of science properly, and thus fails to specify the need for science to improve its aims and methods as it proceeds. Popper's notion of critical rationalism is defective in an analogous way. It does not make improving aims and methods, when aims are problematic, an essential aspect of rationality.[11]

If, however, we take the aim-oriented empiricist conception of scientific method as our starting point, and generalize that, the outcome is quite different. It is not just in science that aims are problematic; this is the case in life too, either because different aims conflict, or because what we believe to be desirable and realizable lacks one or other of these features, or both. Above all, the aim of creating global civilization is inherently and profoundly problematic.[12] Quite generally, then, and not just in science, whenever we pursue a problematic aim we need to represent the aim as a hierarchy of aims, from the specific and problematic at the bottom of the hierarchy, to the general and unproblematic at the top. In this way we provide ourselves with a relatively unproblematic framework within which we may improve more or less specific and problematic aims and methods as we proceed, learning from success and failure in practice what is both of most value and most realizable. Such an "aim-oriented" conception of rationality is the proper generalization of the aim-oriented, progress-achieving methods of science – or rather of natural philosophy.[13]

So much for the second blunder, and how it is to be put right. We come now to the *third* blunder.

This is by far the most serious of the three mistakes made by the traditional Enlightenment. The basic Enlightenment idea, after all, is to learn from our solution to the first great problem of learning how to solve the second problem – to learn, that is, from scientific progress how to make social progress towards an enlightened world. Putting this idea into practice involves getting appropriately generalized progress-achieving methods of science *into social life itself*. It involves getting progress-achieving methods into our institutions and ways of life, into government, industry, agriculture, politics, commerce, international relations, the media, the arts, education. But in sharp contrast to all this, the traditional Enlightenment has sought to apply generalized scientific method, not to social *life*, but merely to social *science*! Instead of helping humanity learn how to become more civilized by rational means, the traditional Enlightenment sought merely to help social scientists improve knowledge of social phenomena. The outcome is that today academic inquiry devotes itself to acquiring knowledge of natural and social phenomena, but does not attempt to help humanity learn how to become more civilized. This is the blunder that is at the root of our current failure to have solved the second great problem of learning.[14]

In order to correct this third, disastrous blunder, we need, as a first step, to bring about a revolution in the nature of academic inquiry, beginning with social inquiry and the humanities (as set out in some detail in my *From Knowledge to Wisdom*).[15] Social inquiry is not primarily social *science*. Its proper basic task is to help humanity build into institutions and social life quite generally the progress-achieving methods of aim-oriented rationality (arrived at by generalizing the progress-achieving methods of science as indicated above). Social inquiry (sociology, economics, anthropology, and the rest) is thus social *methodology* or social *philosophy*. Its task is to help diverse, valuable human endeavours and institutions gradually improve aims and methods so that the world may make social progress towards global enlightenment. And the primary task of academic inquiry, more generally, becomes to help humanity solve its problems of living in increasingly rational, cooperative, enlightened ways, thus

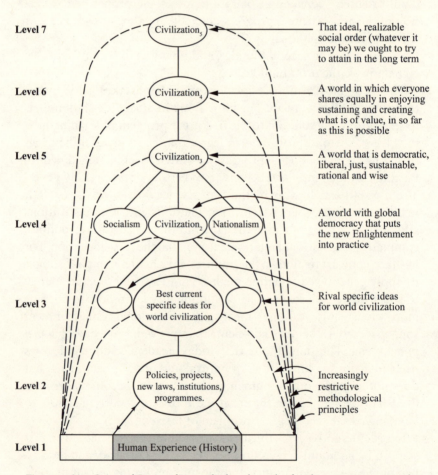

Figure 4 Aim-Oriented Rationality applied to the task of making progress towards a civilized world

helping humanity become more civilized. The basic aim of academic inquiry becomes to promote the growth of *wisdom* – wisdom being defined as the capacity to realize what is of value in life, for oneself and others, thus including knowledge and technological know-how, but much else besides. Those parts of academic inquiry devoted to improving knowledge, understanding and technological know-how contribute to the growth of wisdom. The outcome is a new kind of academic endeavour: *wisdom-inquiry*.

As I have already remarked, the aim of achieving global civilization is inherently problematic. This means, according to aim-oriented rationality, that we need to represent the aim at a number of levels, from the specific and highly problematic to the unspecific and unproblematic. Thus, at a fairly specific level, we might, for example, specify civilization to be a state of affairs in which there is an end to war, dictatorships, population growth, extreme inequalities of wealth, and the establishment of a democratic, liberal world government and a sustainable world industry and agriculture. At a rather more general level we might specify civilization to be a state of affairs in which everyone shares equally in enjoying, sustaining, and creating what is of value in life *in so far as this is possible*. At a still more general level, civilization might be specified simply as that realizable world order we should seek to attain in the long term: see figure 4.

As a result of building into our institutions and social life such a hierarchical structure of aims and associated methods, we create a framework within which it becomes possible for us progressively to improve our real-life aims and methods in increasingly cooperative ways as we live. Diverse philosophies of life – diverse religious, political, economic, and moral views – may be cooperatively developed, assessed, and tested against the experience of personal and social life. It becomes possible progressively to improve these diverse philosophies of life (diverse views about what is of value in life and how it is to be realized) much as *theories* are progressively and cooperatively improved in science. In doing this, humanity would at last have learned from the solution to the first great problem of learning how to go about solving the second problem.[16]

OBJECTIONS

I now consider, briefly, some objections that may be raised against the thesis and argument of this chapter.

It may be objected that the traditional Enlightenment – knowledge-inquiry – does not dominate current academic inquiry to the extent that I have assumed. For the last thirty years I have done what I can to see to what extent this is, or is not, the case. I have found that, over the years, there has been a gradual, muddled, piecemeal, partial drift away from knowledge-inquiry towards what could be held to be wisdom-inquiry, at least in some respects. In chapter 6 of my *From Knowledge to Wisdom*, published in 1984, I looked at the following: (1) books about the modern university; (2) the philosophy and sociology of science; (3) statements of leading scientists; (4) Physics Abstracts; (5) Chemistry, Biology, Geo and Psychology Abstracts; (6) journal titles and contents; (7) books on economics, sociology, and psychology; (8) philosophy. In 1984, there could be no doubt whatsoever that the traditional Enlightenment (or "the philosophy of knowledge" as I called it in the book) dominated academic inquiry. In 2000, I examined thirty-four introductory books on sociology published between 1985 and 1997. All defined sociology as a discipline that seeks to acquire knowledge of society, and most held sociology to be a *scientific* discipline.[17] For the second edition of *From Knowledge to Wisdom*, published in 2007, I looked again at the eight aspects of academic inquiry I had examined in the first edition, and I found that in some respects there had been movement towards wisdom-inquiry, although knowledge-inquiry still overwhelmingly prevailed.[18] In the fourth chapter of Maxwell (2014a), I discuss a number of recent developments that have moved academia, somewhat, in the direction of wisdom-inquiry. There has been, for example, a considerable growth in academic departments and institutions devoted to tackling problems of living – problems of development, peace, poverty, injustice, global health, well-being, climate change, and the environment. My own university – University College London – has created the Grand Challenges Programme, which seeks to bring together specialists to tackle global problems. It even speaks of "the wisdom agenda" and "developing a culture of wisdom" on the UCL website[19] (the influence of my own work). In the last decade or so, there has been an upsurge in research devoted to wisdom, and the University of Chicago seeks to keep track of this research via its "Wisdom Research Network."[20] In recent years, there has been far more emphasis on scientists and other academics engaging in dialogue with the public about matters related to their research and discipline, and research councils and other fund-giving bodies stress the importance of social "impact."

These developments do indicate, I think, a growing awareness of the need for academia to change so that it becomes more responsive to the problems of the modern world. They do not, however, amount to the rejection of knowledge-inquiry and the adoption of wisdom-inquiry in its stead. The growth of university departments concerned with problems of living does not in itself amount to a movement away from knowledge-inquiry to wisdom-inquiry: knowledge-inquiry seeks to help solve problems of living (even if primarily by the application of knowledge). Again, the upsurge in research on wisdom conducted within the framework of knowledge-inquiry is neither the same as, nor an adequate substitute for, wisdom-inquiry.[21] The demand that research should have social "impact" is not remotely the same as, or an adequate substitute for, sustained imaginative and critical discussion of actual and possible aims and priorities for scientific research, conducted by scientists and non-scientists alike. Indeed, the requirement that research has social "impact" is all too likely to be damaging. Much potentially valuable research may not have social impact for decades; or, indeed, it may never have "impact." The "impact" demand is likely to block research of great potential value. Despite the recent developments just indicated, knowledge-inquiry still dominates in universities around the world; some of these recent developments, conducted within the framework of knowledge-inquiry, have not had desirable outcomes.

It may be objected that it is all to the good that the academic enterprise today does give priority to the pursuit of knowledge over the task of promoting wisdom and civilization. Before problems of living can be tackled rationally, knowledge must first be acquired.[22]

I have six replies to this objection.

First, even if the objection were valid, it would still be vital for a kind of inquiry designed to help us build a better world to include rational exploration of problems of living, and to ensure that this guides priorities of scientific research (and is guided by the results of such research).

Second, the validity of the objection becomes dubious when we take into account the considerable success people met with in solving problems of living in a state of extreme ignorance, before the advent of science. We still today often arrive at solutions to problems of living in ignorance of relevant facts.

Third, the objection is not valid. In order to articulate problems of living and explore imaginatively and critically possible solutions (in accordance with Popper's conception of rationality) we need to be able to act in the world, imagine possible actions, and share our imaginings with others: insofar as some common sense knowledge is implicit in all this, such knowledge is required to tackle rationally and successfully problems of living. But this does not mean that we must give intellectual priority to acquiring new relevant knowledge before we can be in a position to tackle rationally our problems of living.

Fourth, simply in order to have some idea of what kind of knowledge or know-how it is *relevant* for us to try to acquire, we must first have some provisional ideas as to what our problem of living is and what we might do to solve it. Articulating our problem of living and proposing and critically assessing possible solutions needs to be intellectually prior to acquiring relevant knowledge simply for this reason. A slight change in the way we construe our problem may lead to a drastic change in the kind of knowledge it is relevant to acquire: changing the way we construe problems of health, to include *prevention* of disease (and not just curing of disease) leads to a dramatic change in the kind of knowledge we need to acquire (importance of exercise, diet, etc.). Including the importance of avoiding *pollution* in the problem of creating wealth by means of industrial development leads to the need to develop entirely new kinds of knowledge.

Fifth, relevant knowledge is often hard to acquire; it would be a disaster if we suspended life until it had been acquired. Knowledge of how our brains work is presumably highly relevant to all that we do, but suspending rational tackling of problems of living until this relevant knowledge has been acquired would clearly not be a sensible step to take. It would, in any case, make it impossible for us to acquire the relevant knowledge (since this requires scientists to act in doing research). Scientific research is itself a kind of action carried on in a state of relative ignorance.

Sixth, the capacity to act, to live, more or less successfully in the world, is more fundamental than (propositional) knowledge. Put in Rylean terms, "knowing how" is more fundamental than "knowing that."[23] All our knowledge is but a development of our capacity to act. Dissociated from life, from action, knowledge stored in libraries is just paper and ink, devoid of meaning. In this sense, problems of living are more fundamental than problems of knowledge (which are but an aspect of problems of living); giving intellectual priority to problems of living quite properly reflects this point.[24]

It deserves to be noted that a kind of inquiry that gives priority to tackling problems of knowledge over problems of living violates the most elementary requirements of rationality conceivable. If the basic task is to help humanity create a better world, then the problems that need to be solved are, primarily, problems of living, problems of action, not problems of knowledge. This means that to comply, merely, with Popper's conception of critical rationalism (or problem-solving rationality) discussed above, the basic intellectual tasks need to be (1) to articulate problems of living, and (2) to propose and critically assess possible solutions, possible more or less cooperative human *actions*. (1) and (2) are excluded, or marginalized, by a kind of inquiry that gives priority to the task of solving problems of knowledge. And the result will be a kind of inquiry that fails to create a reservoir of imaginative and critically examined ideas for the resolution of problems of living, and instead develops knowledge often unrelated to, or even harmful to, our most basic human needs.

It may be objected that in employing aim-oriented rationality in an attempt to help create a more civilized world, in the way indicated above, the new Enlightenment falls foul of Popper's strictures against utopian social engineering. Popper distinguished two approaches to tackling problems of living: piecemeal social engineering, which seeks to solve specific cases of human suffering and deprivation by means of specific actions; and utopian social engineering, which seeks to transform the whole of society. Popper condemned the latter as, invariably, having disastrous outcomes.[25] I have three replies to this objection. First, to the extent that piecemeal social engineering, of the kind advocated by Popper, is indeed the rational way to make progress towards a more civilized world, this will be advocated by the New Enlightenment. Second, when we take into account the unprecedented *global* nature of many of our most serious problems, indicated at the beginning of this chapter (the outcome of solving the first great problem of learning but failing to solve the second), we may well doubt that piecemeal social engineering is sufficient. Third, Popper's distinction between piecemeal and utopian social engineering is altogether too crude: it overlooks entirely what has been advocated here, aim-oriented rationalistic social engineering, with its emphasis on developing increasingly cooperatively rational resolutions of human conflicts and problems in full recognition of the inherently problematic nature of the aim of achieving greater civilization.[26]

All those to any degree influenced by Romanticism and the Counter-Enlightenment will object strongly to the idea that we should learn from scientific progress how to achieve social progress towards civilization; they will object strongly to the idea of allowing conceptions of rationality, stemming from science, to dominate in this way; and they will object even more strongly to the idea, inherent in the new Enlightenment, that we need to create a more aim-oriented rationalistic social world.[27]

Directed at the traditional Enlightenment, objections of this kind have some validity; but directed at the new Enlightenment, they have none. As I have emphasized elsewhere, aim-oriented rationality amounts to a synthesis of traditional rationalist and romantic ideals, and not to the triumph of the first over the second. In giving priority to the realization of what is of value in life, and in emphasizing that rationality demands that we seek to improve aims as we proceed, the new Enlightenment requires that rationality integrates traditional Rationalist and Romantic values and ideals of integrity. Imagination, emotion, desire, art, empathic understanding of people and culture, the imaginative exploration of aims and ideals, which tend to be repudiated as irrational by traditional Rationalism but which are prized by Romanticism, are all essential ingredients of aim-oriented rationality. Far from crushing freedom, spontaneity, creativity, and diversity, aim-oriented rationality is essential for the desirable flourishing of these things in life.[28]

Some historians and sociologists of science deny that there is any such thing as scientific method or scientific progress, and will thus find the basic idea of this chapter (and this book) absurd.[29] These writers are encouraged in their views by the long-standing failure of scientists and philosophers of science to explain clearly what scientific method is, and how it is to be justified. This excuse for not taking scientific method and progress seriously is, however, no longer viable: as we have seen, reject standard empiricism in all its forms, and it becomes clear how scientific method and progress are to be characterized and justified, in a way which emphasizes the rational interplay between evolving knowledge and evolving aims and methods of science.[30] In a world dominated by the products of scientific progress it is quixotic in the extreme to deny that such progress has taken place.

Finally, those of a more rationalist persuasion may object that science is too different from political life for there to be anything worthwhile to be learnt from scientific success about how to achieve social progress towards civilization.[31] Here are six arguments in support of this objection. (a) In science there is a decisive procedure for eliminating ideas, namely, empirical refutation: nothing comparable obtains, or can obtain, in the political domain. (b) In science experiments or trials may be carried out relatively painlessly (except, perhaps, when new drugs are being given in live trials); in life, social experiments, because they involve people, may cause much pain if they go wrong, and may be difficult to stop once started. (c) Scientific progress requires a number of highly intelligent and motivated people to pursue science on the behalf of the rest of us, funded by government and industry; social progress requires almost *everyone* to take part, including the stupid, the criminal, the mad or otherwise handicapped, the ill, the highly unmotivated; and in general there is no payment. (d) Scientists, at a certain level, have an agreed, common objective: to improve knowledge. In life, people often have quite different or conflicting goals, and there is no general agreement as to what civilization ought to mean, or even whether it is desirable to pursue civilization in *any* sense. (e) Science is about fact, politics about value, the quality of life. This difference ensures that science has nothing to teach political action (for civilization). (f) Science is male-dominated, fiercely competitive, and at times terrifyingly impersonal;[32] this means it is quite unfit to provide any kind of guide for life.

Here, briefly, are my replies. (a) Some proposals for action can be shown to be unacceptable quite decisively as a result of experience acquired through attempting to put the proposal into action. Where this is not possible, it may still be possible to assess the merits of the proposal to some extent by means of experience. If assessing proposals for action by means of experience is much more inconclusive than assessing scientific theories by means of experiment, then we need, all the more, to devote our care and attention to the former case. (b) Precisely because experimentation in life is so much more difficult than in science, it is vital that in life we endeavour to learn as much as possible from (i) experiments that we perform in our imagination, and (ii) experiments that occur as a result of what actually happens. (c) Because humanity does not have the aptitude or desire for wisdom that scientists have for knowledge, it is unreasonable to suppose that progress towards global wisdom could be as explosively rapid as progress in science. Nevertheless progress in wisdom might go better than it does at present. (d) Cooperative rationality is only feasible when there is the common desire of those involved to resolve conflicts in a cooperatively rational way. (e) Aim-oriented rationality can help us improve our decisions about what is desirable or of value, even if it cannot reach decisions for us. (f) In taking science as a guide for life, it is the progress-achieving methodology of science to which we need to attend. It is this that we need to generalize in such a way that it becomes fruitfully applicable, potentially, to all that we do. That modern science is male-dominated, fiercely competitive, and at times terrifyingly impersonal should not deter us from seeing what can be learned from the progress-achieving methods of science – unless, perhaps, it should turn out that being male-dominated, fiercely competitive and impersonal is essential to scientific method and progress. (But this, I submit, is not the case.)

CONCLUSION

Having solved the first great problem of learning, it has become a matter of extreme urgency, as far as the future of humanity is concerned, that we discover how to solve the second problem. In order to do this we need to correct the three blunders of the traditional Enlightenment. This involves changing the nature of social inquiry, so that social *science* becomes, primarily, social *methodology* or social *philosophy*, concerned to help us build into social life the progress-achieving methods of aim-oriented rationality, arrived at by generalizing the progress-achieving methods of science.[33] It also involves, more generally, bringing about a revolution in the nature of academic inquiry as a whole, so that it takes up its proper task of helping humanity learn how to become wiser by increasingly cooperatively rational means. The scientific task of improving knowledge and understanding of nature becomes a part of the broader task of improving global wisdom. The wholesale intellectual defects of knowledge-inquiry need to be put right: the outcome would be wisdom-inquiry.

During the course of this book, I have in effect argued for five revolutions. The first is a revolution in the philosophy of science: we need to reject all versions of standard empiricism and accept aim-oriented empiricism in their stead. The second is a revolution in science: science needs to be transformed so that it implements aim-oriented empiricism and becomes natural philosophy. The third is a revolution in philosophy: philosophy needs to devote itself to tackling our most fundamental problems, above all our most fundamental problem of all: it needs to transform itself so as to become a fruitful part of natural philosophy. And it needs to put aim-oriented rationality into practice in pursuing the philosophy of life-endeavours. The fourth is a revolution in the whole academic enterprise: knowledge-inquiry needs to become wisdom-inquiry. And the fifth is a revolution in our human world: we need to start putting cooperative problem-solving rationality and aim-oriented rationality into practice in personal and social life so that we may begin to learn how to make progress towards as good, as wise, a world as possible.

My hope is that this book will help spread awareness of the cogent case, and urgent need, for the first three revolutions. But it is the fifth revolution that really matters. And for that to get going, it is absolutely essential, in my view, that we bring about the fourth revolution – the revolution in academia, so that we come to acquire universities rationally devoted to helping us realize what is of value in life, make progress towards as good a world as possible.[34]

In order to make progress towards a better, wiser world, we need to learn how to do it. That in turn requires that our institutions of learning are rationally designed, well-designed, for the task. At present they are not. There can hardly be any more important thing for us to do, as far as the long-term interests of humanity are concerned, than to bring about the fourth of the above five revolutions, so that we at last have what we so urgently need, institutions of learning rationally devoted to promoting world civilization. I conclude with a list of changes that need to be made to academia if what we have at present, academic inquiry devoted in the first instance to the pursuit of knowledge (knowledge-inquiry as I have called it) is to become the kind of inquiry we really need, devoted to the pursuit of wisdom (wisdom-inquiry as I have called it).

1 There needs to be a change in the basic intellectual *aim* of inquiry, from the growth of knowledge to the growth of wisdom — wisdom being taken to be the capacity and active endeavour to realize what is of value in life, for oneself and others, and thus including knowledge, understanding, and technological know-how (but much else besides).

2 There needs to be a change in the nature of academic *problems*, so that problems of living are included, as well as problems of

knowledge – the former being treated as intellectually more fundamental than the latter.

3 There needs to be a change in the nature of academic *ideas*, so that proposals for action are included as well as claims to knowledge – the former, again, being treated as intellectually more fundamental than the latter.

4 There needs to be a change in what constitutes intellectual *progress*, so that progress in ideas relevant to achieving a more civilized world is included as well as progress in knowledge, the former being indeed intellectually fundamental.

5 There needs to be a change in the idea as to where inquiry, at its most fundamental, is located. It is not esoteric theoretical physics, but rather the thinking we engage in as we seek to achieve what is of value in life. Academic thought is a (vital) adjunct to what really matters, personal and social thought active in life.

6 There needs to be a dramatic change in the nature of social inquiry (reflecting points 1 to 5). Economics, politics, sociology, and so on, are not, fundamentally, *sciences*, and do not, fundamentally, have the task of improving knowledge about social phenomena. Instead, their task is threefold. First, it is to articulate problems of living, and propose and critically assess possible solutions, actions, or policies, from the standpoint of their capacity, if implemented, to promote wiser ways of living. Second, it is to promote such cooperatively rational tackling of problems of living throughout the social world. And third, at a more basic and long-term level, it is to help build the hierarchical structure of aims and methods of aim-oriented rationality into personal, institutional and global life, thus creating frameworks within which progressive improvement of aims and methods of personal and social life becomes possible. These three tasks are undertaken in order to promote cooperative tackling of problems of living — but also in order to enhance empathic or "personalistic" understanding between people as something of value in its own right. Acquiring knowledge of social phenomena is a vital but subordinate activity, engaged in to facilitate the above three fundamental pursuits.

7 Natural science needs to change, so that it includes at least three levels of discussion: evidence, theory, and research aims. Discussion of aims needs to bring together scientific, metaphysical and evaluative consideration in an attempt to discover the

most desirable and realizable research aims. It needs to influence, and be influenced by, exploration of problems of living
undertaken by social inquiry and the humanities, and the public.

8 There needs to be a dramatic change in the relationship between
   social inquiry and natural science, so that social inquiry becomes
   intellectually more fundamental from the standpoint of tackling
   problems of living, promoting wisdom. Social inquiry influences
   choice of research aims for the natural and technological sciences, and is in turn influenced by the results of such research.
   (Social inquiry also, of course, conducts empirical research, in
   order to improve our understanding of what our problems of
   living are, and in order to assess policy ideas whenever possible.)

9 The current emphasis on specialized research needs to change
   so that sustained discussion and tackling of broad, global problems that cut across academic specialities is included, both influencing and being influenced by specialized research.

10 Academia needs to include sustained imaginative and critical
   exploration of possible futures, for each country and for
   humanity as a whole, with policy and research implications
   being discussed as well.

11 The way in which academic inquiry as a whole is related to the
   rest of the human world needs to change dramatically. Instead of
   being intellectually dissociated from the rest of society, academic
   inquiry needs to be communicating with, learning from, teaching
   and arguing with the rest of society — in such ways as to promote cooperative rationality and social wisdom. Academia needs
   to have just sufficient power to retain its independence from the
   pressures of government, industry, the military, and public opinion, but no more. Academia becomes a kind of civil service for
   the public, doing openly and independently what actual civil
   services are supposed to do in secret for governments.

12 There needs to be a change in the role that political and religious ideas, works of art, expressions of feelings, desires, and
   values have within rational inquiry. Instead of being excluded,
   they need to be explicitly included and critically assessed, as
   possible indications and revelations of what is of value, and as
   means of unmasking of fraudulent values in satire and parody,
   vital ingredients of wisdom.

13 There need to be changes in education so that, for example,
   seminars devoted to the cooperative, imaginative, and critical

discussion of problems of living are at the heart of all education from five-year-olds onwards. Politics, which cannot be taught by knowledge-inquiry, becomes central to wisdom-inquiry, political creeds and actions being subjected to imaginative and critical scrutiny.

14 There need to be changes in the aims, priorities, and character of pure science and scholarship, so that it is the curiosity, the seeing and searching, the knowing and understanding of individual persons that ultimately matters, and the more impersonal, esoteric, purely intellectual aspects of science and scholarship are means to this end. Social inquiry needs to give intellectual priority to helping empathic understanding between people to flourish (as indicated in 6 above).

15 There need to be changes in the way mathematics is understood, pursued, and taught. Mathematics is not a branch of knowledge at all. Rather, it is concerned to explore problematic *possibilities*, and to develop, systematize, and unify problem-solving methods.

16 Literature needs to be put close to the heart of rational inquiry, in that it explores imaginatively our most profound problems of living and aids personalistic understanding in life by enhancing our ability to enter imaginatively into the problems and lives of others.

17 Philosophy needs to change so that it ceases to be just another specialized discipline and becomes instead that aspect of inquiry as a whole that is concerned with our most general and fundamental problems — those problems that cut across all disciplinary boundaries. Philosophy needs to become again what it was for Socrates: the attempt to devote reason to the growth of wisdom in life.

18 Academic contributions need to be written in as simple, lucid, jargon-free a way as possible, so that academic work is as accessible as possible across specialities and to non-academics.

19 There needs to be a change in views about what constitute academic contributions, so that publications which promote (or have the potential to promote) public understanding as to what our problems of livings are and what we need to do about them are included, in addition to contributions addressed primarily to the academic community.

20 Every university needs to create a seminar or symposium devoted to the sustained discussion of fundamental problems that cut across all conventional academic boundaries, global problems of living being included as well as global problems of knowledge and understanding.

The above changes all come from my "from knowledge to wisdom" argument spelled out above, and in detail elsewhere. The following three institutional innovations do not follow from that argument, but, if implemented, would help wisdom-inquiry to flourish.

21 Natural science needs to create committees, in the public eye, and manned by scientists and non-scientists alike, concerned to highlight and discuss failures of the priorities of research to respond to the interests of those whose needs are the greatest – the poor of the earth – as a result of the inevitable tendency of research priorities to reflect the interests of those who pay for science, and the interests of scientists themselves.

22 Every national university system needs to include a national shadow government, seeking to do virtually, free of the constraints of power, what the actual national government ought to be doing. The hope would be that virtual and actual governments would learn from each other.

23 The world's universities need to include a virtual world government which seeks to do what an actual elected world government ought to do, if it existed. The virtual world government would also have the task of working out how an actual democratically elected world government might be created.[35]

APPENDICES

Degrees of Theory Unity

What does it mean to say of a physical theory that it is *unified*? How can one capture this notion of the unity of a theory when an apparently beautifully unified theory can always be reformulated so that it becomes horribly disunified, and vice versa, a horribly disunified theory can be reformulated to become unified?[1] How are *degrees* of unity to be specified? These problems of "unification," or of "simplicity" as they are sometimes called, are widely understood to be fundamental problems of the philosophy of science.[2] In chapter 5, section 4, I indicated briefly how aim-oriented empiricism solves the problem. Here I go into a bit more detail.

It is worth noting in passing that Einstein fully recognized the importance of the problem of what the unity of a theory is, and yet did not know how to solve it. This is apparent from a passage of Einstein's "Autobiographical Notes" in which he discusses ways that physical theories, quite generally, can be critically assessed.[3]

Einstein emphasizes that theories need to be critically assessed from *two* distinct points of view: from the standpoint of their empirical success, and from the standpoint of their "inner perfection," the "naturalness" or "logical simplicity" of the postulates. Einstein stresses that the theories that need to be considered are those "whose object is the *totality* of all physical appearances," that is, "theories of everything" in modern parlance. And Einstein acknowledges that "an exact formulation" of the second point of view (having to do with the "inner perfection" of theories) "meets with great difficulties" even though it "has played an important role in the selection of theories since time immemorial."[4] He continues:

The problem here is not simply one of a kind of enumeration of
the logically independent premises (if anything like this were
at all unequivocally possible), but that of a kind of reciprocal
weighing of incommensurable qualities ... The following I
reckon as also belonging to the "inner perfection" of a theory:
We prize a theory more highly if, from the logical standpoint,
it is not the result of an arbitrary choice among theories which,
among themselves, are of equal value and analogously
constructed.[5]

And Einstein comments:

I shall not attempt to excuse the meagre precision of these assertions ... by lack of sufficient printing space at my disposal, but
confess herewith that I am not, without more ado, and perhaps
not at all, capable of replacing these hints with more precise defi-
nitions. I believe, however, that a sharper formulation would be
possible.[6]

Since Einstein's day, many attempts have been made to solve the
problem, none successful.[7] How is the problem to be solved – a problem which baffled even Einstein?

The key to the solution is to appreciate that standard attempts to
solve the problem have been looking at entirely the wrong thing.
They have been looking at the *theory itself*, its axiomatic structure,
its number of postulates, its formulation, its characteristic deriva-
tions, the language in which it is formulated. (Even Einstein made
this mistake.) But all this is wrong. What one needs to look at is not
the theory itself, but rather what the theory says about the world, the
content of the theory in other words. One needs to look at the world
as depicted by the theory. At a stroke the worst aspect of the problem
of what unity *is* vanishes. No longer does one face what may be called
the *terminological* problem of unity – the problem, namely, that the
extent to which a theory is unified appears to be highly dependent on
the way it is *formulated*. Suppose we have a given theory T, which is
formulated in N different ways, some formulations exhibiting T as
beautifully unified, others as horribly complex and disunified, but all
formulations being interpreted in precisely the same way, so as to
make precisely the same assertion about the world. If unity has to do
exclusively with *content*, then *all these diverse formulations of T,*

having the same content, have precisely the same degree of unity. The variability of apparent unity with varying formulations of one and the same theory, T (given some specific interpretation) – which poses such an insurmountable problem for traditional approaches to the problem – poses no problem whatsoever for the thesis that unity has to do with content. Variability of formulation of a theory which leaves its content unaffected is wholly irrelevant: the unity of the theory is unaffected.

But now we have a new problem: How is the unity of the content of a theory to be assessed? What exactly does it mean to assert that a dynamical physical theory has a unified content?

What it means is that the theory has *the same* content throughout the range of possible phenomena to which the theory applies. Unity, in other words, means that there is just *one* content throughout the range of possible phenomena to which the theory applies. If the theory postulates *different* contents, *different* laws, for different ranges of possible phenomena, then the theory is *disunified*, and the more such different contents there are, the more disunified the theory is. Thus "unity" means "one," and "disunity" means "more than one," the disunity becoming worse and worse as the number of different contents goes up, from two to three to four, and so on. Not only does this enable us to distinguish between "unified" and "disunified" theories; it enables us to assign degrees of unity to theories, or to partially order theories with respect to their degree of unity.[8]

All this can be illustrated by considering the disunified "patchwork quilt" theories indicated in figure 1, page 77. Whereas an accepted, unified theory, T, asserts that the same dynamical laws (as far as their content is concerned) apply in ranges of phenomena A, B, and C, a "patchwork quilt" rival, T*, asserts that distinct laws, L_A, L_B, and L_C, apply in A, B, and C, T* being disunified as a result.

To take a specific example, Newton's theory of gravitation, $F = Gm_1m_2/d^2$, is unified in that what it asserts is *the same* throughout all possible phenomena to which it applies. Bodies attract each other in proportion to their masses and inversely proportional to the square of the distance between them, and this remains the same, according to the theory, for all the phenomena to which the theory applies, whatever the masses of the bodies may be, whatever their constitution, shape, relative velocity, distance apart, place, and time. One kind of disunified version of Newton's theory would assert that Newton's law becomes an inverse cube law after some definite time, the last moment of 2050 let us say – the theory asserting that $F = Gm_1m_2/d^2$ up to that moment, and $F = Gm_1m_2/d^3$ for times after the last moment of 2050. This theory is disunified because what it asserts is blatantly *not* the same throughout the range of possible phenomena to which it applies.

If a theory asserts that N distinct laws apply in N distinct regions of phenomena, actual and physically possible, to which the theory applies, then the theory is disunified to degree N. For unity we require that N = 1.

This account of unity needs to be refined further. In assessing the extent to which a theory is disunified we may need to consider *in what way* we need to move from phenomenon to phenomenon in order to reveal a change in the content of the theory. We may need to move through *time* or *space*. Or the content of the theory may be the same at all times and places, but may change as we change the *masses, substances, relative velocities, temperature*, or *kinds of particle* of the phenomena in question.[9] A theory that postulates different laws at different times and places is disunified in a much more serious way than a theory which postulates the same laws at all times and places, but also postulates that distinct kinds of physical particle exist, with different dynamical properties, such as charge or mass. This second theory still postulates *different* laws for different ranges of phenomena: laws of one kind for possible physical systems consisting of one kind of particle, and slightly different laws for possible physical systems consisting of another kind of particle. But this second kind of difference in content is much less serious than the first kind (which involves different laws at different times and places). In other words, the contents of disunified theories may change as we make *different* sorts of change (in imagination) to the phenomena to which the theory applies. Some of these changes of content of theory are more serious than others.

What this means is that there are different *kinds* of disunity, some worse than others, but all facets of the same basic idea. One kind of disunified theory – the most serious kind perhaps – postulates that there are different laws in different regions of space and time. An example of a theory disunified in this way is the version of Newtonian theory considered above, which differs before and after the last moment of 2050. A version of Newton's law disunified in a different way might assert: everything occurs in accordance with $F = Gm_1m_2/d^2$, except for spheres of pure gold, each of mass greater than 1,000 tons, moving in a vacuum, in which case $F = Gm_1m_2/d^5$. And there are a number of other ways in which Newton's law, or indeed any law, might differ from one range of phenomena to which the theory applies to another range. A theory may, for example, postulate two different forces: in one region of phenomena one force applies, and in another region the other force applies. Or, again, a theory might postulate one force but different kinds of particle, of different charge or mass. In one region of possible phenomena, there is just one kind of particle, whereas in another region there is another kind of particle, slightly different laws applying as a result in these two regions.[10]

Elsewhere, I have distinguished eight different kinds of disunity along these lines,[11] all however aspects of the same underlying idea: a physical theory is disunified to degree N if there are N distinct regions of possible phenomena to which the theory applies, each region having its own distinct laws, different from the laws applicable to all the other regions. For unity we require, as I have said, that $N = 1$.

One final point. Degrees of unity can be made relative to a blueprint B as follows. A theory T is B-unified to degree N if the space of all possible physical states to which T applies divides up into N subspaces, and T asserts that, in each subspace, there is just one set of dynamical laws compatible with B which differ from those in all the other subspaces. As the blueprint B for physics evolves, so B-unity evolves as well. A theory T can be said to be P-unified (where P stands for perfect physicalism or perfect physical comprehensibility of the universe) if T is unified in all eight ways, and $N = 1$.

The Problem of Induction

For centuries, philosophers have struggled to solve the problem of induction, and have failed.[1] As long as we cling to standard empiricist science, the problem cannot be solved. What Hume in effect demonstrated, long ago in 1738, is that standard empiricism is untenable. In order to solve the problem it is essential that we construe science as *authentic natural philosophy*, as I have called the endeavour I argue for in this book. More specifically, in order to solve the problem we need to adopt aim-oriented empiricism (AOE). Here I show that AOE does indeed solve the problem, and it is required in order to solve the problem.[2]

That centuries of efforts to solve the problem of induction granted standard empiricism have all failed, and AOE solves the problem with ease, constitutes very strong grounds indeed for rejecting standard empiricism and adopting AOE in its stead – the key step that provides the reason for holding that science needs to become authentic natural philosophy.

In what follows I concentrate on the problem of induction as it arises in the context of physics. In other branches of natural science – chemistry, biology, geology, astronomy – there is always some other, more fundamental science, some results of which influence choice of theory in addition to evidence. Thus biology presupposes chemistry, and chemistry, geology, and astronomy presuppose parts of physics. It is only when we come to physics itself, the fundamental natural science, that there is no more fundamental natural science to constrain what theories are to be accepted. Only in physics does the problem of induction arise in a pure, naked form.

The solution to the problem as it arises in physics will, however, lead to the solution for all of natural science.

Given the failure to solve the problem of induction despite centuries of effort, is my claim that AOE solves the problem really credible? It is. There is a *reason* why previous attempts to solve the problem have failed. Almost all these attempts have tried to solve the problem taking some version of the orthodox conception of science, standard empiricism (SE), for granted. That scientific theories are selected (almost) exclusively on the basis of evidence – on the basis of empirical success and failure – has seemed so utterly obvious that it has hardly occurred to anyone to call it into question. And that is the reason why all these previous attempts have failed. For what the long-standing failure to solve the problem of induction is trying to tell us is that SE is untenable. The problem simply cannot be solved granted SE. In order to solve the problem, we need to reject this orthodox conception of science, and accept AOE, and authentic natural philosophy, instead. We need to recreate something like the pre-Newtonian conception of natural philosophy. At once, the problem of induction can be solved. But it is just this step, this return to something like pre-Newtonian natural philosophy, that philosophers, struggling with the problem of induction after Hume, have been unwilling to take. Indeed, such a step has been all but inconceivable. The immense success of Newtonian science, and natural science after Newton, has seemed wholly to vindicate the *conception* of science associated with this success, namely that scientific theories are selected on the basis of evidence, empirical success and failure. It has seemed inconceivable that this could be fundamentally wrong. And so, a vast literature has grown up recording endless struggles to solve the problem of induction within the framework of this orthodox conception of science of SE. Even Karl Popper tried to solve the problem within the constraints of a version of SE.[3] Just that which one needs to do to solve the problem – reject SE and accept AOE and authentic natural philosophy – has seemed inconceivable. And so the philosophical tradition has condemned itself repeatedly to attempt the impossible.

Here, then, is the nub of the reason why all those previous attempts to solve Hume's problem have failed. They have failed because they have tried to solve the problem taking some version of SE for granted. It cannot be done. They have failed because they have not been prepared to consider that s e is untenable, and we need a more rigorous conception of science in its stead.

s e holds that evidence determines what theories are accepted, but recognizes that considerations that have to do with the simplicity, unity, or explanatory character of a theory may influence choice of theory as well, but not in such a way that this commits science to assuming that the universe, or the phenomena, are simple, unified, or comprehensible. The key tenet of s e is that *no factual thesis about the nature of the universe can be permanently accepted as a part of scientific knowledge independently of evidence, let alone against the evidence.*[4]

In chapter 3, I refuted s e decisively. We saw that, given any accepted physical theory, however well corroborated empirically, we can always easily concoct endlessly many rival theories that fit the facts even better. There are, in fact, infinitely many such empirically more successful theories. But, in scientific practice, these rivals never get considered for a moment. Why not? Because they are all horribly disunified. In physics, two considerations govern acceptance of a theory: it must be (a) sufficiently empirically successful, and (b) sufficiently *unified*. (b) is as important as (a). Indeed, (b) persistently overrides (a), in that endlessly many disunified rivals to any accepted theory are not even considered even though they fit the phenomena even better!

It is this that refutes s e. In persistently ignoring infinitely many empirically more successful, disunified rivals to an accepted theory, physicists thereby reveal that they make a persistent, substantial assumption about the nature of the universe: the universe is such that all disunified theories are false.[5] Physics seeks truth, at least at the empirical level. Given this aim, persistently to ignore infinitely many empirically more successful theories than the ones we accept merely on the grounds that they are all disunified *is* persistently to assume that all disunified theories are false.[6] It is to assume that the universe is such that all disunified theories are false.[7] And this is an item of implicit scientific knowledge that is upheld so firmly that it invariably overrides empirical considerations.[8] It doesn't matter how empirically successful a disunified theory might be, of the kind we are considering: it is presumed to be false!

And as we have seen, this is in flat contradiction with the key tenet of s e that no factual thesis about the nature of the universe can be permanently accepted as a part of scientific knowledge independently of evidence, let alone against the evidence.

SE lacks rigour and is untenable for two reasons. It is inconsistent, in that it denies that physics accepts any metaphysical thesis about the universe, when actually physics does and must accept such a thesis. And secondly, in denying that physics accepts this substantial, problematic, and influential metaphysical thesis, SE fails to make that thesis explicit, and so open to criticism and, we may hope, improvement. SE fails, in other words, to meet the elementary requirement for intellectual rigour that assumptions that are substantial, problematic, influential, and implicit must be made explicit so that they can be critically assessed and improved.

All attempts to solve the problem of induction within the framework of SE are clearly doomed. Far better to adopt the view that physics does accept a substantial metaphysical thesis about the nature of the universe, even if this thesis is a pure conjecture. J.S. Mill, Bertrand Russell, and one or two others have indeed adopted something like this approach, as I mentioned in chapter 3.[9] But most philosophers have treated this approach with scorn. Bas van Fraassen called it "a mug's game."[10] It has been dismissed because the metaphysical conjecture in question cannot be verified, or even rendered probable.

But this response profoundly misses the point. Physics cannot help but accept a substantial metaphysical conjecture concerning underlying unity in the universe, whether this is explicitly acknowledged or not. Precisely because this conjecture is a pure conjecture, very likely to be false, and yet such that it exercises a profound influence over what theories physicists accept and try to develop, it is vital that it be made thoroughly explicit, within the context of physics, so that it may be critically assessed, developed and, we may hope, improved. (This is the key argument for authentic natural philosophy.)

But we need more. We need a methodology which gives us the best possible help with improving the metaphysical conjecture of physics. That methodology is aim-oriented empiricism (AOE). As I indicated in chapter 3, the basic idea behind AOE is that we need to represent the metaphysical conjecture inherent in the enterprise of physics in the form of a hierarchy of conjectures, these becoming less and less substantial as we go up the hierarchy, and thus more and more likely to be true,[11] and more and more such that their truth is required for physics, or even the pursuit of knowledge, to be possible at all. As a result, we provide ourselves with a framework of relatively unproblematic, secure conjectures and associated methods, high up in the hierarchy, within which more substantial, problematic, and insecure conjectures and associated methods, low down in the hierarchy, can be improved, in the light of what best accords with conjectures higher up in the hierarchy, and what best promotes empirically progressive physics at levels 1 and 2, or at least holds out the best promise of doing so. The seven levels of A O E are depicted in figure 2: see page 85 and associated text.[12]

I now summarize arguments designed to show that, at each level, from 7 to 3, the conjecture at that level is the best one to accept. No attempt is made to argue that any of the conjectures, from level 7 to 3, is true, or probably true. The arguments seek to establish merely that the conjecture at this level is the best to adopt, granted that our concern is to acquire (conjectural) knowledge of truth at levels 1 and 2. A key feature of the overall argument is that quite *different* arguments are employed at different levels. Mill and Russell both failed to solve the problem of induction because they put their metaphysical theses on one level, and were thus unable to provide different arguments for the acceptability of theses at different levels. They failed to appreciate that we need a methodology designed to facilitate criticism, development, and improvement of the metaphysical assumptions of physics.

Level 7. Partial knowability: The universe is such that we possess and can acquire some knowledge of our immediate environment as a basis for action.

Even if we have no grounds whatsoever for holding that this cosmological conjecture is true, we are nevertheless justified in accepting it as a permanent part of our scientific knowledge. To do so can only help, and cannot harm, the pursuit of knowledge in any circumstances whatsoever. If the conjecture is false, we cannot acquire knowledge whatever we assume. We will not exist to contemplate the possibility.

Level 6. Meta-knowability: The universe is such that there is some rationally discoverable assumption about it which, if accepted, makes it possible to improve methods for the improvement of knowledge. Not only can we acquire knowledge; we can acquire knowledge about how to acquire knowledge.

The idea of a "rationally discoverable" assumption is somewhat problematic. I take it to mean, at least, that the assumption in question must not be one among infinitely many analogous, equally viable assumptions, like some of the horribly disunified theories considered in chapter 3.

Meta-knowability divides possible universes up into three kinds. Type A universes are such that, relative to our existing knowledge and culture, we can discover a conjecture about the nature of the universe which, if accepted, makes it possible for us to *improve* methods for the improvement of knowledge. Type B universes are such that, relative to our existing knowledge and culture, we can discover a conjecture about the nature of the universe which, if accepted, makes it possible, apparently, for us to improve methods for the improvement of knowledge; this apparent success is illusory, however, and the illusory character of the knowledge acquired could not even in principle be discovered, until eventually it becomes all too apparent. Type C universes are such that there is no rationally discoverable conjecture such that, if accepted, it makes it possible to improve methods for the improvement of knowledge.

The cosmological conjecture of meta-knowability can be interpreted as asserting that the universe is not a B-type universe.[13]

A major problem that confronts any attempt to solve the problem of induction by appealing to metaphysical conjectures is that such an attempt must, it seems, be viciously circular, and thus hopelessly invalid. Acceptance of some metaphysical principle is justified on the grounds that it leads to the great success of science, and then the great success of science is justified by an appeal to the metaphysical principle. X is justified by an appeal to Y, and then Y is justified by an appeal to X.

Aim-oriented empiricism (AOE) seems peculiarly vulnerable to this intellectual sin of vicious circularity. As I have emphasized (in chapter 3 especially), the hierarchical character of AOE makes it possible to revise metaphysical conjectures and associated methods, low down in the hierarchy of conjectures, based on which seem best to promote progress in empirical knowledge at levels 1 and 2. This progress in knowledge in turn makes possible further improvement in accepted metaphysical conjectures. AOE enables science to improve its methods in the light of what it finds out about the nature of the universe, there being a kind of positive feedback between improving knowledge, and improving knowledge about how to improve knowledge, which helps explain the explosive growth in scientific knowledge and understanding. But this great success of AOE is actually, it seems, its great disaster: it reveals, so it would seem, that AOE suffers from vicious circularity.

Meta-knowability, as interpreted above, rescues AOE from this disaster. For what meta-knowability asserts is that this universe is a type A or type C universe. The universe is such that it is entirely legitimate to try to *improve* metaphysical conjectures, and associated methods, in the light of which seem best able to promote the growth of empirical knowledge at levels 1 and 2. Meta-knowability asserts, in other words, that the universe is such that it is legitimate to put the positive feedback procedure of AOE into scientific practice. This circularity or positive feedback procedure can only lead to undetectable disaster in type B universes, but meta-knowability asserts that this is *not* a type B universe. Of course, in improving our metaphysical conjectures in the light of which best promote the growth of empirical knowledge, and vice versa, we may deceive ourselves, and take for knowledge and progress what is nothing of the kind. The all-important point, however, is that, granted meta-knowability – granted that this is not a type B universe – such self-deception is always in principle discoverable. And furthermore, putting AOE into practice gives us our best hope of discovering such self-deception, because it requires us to explore the widest range of possible metaphysical conjectures, and associated methods, at different levels, and thus look critically at the metaphysical conjectures and methods that have been put into scientific practice in an apparently successful way.

This justification of the positive feedback, circularity feature of AOE depends on one crucial point: reasons for accepting meta-knowability must not in any way appeal to the success of science (at levels 1 and 2). Such an appeal would immediately reintroduce vicious circularity, just that which the above considerations banish. Meta-knowability implies that the universe is such that methodological circularity and positive feedback are valid and legitimate, but only if arguments for meta-knowability itself do not appeal to the success of science!

What grounds are there, then, for accepting meta-knowability? There are two.

First, if we consider the great sweep of the human endeavour to improve knowledge – from the earliest times of belief in gods, spirits, and demons, via the ideas of the Presocratic philosophers, Plato, Aristotle, Arabic and Medieval science, to the Renaissance, the scientific revolution, the emergence of modern science and the subsequent evolution of metaphysical ideas about the nature of the universe associated with physics – it becomes apparent that, increasingly, there has been positive feedback between metaphysical conjectures and associated methods, on the one hand, and the growth of empirical scientific knowledge at levels 1 and 2, on the other. If we had not revised metaphysical conjectures in the light of empirical progress in science, we would still be stuck with Aristotelian science, or even the practices of witch doctors and shamans. Meta-knowability has only been *implicit* in the endeavour to acquire knowledge, and has not been acknowledged *explicitly*, because widespread acceptance of s E has suppressed it.

Given that meta-knowability has been accepted implicitly, physics becomes all the more rigorous intellectually if this implicit assumption is acknowledged explicitly as an accepted metaphysical conjecture about the nature of the universe. This, then, is the first argument for accepting meta-knowability.

Note, this argument does not appeal to the empirical *success* of physics, or of the pursuit of knowledge more generally. It appeals only to the principle that inquiry becomes more rigorous intellectually if implicit assumptions are acknowledged explicitly – even if inquiry meets with no success whatsoever!

The second argument is that, as a result of accepting meta-knowability, our pursuit of knowledge may have much to gain and little to lose. In accepting meta-knowability we decide, in effect, that it is worthwhile to try to improve knowledge about how to improve knowledge. We take seriously the possibility that the universe is such that we can discover something rather general about its nature which will enable us to *improve* our methods for improving knowledge. Not only do we hope to learn about the world; we hope to learn about how to learn about the world, and we are prepared to put into practice a meta-methodology which capitalizes on this possibility should it turn out to be actual. To fail to try to *improve* methods for improving knowledge on the grounds that apparent success might prove to be illusory is surely to proceed in a cripplingly overcautious fashion. Any attempt at improving knowledge may unexpectedly fail, including the attempt to improve methods for improving knowledge. But abandoning the attempt to learn – and to learn how to learn

– because it may fail cannot be sound: such an excuse for not making the attempt always exists. In accepting meta-knowability we do not assume that the universe *is* such that AOE, or something like it, will meet with success. We assume, merely, that it is such that *if* AOE, or something similar, appears to meet with empirical success, this success will not be illusory in a way which could not have been discovered before the illusory character of the success becomes all too apparent. But this is an entirely sensible assumption to make. Nothing is to be gained from foregoing the attempt to acquire knowledge merely because there is the possibility, as far as we can know for certain, that in the future intrinsically unpredictable changes in the laws of nature may occur which render our current knowledge obsolete.

Neither partial knowability nor meta-knowability excludes the possibility that such inherently unpredictable events occur. Even though we accept these conjectures, it is still conceivable that we might discover that unpredictable changes in the laws of nature do occur. It is conceivable that we might come to live in a world in which inherently inexplicable, unpredictable events occur quite often. Objects vanish, or abruptly appear; substances abruptly change their properties; bridges collapse, houses turn into giraffes, mountains vanish, trees become hedgehogs. People die as a result, but life might nevertheless continue, and it might be possible, not just to improve knowledge, but to improve knowledge about how to improve knowledge. Meta-knowability implies that, if we have had no such experience of them, we are entitled to assume that such events do not occur. We are justified in ignoring the possibility that such events may occur in the future in both science and life because, if they occur in the future, nothing in the nature of things can be done to anticipate their occurrence, or evade the harm they may cause.

Hume famously argued that what exists at one moment cannot necessarily determine what exists at the next moment. If he is right, we may well feel that anything may happen at any moment – just because there can be nothing in existence now to *determine* (perhaps probabilistically) what will exist next. I have shown, however, that Hume is wrong, and it *is* possible that what exists at one instant necessarily determines what exists at the next moment.[14] Since this is possible, it is, in my view, absurd not to assume that what exists now *does* necessarily determine what exists next. Recognizing that Hume's arguments, here, are invalid is bound to affect ideas about how likely it is that utterly inexplicable, inherently unpredictable events will occur in the future, events of which we have had no experience.

Accepting meta-knowability, then, puts on record our decision that this universe is such that it is worthwhile to try to learn how to learn – to try to improve assumptions and associated methods in the light of improving knowledge and understanding, in the light of which seem best to promote empirical progress. This goes on, after all, in a thoroughly acknowledged and uncontroversial manner at the empirical level. New knowledge can give rise to new technology, new instruments and experimental techniques – from the telescope and microscope to the cyclotron – which in turn are used to help create new knowledge. At the empirical level, uncontroversially and fruitfully, there is a kind of circular, positive feedback between improving knowledge and improving observational and experimental methods for the further improvement of knowledge. Something analogous has long gone on, too, implicitly, in scientific practice, at the theoretical level. Science would be more rigorous, and even more successful, if this latter was explicitly recognized and acknowledged. Meta-knowability asserts that the universe is such that it is legitimate to proceed in such a way that there is positive feedback between improving metaphysical conjectures and improving empirical knowledge. If apparent knowledge acquired in this way turns out subsequently to be illusory, this could have been discovered ahead of time.

This concludes my discussion of the solution to the circularity problem, and the reasons for accepting meta-knowability in preference to any rival thesis at this level.

Level 5. Comprehensibility: The conjecture that the universe is comprehensible in some way or other, there being *something*, or an aspect of something (a kind of physical entity, God, society of gods, cosmic purpose, cosmic programme, or whatever) that runs through all phenomena, and in terms of which all phenomena can, in principle, be explained and understood.

Almost all (perhaps all) cultures possess a myth, cosmology, or religious view which is held to explain natural phenomena, and is presupposed by attempts to improve knowledge. Almost all of these are animistic or purposive in character: natural phenomena are explained in terms of the actions of gods, demons, spirits, God, or other purposes. Acceptance of some version of the conjecture of comprehensibility is often combined, however, with a clause that places strict limits on knowability (this clause being required, perhaps, to protect the thesis against criticism, and to explain away the lack of success of the view in promoting acquisition of knowledge). Thus God is said to be mysterious and unknowable. That the universe is held to be (more or less) comprehensible in almost all cultures is not, however, a good reason to hold it to be worthy of acceptance.

Acceptance of the conjecture of comprehensibility can be justified by appealing to meta-knowability. Comprehensibility is just the kind of general idea about the nature of the universe that meta-knowability encourages us to adopt and explore. For comprehensibility, especially if held in one or other more or less specific version, requires us to put forward and critically assess hypotheses of a more or less specific type – namely hypotheses that accord with the general comprehensibility conjecture. In other words, comprehensibility suggests the kind of more or less specific explanatory hypotheses we need to put forward and assess. But meta-knowability also requires us to accept that version of comprehensibility which leads to the most successful specific explanatory hypotheses, and best supports the growth of empirical knowledge. In order to accord with the spirit of meta-knowability, we need to modify the conjecture of comprehensibility in the direction of that version which seems to be the most fruitful from the standpoint of the growth of empirical knowledge.

It may be argued that it is just this process of positive feedback, licensed and endorsed by meta-knowability, which has led to the emergence of natural philosophy and modern science from a background of primitive, animistic cosmologies, myths, and religious views. If so, it must also be acknowledged that this process has unfolded in a painfully slow and muddled way over millennia,[15] and in a way that is still, today, not generally understood (or this book would not be necessary).

No version of the comprehensibility conjecture seemed to be of much help in improving knowledge until one version of this conjecture emerged in Europe around 1600, namely *physicalism*, initially as an adjunct, primarily, to Christianity.

Level 4. Physical comprehensibility (physicalism): The conjecture that the universe is physically comprehensible, everything being made up of just one kind of physical entity (or perhaps just one entity), all change and diversity being capable, in principle, of being explained in terms of this one kind of entity. This conjecture asserts that the universe is such that some yet-to-be-discovered physical "theory of everything" (in the jargon of theoretical physicists) is both true and *unified*.[16]

Granted meta-knowability, we are justified in accepting that thesis, other things being equal, which holds out the greatest hope, if true, for progress in empircal knowledge. Granted the level 5 conjecture of comprehensibility, we are justified in accepting that version of this conjecture which provides the greatest promise for progress in empirical knowledge. Physicalism satisfies these requirements better than any rival conjecture at this level, in that it places more demanding restrictions on any testable theory that is to be ultimately acceptable. (Such a theory must, in principle, predict and explain all physical phenomena, and must be unified in the strongest way possible.) Physicalism also specifies how physics should proceed in order to improve empirical knowledge: testable theories need to be put forward and tested that, as far as possible, (a) predict ever wider ranges of phenomena, and (b) are ever more unified.

But it is not just that physicalism holds out the promise of progress; it has been associated, implicitly, with all the great advances in theoretical knowledge and understanding in physics since Kepler and Galileo.

All advances in theory in physics since the scientific revolution have been advances in unification, a point I stressed in chapter 3.[17] The whole way theoretical physics has developed points towards physicalism, in other words, as the goal towards which physics has made progress, and towards which it seeks to make progress. Granted the level 6 and 5 conjectures of meta-knowability and comprehensibility, and granted the entire history of theoretical physics since Galileo and its current strivings to unify general relativity and the standard model, the argument for accepting the conjecture of physicalism becomes all but irresistible.

In response to this claim it may be objected that theoretical physics could equally well be regarded as pointing towards a less restrictive version of physicalism – for example, one which demands no more than that there are three distinct forces, so that the true theory of everything is only unified to the extent that N = 3. What reasons are there for accepting the strongest possible version of physicalism in preference to weaker versions, which demand a less stringent kind and degree of unity? There are four, none of course decisive.

Fundamental to the whole argument for AOE is that physics needs to put the *principle of rigour* into practice, formulated on page 81 of chapter 3. (AOE can be construed to be the outcome of successive applications of this principle.) In considering what conjecture ought to be accepted at level 4, then, we need to consider what is implicit in those current methods of physics that influence what theories are to be accepted on non-empirical grounds – having to do with simplicity, unity, explanatoriness. There can be no doubt that, as far as non-empirical considerations are concerned, the more nearly a new fundamental physical theory satisfies unity of the strongest kind with $N = 1$, so the more acceptable it will be held to be. Furthermore, failure of a theory to satisfy elements of these criteria is taken to be grounds for holding the theory to be false even in the absence of empirical difficulties. For example, high energy physics in the 1960s kept discovering more and more different hadrons (fundamental particles similar to protons and neutrons), and was judged to be in a state of crisis as the number rose to over one hundred. Again, even though the standard model (the current quantum field theory of fundamental particles and forces) does not face serious empirical problems, it is nevertheless regarded by most physicists as unlikely to be correct just because of its serious lack of unity. In adopting such non-empirical criteria for acceptability, physicists thereby implicitly assume that the best conjecture as to where the truth lies is in the direction of physicalism in the strongest sense. The principle of rigour requires that this implicit assumption – or conjecture – be made explicit so that it can be critically assessed and, we may hope, improved. Theoretical physics with physicalism in the strongest sense explicitly acknowledged as a part of conjectural knowledge is more rigorous than physics without this being acknowledged, because physics pursued in the former way is able to subject non-empirical methods to critical appraisal as the strongest version of physicalism is critically appraised, whereas physics pursued in the latter way is not able to do this as well. Because the strongest version of physicalism makes more definite, substantial claims than any rival version of physicalism, it is more open to critical appraisal than rival versions.

A second point to note is that it may well be that, even if some other, weaker version of physicalism is true, with $N > 1$, nevertheless our best hope of discovering the truth may still lie in attempting to discover a theory that exemplifies physicalism with $N = 1$, and failing in the attempt. As N becomes bigger, the number of possible theories of everything compatible with that version of physicalism rapidly increases. It makes sense to seek the simplest, most discoverable possibility, and design our methodology accordingly. One can imagine a universe in which we might have reasons for adopting a methodological rule different from: (A) In order to be ultimately acceptable, a theory must be comprehensive and unified in the strongest possible way, with $N = 1$. An example of such a rule is: (B) In order to discover the true theory of everything, there need to be infinitely many theoretical revolutions, the number of forces increasing by one at each revolution. We might come to adopt (B) if we found the number of forces goes up by one every time there is a revolution in theoretical physics. We cannot, therefore, just argue that, even if only a weaker version of physicalism is true, nevertheless our best hope of discovering the truth is to adopt (A), try to discover a theory that exemplifies the strongest version of physicalism, and fail in the attempt. But we can argue that, *in our current state of ignorance*, our best bet is to adopt (A), and revise our conjecture and methods if some other version of physicalism should emerge that appears to fit the progress of physics better (for example, a number of revolutions have taken place, and each time, the number of forces has gone up by one).

Third, it may be argued that any version of physicalism with $N > 1$ fails to accord with meta-knowability, in that such a version of physicalism is one among endlessly many analogous theses, just that which meta-knowability prohibits. If meta-knowability is interpreted as asserting that the universe is not one among endlessly many analogous possible universes, this argument becomes even stronger, since any physicalistic universe with $N > 1$ must be one among infinitely many analogous possible universes.

In short, the strongest version of physicalism with $N = 1$ seems to be the best bet when one takes into account (a) its inherent promise of progress, (b) the manner in which it is exemplified in every accepted new fundamental theory in physics, (c) the way it is implicit in non-empirical criteria in physics for a theory to be ultimately acceptable, (d) its greater fruitfulness for progress even if some other version of physicalism is true, and (e) the manner in which it accords with meta-knowability.

Finally, it needs to be remembered that what we are discussing is reasons for accepting physicalism at level 4 *within the context of* AOE. If physicalism was a candidate for the *only* metaphysical thesis to be accepted by physics, it might well be thought to be much too specific and risky to be regarded as a part of scientific knowledge. But the whole point of AOE is that, as we descend the hierarchy,

conjectures become increasingly specific, risky, tentative, and likely
to require rejection, or at least revision. Physicalism is bound to
have a much more dubious epistemological status than partial
knowability at level 7, let us say.

This concludes my discussion of reasons for accepting physicalism
at level 4.

Level 3. Best blueprint: The best available more or less specific
metaphysical conjecture as to how the universe is physically comprehensible, a conjecture which asserts that everything is composed
of some more or less specific kind of physical entity, it being in principle possible to explain all change and diversity in terms of this
kind of entity. As we have seen, examples taken from the history of
physics include: the corpuscular hypothesis of the seventeenth century, according to which the universe consists of minute, infinitely
rigid corpuscles that interact only by contact; the view, associated
with Newton and Boscovich, according to which the universe consists of point-atoms that possess mass and interact at a distance by
means of rigid, spherically symmetrical, centrally directed forces;
and the unified field view, associated with Faraday and Einstein,
according to which everything is made up of one self-interacting
field, particles of matter being especially intense regions of the field.
Many theoretical physicsts would argue that the best blueprint available today is the basic metaphysical idea of superstring theory or
M-theory: the universe consists of minute quantum strings that move
in ten or eleven dimensions of space-time, all but four of which are
curled up into a minute size, thus escaping detection. Elsewhere I
have argued, however, that the best available blueprint is a somewhat
more general thesis that I call *Lagrangianism*.[18] What one requires,
of course, is a metaphysical idea which unifies key ideas taken from
quantum theory and general relativity. My suggestion, along these
lines, is probabilistic dynamic geometry of space-time.[19]

Level 2. Accepted fundamental physical theory: All accepted fundamental dynamical theories, or accepted laws governing the way
physical phenomena occur if no dynamical theory has been developed that applies to the phenomena in question. In terms of current
scientific knowledge, this level consists of the so-called standard
model (s m) – the quantum field theory of fundamental particles and
the forces between them – plus general relativity (g r).[20] We are justified in accepting these theories because, better than any available
rivals, they satisfy the two requirements of (a) empirical success, and

(b) unity, as explicated above, thus exemplifying (in the best available way) the best level 4 thesis – the strongest version of physicalism with $N = 1$.[21]

This concludes my discussion of reasons for preferring theses at levels 7 to 2 of the version of AOE depicted in figure 2 (on page 85).

It may be conceded that AOE solves the problem of induction as far as pure theoretical physics is concerned – physics pursued for the sake of theoretical knowledge and understanding for its own sake, without a thought for practical applications. The reason given for accepting metaphysical conjectures at levels 7 to 3 has to do, not with the truth or reliability of these conjectures, but rather with their capacity to promote the growth of theoretical knowledge – to help promote the aims of pure theoretical physics, in other words. But this means that the above does not, and cannot, solve the problem of induction as far as *practical applications* are concerned. Here, it is all-important that standard empirical predictions of accepted theories are reliable, and sufficiently accurate for practical purposes. If such predictions are seriously false, bridges will collapse, aeroplanes will fall out of the sky, medicines will poison, and people will die. But we have no reason to suppose that physical theories – accepted because (a) they are empirically successful and (b) they accord better with accepted metaphysical conjectures at levels 3 and 4 – give more reliable empirical predictions than rival theories which meet requirement (a) even better, even if they clash with requirement (b).

In brief, according to the above, theories in physics are accepted in part because they accord with *metaphysical conjectures*. But when lives are at stake, we cannot rely on mere metaphysical conjectures being true, especially when no argument whatsoever has been given for their truth.

I have three points to make in support of the claim that the above does succeed in solving the practical problem (insofar as it is capable of being solved).

The first is this. Accept AOE, accept that the level 4 thesis of physicalism is a part of our knowledge, and a sharp distinction can be drawn between *certainty* and *speculation* – a distinction that eludes Popper's account of the matter. Briefly, and roughly, factual propositions which are sufficiently well-corroborated and sufficiently in accord with physicalism fall into the category of trustworthy knowledge; all other factual theories that have not been falsified fall into the category of mere speculation. This, I claim, reflects the way we actually demarcate *trustworthy knowledge* from *mere speculation*. To take an example considered by John Worrall (1989), we do not jump off the top of the Eiffel Tower, entrusting our life to the truth of the conjecture that we, exceptionally, will float gently down to the ground, because this conjecture fails to satisfy the two requirements for trustworthy knowledge. It is no doubt possible to concoct a theory that is more acceptable, according to the methodology of Popper,[22] than Newton's or Einstein's theory of gravitation – an ad hoc theory concocted to have greater empirical content and success than either, and which predicts that we will float gently down to the ground – but such a theory would clash severely with physicalism.[23]

This demarcates trustworthy knowledge from speculation, but does not provide a *justification* for the distinction. For that, some kind of justification of physicalism is required. Is any forthcoming?

This leads me to my second point. Even our most humdrum, particular, factual items of knowledge about our immediate circumstances, presupposed by our ordinary actions in life, have a cosmological dimension. I assume, at the time of writing, that I can rise from my chair and walk out of the room at any time during the next two minutes. But this very modest item of common sense knowledge makes an assumption about the entire cosmos. It presupposes that nowhere, in the entire cosmos, is there a vast explosion taking place which will spread at almost infinite speed to engulf the earth, and me with it before the two minutes are up. My modest item of common sense knowledge is only true if this cosmological presupposition is true as well. Thus, even our most modest items of common sense knowledge which edge into the future by a mere two minutes make cosmological presuppositions. It should occasion no surprise, then, that physics, with its vastly greater burden of empirical content, should make cosmological presuppositions as well. Cosmological assumptions, or conjectures, are an inevitable part of almost all that we take to be factual knowledge, whether commonsensical or scientific. The crucial question, in the context of practical life, is: which cosmological conjecture, of those available, is to be preferred? The only guideline we have available as to which is most likely to be true is: which seems best to promote acquisition of empirical knowledge? The answer, as we have seen, is physicalism.

We have before us, let us suppose, a number of candidate cosmological theses: physicalism, and theses A, B, C … (which might include the Aristotelian thesis that everything is to be explained in terms of some overall cosmological purpose, the thesis that natural phenomena exemplify a cosmological computer programme, and the thesis that phenomena occur as a result of the will of God). How should we choose? (We assume these theses are all consistent, and that they are viable cosmological theses in that each can apparently accommodate everything that we know to exist.) One consideration, clearly, is to see which is implicit in our everyday actions, and is presupposed by that part of what we take to be knowledge upon which we base our actions. Let us suppose all the candidates pass this test. The only remaining relevant consideration is: which thesis holds out the greatest hope of empirical progress, if true, and is actually associated with what seems to be progress in empirical knowledge? Metaphysical conjectures, though untestable empirically, can nevertheless be more or less *empirically fruitful*, as we saw in chapter 5, section 4. An untestable, metaphysical thesis that holds out the promise of progress in empirical knowledge, if true, has a kind of quasi-testable status. If it is adopted as the blueprint of an actively pursued research programme, and this programme, even after decades or centuries of endeavour, makes no substantial progress, this tells against the blueprint. But if, on the other hand, the research programme seems to make rapid, even ever-accelerating progress, this tells in favour of that blueprint. What better indication could we have of the truth of the blueprint than that assuming it to be true is uniquely fruitful for the acquisition of knowledge? Given this way of assessing cosmological theses, the grounds for preferring physicalism to all other candidates are very good.

But the above argument has, of course, a built-in circularity (which no doubt explains why philosophers ignore it). It is perfectly possible, in other words, for physics to appear to achieve spectacular progress in empirical knowledge – this success being uniquely associated with physics presupposing physicalism – and yet for physicalism to be grossly false. The success might be illusory, either in a way which could in principle be discovered, or in a way which could not, even in principle, until some specific time in the future (when the laws of nature abruptly change).

This circularity problem was solved above. If apparent progress in physics is illusory in a discoverable way, well, AOE is uniquely equipped to discover it. The circularity feature of AOE (as far as discoverable illusory success is concerned) provides no grounds whatsoever for not implementing AOE, and accepting the results of AOE science as a basis for action, when these results are sufficiently well-corroborated empirically. If, on the other hand, progress in physics is illusory in a way which is not discoverable (until all is revealed), then nothing can be done to guard us against such possible future disasters. Not just A O E science, but *any* methodology, *any* procedure or way of life, must be vulnerable to such undiscoverable illusory success. That A O E is vulnerable to it, and cannot guard against it, is thus no reason whatsoever for not accepting, as a basis for action, the well-established results of A O E science. Since *nothing* can anticipate, and protect us from, such unanticipatable disaster, it is foolish to blame A O E for being unable to anticipate, and protect us from, such disaster. There is here no reason not to accept well-established results of A O E science as a basis for action.

My third and final point is this. Before the scientific revolution, there was much more general awareness than there is today that what may be called cosmological circumstances could impact, in perhaps drastic and dreadful ways, on the ordinary circumstances of life. Evil spirits might cast spells and bring catastrophe, even death; comets might bring disaster; the gods might send drought, locusts, storm, the plague, and might even destroy the world. Then came science, and with it the assurance that the natural world is governed by impersonal, utterly reliable physical law. This, it seemed, had been securely established by Newtonian science. Had not Newton himself demonstrated how physical laws can be verified by induction from phenomena? There remained the niggling philosophical puzzle as to how it is possible to verify laws by means of induction, but this irritating puzzle of induction is best left to philosophers to waste their time on.

This rather common attitude – common at least until recently (skepticism about science having recently become much more widespread) – rests on an illusion. As we have seen, Newton did not establish his law of gravitation by induction from the phenomena, as he claimed to have done. He could not have done this, because it cannot be done.

Newton himself, in the first edition of the *Principia* at least, anticipated a basic feature of A O E, as we saw in chapter 2. He recognized explicitly that scientific method makes presuppositions about nature. His first three rules of reason, concerned with simplicity, quite explicitly make assumptions about the nature of the universe. Newton understood that persistently preferring simple theories means that Nature herself is being persistently assumed to be simple.

But this aspect of Newton's thought came to be overlooked. The immense, unprecedented success of natural science after Newton was taken to demonstrate that humanity had somehow discovered the secret of wresting truth and certainty from nature, and only the incompetence of philosophers prevented everyone from knowing exactly what this secret amounted to. Even today there are philosophers who think that the problem of induction will only be solved when this secret of how scientists manage to capture truth and certainty is laid bare for everyone to see and understand.

But this is an illusion. Even our most humdrum, particular, practical knowledge of aspects of our immediate environment, as we have seen, let alone the mighty claims to knowledge of physics, contains a cosmological element which must remain conjectural. Modern science has, it seems, made a profound discovery about the ultimate nature of the cosmos, namely that it is physically comprehensible. Once AOE is accepted, it becomes clear that this thesis, despite its *metaphysical* and *cosmological* character, is one of the most firmly established theoretical propositions of science (in that physical theories, in order to be accepted, must accord with this proposition as far as possible, and theories which clash with it too stridently are not even considered, even though they would be much more empirically successful than accepted theories if considered). Given this cosmological thesis that the universe is physically comprehensible, the way we in practice distinguish trustworthy knowledge from mere speculation becomes clear. Nevertheless, despite its central place and role in science, the thesis remains inherently conjectural in character. Practical certainty has this usually unacknowledged conjectural and cosmological dimension inherent in it.[24]

As it is, our attitude towards the thesis that the universe is physically comprehensible is highly hypocritical. The fundamental role that it plays in science, in technology, in our whole culture and way of life, is denied. Non-scientists deny it because they do not want to confront the grim implications the thesis has for the meaning and value of human life – the difficulty of seeing how there can be consciousness, freedom, meaning, and value if the universe really is physically comprehensible.[25] Scientists deny it, because they do not want to acknowledge that there is an element of *faith* in science. They confidently distinguish science from religion on the grounds that, whereas

religion appeals to dogma and faith, in science there is no faith and
everything is assessed impartially with respect to evidence. But this,
as we have seen, is nonsense. There is an element of faith in science
too. The real difference between science as it ought to be, natural
philosophy, and religion – most dogmatic religions that is – is that
whereas natural philosophy subjects its articles of faith to sustained
critical scrutiny, modifying them in the direction of that which seems
most fruitful from the standpoint of the growth of knowledge, dogmatic religion does nothing of the kind. We are justified in accepting
physicalism as a part of our knowledge, even in the context of practical action, because some such cosmological conjecture must be
accepted, and physicalism has proved more fruitful for progress in
knowledge than any rival. It is always possible that this success is
illusory, and physicalism is no more than a kind of scientific halluci-
nation. But if the success of science is illusory in a way we could not
in principle discover, then this is a possibility we face whatever we
assume; it is not something we can do anything about, and deserves
to be ignored. If, on the other hand, the success of science is illusory
in a way which can in principle be discovered, then A O E science provides us with the best means of unmasking the illusion. Either way,
physicalism deserves to be accepted even in practical contexts.

A more honest recognition of the presence of cosmological conjectures inherent in physics, in science more generally, and even in our
most humble items of practical knowledge would involve recognizing that all our knowledge is indeed conjectural in character, without
thereby destroying the distinction we make between practical certainty and speculation.

Popper has done much to create an awareness of the conjectural character of scientific knowledge – helped, of course, by the
dethronement of Newtonian science and classical physics with the
advent of general relativity and quantum theory. But in one crucial
respect, Popper helped sustain the Newtonian tradition, the status
quo. He fiercely defended, to the last, the highly traditional, and mistaken, idea that the scientific character of science depends on it being
dissociated from metaphysics.[26] Actually, it is all the other way round.
If science is to be rigorous, it is essential that it acknowledge – and so
throw open to criticism and improvement – metaphysical and cosmological theses implicit in the persistent scientific selection of unified, explanatory theories. And that is just the start of one line of
argument leading to wisdom-inquiry: not just metaphysics, but

values, and political commitments too, implicit in the scientific endeavour, need to be made explicit, if science is to be rigorous, so that these problematic assumptions and commitments can be criticized and, we may hope, improved.

One final remark. Not only does A O E suffice to solve the problem of induction; it is required to solve the problem. There are three reasons why the problem can only be solved within the framework of A O E.

1 The hierarchical structure of A O E is essential for the solution to the problem. It is needed, because quite *different* reasons need to be given for accepting theses, at the five different levels of the view. If these different levels become just *one* level, this cannot be done.

2 A O E is required to solve the problem of vicious circularity involved in justifying acceptance of physical theory by an appeal to metaphysics, and then justifying acceptance of this same metaphysics by an appeal to the empirical success of physical theory. A O E alone solves this problem by accepting, at level 6, a conjecture which asserts, in effect, that the universe is such that this apparently viciously circular procedure is justified and can meet with success, acceptance of this conjecture being justified in a way which makes no appeal to the empirical success of science.

3 In order to solve the problem, we need an intellectually rigorous conception of science. A O E alone has the required rigour, in that it alone acknowledges and provides the means to improve problematic metaphysical conjectures of physics – only possible because of the hierarchical structure of A O E.[27]

For a more detailed exposition of the argument that A O E solves the problem of induction, see N. Maxwell 2017. For earlier expositions see N. Maxwell 1998 (chapter 5), 2004a (appendix, section 6), 2007a (chapter 14, section 6), 2011b, and 2013a.

Notes

CHAPTER ONE

1 Aspects of these philosophical blunders are discussed in N. Maxwell 1984 (second edition 2007a), 2004a, 2014a, 2014b, and 2017. See also N. Maxwell 2009a, 2010a, and 2012.
2 For an excellent recent detailed account of the origins of modern science see Cohen 2010. Classic works on the scientific revolution include Burtt 1980; Koyré 1957; Butterfield 1949; Dijksterhuis 1969; and Westfall 1977. See Cohen 1994 for a fascinating, comprehensive discussion of various approaches of historians of science to the scientific revolution up to around 1991. More recent works on the scientific revolution include: Lindberg and Westman 1990; Shapin 1998; Rossi 2001; Henry 2002; Gaukroger 2006 and 2010; and Cohen 2015.
3 This point was well made long ago by Burtt 1932.
4 Aspects of the picture of the scientific revolution I depict in this chapter have been called into question by some historians of science in recent decades. I discuss this issue briefly in the final section of this chapter.
5 Galileo, *The Assayer* 1623: see Drake 1957, 274.
6 Drake 1957, 276.
7 A slightly modified version of a translation quoted in Guthrie 1978, 440, where an account of Democritus's life and work is to be found.
8 The first person to publish the correct version of the law of inertia was Pierre Gassendi, who also tested it experimentally by dropping weights on moving ships and carriages. Descartes formulated the law earlier in a treatise on natural philosophy called *Le Monde* which he decided not to publish at the last minute because he received news of Galileo's

trial. *Le Monde* defended a Copernican theory. Descartes finally published the law in his *Principia Philosophiae* (*Principles of Philosophy*)
which appeared in 1644, published after Gassendi: see Cohen 1985,
210–11.

9 That the particles fill all of space and are rigid creates a problem for
motion.

10 Locke 1961, xxxv.

11 A *metaphysical* thesis, as I use the term, is one that is not testable
empirically. It is neither verifiable nor falsifiable by means of observation or experiment. This definition is not entirely satisfactory. One
might well hold that the corpuscular hypothesis – the doctrine that
matter is made up of minute, invisible, rigid corpuscles – is a metaphysical doctrine. But versions of the corpuscular hypothesis that hold
that corpuscles interact only by colliding – there thus being only repulsive forces in the world – can be regarded as being not just falsifiable
empirically, but falsified by the observation that there are cohesive and
attractive forces in nature (forces that hold pieces of rock and metal
together, for example, and magnetic and gravitational forces). In the
seventeenth century, attempts were made to explain cohesive and
attractive forces within the framework of the corpuscular hypothesis,
but these attempts were not very successful! We may, alternatively,
characterize metaphysical theses as imprecisely formulated physical
theories. The metaphysical theses that we will be concerned with in
this book are all theses put forward in an attempt to anticipate what
theoretical physics may subsequently discover. Examples of such theses
from the history of physics and its associated metaphysics are the corpuscular hypothesis just mentioned; the thesis that the world is made
up of point-particles that have mass and are surrounded by a centrally
directed, rigid, spherically symmetric field of force that varies from the
repulsive to the attractive as one moves away from the point-particle.
For further examples, see chapter 5, section 5.

12 See Galileo, *The Assayer* in Drake 1957, 237–8.

13 In what follows I give a very brief account of the contributions of
Copernicus, Kepler, Galileo, and Newton, not with the intention of
saying anything new about these contributions, but rather to highlight
the vital role that a certain metaphysical view about the nature of the
universe played in these discoveries – the view, as Galileo put it, that
"the book of nature is written in the language of mathematics." This
metaphysical view is not just psychologically important, important in
suggesting fruitful hypotheses – important in the context of discovery,

as philosophers of science would put it. The view is *methodologically* important – indeed essential. It is vital in the context of verification, the context of accepting and rejecting hypotheses. It is as important as *evidence* is – observation and experiment. There were two vital ingredients in the new natural philosophy: the appeal to *observation* and *experiment*; and the appeal to the metaphysical thesis that the universe has some kind of mathematical structure or reality. A new hypothesis in physics or astronomy, in order to be acceptable as new knowledge, had to satisfy *both*.

14 Copernicus differs from Ptolemy, not only in holding that the earth goes round the sun every year, but also in holding that the earth rotates on its axis every twenty-four hours – instead of the heavens rotating every twenty-four hours around a stationary earth.

15 Galileo cleared up the first of these two empirical problems facing Copernicus's theory. A stone thrown into the air continues to possess the motion of the earth it had before it was thrown. The second empirical problem was not cleared up until 1838, when Friedrich Bessel, a German mathematician and astronomer, observed stellar parallax predicted by Copernican theory.

16 Ptolemy's theory postulated some eighty epicycles (plus other devices), whereas Copernicus postulated only thirty-four.

17 Burtt 1932, 42–3.

18 The Platonic, regular or perfect solids are polyhedra whose faces are all the same, edges all the same length. Thus the cube has six faces, each face a square. The tetrahedron has four faces, each an equilateral triangle; the octahedron has eight faces, each also an equilateral triangle; the dodecahedron twelve faces each with five edges; and the icosahedron has twenty faces each an equilateral triangle. And these are all that there are, granted that space is Euclidean and three-dimensional.

19 From a modern perspective, of course, Kepler's idea faces the further difficulty that there are nine planets (taking Pluto to be a planet), not five. In addition, we have no particular reason to suppose that the distances planets have from the sun will obey any precise law. There is, however, Bode's law, which states that the distance from sun to planet is $4 + N$, where 10 is taken to be the distance from the sun to the earth, and $N = 0, 3, 6, 12, 24, 48, \ldots$, where for $N \geq 3$ each value of N is twice the previous value. This rule works quite well, as long as we take Ceres in the asteroid belt to be a planet (or failed planet), until we get to the two final planets, Neptune and Pluto, when it goes badly astray.

20 A few words of explanation. In order to draw an ellipse, fix the ends
    of a piece of string to two drawing pins stuck into a board, and trace
    out a curve with a pencil pressed hard against the string so as to keep
    the string taut. The drawing pins are at the two foci of the ellipse that
    results. The ellipse, it should be noted, is a generalization of the circle.
    As the drawing pins are put closer and closer together, so the ellipse
    tends towards the circle. Kepler's 2nd law amounts to a generalization,
    for the ellipse, of the statement that planets move uniformly in circles
    round the sun. The semi-major axis of an ellipse is the line drawn from
    the centre of the ellipse, halfway between the foci, through one focus
    and on to the ellipse itself. It is, as it were, the longest radius of the
    ellipse, as opposed to the shortest radius, the "semi-minor" axis. (The
    difference between these two axes becomes less and less as the two
    foci are put closer and closer together.) Kepler's 3rd law can be formu-
    lated thus: $T^2 = kR^3$, where T is the time it takes for the planet in ques-
    tion to orbit the sun, R is the length of the semi-major axis of the
    ellipse the planet traces out on its journey round the sun, and k is
    a constant.

21 Tycho Brahe's theory of the solar system was a compromise between
    Ptolemy and Copernicus. He held that the sun goes round the earth,
    but all the other planets go round the sun.

22 I should make clear that "implications" of Copernicus's theory here
    means no more than "what might be taken to be reasonable modifica-
    tions of Aristotelianism in the light of Copernicus's theory." The
    Aristotelian contrast between the unchanging mathematical perfection
    of the heavens and the rather more arbitrary processes of change,
    growth, and decay here on earth can hardly be maintained once it is
    acknowledged that the earth is, as it were, in the heavens itself as it
    goes round the sun with the other planets. It is not unreasonable to
    conclude that other planets, other heavenly bodies, exhibit change,
    imperfection, growth, and decay just as the earth does. And, on the
    other hand, if we hold onto the Platonic and Aristotelian idea that
    mathematics governs what goes on in the heavens, and we hold that
    the earth is now itself in the heavens, it is reasonable to conclude that
    phenomena on earth occur in accordance with (unknown) mathemati-
    cal laws.

23 An Englishman called Leonard Digges seems to have been the first per-
    son to invent the telescope around 1551. His son, Thomas Digges, was
    the first person to give an account of Copernicus's theory in English
    in 1576: see Gribbin 2003, 15–17. The telescope was reinvented by

accident by a Dutch spectacle maker, Hans Lipershey, in 1608. Galileo, on hearing of the invention, reinvented an improved telescope, one which included a convex lens, and thus kept the image upright instead of inverting it as Lipershey's telescope did.

24 For a summary of Galileo's discoveries concerning terrestrial motion see Cohen 1985, 214–17.

25 Galileo wrote: "Aristotle says that a hundred-pound ball falling from a height of one hundred cubits hits the ground before a one-pound ball has fallen one cubit. I say they arrive at the same time. You find, on making the test, that the larger ball beats the smaller ball by two inches. Now, behind those two inches you want to hide Aristotle's ninety-nine cubits and, speaking only of my tiny error, remain silent about his enormous mistake" (quoted in Gribben 2003, 77).

26 For discussion of the grounds for holding that Galileo really did perform the experiments he claimed to have performed, and further references, see Cohen 1985, 188–209, 212–13.

27 The law of inertia and Galilean invariance may be understood to be consequences of, or at least closely related to, the idea that all motion is relative, there being no such thing as motion relative to space itself but only relative to some other body. If this is the case, then whether a body is at rest or in motion depends solely on one's frame of reference. So, if we agree that a body at rest stays at rest unless a force impressed on it causes it to move, it follows from this that a body in motion will continue in that state of motion unless a force impressed on it changes its state of motion. For the body at rest with respect to another body, A, is also in motion with respect to another body, B, in motion with respect to A. Even though all this can be regarded as key components of Newtonian theory, Newton himself would have disagreed. Newton held that there is such a thing as absolute space, and absolute motion with respect to it. And there is the following consideration ostensibly in favour of this view. Even though there is no way of measuring whether one is in uniform motion or at rest with respect to absolute space, one can, it seems, determine whether one is accelerating or not – without it being necessary to refer to any external body. If you are travelling in a train that hits the buffers as it comes into the station, what you experience inside the train tells you that you have experienced a sudden deacceleration. Only with Einstein's general theory of relativity is there a suggested explanation as to why you may not know whether you have suffered a sudden deacceleration or not. At first sight it seems impossible to declare, in the spirit of the relativity

of motion, that the train is stationary throughout and it is the platform and station (and earth) which come hurtling towards the train,
to suffer sudden deacceleration when the buffers hit the train. It is
only people in the train who feel the effects of sudden deacceleration;
people on the platform feel no effects whatsoever. But Einstein suggests a way in which it is possible to declare that the train is stationary
throughout and it is the station that deaccelerates. At the very moment
that the station buffers hit the stationary train, a powerful gravitational field comes into existence for the brief period of the collision.
This exactly cancels out the effects of deacceleration of the platform
and the people on it. Acceleration due to the gravitational field and
deacceleration due to the collision with the train cancel each other out,
and people on the platform feel nothing. But people in the train, being
stationary (according to this surreal account), feel powerfully the
effects of the sudden gravitational field at the moment of impact. They
are thrown forward, and cups of coffee fly off tables. It is just as if the
train has come to an abrupt halt, even though it has been stationary
throughout. All the effects of acceleration, in other words, can be
mimicked by gravitational forces appropriately switched on and off,
and vice versa. No experiment performed in a lift can distinguish
between effects of (a) acceleration or (b) appropriate gravitational
field. But all this lies far into the future of Galileo. Nevertheless, that
Galileo's work prompts such reflections is an indication of just how
fundamental his contribution is.

28 The first to publish the correct form of the law was Pierre Gassendi:
    see note 8.

29 Gary Hatfield has argued that Galileo adopted, and argued for, a
    mathematical approach to nature, but this does not amount to adopt-
    ing a metaphysical view of nature: see Hatfield 1990. But Hatfield's
    argument strikes me as unconvincing. There is, implicit in Galileo's
    methods and approach, a view of the natural world dramatically dif-
    ferent from Aristotle's – a view that becomes explicit in Galileo's
    remark about the book of nature – "this grand book, the universe" –
    and in the distinction he draws between what came to be called after
    Locke "primary" and "secondary" qualities, only the former being real.

30 For a famous articulation of this sense of bafflement see Eugene
    Wigner's essay "The Unreasonable Effectiveness of Mathematics in the
    Natural Sciences" (in Wigner 1967). Related is Einstein's pronounce-
    ment, "The eternal mystery of the world is its comprehensibility"
    (Einstein 1973, 292).

31 A "dynamical" theory, as I use the term, is a theory that provides a law for the operations of a *force*.

32 The other five are classic electrodynamics, general relativity, quantum electrodynamics, quantum electroweak theory, and quantum chromodynamics. Classical electrodynamics is the theory of the electromagnetic field. It was created by James Clerk Maxwell in the nineteenth century, building on the work of Michael Faraday and others. General relativity is Einstein's theory of gravitation, put forward in 1915. It holds, roughly, that matter (or energy more generally) curves space-time, and bodies then move along what is nearest to straight lines (called geodesics) in the resulting curved space-time. Quantum electrodynamics, as its name suggests, is the quantum version of Maxwell's classical electrodynamics. It was created by Paul Dirac, Richard Feynman, and others in the twentieth century. Quantum electroweak theory unifies the electromagnetic and so-called weak forces (the latter a nuclear force). And chromodynamics is the quantum field theory of the so-called strong nuclear force.

33 For a recent, detailed, and very impressive analysis (and, in a way, defence) of Newton's achievement, see Harper 2011.

34 As I have already mentioned, the calculus was also invented independently by Leibniz. Newton invented his version of the calculus first in 1666 when he was twenty-three, but did not publish at the time. Leibniz invented his version later and published before Newton. Newton's supporters accused Leibniz of stealing Newton's work from unpublished letters and manuscripts.

35 Full title: *Philosophiae Naturalis Principia Mathematica* (*Mathematical Principles of Natural Philosophy*).

36 Newton (1687) 1962, vol. 1, xvii–xviii.

37 One needs of course the physical theories of these forces to predict phenomena – the theories mentioned in note 32. And in practice only the simplest phenomena can be predicted because of the extreme difficulty of solving the equations of the theories. The nature of dark matter remains a mystery – a form of matter conjectured to exist on the basis of its gravitational effects on the rotation of stars in galaxies.

38 Newton (1687) 1962, vol. 1, 13.

39 Newton (1687) 1962, vol. 2, 398–400. These rules were modified, and even added to, by Newton in successive editions of the *Principia*, as we shall see in chapter 2.

40 All this is established in the first twenty-four pages of Book 3 of the *Principia*: see ibid., 399–422.

41 Ibid., 547.

42 See Burtt 1980; Koyré 1957, 1965, 1968; Butterfield 1949; and Westfall 1977.

43 Duhem 1954–58, 1991.

44 The very distinction, as customarily drawn – factors "internal" to the discipline versus "external" social factors (see, for example, Henry 2002, 7) is doubly misconceived. In the first place, the rationality, the scientific character, of science depends crucially on its *social* character (Popper 1962, 217–20), and on having the right kind of *institutional* structure (Popper 1961, 154–9). In ignoring *methodological* aspects of science (as "internalist"), social constructivists ignore vital *social* and *institutional* aspects of science! Secondly, it is absurd to hold that *intellectual* aspects of science are *internal* to it. Very crudely, we might say that the intellectual aspects of the social phenomenon that is science are those aspects that have to do with fact, truth, knowledge and explanation, and methods relevant to the assessment of these things. But it is quite wrong to characterize these as "internal" to science: they are of concern throughout the social world, in courts of law, in journalism, and throughout social life quite generally. Whether a statement or belief is true or not – or whether there are good grounds to hold it to be true or not – can be a matter of great concern in all sorts of social contexts. It is an aspect of social life that no social scientist can ignore – including, of course, sociologists and historians of science.

45 The notion of "Whiggish" history as something intellectually disreputable comes from Butterfield 1951 – a rather bad book that ignores that history is always about something more or less specific, and may, quite legitimately, be about the more or less specific topic of an endeavour that seeks to make progress towards some aim, and may even achieve it.

46 Popper 1962, 270.

47 For a more detailed refutation of the idea that history that sees science as a progress-achieving endeavour must be Whiggish history in an intellectually disreputable sense, see N. Maxwell 2014b, 65–85.

48 We need to distinguish two kinds of discovery associated with the birth of modern science: (1) discoveries about the world, such as Kepler's, Galileo's, and Newton's laws, and Harvey's discovery of the function of the heart, and (2) the discovery of how to do science. If (2) is to be attributed to any one individual – and of course it cannot be – that individual would be Galileo. But Galileo made the discovery primarily

in practice, in the way he *did* natural philosophy, not in a formulated view as to how natural philosophy ought to be pursued.

49 Shapin 1998, 3–4.

50 For a decisive criticism of social constructivism see N. Maxwell 2014b, chapter 4.

51 Gaukroger 2006, 17–18.

52 Ibid., 18.

53 The view I have in mind is that *evidence* decides what theories are accepted and rejected in science, metaphysical assumptions playing no role. This orthodox view of *standard empiricism*, as I call it, is expounded and refuted in chapter 3.

54 How are metaphysical theses associated with physics to be assessed and improved even though they are not empirically testable? First, there are theses which are required to be true if science is to be possible at all: these deserve to be accepted even though we have no grounds to hold that they are true. An example is the thesis: the universe is such that it is possible for us to acquire some knowledge of our local circumstances. If this thesis is false, we have had it, whatever we assume. Nothing can ever be gained by rejecting this thesis. Second, from a number of candidates, we accept that thesis which (a) best accords with theses of the type just mentioned, and (b) is associated with the most empirically successful research programme in physics, or at least holds out the best hope of leading to such an empirically successful research programme. For details, see chapter 3, appendix 2, and above all chapter 5, section 5. See also N. Maxwell 2017.

55 See N. Maxwell 1993a, part III.

56 Einstein 1973, 270.

CHAPTER TWO

1 Various dates may be proposed, no doubt, for the demise of natural philosophy and the birth of modern science as we know it today. Modern science may be characterized, in part, in terms of its institutional and social aspects. These must develop, it may be held, before modern science can be held to have emerged. My concern, however, is with the splitting of natural philosophy into science on the one hand, philosophy on the other. This split can no doubt be assigned various dates, and it is, to some extent, a matter of degree. My claim is that the intellectual origins of the split go back to Newton, and his claim

to have derived his law of gravitation from the phenomena without recourse to hypotheses "whether metaphysical or physical."

2 These are quoted towards the end of chapter 1.

3 Newton (1687) 1962, 398.

4 Ibid.

5 In recent years, a number of historians of science have explored in detail Newton's methodology as this is revealed in his *Principia* (see Cohen 1983; Smith 2002; Harper 2011; and Ducheyne 2012). Ducheyne in particular argues that Newton's methodology is not the crude inductivism that Duhem and Popper attribute to him, and then criticize (Duhem 1962, 190–5; Popper 1972, chapter 5): see Ducheyne 2012, xiv–xv. (Harper makes a similar point: see Harper 2011, 126–30.) Ducheyne goes on to argue that Newton's methodology is more sophisticated than hypothetico-deductivism, in that it includes methods which check the adequacy of empirically confirmed hypotheses – methods that hypothetico-deductivism does not provide (103–6, 159–69). Whether Ducheyne is correct about this last point depends crucially on how sophisticated a version of hypothetico-deductivism one considers. But even if Ducheyne is correct, this leaves untouched my central claim about Newton: his methodology makes substantial problematic metaphysical presuppositions, a point that is progressively obscured in successive editions of the *Principia*. Furthermore, Newton was subsequently interpreted to have derived his law of gravitation from the phenomena by induction without recourse to "hypotheses, whether metaphysical or physical," as he claimed to have done in the third edition of the *Principia*.

6 In chapter 3 I show decisively that it is not just Newton's law of gravitation which requires an appeal to both *empirical success* and a *metaphysical assumption about the nature of the universe* if valid grounds are to be given for its acceptance. This is the case for *all* laws and theories of physics.

7 What Newton in effect asserted, in the *Principia*, was that what he was *against* was recourse to hypotheses during the course of establishing scientific knowledge based on evidence (as might be said these days). Newton was not against putting forward hypotheses in natural philosophy as such (in the context of discovery), and he put forward many hypotheses himself.

8 Newton's "derivation" of his law of gravitation from the phenomena also requires, of course, his three laws of motion (formulated towards the end of chapter 1). These may not be metaphysical, but they are

certainly hypothetical when interpreted as applying to all objects everywhere, at all times and places.

9 Hypothesis III asserts that any body can be transformed into any other. Koyré suggests that it was dropped from subsequent editions because it clashes with Newton's assertion in his *Opticks* that God in the beginning created atoms of different shapes and sizes, which implies they cannot be transformed into one another (Koyré 1965, 263n2).

10 What becomes of the nine hypotheses of the first edition of the *Principia* in the subsequent two editions is clearly laid out in a table in Newton 1999, 794, note aa. For an excellent discussion see Cohen 1999, 198–204.

11 Koyré 1965, 266. My remarks concerning the changes that Newton made to later editions of his *Principia* are based on what Koyré has to say in ibid., 261–72.

12 It comes towards the end of the General Scholium, which was added at the end of Book III of the second edition of the *Principia*, edited by Roger Cotes.

13 It appeared in Newton's own copy of the second edition of the *Principia*: see Harper 2011, 260n6.

14 Newton (1687) 1962, 400.

15 If we take the first edition of the *Principia* at its face value, and attend to what Newton actually claimed in it, there can be no doubt that it is emphatically a work of natural philosophy in the sense of Kepler and Galileo. Newton explicitly acknowledges that his "derivation" of his law of gravitation from the phenomena makes essential use of *metaphysical hypotheses* about the nature of the universe, there called "hypotheses" and not "rules of reasoning in philosophy." It is only with the second and third editions that the picture changes, and Newton decisively denies that he adopts any such metaphysical hypotheses. Thus, it is not the first edition of the *Principia*, but the second edition onwards, and the way they came to be understood, that killed off natural philosophy.

16 Koyré 1965, 117–18.

17 See quotation from Huygens in Harper 2011, 205.

18 Burtt 1932, 265–6.

19 See Cajori's appendix to Newton's *Principia* (Newton [1687] 1962, 674). Cajori there remarks, "My quotations from Newton suggest the motive which induced him to take a stand against the use of hypotheses, namely the danger of becoming involved in disagreeable controversies."

20 Newton (1687) 1962, 544.

21 This idea was ridiculed by Leibniz. In a letter to Caroline of Ansbach
    (Queen of Great Britain, wife of King George II), Leibniz poured scorn
    on the Newtonian idea that God might be such an incompetent crafts-
    man that He might find it necessary to adjust the working of the uni-
    verse. It was this letter which sparked off a famous exchange between
    Leibniz and Clarke, as we shall see later on.

22 Newton (1687) 1962, 669.

23 Stephen Inwood, during his account of the dispute between Newton
    and Hooke, describes Newton, I think fairly, as "neurotic, self-centred,
    ambitious, intolerant, oversensitive, secretive, unforgiving, and highly
    argumentative" (Inwood 2003, 299).

24 Inwood 2003, 82–5.

25 Ibid., 84.

26 Ibid., 289–90, 291–9.

27 Ibid., 289–90, 461n15.

28 Ibid., chapter 22.

29 But the word "science," stemming from the Latin "scientia" (which
    meant knowledge), was in use centuries earlier. Galileo's *Two New
    Sciences*, first published in 1638 in Italian, referred in the title to
    Due Nuove Scienze. The French Academy was called "La première
    Académie des sciences" when first formed in 1666, and was
    renamed "L'Académie royale des sciences" in 1699. The Royal
    Society, on the other hand, was referred to in the Royal Charter of
    1663 as "The Royal Society of London for Improving Natural
    Knowledge."

30 Some historians of science employ the term "natural philosophy" to
    refer, merely, to what others call "pure science" – science devoted to
    the pursuit of knowledge for its own sake without any suggestion that
    natural philosophy, in that sense, makes substantial metaphysical
    assumptions about the nature of the universe and intermingles science
    and philosophy: see for example Dear 2006. "Natural philosophy,"
    interpreted to mean merely "pure science," is quite different from
    authentic natural philosophy as I have characterized it, the endeavour
    I seek to resurrect in this book.

31 Voltaire 1980, 68.

32 In subsequent chapters I will, however, argue against this conclusion.

33 The reasons I have given for doubting the veracity of the senses are
    not the ones Descartes gives in his *Discourse on Method*, and else-
    where: see Descartes 1949. My claim is, nevertheless, that the reasons

I have given are the real, powerful grounds for doubting the senses
that emerge from the corpuscular hypothesis associated with the new
natural philosophy; these grounds would almost certainly have influenced Descartes.

34 Koyré 1965, 63.

35 For a very detailed and lucid account of the battle between Newtonians
and Cartesians see Shank 2008. My account of the Newton wars in
France owes much to Shank's book. For a good, brief account, see
Heilbron 1979, 39–43, 55–63. See also Koyré 1965, chapter 3.

36 For an account of this dispute see Hall 1980.

37 See, for example, the Leibniz-Clarke correspondence edited by H.G.
Alexander, 1956.

38 For Maupertuis's life and work see Terrall 2002.

39 The full title is *Discours sur les différentes figures des astres d'ou l'on
tire des conjectures sur les étoiles qui paraissent changer de grandeur,
et sur l'anneau de Saturne*, which can be translated as *Discourse on
the different shapes of heavenly bodies from which conjectures can be
drawn about planets which appear to change in size, and on the ring
of Saturn*.

40 Quoted in Shank 2008, 288.

41 There is a wonderful, hilarious account of their life together in
Mitford 1957.

42 See Shank 2008, 372–5 for extended quotations from her review.

43 See Kuhn 1970, 151.

44 See Shank 2008, 242.

45 So unassailable did Newton's authority become, that it was not until
the early twentieth century that Newton's argument for his law of
gravitation was seriously challenged. Pierre Duhem argued around
1906 that Newton could not have derived his law from Kepler's laws,
since Newton went on to show that his law *corrects*, and is thus
incompatible with, Kepler's laws: see Duhem 1962, 190–5. For a discussion see N. Maxwell 2014c. Recently, as we saw in note 5, Newton
has been defended against Duhem's criticisms: see Harper 2011, 126–
32; Ducheyne 2012, xiv–xv.

46 Rationalism did not die out entirely, however: see Darrigol 2014. It is
significant that Darrigol, in exploring hints of rationalism associated
with physics up to the twenty-first century, as a potential rival to
empiricism, overlooks *authentic natural philosophy*, as I have characterized it.

47 William Whewell coined the term *scientist* in 1833.

48 There are 118 elements, but elements at the top end of the scale tend to decay rapidly, being short-lived. Ninety-eight elements are found naturally on earth, some in minute quantities.

49 One billion = one thousand million = 1,000,000,000 = 10^9.

50 A light year is the distance light travels in one year. In one second light travels 186,000 miles. A light year is roughly 6 million million miles (10^{12} miles).

51 Viewed from the perspective of Einstein's theory, Newton and his critics were right to be suspicious of the idea that gravitation could exert a force at a distance through empty space. Einstein's theory explains the motion of bodies acting in response to gravitation in such a way that there is no appeal to such a gravitational force acting at a distance.

52 I have suggested that these paradoxical features of quantum theory can be resolved by a reformulation of the theory as a fundamentally *probabilistic* theory – a suggestion that will be discussed in chapter 5.

53 According to string theory, all fundamental particles are the same kind of tiny closed string, different vibrations going round the string accounting for the different properties of the different kinds of particle.

54 It has also led to the grave global problems of the modern world: population growth, pollution of earth, sea, and air, destruction of natural habitats and extinction of species, vast inequalities of wealth and power around the globe, the lethal character of modern war, and, most serious of all, the impending disasters of climate change. These adverse consequences of modern science and technology will be discussed in chapter 8.

CHAPTER THREE

1 The story is told briefly in Russell 1982, 90, although Russell does go on to suggest that philosophy has the task of tackling fundamental problems even though truth may here be unattainable. Versions are also told in Kuhn 1970, chapter 2, and Ayer 1982, 14.

2 A key purpose of the present book is, of course, to establish that problematic metaphysical assumptions about how the fundamental problem "What kind of universe is this?" is to be answered inevitably play an influential role in science. Precisely because these assumptions are highly conjectural and problematic – almost bound to be false – they need to be made explicit within science so that they may be critically

assessed and, we may hope, improved. Imaginative and critical thought about this fundamental problem of science is important for the rigour, the health, of science! In chapter 6 I argue that ideas about what is of value play a role in science too – in influencing choice of research aims.

3   See N. Maxwell 2014b, chapters 1 and 5.

4   For what it means to say of a physical theory that it is unified, see appendix 1. For more detailed, technical accounts, see N. Maxwell 1998 (chapters 3–4), 2004a (appendix, section 2), 2007 (chapter 14, section 2), 2013a (section 4), 2017 (chapter 5).

5   I have devoted two books to articulating, and trying to help solve, this fundamental problem: N. Maxwell 2001 and 2010a. I there argue that this is our fundamental problem. See also N. Maxwell 1966, 1968a, 1968b, 1984 (chapter 10), 2000b, 2011a. For my discussion of that aspect of the problem concerned primarily with the *flourishing* of what is of value in our human world, see N. Maxwell 1984, 2004a, 2007a, 2014a; for summaries, see N. Maxwell 1980, 1992, 2000a, 2007b, 2009a, 2012.

6   The moment it is accepted that philosophy has, as its basic task, to tackle fundamental problems, it is clear that philosophy education must be transformed. Instead of learning philosophy via the history of philosophy, rather one needs to plunge, from the outset, into the fundamental problem as it confronts us today, relevant background knowledge in physics, biology, climate science, social inquiry, and the humanities, politics, economics, and international affairs being acquired as one goes along. That the history of philosophy is the wrong way to learn philosophy becomes all the more obvious granted the points to be made below – namely, that much of philosophy in the past has been alienated from concern with our fundamental problems. For hints as to what is required, see N. Maxwell 2005b and 2010a.

7   N. Maxwell 2014b, chapter 2.

8   Unquestionably, philosophers in recent decades have grappled with problems about the existence and nature of our human world – the world as we experience it – in the light of what physics seems to tell us about the nature of the universe. See, for example, Smart 1963, Nagel 1986, and Chalmers 1996. To this extent, academic philosophy already puts into practice the conception of philosophy I am arguing for here. The whole question of whether contemporary philosophy does do what I argue it ought to do will be considered towards the end of chapter 4.

9 In Maxwell 1980 I argued that academic inquiry needs to grapple
with fundamental problems in a way which interacts with more specialized research, the former both influencing and being influenced
by the latter. I argued that, in order to do this rigorously, academic
inquiry needs to put the four rules of problem solving, 1 to 4, into
practice. I failed, however, to argue for the reform of philosophy, so
that it takes up the basic task of ensuring that academic inquiry tack-
les both fundamental and specialized problems in a way that puts 1 to
4 into practice. I left philosophy as a specialized discipline alongside
the others. For a later and somewhat more detailed discussion of the
rules 1 to 4 and other rules of rational problem solving see N.
Maxwell 1984, 67–71, or 2007a, 79–84.

10 N. Maxwell 1980.

11 Huxley 1937, 276–7.

12 Huxley 1980, 9. Huxley goes on to describe a number of attempts to
solve the problem that have been made over the years which do not
succeed, and then argues for an approach "in terms of fundamental
human problems," not so very different from what I am arguing for
here, except Huxley does not set human problems into the context of
what science seems to be telling us about the nature of the universe:
see ibid., 9–10.

13 In my own university, University College London, the recently founded
"Grand Challenges Programme" successfully puts a form of multi-
disciplinarity into practice. The idea is to bring specialists together to
help solve global problems: see http://www.ucl.ac.uk/grand-challenges
(accessed 4 July 2015).

14 When it comes to rampant specialization, academic philosophers are
themselves among the worst offenders. They have done the opposite
of seeking to check rampant specialization.

15 See, however, N. Maxwell 1980. Much of my work, from 1966
onwards, has sought, either to tackle fundamental problems, or urge
the importance of doing just that. And of course I am not alone in
pursuing philosophy so as to tackle fundamental problems of thought
and life.

16 See N. Maxwell 2014b, chapter 1.

17 See Popper 1959, 1962, 1963, 1969. See also Popper 1976.

18 See my "Popper's Paradoxical Pursuit of Natural Philosophy" (2016b).
Much of my own work – including the present book – can be regarded
as arising out of a concern to solve problems that confront Popper's

philosophy: see N. Maxwell 1972a, 2009a, 2009b (preface), 2012, 2016b.

19 Kant scholars will no doubt complain that my thumbnail sketch of
The Critique of Pure Reason fails hopelessly to do Kant justice. It does
not matter. However detailed and faithful a representation of Kant's
view one may have, it will still fall victim of the elementary criticism
I have stated in the text. In defence of my simple exposition of Kant,
I would like to say just this. Some philosophers almost see obscurity
as a virtue. Actually, it is a vice. Philosophy should strive to keep
things as simple as possible.

20 I exclude my own contributions from consideration.

21 "I think I have solved a major philosophical problem: the problem of
induction" (Popper 1972, 1).

22 See N. Maxwell 1972a, 1974 (133–4), 2005a, 2016b.

23 See my *Understanding Scientific Progress* (2017, chapters 1–9). In that
book I set out to solve eight fundamental philosophical problems that
arise in connection with scientific progress: the problem of underdeter-
mination of theory by evidence; the problem of what it means to say
of a physical theory that it is unified; the problem of why we are justified in preferring unified theories even against the evidence; the problem of what scientific progress means if physics advances from one
false theory to another; the problem of induction; the problem of the
nature of scientific method; the problem of how it is to be justified;
and the problem of how new theories are discovered. For some of my
earlier attempts at solving these problems see N. Maxwell 1974, 1984
(chapters 5 and 9), 1993a, 1998, 2004a, 2005a, 2006a, 2007a (chapters 5, 9, and especially 12), 2011b, 2013a, 2016b.

24 For discussion of the claim that Kuhn and Lakatos defend versions
of standard empiricism see N. Maxwell 1998, 40, and N. Maxwell
2005a. Bayesianism might seem to reject standard empiricism, in
acknowledging both prior and posteriori probabilities. But
Bayesianism tries to conform to the spirit of standard empiricism as
much as possible, by regarding prior probabilities as personal, subjective, and non-rational, their role in theory choice being reduced as
rapidly as possible by empirical testing: see N. Maxwell 1998, 44.

25 See Mill 1973–4, book III, chapter III, section 1. For an interesting
exposition and partial defence of Mill's view, see Graves 1974.

26 Russell 1948.

27 Atkins 1983, xiv.

28 Poincaré 1952, 140.

29 See Holton 1973, 262.

30 Popper 1963, 54. For more detailed discussion of the point that standard empiricism is widely taken for granted see N. Maxwell 1984 (chapters 2 and 6), 1998 (chapter 2), 2004a, 13-14n14.

31 Ramakrishnan 2016.

32 For a more detailed exposition of standard empiricism, see N. Maxwell 1984, 21–38, or 2007a, 32–51. For grounds for holding scientists do, by and large, accept standard empiricism, see N. Maxwell 1998 (38–45), 2007a (145–56), 2004a (5–6n5).

33 An aberrant theory of this type was indicated in chapter 2.

34 Even if no phenomena ostensibly refute T, each of $T_1^*, T_2^*, \dots T_\infty^*$ is still more successful empirically than T in successfully predicting phenomena B and D.

35 Consider disunified theories whose contents are specified by continuous functions. There is a famous theorem, the Stone-Weierstrass theorem (Dieudonné 1960, 131–4), which tells us that any continuous function can be approximated arbitrarily closely by an analytic function throughout a finite interval. An analytic function has the remarkable property that any bit of it, through a restricted range of values, determines uniquely the rest of the function for all the values of the variables for which it exists. Thus, a theory based on an analytic function would seem to have just the feature required of a *unified* theory, in that any bit of the theory, for any restricted range of phenomena, determines uniquely the rest of the theory for all the possible phenomena to which the theory applies. An analytic function is one that can be represented by a Taylor series. It must be infinitely differentiable.

36 As we saw in connection with Newton's first three rules of reasoning in philosophy!

37 van Fraassen 1985, 259–60.

38 Empiricists judge that it cannot be done, and so conclude that appealing to metaphysics cannot help. Rationalists, from Descartes, Leibniz, and Kant onwards, try to provide reasons for holding the metaphysical thesis to be true, but fail. Both parties miss the crucial point that the principle in question is a *conjecture*!

39 For earlier, and in many cases more detailed, formulations of this argument, see N. Maxwell 1972a, 1974, 1984 (chapter 9), 1993a, 1998, 2004a, 2005a, 2006a, 2007a (chapters 9 and 14), 2010a (chapter 5), 2011b, 2013a. See especially the last two references, and N. Maxwell 2017.

40 In Maxwell 1998, 4–6, I called it "The Fundamental Epistemological Dilemma of Science."

41 More precisely, the view that the universe is such that some kind of (more or less) unified pattern of physical law governs all phenomena.

42 An additional factor leads to the toleration of failure, given a metaphysics of spirits and gods. Such a metaphysics holds out no great promise of rapid increase in knowledge of natural phenomena: spirits and gods may change their moods, so that knowledge acquired yesterday may have no relevance today – and besides, acquiring knowledge of the intentions of gods can easily be understood to be difficult, and liable to fail. All this is to be contrasted with a metaphysics which holds that fixed laws determine natural phenomena. Such a metaphysics, by contrast, does hold out the promise that it will be possible to improve knowledge of natural phenomena rapidly, if one goes about it in the correct way.

43 Even when the assumption that sustains the methodology is a falsifiable theory rather than an unfalsifiable metaphysical thesis, it still may be difficult to reject the theory in the light of empirical difficulties, as Kuhn has shown in his account of the resistance encountered within science to the overthrow of paradigms that have encountered anomalies: see Kuhn 1970, chapters 8–9 and 12.

44 Adoption of such a metaphysical view is necessary for science, but not, of course, sufficient. One also needs a tradition of proposing and empirically testing hypotheses that accord with the basic metaphysical view – and perhaps other essential ingredients such as instrument-making, appropriate institutions of education and communication, and government tolerant of free exploration of ideas about nature. Anaximander, Democritus and other ancient Greek philosophers developed versions of physicalism, but did not develop science.

45 An additional difficulty involved in creating modern science has to do with the nature of the metaphysical conjecture that needs to be adopted for science to succeed, namely that some kind of impersonal unified pattern of physical law determines how events occur. This is an inherently difficult idea to make precise; it requires, amongst other things, the mathematical theory of differential equations. It has disturbing consequences for the nature and value of human life, having to do especially with consciousness and free will as we saw in the last chapter. And the mode of explanation for natural phenomena that it makes possible is profoundly unintuitive for human beings. Human consciousness evolved within the context of social life, in part as a

result of the need to understand others in terms of their desires, inten-tions, beliefs, feelings. This personalistic mode of understanding, being intimately bound up with our existence as conscious beings, is the "natural," intuitive way for us to understand things. It is not surpris-ing, then, that humanity should (initially) try to understand the natural world in the same sort of way, in terms of the desires, intentions of gods. It has been extraordinarily difficult and painful for humanity to discover that the universe is not comprehensible in this personalistic fashion but, on the contrary, is only physically comprehensible in terms of some unified pattern of physical law. In many ways, indeed, the discovery has not yet been made; hence the need for this book.

46 Technological discoveries first made in China include: cast iron (fifth century BC), crossbow (fifth century BC), pinhole camera (fourth cen-tury BC), chromium (second century BC), paper (second century BC), compass (first century AD), seismometer (second century AD), steel (sixth century AD), porcelain (seventh century AD, and possibly much earlier), printing (seventh century AD), and finally gunpowder (tenth century AD).

47 See Needham 1979. The question is asked on page 11.

48 Chinese views of nature excluded physicalism as a possibility. For the Chinese, this vital element of *authentic natural philosophy* simply did not exist.

49 I first expounded and defended a version of this hierarchical view in N. Maxwell 1974. It was further elaborated in N. Maxwell 1984 (chapter 9), and 1993a. A more elaborate version still is expounded and defended in great detail in N. Maxwell 1998. For a more detailed defence of the version indicated here, see N. Maxwell 2004a (chapters 1–2 and appendix). In N. Maxwell 2005a I argue that this view is a sort of synthesis of the views of Popper, Kuhn, and Lakatos, but an improvement over the views of all three. In N. Maxwell 2006a I tackle the question of how science can deliver apparently secure items of knowledge if the whole enterprise must presuppose a conjecture about the entire cosmos. In N. Maxwell 2007a (chapter 14), I give a detailed exposition of AOE, and argue, in some detail, that AOE succeeds in solving major problems in the philosophy of science, including the problems of induction, simplicity, and verisimilitude. For more recent expositions of, and arguments for, aim-oriented empiricism, see N. Maxwell 2011b, 2013a, and especially 2017. For accounts of how I developed AOE, partly as a result of criticizing Popper's

falsificationism, see N. Maxwell 2009a, 2012a, or 2014b (chapter 5). For refutations of objections to AOE see N. Maxwell 2015.

50 In chapter 5 I do what I can to illustrate the way in which knowledge and understanding in theoretical physics can be improved as a result of active improvement of metaphysical assumptions.

51 Aim-oriented empiricism implies that the philosophy of physics needs to become a vital, integral part of physics itself, insofar as philosophy of physics is about what the aims and methods of physics ought to be. And more generally, as I argue in chapter 7, the philosophy of science needs to become a vital, integral part of science itself – or of natural philosophy. Indeed, as we shall see, the philosophy of any worthwhile human endeavour with problematic aims needs to become a vital, integral part of that endeavour – if that endeavour is to be rational, and to give itself the best chances of achieving authentic success.

52 It is this positive feedback feature of AOE that is illustrated in chapter 5.

53 See N. Maxwell 1993a, 275–305.

54 Einstein 1973, 270.

55 N. Maxwell 1993a, 275–305.

56 As we shall see in chapter 5, Maxwell learnt much from Faraday in creating his theory of the electromagnetic field, and Faraday did develop metaphysical ideas relevant to the new theory, as we shall see, even if Maxwell did not.

57 See Einstein 1973, 357. See, also, N. Maxwell 1993a, 275–305.

58 Wigner 1970, 15.

59 Aim-oriented empiricism can be generalized in a number of ways. First, it can be reformulated so that it depicts a hierarchy of *aims* and methods, rather than *assumptions* and methods. We can interpret the aim of physics, at each level, from 3 to 7, to be to turn the assumption, at that level, into the precise, true physical theory of everything. Second, we need to recognize that there are not just *metaphysical* assumptions inherent in the aims of science, but also *value* assumptions, and *humanitarian* or *political* assumptions. The level 4 aim of seeking explanatory truth – truth presupposed to be explanatory – is a special case of the more general aim of seeking truth that is *of value*, intellectually or practically. And this in turn is sought so that it may be *used* by people to enrich life, in either cultural or practical ways. These value and political assumptions inherent in the aims of science are almost more problematic than metaphysical assumptions. Here, too, aims and assumptions need to be made explicit so that they may be

critically assessed and, we may hope, improved. Third, aim-oriented empiricism can be generalized so that it applies to *all* the diverse branches of natural science, and not just to theoretical physics. Each science has its own specific, problematic aims which need to be made explicit and subjected to sustained critical scrutiny. Finally, it is not just in science that aims are problematic; this is the case in life too, at all levels, from the individual and personal, to the institutional, social and global. Aim-oriented empiricism needs to be generalized to become a conception of rationality – *aim-oriented rationality* – which stresses that problematic aims need to be represented in the form of a hierarchy, so that aims can be improved as we act, as we live. These generalizations of aim-oriented empiricism will be discussed in more detail in chapters 6 and 8.

60 N. Maxwell 2017. The best earlier formulation of the argument is probably N. Maxwell 2007a, 400–30. See also N. Maxwell 2013a, 2011b, 2004a (appendix, section 6), and 1998 (especially chapter 5).

61 See Kuhn 1970; Laudan 1980.

62 It does this by revealing that how the electromagnetic field divides up into the electric part of the field and the magnetic part differs for different reference frames moving with respect to each other. According to special relativity, any one inertial reference frame is as good as any other, so there can be no privileged division of the field into electric and magnetic fields. We are obliged to think of the electromagnetic field as one unified entity: for further discussion see my 1998, 125–32.

63 For a more detailed discussion of theoretical unification in theoretical physics see my 1998, chapter 4.

64 Ibid., 181.

65 Newton-Smith 1981, 14.

66 Kuhn 1970, chapter 8.

67 Popper discovered the "problem of verisimilitude," and attempted to solve it: see Popper 1963, chapter 10 and 391–7. Popper's proposed solution was subsequently found to be defective: see Miller 1974 and Tichý 1974; see also N. Maxwell 1998, 70–2, for a simple discussion of the problem.

68 See N. Maxwell 2017, chapter 8. For earlier accounts, see N. Maxwell 2007a, 393–400, 430–3.

69 In appendices 1 and 2, I give an informal outline of the solutions to the problems of unity and induction. In my 2017 I argue in detail that aim-oriented empiricism solves, and is required to solve, fundamental problems of scientific progress, including the problem of induction.

This provides decisive grounds for accepting aim-oriented empiricism. The problems of simplicity and unity, verisimilitude, and induction are tackled in turn in N. Maxwell 2007a, 373–86, 393–400, 400–30, 430–3. For more details, see works referred to in notes 49 and 60. For what aim-oriented empiricism has to say about scientific method, see chapter 6, and N. Maxwell 2004a (39–47), 2017 (chapter 10).

CHAPTER FOUR

1 In my attempt, in this chapter, to jolt philosophers out of too complacent an attitude of satisfaction with the state of their discipline, I may have overstated my case somewhat. Academic philosophy has, undoubtedly, improved in recent decades, and has included discussion of aspects of our fundamental problem, as I have just formulated it. Nevertheless, academic philosophy has failed to establish sustained discussion of our fundamental problem as an important, integral part of academic inquiry and education, both influencing and being influenced by more specialized research from physics to the humanities. Academic philosophy has not even conceived of its task in such terms. This is an issue I return to in the final section of the present chapter. The most serious failing of modern philosophy, however, is its failure to appreciate that academic inquiry suffers from the implementation of a damagingly irrational philosophy of inquiry: see chapter 8.

2 It may be objected that the three problems I have described as being generated by Cartesian dualism arise whether one accepts Cartesian dualism or not. In what follows I will argue, however, that in order to solve these problems it is essential to put them into the context of our fundamental problem. Philosophy since Descartes has failed to arrive at an agreed resolution of these three problems in part because it has failed to do just that.

3 Locke 1961, book II, chapter VIII.

4 Berkeley 1957.

5 Hume 1959.

6 Kant 1961, Transcendental Analytic, Book II, chapter III. In order to refute Kant, all one needs to do is formulate a proposition about the *noumenal* world that says so little it is almost bound to be true (and so will certainly be meaningful). "The cosmos is not a chicken" is an example of such a proposition. Just conceivably, galaxies are molecules in the wattle of the cosmic chicken, but this seems very, very, very

unlikely. The proposition stands a very good chance of being true because it asserts so little. It permits the universe to be anything *just as long as it is not a chicken.* Not only can we make a *meaningful* assertion about the noumenal world, the world of ultimate reality; we can make one that is almost certainly *true*, that constitutes *knowledge.*

7 Kant contributed to the nebula hypothesis concerning the origins of the solar system: according to this hypothesis, a mass of particles surrounding the sun gradually coalesced to form the planets.

8 Moore 1959.

9 Russell 1956; Wittgenstein 1960.

10 The point of the analysis is to make clear that the sentence is false because there is no King of France: see Russell 1905.

11 Logical positivism became well-known in the English speaking world as a result of A.J. Ayer's racy exposition in his *Language, Truth and Logic* (1960).

12 One of the persistent intellectual sins of philosophy is the idea that philosophical problems need to be solved, can be solved, by an analysis of language, meaning, or concepts. Wittgenstein 1958 is the worst offender. But the idea goes all the way back to Hume, and to Locke – if not to Aristotle and Plato.

13 Ryle 1949.

14 Popper has decisively criticized doing philosophy via analysis of concepts: see Popper 1963 (chapter 2), 1976 (section 7).

15 Popper 1959, 1962, 1963, 1969.

16 See, for example, Smart 1963, Nagel 1989, Dennett 1991, Singer 1995, Chalmers 1996, Maudlin 2010.

17 Recent philosophy of science, and science and technological studies, may seem to be branches of philosophy more engaged with science, and with the view of the universe presented to us by science. But these disciplines suffer from the general malaise of rampant specialization, or *specialism* as I have called it (1980), and fail in their primary philosophical task to try to ensure that academia keeps alive sustained exploration of global problems. See N. Maxwell 2014b, chapter 4 for critical remarks concerning these specific disciplines, and for proposals as to what they ought to do.

18 For details of my publications related in one way or another to this theme – eight books and over eighty articles (many available online) – see: http://discovery.ucl.ac.uk/view/people/ANMAX22.date.html; and http://philpapers.org/profile/17092. See also my website: http://www.ucl.ac.uk/from-knowledge-to-wisdom.

19 See especially N. Maxwell 2001, 2010a. See also N. Maxwell 1966,
    1968a, 1968b, 1984 or 2007a (chapter 10), 2000b, 2009a, 2011a. For
    my discussion of that aspect of the problem concerned primarily with
    the *flourishing* of what is of value in our human world, see my 1984,
    2004a, 2007a, 2014a, 2014b, 2016a, 2017 (chapter 14). For summa-
    ries, see N. Maxwell 1980, 1992, 2000a, 2007b. In N. Maxwell 2009a
    and 2012 I outline my contributions to both aspects of the problem.

20 For an account of Darwinian evolution along these lines see N.
    Maxwell 1984, 269–73; 2010a (chapter 8). See also Maxwell 2001
    (chapter 7), 2009a (50–6); Avital and Jablonka 2000; and Jablonka
    and Lamb 2005. And see chapter 6 below.

21 Maxwell 1968a and 1998, 141–55.

22 This argument was first spelled out in N. Maxwell 1966, 1968a,
    1968b. See especially N. Maxwell 1966, 303–8, and 1968b, 127 and
    134–7. The argument became much better known when spelled out
    later by Nagel 1974 and Jackson 1986.

23 N. Maxwell 2000b, 2010a (chapter 3), 2011a.

24 See Spinoza (1677) 1955.

25 See especially N. Maxwell 2010a, chapter 3. See also N. Maxwell
    1966, 1968a, 1968b, 1984 (chapter 10), 2000b, 2001 (chapter 5),
    2011a.

26 See N. Maxwell 2010a, 77–82. See also N. Maxwell 2000b and 2011a.

27 In order to tackle it, we need natural philosophy, both science and phi-
    losophy working together, a point I say a bit more about in chapter 6.
    The conceptual part of the problem has to do primarily with how it
    can be possible both for the *person* and the *brain* to be in control –
    how free will is possible if physicalism is true. For my suggestions as
    to how this problem is to be solved see N. Maxwell 2001, chapters
    6–8, and 2010a, chapters 7 and 8.

28 Some ordinary language philosophers have argued that what we see
    most immediately and directly are not sense data, but rather objects in
    the world around us: see Austin 1962 and Ryle 1949. These philoso-
    phers base their arguments on an appeal to ordinary language – not a
    convincing way to establish the point. And, being constrained by the
    crippling straightjacket of conceptual analysis, these philosophers
    failed to return philosophy to our fundamental problem – and were
    entirely incapable of doing that.

29 Popper 1963, 72.

30 Ibid., 67. For further quotations indicating Popper's commitment to
    tackling fundamental problems that cut across disciplinary boundaries

see N. Maxwell 2016b. For an interpretation of Popper's work along
these lines see N. Maxwell 2002.

31 See for example Kane 1998.

32 See for example Dupré 1993.

33 See van Fraassen 1980.

34 It is important, in this context, to take note of a crucial ambiguity in
the meaning of "objective": see N. Maxwell 1966, 310–11.

35 See above and works referred to in the next note.

36 I have expounded and developed this "two-aspect" approach to the
human world/physical universe problem in N. Maxwell 1966, 1968a,
1968b, 1984 (chapter 10), 2000b, 2001, 2010a, 2011a. For a summary see N. Maxwell 2009a, 38–56.

37 Sellars 1963, 1–40.

38 Ibid., 1.

39 Ibid., 2.

40 Whitehead 1932, chapter 5.

41 See N. Maxwell 1980.

42 This theme will be taken up again in chapter 8. Humanity suffers from
the fact that academia has built into its intellectual/institutional structure a profoundly irrational and damaging philosophy of inquiry.
Modern philosophy has singularly failed to bring the world's attention
to this disastrous state of affairs. Most philosophers, indeed, seem
entirely unaware of it. For the last forty years I have done what I can
to highlight the situation: see Maxwell 1976a, 1980, 1984, 1992,
2000a, 2004a, 2007a, 2007b, 2009b, 2012, 2014a, 2014b. For
thumbnail sketches of the argument highlighting the role of philosophy see N. Maxwell 2008, 2013c.

CHAPTER FIVE

1 Popper 1963, 54. For more detailed discussion of the point that standard empiricism is widely taken for granted see N. Maxwell 1984
(chapters 2 and 6), 1998 (chapter 2), 2004a (13–14n14).

2 Science is all about progress and improvement. We need to appreciate
that science itself, our working conception of it, may improve as well
(an idea inherent in AOE in any case).

3 By "SE science" I mean invariably "science pursued by a community of
scientists who take SE for granted and do their best to put SE into scientific practice."

4 Dirac 1963, 47.

5 See appendix 1.

6 In appendix 1, I explicate two notions, P-unity, and B-unity. The latter changes as B changes.

7 The theses at levels 6 and 7, however, are accepted on non-empirical grounds – on the grounds that their acceptance can only help and cannot seriously harm the search for knowledge.

8 Level 4 played a role in the past when Aristotelianism was abandoned, and Galileo's vision was adopted instead. In exceptional circumstances, level 4 might have a role again in the future if the need arises to find an alternative to the current version of physicalism: see point 10 of the present chapter.

9 d'Alembert might not have been entirely hostile to the idea of blueprint articulation. At one point in his *Preliminary Discourse* he declares, "The universe … would only be one fact and one great truth of whoever knew how to embrace it from a single point of view" (d'Alembert 1963, 29), which almost sounds like a formulation of physicalism. Oersted, Ampère, and Faraday held somewhat similar views to the extent, at least, of believing in underlying unity in nature.

10 This is counterfactual intellectual history of science, of course, a deeply heretical endeavour these days. It is rarely appreciated that if counterfactual considerations are banned from history, explanation is banned as well. An explanation, in order to be an explanation, must have counterfactual implications. It must tell us, not just what did happen, but what *would have* happened had circumstances been slightly different. In any case, the present book is, in a sense, in its entirety an exploration in counterfactual intellectual history, in that it seeks to indicate how and why the history of science – and the history of philosophy – would have been different if AOE had been explicitly accepted, from Newton's time onwards.

11 For an account of the emergence of the corpuscular hypothesis from the views of ancient Greece see Dijksterhuis 1969.

12 See Boscovich 1966, first published in 1758.

13 In 1756 in his *Physical Monadology*, Kant arrived at the idea of particles as non-extended centres of attractive and repulsive forces as a result of seeking a synthesis of the views of Newton and Leibniz. In his *Metaphysical Foundations of Natural Science* of 1786 Kant developed the view further by reducing the point-particle to a mere centre of forces, so that this latter Kantian view becomes almost a field theory: see Hendry 1986, 14–15 for an account. Boscovich and Kant were

anticipated to some extent by Newton 1952, 395 and Jean
Desaguliers: see Heilbron 1979, 64, 66.

14 The infinitely repulsive forces of B_1 and B_2 could of course be eliminated by attributing elasticity to corpuscles, so that they deform and
bounce apart, in a continuous way, when they collide. This introduces
a new arbitrariness into theoretical physics at a fundamental level, in
that two constants (Young's modulus and Poisson's ratio) are required
to specify the elasticity of the corpuscles. It could be argued that such
a view violates the very idea of corpuscles being fundamental physical
entities. An explanation is required as to why the corpuscles are elastic, to the degree that they are. In any case, such a blueprint lacks the
far greater generality and potential explanatory power of the
Boscovich blueprint, B_3. And once B_2 is accepted, any rationale behind
adopting the idea of elastic corpuscles seems to vanish.

15 N. Maxwell 1968a and 1998, 141–55.

16 B_5 does not face this problem, because each particle has its own distinct field, and so the velocity of transmission of changes in the field
can be postulated to be relative to the velocity of the source particle.
Once the unified field blueprint is adopted, B_6, this option is no longer
available.

17 In chapter 1, on page 18, I raised the question of why mathematics can
sometimes anticipate subsequent physics. The answer is that mathematicians who do this engage in blueprint articulation without realizing
it, and such blueprint articulation can sometimes anticipate subsequent physics because the universe is physically comprehensible. But
this leaves unsolved the profound mystery as to *why* the universe is
physically comprehensible, especially why it should be comprehensible
to us. Einstein was well aware of the problem; as I indicated in chapter
1, he once remarked, "the eternal mystery of the world is its comprehensibility" (1973, 292). For my proposal as to how this mystery is to
be solved, see N. Maxwell 2001, 254–8.

18 Hunt 1991, 122–8.

19 See Chalmers 1973.

20 Hunt 1991, 33–47.

21 For an excellent account of the development of electrodynamics see
Darrigol 2000.

22 See Hunt 1991, chapter 4. See also Schaffner 1972, and Klein 1972.

23 Duhem 1962, 70–1. Duhem's book was first published in 1906, based
on articles published earlier.

24 See his article on the aether: J.C. Maxwell 1878. At one point
   Maxwell writes, significantly: "light is not a substance but a process
   going on in a substance."

25 Quoted in Hunt 1991, 104.

26 It may be objected that it was only acceptance of Maxwell's theory
   given a certain physical interpretation that was delayed, not the theory
   as such. But Maxwell's theory (a) interpreted in terms of the aether,
   and (b) interpreted as a field theory devoid of the aether, are not the
   same theory. Theory (a) predicts that elecromagnetic waves travel at
   the velocity of light relative to the aether, whereas theory (b) can make
   no such prediction. In any case, the tendency of outdated metaphysics
   to retard correct *interpretations* of new theories will be discussed in
   the next section.

27 See Hunt 1991, 94–5.

28 "Heaviside affirmed many times that there must be a mechanical
   ether; to deny it, he said, would be 'thoroughly anti-Newtonian, anti-
   Faradaic, and anti-Maxwellian.' But attempting to find the actual
   structure of the ether was, he thought, too ambitious and speculative a
   task to be worthwhile" (Hunt 1991, 104).

29 Quoted in Hendry 1986, 260.

30 See Hendry 1986, 259.

31 OQT is not a relativistic theory. But relativistic versions of OQT have
   subsequently been developed, that have also achieved astonishing
   empirical success: Dirac's relativistic theory of the electron, quantum
   electrodynamics, quantum electroweak theory, and the current so-
   called standard model, the quantum field theory of fundamental particles, quarks and leptons, and the forces between them, the
   electromagnetic, weak, and strong force.

32 Einstein, "Letter to Schrödinger, 1950," in Przibram 1967, 39. One of
   the myths about Einstein is that he opposed OQT on the grounds that
   it makes probabilistic predictions only. "God does not play dice," he is
   reported to have said. Actually, Einstein's fundamental objection was
   the one emphasized here: OQT abandons realism. It does not solve the
   wave/particle problem – a problem discovered by Einstein, with his
   light quanta hypothesis of 1905. See also Einstein 1982, 667. Another
   myth is that Bohr won his great argument with Einstein over QT. He
   did not. Einstein was right, and Bohr was disastrously wrong.

33 It is astonishing that, ninety years after QT was first put forward by
   Heisenberg and Schrödinger in 1925 and 1926, theoretical physicists

still fudge the fundamental question raised by the theory: Is nature deterministic or probabilistic?

34 I first argued for the need to eliminate the notion of "measurement" from the postulates of QT and specify precise quantum mechanical conditions for probabilistic transitions to occur in my 1972b. The many defects of OQT arising from the failure to solve the wave/particle problem and the resulting need to interpret the theory as being about measurement were further elaborated in subsequent papers: N. Maxwell 1976b and 1988. John Bell has argued, independently, for the need to develop QT as a theory about *beables* rather than *observables*: see Bell 1987. Bell tended to stress, however, that OQT is satisfactory "for all practical purposes" (FAPP), but lacks precision because the notion of measurement is imprecise.

35 It is this that I have argued in a long series of papers: see N. Maxwell 1972b, 1976b, 1982, 1988, 1993b, 1994, 1995, 2004b, 2011c.

36 See Jammer 1974.

37 This statement will be qualified in a moment.

38 In recent decades there has, however, been a growing awareness among physicists that the interpretation of quantum theory poses a problem. But, at the time of writing (2016) there still seems to be hardly any serious discussion of the basic wave/particle problem, or even awareness that this is the basic problem confronting quantum theory. It was generally recognized to be *the* basic problem by those involved in creating quantum theory during the first three decades of the twentieth century. It was said, in ironic despair, "On Mondays, Wednesdays, and Fridays the electron is a wave, on Tuesdays, Thursdays, and Saturdays it is a particle." A century later, the problem has almost been forgotten.

39 In the context of quantum theory, this "stuff" is called *position probability density*.

40 Some hold that quantum field theory solves the wave/particle problem in depicting quantum entities as excitations of the quantum field. But this view is untenable. Quantum field theory is just as much a theory about measurement as non-relativistic OQT is; it suffers from all the defects of OQT. In order to solve the problem, quantum field theory must either specify precisely, in field theoretic terms, when probabilistic events occur, and what the possible outcomes are; or it must explain how the theory can account for the world we observe even in the absence of measurement.

41 This is the version of QT I have developed in papers referred to in note 35.

42 I first put this idea forward in N. Maxwell 1982.

43 In the case of the photographic plate, a silver bromide molecule is dissociated, leaving the dot of a silver atom.

44 Or rather, very nearly at an end. I have specified precisely what this means: see N. Maxwell 1994.

45 It is important to distinguish measurement, in this sense, from *preparation* – a procedure which arranges for quantum systems to have a definite quantum state *if found* in a certain spatial region.

46 Consider a nucleus which decays, emitting an α-particle. OQT predicts that the nucleus goes into a superposition of the decayed and undecayed state, the decayed state becoming continuously more probable to be found, until a measurement is made, and then the nucleus is found either to be decayed or undecayed. PQT predicts that the nucleus goes into a superposition of emitting the α-particle and not emitting it, and then collapses back into the undecayed state, again and again, in the absence of measurement, until eventually the superposition collapses into the decayed state. These processes predicted by OQT and PQT seem very different, but there is just one circumstance in which they give the same answer: if the law governing decay is exponential. As it happens, it is exponential, as Rutherford found out in 1900. But not precisely exponential, for long times. This creates the possibility of a test between OQT and PQT: see N. Maxwell 1988.

47 N. Maxwell 1972b.

48 Band and Park 1973.

49 N. Maxwell 1973.

50 N. Maxwell 1982, 1988.

51 N. Maxwell 1985. See also N. Maxwell 2006b.

52 Squires 1989.

53 N. Maxwell 1994, 1995, 1998 (chapter 7), 2004b, 2011c.

54 See Haag 2013.

55 Ghirardi, Rimini, and Weber 1986.

56 Penrose 1996. See also Penrose 2007, 846–60, and 2014.

57 In the case of Ghirardi, Rimini, and Weber, their idea grew out of a failed attempt to solve the (absurd) measurement problem. Furthermore, their indifference to probabilism is indicated by their attempt to explain ostensibly probabilistic localizations by means of a background field which interacts with quantum systems to produce

occasional localizations, somewhat in the same way as molecules interact with a pollen grain to produce apparently haphazard Brownian motion.

58 de Broglie's original papers, published in 1926 and 1927, are republishd in de Broglie 1953.

59 Bohm 1952.

60 See Bacciagaluppi 2012 for an account of decoherence.

61 Everett 1957. For a recent exposition and defence see Wallace 2012.

62 Strictly speaking, a quantum system, such as an electron, has additional physical properties, such as electric charge and mass: Everett QT fails to tell us, however, how the complex numbers of the state function Ψ specify how the charge and mass of the electron are situated in space. Bohmian mechanics, by contrast, is free of this objection. It does tell us how charge and mass are located in space.

63 Even if probabilism turns out one day to be false, it would still have been a possibility that would have deserved serious theoretical and empirical exploration. My argument does not require probabilism to be true, merely a possibility worth exploration.

64 Hume 1959, volume 1, part III.

65 For a decisive refutation of Hume on causation, an account of how necessary connections between successive states of affairs are possible, and the need to interpret fundamental physical theories essentialistically, as specifying necessitating physical properties attributed to fundamental physical entities, see N. Maxwell 1968a. For updated accounts see N. Maxwell 1993a (81–101), 1998 (141–55).

66 See N. Maxwell 1976b (283–9), 1988 (10–22), 2011c.

67 As far as the following discussion of theoretical physics is concerned, instead of always referring to "fundamental theory" or fundamental physical theory," I shall just speak of "theory" – but this must be taken to mean "fundamental physical theory."

68 Popper 1959, 31.

69 Whereas AOE holds that there are metaphysical theses, incompatible with accepted theories, that are a part of scientific knowledge, and thus may provide a rational guide for the development of new theories, SE holds that no such metaphysical theses can be a part of scientific knowledge. It is this difference which ensures that AOE provides a rational method of discovery while SE does not.

70 In more recent times, Erwin Schrödinger took the wave equation of classical physics as a model for his time-dependent equation of quantum theory; Abdus Salam and Steven Weinberg took quantum

electrodynamics as a model for their quantum electroweak theory, which in turn became a partial model for quantum chromodynamics.

71 Boscovich's idea that force varying with distance is fundamental was anticipated, to some extent, by some Newtonians, for example by Jean Desaguliers: see Heilbron 1979, 66.

72 He was anticipated to some extent by John Mitchell, a Cambridge mathematician, who announced the inverse square law for magnets in 1750; ten years later Tobias Mayer, a professor of mathematics at the university of Göttingen, announced the same result. See Heilbron 1979, 91–3.

73 Darrigol 2000, 7.

74 Quoted in Hendry 1986, 125.

75 J.C. Maxwell 1856.

76 The closer together the lines of force, the stronger the field.

77 J.C. Maxwell 1861 and 1862, 1865.

78 This is to take two fundamental theories that conflict, T_1 and T_2, pare away from T_1 and T_2 everything not involved in the clash until two principles contradicting each other are arrived at, p_1 from T_1, p_2 from T_2, the idea being then to modify p_1, or p_2, or both, or some background assumption, so that a new unified idea, U, emerges, a synthesis of p_1 and p_2, and a possible core idea for a new theory, T_{1+2}, that unifies T_1 and T_2.

79 These papers are all republished in English in Einstein 1998.

80 He argued that MT interpreted in terms of the aether introduces an implausible asymmetry in the explanation of electromagnetic induction, implausible because of the symmetry in the phenomena to be explained. The theoretical explanation for the current in a conductor moving near a magnet at rest is strikingly different from the explanation of the current if the conductor is at rest and the magnet moves, even though all that matters is the relative motion as far as the effect is concerned. He also argued that the aether view runs into empirical difficulties in that all attempts to detect the motion of the earth relative to the aether have failed. Einstein concluded that "the phenomena of electrodynamics as well as of mechanics possess no properties corresponding to the idea of absolute rest" (1998, 124). Einstein was of course well aware that the null result of the Michelson-Morley experiment does not decisively demolish the aether; he knew of Lorentz's efforts to employ the FitzGerald contraction hypothesis to develop a version of electrodynamics which both presupposes the aether and is compatible with observation. In a paper published in 1907, however,

Einstein remarked of the FitzGerald-Lorentz approach (surely with
some justice) that it is "ad hoc" and "artificial" (Holton 1973, 334).

81 This is implicit in a "paradox" that Einstein discovered when sixteen,
and which he later saw as the germ from which special relativity grew.
In his "Autobiographical Notes," first published in 1949, Einstein
describes the paradox thus: "If I pursue a beam of light with the velocity c ... I should observe such a beam of light as a spatially oscillatory
electromagnetic field at rest. However, there seems to be no such thing,
whether on the basis of experience or according to Maxwell's equations. From the very beginning it appeared to me intuitively clear that,
judged from the standpoint of such an observer, everything would
have to happen according to the same laws as for an observer who,
relative to the earth, was at rest" (1982, 53). This only makes intuitive
sense as a paradox insofar as electromagnetism is being conceived of
in the absence of the aether.

82 More precisely, Einstein took, as the light postulate, that the velocity
of light is c in some "resting" frame, and then derived the principle
that it is c in all inertial reference frames.

83 Just as velocity may be thought of either as an absolute, intrinsic property of an object, or as a relational property between two objects, so
too length and time-intervals may be thought of as absolute or relational. We ordinarily think of length and time-intervals as absolute; s r
demands that they be construed as relational, so that one and the same
rod or clock can have different lengths or rates relative to different
frames, just as they can have different velocities relative to different
frames.

84 See Minkowski 1952.

85 Here, x, y, z are distances measured along the X, Y and Z axes of some
reference frame, and t is the time interval between two events measured in the reference frame.

86 Special relativity presupposes determinism. Probabilism might change
things dramatically, in that probabilistic transitions might be cosmic
wide, thus providing an objective, cosmic "now": see N. Maxwell
1985 and 2006b.

87 Eugene Wigner has stressed how important special relativity is in this
respect: see his 1970, chapter 2.

88 Global and local gauge invariance, and supersymmetry, are examples
of symmetry principles that have had important roles to play in physics after special relativity. Invariance with respect to spatial position
and orientation, time of occurrence, and direction of time, are all

symmetries of fundamental significance in physics, associated with the nature of space and time.

89   See N. Maxwell 1998 (91–5, 262–4), 2017 (chapter 5 and appendix 1).

90   See N. Maxwell 1993a, 297–303.

91   Einstein 1973, 357.

92   A geodesic is the shortest distance between two points in a curved space: it reduces to a straight line in flat, Euclidean space.

93   Einstein 1982, 27–33.

94   For a discussion of Einstein's failure to employ his own method of discovery properly during the last thirty years of his life, and for a discussion of Einstein's largely correct criticisms of OQT, see N. Maxwell 1993a, 288–96.

95   Feynman 1963, 1–2.

96   For an excellent account of the quantum theory of the vacuum, see Aitchison 1985.

97   I first put forward cosmic physicalism as a possibility in N. Maxwell 2004a, 198–205.

98   Popper highlighted the problem and proposed a solution: see Popper 1963, chapter 10, and 391–7. David Miller 1974 and Pavel Tichý 1974 independently discovered that Popper's proposed solution does not work, and for decades the problem remained an open one.

99   See Laudan 1980; Kuhn 1970, chapter 13.

100   See N. Maxwell 2007a (393–400, 430–3) and 2017 (chapter 8).

101   For a fascinating, non-technical account of string theory see Greene 1999. Chapter 9 discusses the question of empirical predictions of the theory.

102   See Sheldon Glashow, 180–91, and Richard Feynman, 192–210, in Davies and Brown 1988; Smolin 2006; Woit 2006.

103   This point is made in Smolin 2000, chapter 13. In particular, Smolin describes the way string theorists, and those pursuing the rather different approach to unifying quantum theory and general relativity called "loop quantum gravity," have tended to ignore, and even unjustly disparage, each others' work.

104   For attempts to do this see Isham 1997, Smolin 2000, and Penrose 2004.

105   Elsewhere, I have suggested a doctrine that might be called *Lagrangianism* could be regarded as an acceptable blueprint for physics today: see N. Maxwell 1998, 88–9. All fundamental, dynamical theories accepted so far in physics can be formulated in terms of a Lagrangian and Hamilton's principle of least action. In the case of

Newtonian theory (NT), this takes the following form. Given any system, we can specify its kinetic energy, KE (energy of motion), and its potential energy, PE (energy of position due to forces), at each instant. This enables us to define the Lagrangian, L, equal at each instant to KE – PE. Hamilton's principle states that, given two instants, t_1 and t_2, the system evolves in such a way that the sum of instantaneous values of KE – PE, for times between t_1 and t_2, is a minimum value (or, more accurately, a stationary value, so that it is unaffected to first order by infinitesimal variations in the way the system evolves). From the Lagrangian for NT (a function of the positions and momenta of particles) and Hamilton's principle of least action, we can derive NT in the form familiar from elementary textbooks. It is this way of formulating NT, in terms of a Lagrangian, L, and Hamilton's principle, that can be generalized to apply to all accepted fundamental theories in physics. Lagrangianism, then, asserts that the universe is such that all phenomena evolve in accordance with Hamilton's principle of least action, formulated in terms of some unified Lagrangian (or Lagrangian density), L. We require, here, that L is not the sum of two or more distinct Lagrangians, with distinct physical interpretations and symmetries, for example one for the electroweak force, one for the strong force, and one for gravitation, as at present; L must have a single physical interpretation, and its symmetries must have an appropriate group structure. We require, in addition, that current quantum field theories and general relativity emerge when appropriate limits are taken. However, even if the level 4 thesis of physicalism is true, it is more than likely that Lagrangianism is false. This is the case if space-time is discontinuous in the very small. In fact developments in quantum gravity, having to do with "duality," suggest that Lagrangianism may well be false: see Isham 1997, 194–5.

CHAPTER SIX

1 Judgements of triviality are fallible, of course. That which seems trivial may not be. In 1958 Charles Keeling began his profoundly important measurements of the increase of carbon dioxide in the atmosphere. In the early 1960s, the National Science Foundation of the USA withdrew funding on the grounds that the work was merely "routine," that is, too trivial to be worth continuing – although actually the measurements concerned the future of humanity!

2 See http://www.rcuk.ac.uk/ (accessed 15 July 2014).

3 Scientific research councils and funding bodies these days tend to demand that research proposals will lead to results that have social *impact*. But however intelligently·this demand is formulated – even if it is *potential* impact that is required, and the diversity of the ways science can have impact of value is recognized – still this demand for impact is not an adequate substitute for creating a tradition of rational discussion of problems associated with aims and priorities of research. This discussion would of course seek to discover new aims for research likely to lead to science of value; it would not be restricted to criticizing existing research aims. The task would be to create a literature about actual and possible research aims from which scientists and funding bodies can *learn*.

4 It is not enough to predict more and more phenomena more and more accurately (as we saw in connection with orthodox quantum theories, in chapter 5, section 6). We should require, in addition, that theories which successfully predict, also *explain* and enhance *understanding*; or we should require that predictions are relevant to the achievement of other goals of value: health, prosperity, and so on. It is of course true that we cannot always tell in advance whether new predictions will turn out to be useful or not.

5 See Langley 2005, and Smith 2003.

6 Quoted in N. Maxwell 1984, 54, and 2007a, 66.

7 But see Firestein 2012.

8 Einstein 1973, 80.

9 It could only be the theoretical aspect of our fundamental problem that could be definitively solved. The practical, personal, and social aspects come to life again, afresh, every time a baby is born. These aspects of the problem will only cease to be renewed when sentient life itself disappears for ever from the universe.

10 The experiential and what is of value are inextricably intermingled, as art and music remind us.

11 Monot 1974.

12 Dawkins 1978. To call genes "selfish" sounds as if one is attributing purposes to them, but Dawkins would be the first to deny this imputation. "Selfish" is intended to be metaphorical, not literal. Genes do not have purposes.

13 The "purposeless" view of life gets into great difficulties when it comes to human life. Either an artificial and thoroughly un-Darwinian hiatus is created between pre-human and human life, or all human life must be declared to be devoid of purpose too.

14 Ignore those human beings who are, in part, the outcome of unnatural human interventions.

15 What I have to say here about evolution is spelled out in much greater
    detail in N. Maxwell 2010a, chapter 8; see also chapter 7. I there dis-
    tinguish nine versions of Darwinian theory, each version giving a
    greater role to purposiveness than the previous one. See also N.
    Maxwell 1984 (269–73), 2001 (chapter 7), and 2009a (50–6).

16 Personalistic understanding is somewhat similar to what psychologists
    and neuroscientists call "theory of mind," "empathic understanding"
    or "folk psychology." But there are important differences: see N.
    Maxwell 2001 (chapter 5), 1984 (174–81, 183–9, 264–75).

17 I employ the somewhat clumsy phrase "evolution by cultural means,"
    and not "cultural evolution," because of the ambiguity of the latter.
    "Cultural evolution" might mean "evolution by cultural means," but
    in the relevant literature is generally taken to mean "the evolution of
    culture." Whereas "the evolution of culture" is about the evolution of
    a specific kind of thing – culture – "evolution by cultural means" refers
    to a specific manner in which evolution can proceed – by means of
    individual learning and imitation (or learning from others).

18 See Lloyd Morgan 1896. The idea is much more clearly formulated, it
    must be admitted, by Alister Hardy: see his 1965, 170, or my 2010a,
    287, where I quote Hardy.

19 Baldwin 1986.

20 See Simpson 1953; Dennett 1996, 77–80.

21 See N. Maxwell 2010a, 276–89. My account owes much to Hardy
    1965.

22 It is above all when we come to the evolution of human qualities that
    we especially value – consciousness, free will, the ability to understand
    and speak a language, our capacities for science, art, fairness, civiliza-
    tion, friendship, love – that we need to employ a version of Darwinian
    theory that does justice to the way the mechanisms of evolution them-
    selves evolve, gradually giving increasingly important roles to purpo-
    sive action. I discuss these issues in more detail in N. Maxwell 2001,
    chapter 7, and 2010a, chapter 8.

23 Crick 1984.

24 That consciousness became a respectable topic for research in neuro-
    science in the 1980s was no doubt brought about in part by the
    advent of new brain imaging techniques, which made it possible to
    view brain activity in the conscious human brain non-invasively.

25 As I indicated towards the end of chapter 4, I favour the view that per-
    ceptual qualities do exist in the world around us, and the mental fea-
    tures of brain processes are just that aspect of these processes that we

can only get to know about as a result of these processes occurring
in our own brain. I have called this view *experiential physicalism*: see
N. Maxwell 1966, 1968b, 2000b, 2001 (chapter 5), 2009a, 2010a
(chapter 3), 2011a.

26 See N. Maxwell 2001, 126–9, and 2011a, 6–9.

27 Libet 1985.

28 See for example Dennett 1991, 162–8; Kane 1998, 232.

29 He held that the "volitional process, initiated unconsciously, can either
be consciously permitted to proceed to consummation in the motor
act or be consciously 'vetoed'" (Libet 1985, 536–7). See also Libet
2005, chapter 4.

30 I first spelled out in detail this argument for the urgent need for a revolution in social inquiry, the humanities, and academic inquiry more
generally, in N. Maxwell 1984; second edition 2007a. See also N.
Maxwell 2004a, 2014a, 2014b. For diverse summaries of the argument see N. Maxwell 1992, 2000a, 2007b, and 2009a.

CHAPTER SEVEN

1 This remains true even though some traditions of modern philosophy
have become so alienated from the source of their problems that they
have come to regard science as irrelevant to their concerns – as we saw
in chapter 4. Work in both continental and analytic philosophy is
guilty of this sin.

2 For a suggestion along these lines that puts what Paul Grice 1957 had
to say about meaning into an evolutionary context, see N. Maxwell
2001, 189–90.

3 Smart 1963 defends the view that everything is just physics, but argues
that moral values nevertheless exist: see 152–6.

4 For arguments defending value realism, or at least criticizing objections to the view, see N. Maxwell 1976a (138–46, 242–54), 1984
(chapter 10), 1999, 2001 (chapter 2). See also Brink 1989, 90–8;
Little 1994.

5 See Dunbar 2010.

6 For expositions of this "meta" conception of philosophy, see Melden
1960 and Quinton 1968. Quinton declares, "A comparatively definite
place has now been marked out for philosophy within the total range
of man's intellectual activities … philosophy has the task of classifying
and analysing the terms, statements and arguments of the first-order
disciplines" (1968, 1).

7 This self-imposed sterility of philosophy stems from logical positivism, which held that philosophy concerns problems of conceptual analysis, not problems having to do with the real world and life. Logical positivism is rejected, but its implications linger on.

CHAPTER EIGHT

1 Humans have however been causing some environmental damage for centuries. Aldous Huxley cites the ancient destruction of the cedars of Lebanon as an example; see Huxley 1980, 21–2. For a discussion of the role of early man in causing extinction of species see Holdgate 1996, 1–10.
2 See, for example, Gray 2004.
3 This idea is implicit in much that the *philosophes* did and wrote, but I am not sure any *philosophe* quite articulated the idea explicitly, as I understand it here.
4 The best overall account of the Enlightenment that I know of is still Gay 1973.
5 For the importance of Francis Bacon for the Enlightenment see Gay 1973, volume 1, 11–12 and 322.
6 Mill, Marx, Durkheim, and Weber were all in thrall to the traditional Enlightenment.
7 Berlin 1980, 1–24, and 1999.
8 For a clearly written, sympathetic, but critical discussion of criticisms of the Enlightenment, from Horkheimer and Adorno, via Lyotard, Foucault, and Derrida to MacIntyre and Rorty, see Gascardi 1999. For less sympathetic criticisms of postmodernists' anti-rationalism, see Sokal and Bricmont 1998; Gross et al. 1996; Koertge 1998.
9 Popper 1959, 1963.
10 "inter-subjective *testing* is merely a very important aspect of the more general idea of inter-subjective *criticism*, or in other words, of the idea of mutual rational control by critical discussion" (Popper 1959, 44n*1). See also Popper 1963 (193–200), 1976 (115–16), 1972 (119, 243).
11 Popper's conception, though defective, does nevertheless provide acceptable necessary conditions for rationality. An endeavour or discipline which fails (1) to articulate its problems, and (2) to propose and critically assess possible solutions, violates absolutely elementary requirements for rationality. As we shall see, academic inquiry

dominated by the traditional Enlightenment, giving priority to problems of knowledge over problems of living, violates rationality in just this way.

12 There are a number of ways of highlighting the inherently problematic character of the aim of creating civilization. People have very different ideas as to what does constitute civilization. Most views about what constitutes Utopia, an ideally civilized society, have been unrealizable *and* profoundly undesirable. People's interests, values, and ideals clash. Even values that, one may hold, ought to be a part of civilization may clash. Thus freedom and equality, even though interrelated, may nevertheless clash. It would be an odd notion of individual freedom which held that freedom was for some, and not for others; and yet if equality is pursued too single-mindedly this will undermine individual freedom, and will even undermine equality, in that a privileged class will be required to enforce equality on the rest, as in the old Soviet Union. A basic aim of legislation for civilization, we may well hold, ought to be to increase freedom by restricting it: this brings out the inherently problematic, paradoxical character of the aim of achieving civilization. One thinker who has stressed the inherently problematic, contradictory character of the idea of civilization is Isaiah Berlin 1980, 74–9. Berlin thought the problem could not be solved; I, on the contrary, hold that aim-oriented rationality provides us with the means to learn how to improve our solution to it as we live.

13 For much more detailed expositions of aim-oriented rationality see N. Maxwell 1984 or 2007a, especially chapters 5 and 8. See also N. Maxwell 2004a, especially chapters 3 and 4.

14 For a discussion of the extent to which the traditional Enlightenment dominates academic inquiry see N. Maxwell 1984 or 2007a, chapter 6.

15 N. Maxwell 1984 or 2007a. See also N. Maxwell 1976a, 2004a, 2014a, 2014b. For various summaries of the argument see N. Maxwell 1980, 1992, 2000a, 2007b, 2009a, 2012.

16 It needs to be recognized, however, that social progress towards civilization faces all sorts of difficulties not encountered by scientific progress towards greater knowledge: see N. Maxwell 1984, 157–66, or 2007a, 182–90; and see below.

17 N. Maxwell 2000a, 38.

18 See N. Maxwell 2007a, chapter 6.

19 See http://www.ucl.ac.uk/research/wisdom-agenda (accessed 23 Sept. 2014).

20 See http://wisdomresearch.org/ (accessed 23 Sept. 2014).

21 See N. Maxwell 2013b.

22 This is the objection that most academics will wish to raise against the thesis of this chapter. It will be made by all those who hold that academic inquiry quite properly seeks to make a contribution to human welfare by, first, acquiring knowledge, and then, secondarily, applying it to help solve human problems.

23 Ryle 1949, chapter 2.

24 For a development of this point, see N. Maxwell 1984, 174–81, or 2007a, 197–205.

25 Popper 1969, chapter 9, and 1961, 64–92.

26 For further discussion see N. Maxwell 1984, 189–98, or 2007a, 213–21.

27 For literature protesting against the influence of scientific rationality in various contexts and ways, see for example: Berlin 1999; Laing 1965; Marcuse 1964; Roszak 1973; Berman 1981; Schwartz 1987; Feyerabend 1978, 1987; Appleyard 1992.

28 See N. Maxwell 1984, 63–4, 85–91, 117–18, for further discussion of this issue. See also N. Maxwell 1976a, especially chapters 1 and 8–10.

29 Bloor 1976; Barnes and Bloor 1981; Latour 1987; Feyerabend 1978, 1987. These authors might protest that they do not deny scientific knowledge, method, progress, or rationality as such, but deny, merely, that the sociology of knowledge can legitimately appeal to such things, or deny extravagant claims made on behalf of these things. See, however, the sparkling criticism by Sokal and Bricmont 1998, chapter 4.

30 For earlier arguments in support of aim-oriented empiricism see N. Maxwell 1974, 1998, 2004a, 2005a, 2007a (chapter 14), 2011b, 2013a.

31 N. Rescher, personal communication; Durant 1997.

32 Harding 1986.

33 Social science becomes, primarily, the servant of social methodology or social philosophy: see Maxwell 2014a, 47–55 for a discussion of the role of social science within wisdom-inquiry.

34 I first spelled out the argument for the urgent need for a revolution in academia, from knowledge to wisdom, in N. Maxwell 1976a, and then again, in much greater detail, in N. Maxwell 1984.

35 This is a modified version of the list to be found in N. Maxwell 2004a, 119–21.

APPENDIX ONE

1 Richard Feynman has provided the following amusing illustration of this point (Feynman et al. 1965, vol. 2, 25-10 – 25-11). Consider an

appallingly disunified, complex theory, made up of 10^{10} quite different, distinct laws, stuck arbitrarily together. Such a theory can easily be reformulated so that it reduces to the dazzlingly unified, simple form: A = 0. Suppose the 10^{10} distinct laws of the universe are: (1) F = ma; (2) F = Gm_1m_2/d^2; and so on, for all 10^{10} laws. Let A_1 = $(F - ma)^2$, $A_2 = (F - Gm_1m_2/d^2)^2$, and so on. Let A = $A_1 + A_2 + ... + A_{10^{10}}$. The theory can now be formulated in the unified, simple form A = 0. (This is true if and only if each A_r = 0, for r = 1, 2, ... 10^{10}).

2 See for example Salmon 1989. Elsewhere, I have formulated seven problems of unity or simplicity: see N. Maxwell 1998, 104–5.

3 Einstein 1982, 20–5.

4 Ibid., 21–3.

5 Ibid., 23.

6 Ibid.

7 See my 1998, 56–68, for my criticisms of proposals put forward by Jeffreys and Wrinch 1921; Popper 1959, 62–70, 126–45; Friedman 1974; Kitcher 1981; and Watkins 1984, 203–13. For criticisms of more recent proposals see my 2004c.

8 For earlier accounts of my proposed solution to the problem of unity of physical theory see N. Maxwell 1998 (chapters 3–4), 2004a (chapters 1–2 and appendix), 2004c, 2007a (373–86), and 2011b.

9 Examples of theories that are disunified in these different kinds of way were given in chapter 3, pages 75–8.

10 See chapter 3 for examples.

11 See note 8 above, and N. Maxwell 2013a, 2017 (chapter 5). In these works I discuss a number of further, more technical issues that arise in connection with the unity of physical theory, such as: simplicity, the role of symmetry, content and terminological unity and the connection between the two, unity and metaphysics, unity and the explanatory character of a theory, the unity, or lack of it, of specific physical theories such as quantum theory, general relativity, and the standard model. I also consider objections to the account of unity sketched here.

APPENDIX TWO

1 For references to work on the problem of induction see Kyburg 1970; Swain 1970; Watkins 1984; and Howson 2002.

2 For a much more detailed exposition of the aim-oriented empiricist solution to the problem of induction see N. Maxwell 2017. For earlier expositions see N. Maxwell 1984 (chapter 9), 1993a (Part I), 1998

(especially chapter 5), 2004a (appendix, section 6), 2006a, 2007a
(chapter 9 and 400–30), 2011b, 2013a.

3 One needs to take two steps away from SE, as widely understood, to
   solve the problem of induction. The first step is to appreciate that theories cannot be verified, or rendered probable, by evidence alone.
   Popper took this first step. The second step is to appreciate that theories cannot even be *selected* by evidence alone, even if we forego verification and falsification. Only evidence *plus some metaphysical
   conjecture concerning unity* suffice to select physical theories. This
   second step was firmly resisted by Popper. To the end of his life, he
   defended his principle of demarcation which *excludes* metaphysics
   from science: see Popper 1999, 76–7. Popper did acknowledge that
   metaphysics plays a role in science *in the context of discovery*, especially in connection with what he called "metaphysical research programmes." But to the end, he firmly resisted the idea that metaphysics
   has any role *in the context of acceptance* of theories. For Popper's failure to solve the problem of induction, see N. Maxwell 1972a, 1974
   (133–4), 2005a, 2016b.

4 See chapter 3.

5 Or rather, the assumption is that all *precise* disunified theories are
   false. Even if the true "theory of everything" is unified, it will nevertheless imply endlessly many true approximate, disunified theories. Thus
   Newtonian theory, which, for the sake of argument, we may take to be
   unified, implies the disunified theory made up of Kepler's three laws of
   planetary motion, as long as these laws are interpreted as making sufficiently *approximate* assertions to be true.

6 For discussion of this point see Vicente 2010, 631–40, and N. Maxwell
   2010b, 673–6.

7 Philosophers of science, from Popper to Bayesians, have invented various strategies to bias selection of theories in the direction of unity
   *without thereby committing science to the assumption that the uni-
   verse is such that all disunified theories are false.* All these strategies
   fail. For discussion of some of them, see N. Maxwell 1998 (chapter 2),
   2005a, and 2015.

8 Furthermore, physics *must* accept some such metaphysical thesis since
   otherwise it would be drowned in an infinite ocean of empirically successful but horribly disunified theories.

9 See chapter 3, notes 25 and 26 and associated text.

10 See chapter 3, note 37.

11 The less you assert the more likely it will be, other things being equal, that what you assert is true.

12 See chapter 3, note 49, for a brief account of my development and defence of AOE.

13 In Einstein's words: God is subtle but not malicious. The universe is not designed in such a way as to delude us into thinking we are acquiring knowledge when in reality we are not.

14 See chapter 5, section 7, and N. Maxwell 1968a and 1998, 141–55.

15 Most cultures have maintained their myths, their religious views, in a highly dogmatic fashion, fiercely resisting the kind of critical, flexible, imaginative attitude and approach required by meta-knowability. A key feature of meta-knowability is that we are not just ignorant; we are ignorant about how to go about decreasing our ignorance. Not only do we need to learn; we need to learn how to learn! And that requires that we are skeptical and open-minded about our basic con-jecture of comprehensibility, whatever it may be. Some religions, it should be noted, go so far as to make it a sin to doubt. Blind, dog-matic allegiance to the faith is held to be a virtue!

16 In the last but one paragraph of appendix 1, I mentioned that eight different kinds of unity – or disunity – can be distinguished. Physicalism is here interpreted in such a way that it is unified in all eight ways, with $N = 1$.

17 For further discussion see N. Maxwell 1998, 80–9, 131–40, 257–65, and additional works referred to therein. See also N. Maxwell 2017, chapter 5.

18 See chapter 5, note 105.

19 See N. Maxwell 1985, 40–1, and 2006b, 240–1.

20 At the time of writing, there is no accepted theory of dark matter, and dark energy.

21 The more disunified the totality of fundamental physical theory is, so the more seriously this totality of theory clashes with physicalism.

22 Popper 1959, 1963.

23 This point is argued in more detail in N. Maxwell 2006a.

24 N. Maxwell 2006a.

25 Elsewhere, as I have already noted, I have sought to show how con-sciousness, free will, the experiential world, meaning, and value can exist even though the universe is physically comprehensible: see N. Maxwell 1966, 1968b, 1984 (chapter 10), 2000b, 2001, 2010a, 2011a.

26 For discussion of this defect in Popper's work, see N. Maxwell 2005a, 2016b.

27 The hierarchical structure of AOE is designed to promote progress in knowledge in at least four ways. (1) It concentrates criticism, development, and attempted improvement where it is most likely to promote progress in knowledge, low down in the hierarchy. (2) It constrains what conjectures, low down in the hierarchy, are to be accepted in requiring that these conjectures exemplify conjectures higher up in the hierarchy. (3) It makes possible modification of conjectures, and associated methods, low down in the hierarchy in the light of what is learnt from empirically successful, accepted theories. (4) It provides theoretical physics with a rational, if fallible, method for the discovery of new physical theories, as we saw in chapter 5. Further fruitful implications of AOE for theoretical physics were explored in chapter 5.

References

Aitchison, I.J.R., and A.J.G. Hey. 1982. *Gauge Theories in Particle Physics.* Bristol: Adam Hilger.

Alexander, H.G., ed. 1956. *The Leibniz-Clarke Correspondence.* Manchester: University of Manchester Press.

Appleyard, B. 1992. *Understanding the Present: Science and the Soul of Modern Man.* London: Picador.

Atkins, P.W. 1983. *Molecular Quantum Mechanics.* Oxford: Oxford University Press.

Austin, J.L. 1962. *Sense and Sensibilia.* Oxford: Oxford University Press.

Avital, E., and E. Jablonka. 2000. *Animal Traditions.* Cambridge: Cambridge University Press.

Ayer, A.J. (1936) 1960. *Language, Truth and Logic.* London: Gollancz.

– 1982. *Philosophy in the Twentieth Century.* London: Weidenfeld and Nicolson.

Bacciagaluppi, G. 2012. "The Role of Decoherence in Quantum Mechanics." In *Stanford Encyclopedia of Philosophy.* http://plato.stanford.edu/entries/qm-decoherence/.

Baldwin, J.M. 1896. "A New Factor in Evolution." *The American Naturalist* 30: 354–451 and 536–53.

Band, W., and J.L. Park. 1973. "Comments concerning 'A New Look at the Quantum Mechanical Problem of Measurement.'" *American Journal of Physics* 41: 1021–2.

Barnes, B., and D. Bloor. 1981. "Relativism, Rationalism and the Sociology of Knowledge." In *Rationality and Relativism*, edited by M. Hollis and S. Lukes, 21–47. Oxford: Blackwell.

Bell, J.S. 1987. *Speakable and Unspeakable in Quantum Mechanics.* Cambridge: Cambridge University Press.

Berkeley, G. (1709, 1710, 1713) 1957. *A New Theory of Vision and Other Writings*. London: Dent.

Berlin, I. 1980. *Against the Current*. London: Hogarth Press.

– 1999. *The Roots of Romanticism*. London: Chatto and Windus.

Berman, M. 1981. *The Reenchantment of the World*. Ithaca: Cornell University Press.

Bloor, D. 1976. *Knowledge and Social Imagery*. London: Routledge and Kegan Paul.

Bohm, D. 1952. "A Suggested Interpretation of the Quantum Theory in Terms of 'Hidden' Variables. I and II." *Physical Review* 85: 166–93.

Boscovich, R.J. (1763) 1966. *A Theory of Natural Philosophy*. Cambridge, MA: MIT Press.

Brink, D. 1989. *Moral Realism and the Foundations of Ethics*. Cambridge: Cambridge University Press.

de Broglie, L. 1953. *La Physique Quantique Restera-t-elle Indeterministique?* Paris: Gauthier-Villars.

Burks, A.W. 1977. *Chance, Cause and Reason*. Chicago: University of Chicago Press.

Burtt, E.A. 1980. *The Metaphysical Foundations of Modern Science*. London: Routledge and Kegan Paul.

Butterfield, H. 1949. *The Origins of Modern Science*. London: Bell and Sons.

– 1951. *The Whig Interpretation of History*. London: Bell and Sons.

Chalmers, A.F. 1973. "The Limitations of Maxwell's Electromagnetic Theory." *Isis* 64 (4): 469–83.

Chalmers, D. 1996. *The Conscious Mind*. Oxford: Oxford University Press.

Cohen, H.F. 1994. *The Scientific Revolution: A Historiographical Inquiry*. Chicago: University of Chicago Press.

– 2010. *How Modern Science Came into the World*. Amsterdam: Amsterdam University Press.

– 2015. *The Rise of Modern Science Explained: A Comparative History*. Cambridge: Cambridge University Press.

Cohen, I.B. 1960. *The Birth of a New Physics*. New York: W.W. Norton.

– 1983. *The Newtonian Revolution*. Cambridge: Cambridge University Press.

– 1999. "A Guide to Newton's Principia" in Newton 1999, 3–370.

Cohen, I.B., and G.E. Smith., eds. 2002. *The Cambridge Companion to Newton*. Cambridge: Cambridge University Press.

Crick, F. 1984. "Function of the Thalamic Reticular Complex: The Searchlight Hypothesis." *Proceedings of the National Academy of Sciences USA* 81: 4586–90.

d'Alembert, D. (1751) 1963. *Preliminary Discourse to the Encyclopedia of Diderot*. New York: Bobbs-Merrill.

Darrigol, O. 2000. *Electrodynamics from Ampère to Einstein*. Oxford: Oxford University Press.

– 2014. *Physics and Necessity*. Oxford: Oxford University Press.

Davies, P.C.W., and J. Brown., eds. 1988. *Superstrings: A Theory of Everything?* Cambridge: Cambridge University Press.

Dawkins, R. 1978. *The Selfish Gene*. London: Paladin.

Dear, P. 2006. *The Intelligibility of Nature*. Chicago: University of Chicago Press.

Dennett, D. 1991. *Consciousness Explained*. London: Allen Lane.

– 1996. *Darwin's Dangerous Idea*. London: Penguin.

Descartes, R. 1949. *A Discourse on Method*. London: Dent.

Dieudonné, J. 1960. *Foundations of Modern Analysis*. London: Academic Press.

Dijksterhuis. E.J. 1969. *The Mechanization of the World Picture*. Oxford: Oxford University Press.

Dirac, P. 1963. "The Evolution of the Physicist's Picture of Nature." *Scientific American* 208 (5): 45–53.

Drake, S. 1957. *Discoveries and Opinions of Galileo*. New York: Anchor Books.

Duchayne, S. 2012. *The Main Business of Natural Philosophy*. Dordrecht: Springer.

Duhem, P. 1954–58. *Le système du monde: Histoire des doctrines cosmologiques de Platon a Copernic*. Paris: Hermann.

– 1962. *The Aim and Structure of Physical Theory*. New York: Atheneum.

– 1991. *The Origins of Statics*. Dordrecht: Kluwer.

Dunbar, R. 2010. *How Many Friends Does One Person Need? Dunbar's Number and Other Evolutionary Quirks*. London: Faber and Faber.

Dupré, J. 1993. *The Disorder of Things*. Cambridge, MA: Harvard University Press.

Durant, J. 1997. "Beyond the Scope of Science." *Science and Public Affairs* (Spring): 56–7.

Einstein, A. 1973. *Ideas and Opinions*. London: Souvenir Press.

– (1949) 1982. "Autobiographical Notes, and Reply to Criticisms." In *Albert Einstein: Philosopher-Scientist*, edited by P.A. Schilpp, 3–94 and 665–88. La Salle, IL: Open Court.

– 1998. *Einstein's Miraculous Year*. Edited by J. Stachel. Princeton: Princeton University Press.

Everett, H. 1957. "Relative State Formulation of Quantum Mechanics." *Reviews of Modern Physics* 29: 454–62.

Faraday, M. 1839–1855. *Experimental Researches in Electricity*. London: Taylor and Francis.

Feyerabend, P. 1978. *Against Method*. London: Verso.

– 1987. *Farewell to Reason*. London: Verso.

Feynman, R., R.B. Leighton, and M. Sands 1963. *The Feynman Lectures on Physics*. Vols. 1 and 2. Reading: Addison-Wesley.

Firestein, S. 2012. *Ignorance: How It Drives Science*. Oxford: Oxford University Press.

Friedman, M. 1974. "Explanation and Scientific Understanding." *Journal of Philosophy* 71: 5–19.

Gascardi, A. 1999. *Consequences of Enlightenment*. Cambridge: Cambridge University Press.

Gaukroger, S. 2006. *The Emergence of a Scientific Culture*. Oxford: Clarendon Press.

– 2010. *The Collapse of Mechanism and the Rise of Sensibility*. Oxford: Clarendon Press.

Gay, P. 1973. *The Enlightenment: An Interpretation*. London: Wildwood House.

Ghirardi, G.C., A. Rimini, and T. Weber. 1986. "Unified Dynamics For Microscopic and Macroscopic Systems." *Physical Review* D 34: 470–91.

Goodman, N. 1954. *Fact, Fiction, and Forecast*. London: Athlone Press.

Graves, J.C. 1974. "Uniformity and Induction." *British Journal for the Philosophy of Science* 25: 301–8.

Gray, J. 2004. *Heresies: Against Progress and Other Illusions*. London: Granta.

Greene, B. 1999. *The Elegant Universe*. New York: W.W. Norton.

Gribbin, J. 2003. *Science: A History*. London: Penguin.

Grice, H.P. 1957. "Meaning." *Philosophical Review* 66: 377–88.

Griffiths, D. 1987. *Introduction to Elementary Particles*. New York: John Wiley.

Gross, P., and N. Levitt, eds. 1996. *The Flight from Science and Reason*. New York: Annals of the New York Academy of Sciences.

Guthrie, W.K.C. 1978. *A History of Greek Philosophy: Vol. 2. The Presocratic Tradition from Parmenedes to Democritus*. Cambridge: Cambridge University Press.

Haag, R. 2013. "On the Sharpness of Localization of Individual Events in Space and Time." *arXiv:1303.6431*: 18–19.

Hall, A.R. 1980. *Philosophers at War: The Quarrel between Newton and Leibniz*. Cambridge: Cambridge University Press.

Harding, S. 1986. *The Feminist Question in Science*. Milton Keynes: Open University Press.

Hardy, A. 1965. *The Living Stream*. London: Collins.

Harper, W.L. 2011. *Isaac Newton's Scientific Method*. Oxford: Oxford University Press.

Hatfield, G. 1990. "Metaphysics and the New Science." In *Reappraisals of the New Science*, edited by D.C. Lindberg and R.S. Westman, 93–166. Cambridge: Cambridge University Press.

Heilbron, J. 1979. *Electricity in the 17th and 18th Centuries*. Berkeley: University of California Press.

Hendry, J. 1986. *James Clerk Maxwell and the Theory of the Electromagnetic Field*. Bristol: Adam Hilger.

Henry, J. 2002. *The Scientific Revolution and the Origins of Modern Science*. Basingstoke: Palgrave.

Holdgate, M. 1996. *From Care to Action*. London: Earthscan.

Holton, G. 1973. *Thematic Origins of Scientific Thought: Kepler to Einstein*. Cambridge, MA: Harvard University Press.

Howson, C. 2002. *Hume's Problem*. Oxford: Oxford University Press.

Hume, D. (1738) 1959. *A Treatise of Human Nature*. London: Everyman.

Hunt, B.J. 1991. *The Maxwellians*. London: Cornell University Press.

Huxley, A. 1937. *Ends and Means*. London: Chatto and Windus.

– 1980. *The Human Situation*. St. Albans: Triad/Panther Books.

Inwood, S. 2003. *The Man Who Knew Too Much*. London: Pan Books.

Isham, C.J. 1989. *Lectures on Groups and Vector Spaces for Physicists*. London: World Scientific.

– 1997. "Structural Issues in Quantum Gravity." In *General Relativity and Gravitation: Proceedings*, edited by M. Francaviglia, G. Longhi, L. Lusanna, and E. Sorace, 167–209. Singapore: World Scientific.

Jablonka, E., and M.J. Lamb. 2005. *Evolution in Four Dimensions*. Cambridge, MA: MIT Press.

Jackson, F. 1986. "What Mary Didn't Know." *Journal of Philosophy* 3: 291–5.

Jammer, M. 1974. *The Philosophy of Quantum Mechanics*. London: Wiley.

Jeffreys, H., and D. Wrinch. 1921. "On Certain Fundamental Principles of Scientific Enquiry." *Philosophical Magazine* 42: 269–98.

Kane, R. 1998. *The Significance of Free Will*. Oxford: Oxford University Press.

Kant, I. (1787) 1961. *Critique of Pure Reason*. Second edition. London: Macmillan.

– (1786) 1985. "Metaphysical Foundations of Natural Science." In *Immanuel Kant: Philosophy of Material Nature* (Book II), translated by J.W. Ellington. Indianapolis: Hackett. Indianapolis.

Kitcher, P. 1981. "Explanatory Unification." *Philosophy of Science* 48: 507–31.

Klein, M.J. 1972. "Mechanical Explanation at the End of the Nineteenth Century." *Centaurus* 17: 58–82.

Koertge, N., ed. 1998. *A House Built on Sand: Exposing Postmodernist Myths about Science*. Oxford: Oxford University Press.

Koyré, A. 1957. *From the Closed World to the Infinite Universe*. Baltimore: John Hopkins Press.

– 1965. *Newtonian Studies*. London: Chapman and Hall.

– 1968. *Metaphysics and Measurement*. London: Chapman and Hall.

Kuhn, T.S. (1962) 1970. *The Structure of Scientific Revolutions*. Chicago: University of Chicago Press.

Kyburg, H. 1970. *Probability and Inductive Logic*. London: Collier-Macmillan.

Laing, R.D. 1965. *The Divided Self*. Harmondsworth: Penguin.

Langley, C. 2005. *Soldiers in the Laboratory*. Folkstone: Scientists for Global Responsibility.

Latour, B. 1987. *Science in Action*. Milton Keynes: Open University Press.

Laudan, L. 1980. "A Confutation of Convergent Realism." *Philosophy of Science* 48: 19–48.

Libet, B. 1985. "Unconscious Cerebral Initiative and the Role of Conscious Will in Voluntary Action." *Behavioral and Brain Sciences* 8: 529–66.

– 2005. *Mind Time*. Cambridge, MA: Harvard University Press.

Little, M. 1994. "Moral Realism." *Philosophical Books* 35: 145–53 and 225–33.

Lloyd Morgan, C. 1896. "On Modification and Variation." *Science* 4: 733–40.

Locke, J. (1688) 1961. *An Essay concerning Human Understanding*. London: J.M. Dent.

Mandl, F., and G. Shaw. 1984. *Quantum Field Theory*. New York: John Wiley.

Marcuse, H. 1964. *One Dimensional Man*. Boston: Beacon Press.

Maudlin, T. 2010. "The Geometry of Space-Time." *The Aristotelian Society*. Supplementary vol. 84: 63–78.

Maxwell, J.C. 1856. "On Faraday's Lines of Force." *Transactions of the Cambridge Philosophical Society* 10, Part 1: 27–83. Reprinted in J.C. Maxwell 1890, vol. 1: 155–229.

– 1861 and 1862. "On Physical Lines of Force." *Philosophical Magazine* 21: 161–75, 281–91, and 338–48; and *Philosophical Magazine* 22: 12–24 and 85–95. Reprinted in J.C. Maxwell 1890, vol. 1: 451–513.

- 1865. "A Dynamical Theory of the Electromagnetic Field." *Transactions of the Cambridge Philosophical Society* 155: 459–512. Reprinted in J.C. Maxwell 1890, vol. 1: 526–97, and in J.C. Maxwell 1982.
- 1878. "Aether." *Encyclopædia Britannica*. 9th edition, vol. 8: 568–72.
- 1890. *The Scientific Papers of James Clerk Maxwell*. Edited by W.D. Niven. Cambridge: Cambridge University Press. Reprint, New York: Dover, 1965. Citations refer to the Dover edition.
- 1982. *A Dynamical Theory of the Electromagnetic Field*. Edited by T.F. Torrance. Edinburgh: Scottish Academic Press.

Maxwell, N. 1966. "Physics and Common Sense." *British Journal for the Philosophy of Science* 16: 295–311.
- 1968a. "Can There Be Necessary Connections between Successive Events?" *British Journal for the Philosophy of Science* 19: 1–25.
- 1968b. "Understanding Sensations." *Australasian Journal of Philosophy* 46: 127–46.
- 1972a. "A Critique of Popper's Views on Scientific Method." *Philosophy of Science* 39: 131–52.
- 1972b. "A New Look at the Quantum Mechanical Problem of Measurement." *American Journal of Physics* 40: 1431–5.
- 1973. "The Problem of Measurement – Real or Imaginary?" *American Journal of Physics* 41: 1022–5.
- 1974. "The Rationality of Scientific Discovery." *Philosophy of Science* 41: 123–53 and 247–95.
- 1976a. *What's Wrong with Science?* Hayes, Middlesex: Bran's Head Books.
- 1976b. "Towards a Micro Realistic Version of Quantum Mechanics. Parts I and II." *Foundations of Physics* 6: 275–92 and 661–76.
- 1980. "Science, Reason, Knowledge and Wisdom: A Critique of Specialism." *Inquiry* 23: 19–81.
- 1982. "Instead of Particles and Fields." *Foundations of Physics* 12: 607–31.
- 1984. *From Knowledge to Wisdom: A Revolution in the Aims and Methods of Science*. Oxford: Blackwell.
- 1985. "Are Probabilism and Special Relativity Incompatible?" *Philosophy of Science* 52: 23–43.
- 1988. "Quantum Propensiton Theory: A Testable Resolution of the Wave/Particle Dilemma." *British Journal for the Philosophy of Science* 39: 1–50.
- 1992. "What Kind of Inquiry Can Best Help Us Create a Good World?" *Science, Technology, and Human Values* 17: 205–27.

– 1993a. "Induction and Scientific Realism. Parts I, II and III." *British Journal for the Philosophy of Science* 44: 61–79, 81–101, and 275–305.
– 1993b. "Beyond Fapp: Three Approaches to Improving Orthodox Quantum Theory and an Experimental Test." In *Bell's Theorem and the Foundations of Modern Physics*, edited by A. van der Merwe, F. Selleri, and G. Tarozzi, 362–70. Singapore: World Scientific.
– 1994. "Particle Creation as the Quantum Condition for Probabilistic Events to Occur." *Physics Letters* A 187: 351–5.
– 1995. "A Philosopher Struggles to Understand Quantum Theory: Particle Creation and Wavepacket Reduction." In *Fundamental Problems in Quantum Physics*, edited by M. Ferrero and A. van der Merwe, 205–14. London: Kluwer Academic.
– 1998. *The Comprehensibility of the Universe: A New Conception of Science*. Oxford: Clarendon Press.
– 1999. "Are There Objective Values?" *The Dalhousie Review* 79 (3): 301–17.
– 2000a. "Can Humanity Learn to Become Civilized? The Crisis of Science without Civilization." *Journal of Applied Philosophy* 17: 29–44.
– 2000b. "The Mind-Body Problem and Explanatory Dualism." *Philosophy* 75: 49–71.
– 2001. *The Human World in the Physical Universe: Consciousness, Free Will, and Evolution*. Lanham, Maryland: Rowman and Littlefield.
– 2002. "Karl Raimund Popper." In *British Philosophers. 1800–2000*, edited by P. Dematteis, P. Fosl, and L. McHenry, 176–94. Columbia: Bruccoli Clark Layman.
– 2004a. *Is Science Neurotic?* London: Imperial College Press.
– 2004b. "Does Probabilism Solve the Great Quantum Mystery?" *Theoria* 19/3 (51): 321–36.
– 2004c. "Non-Empirical Requirements Scientific Theories Must Satisfy: Simplicity, Unification, Explanation, Beauty." http://philsci-archive.pitt.edu/1759/ .
– 2005a. "Popper, Kuhn, Lakatos and Aim-Oriented Empiricism." *Philosophia* 32 (1–4): 181–239.
– 2005b. "Philosophy Seminars for Five Year Olds." *Learning for Democracy* 1 (2): 71–7.
– 2006a. "Practical Certainty and Cosmological Conjectures." In *Is There Certain Knowledge?*, edited by M. Rahnfeld, 44–59. Leibzig: Leipziger Universitätsverlag.
– 2006b. "Special Relativity, Time, Probabilism and Ultimate Reality." In *The Ontology of Spacetime*, edited by D. Dieks, 229–45. Amsterdam: Elsevier B.V.

– 2007a. *From Knowledge to Wisdom: A Revolution for Science and the Humanities*. 2nd revised edition. London: Pentire Press.

– 2007b. "From Knowledge to Wisdom: The Need for an Academic Revolution." *London Review of Education* 5 (2): 97–115.

– 2008. "Are Philosophers Responsible for Global Warming?" *Philosophy Now* 65: 12–13.

– 2009a. "How Can Life of Value Best Flourish in the Real World?" In *Science and the Pursuit of Wisdom: Studies in the Philosophy of Nicholas Maxwell*, edited by L. McHenry, 1–56. Frankfurt: Ontos Verlag.

– 2009b. *What's Wrong with Science? Towards a People's Rational Science of Delight and Compassion*. 2nd edition. London: Pentire Press.

– 2010a. *Cutting God in Half – And Putting the Pieces Together Again: A New Approach to Philosophy*. London: Pentire Press.

– 2010b. "Reply to Comments on *Science and the Pursuit of Wisdom*." *Philosophia* 38 (4): 667–90.

– 2011a. "Three Philosophical Problems about Consciousness and Their Possible Resolution." *Open Journal of Philosophy* 1 (1): 1–10.

– 2011b. "A Priori Conjectural Knowledge in Physics." In *What Place for the A Priori?*, edited by M. Shaffer and M. Veber. Chicago: Open Court, 211–40.

– 2011c. "Is the Quantum World Composed of Propensitons?" In *Probabilities, Causes and Propensities in Physics*, edited by M. Suárez, 221–43. Dordrecht: Synthese Library, Springer.

– 2012. "Arguing for Wisdom in the University: An Intellectual Autobiography." *Philosophia* 40 (4): 663–704. Reprinted in Maxwell 2014b.

– 2013a. "Has Science Established That the Cosmos Is Physically Comprehensible?" In *Recent Advances in Cosmology*, edited by A. Travena and B. Soen, 1–56. New York: Nova Publishers.

– 2013b. "Misconceptions concerning Wisdom." *Journal of Modern Wisdom* 2: 92–7.

– 2013c. "Knowledge or Wisdom?" *The Philosophers' Magazine* 62 (3rd quarter): 17–18.

– 2014a. *How Universities Can Help Create a Wiser World: The Urgent Need for an Academic Revolution*. Exeter: Imprint Academic.

– 2014b. *Global Philosophy*. Exeter: Imprint Academic.

– 2014c. "Three Criticisms of Newton's Inductive Argument in the *Principia*." *Advances in Historical Studies* 3 (1): 2–11.

– 2015. "What's Wrong with Aim-Oriented Empiricism?" *Acta Baltica Historiae et Philosophiae Scientiarum* 3 (2): 5–31.

– 2016a. "Can Scientific Method Help Us Create a Wiser World?" In *Practical Wisdom in the Age of Technology: Insights, Issues, and Questions for a New Millennium*, edited by N. Dalal, A. Intezari, and M. Heitz, 147–61. Farnham: Ashgate.

– 2016b. "Popper's Paradoxical Pursuit of Natural Philosophy." In *The Cambridge Companion to Popper*, edited by J. Shearmur and G. Stokes, 170–207. Cambridge: Cambridge University Press.

– 2017. *Understanding Scientific Progress*. Saint Paul, MN: Paragon House.

Melden, A.I., 1960. "On the Nature and Problems of Ethics." In *Ethical Theories*, edited by A.I. Melden, 1–19. Englewood Cliffs: Prentice Hall.

Mill, J.S. 1973–4. *A System of Logic*. In *Collected Works of John Stuart Mill*, edited by J.M. Robson. Vol. 8. Toronto: University of Toronto Press.

Miller, D. 1974. "Popper's Qualitative Theory of Verisimilitude." *British Journal for the Philosophy of Science* 25: 166–77.

Minkowski, H. 1952. "Space and Time." In H.A. Lorentz, A. Einstein, H. Minkowski, and H. Weyl, eds. *The Principle of Relativity*. New York: Dover: 75–91.

Mitford, N. 1957. *Voltaire in Love*. London: Hamish Hamilton.

Monot, J. 1974. *Chance and Necessity*. Glasgow: Fontana.

Moore. G. 1959. *Philosophical Papers*. London: Allen and Unwin.

Moriyasu, K. 1983. *An Elementary Primer for Gauge Theory*. Singapore: World Scientific.

Nagel, T. 1974. "What Is It Like to Be a Bat?" *Philosophical Review* 83: 435–50.

– 1986. *The View from Nowhere*. Oxford: Oxford University Press

Needham, J. 1979. *The Grand Titration*. London: George Allen and Unwin.

Newton, I. (1704) 1952. *Opticks*. New York: Dover Publications.

– (1687) 1962. *Principia*. Translated by A. Motte, revised by F. Cajori. Berkeley: University of California Press.

– 1999. *The Principia*. Translated by I.B. Cohen and A. Whitman. Berkeley: University of California Press.

Newton-Smith, W. 1981. *The Rationality of Science*. London: Routledge and Kegan Paul.

Penrose, R. 1996. "On Gravity's Role in Quantum State Reduction." *General Relativity and Gravitation* 28 (5): 581–600.

– 2004. *The Road to Reality*. London: Jonathan Cape.

– 2014. "On the Gravitization of Quantum Mechanics 1: Quantum State Reduction." *Foundations of Physics* 44: 557–75.

Poincaré, H. 1952. *Science and Hypothesis*. New York: Dover.

Popper, K.R. (1934) 1959. *The Logic of Scientific Discovery*. London: Hutchinson.

- 1961. *The Poverty of Historicism*. London: Routledge and Kegan Paul.

- 1962. *The Open Society and Its Enemies*. Vol. 2. London: Routledge and Kegan Paul.

- 1963. *Conjectures and Refutations*. London: Routledge and Kegan Paul.

- 1969. *The Open Society and Its Enemies*. Vol. 1. London: Routledge and Kegan Paul.

- 1972. *Objective Knowledge*. Oxford: Clarendon Press.

- 1976. *Unended Quest*. London: Fontana.

- 1994. *The Myth of the Framework*. London: Routledge.

- 1999. *All Life Is Problem Solving*. London: Routledge.

Przibram, K., ed.1967. *Letters on Wave Mechanics*. New York: Philosophical Library.

Quinton, A., ed. 1968. *Political Philosophy*. Oxford: Oxford University Press.

Ramakrishnan, V. 2016. "More Than Ever, Science Must Be Central to All Our Lives." *The Observer*, 28 February, 35.

Rossi, P. 2001. *The Birth of Modern Science*. Oxford: Blackwell.

Roszak, T. 1973. *Where the Wasteland Ends*. London: Faber and Faber.

Russell, B. 1905. "On Denoting." *Mind*, new series 14: 479–93.

- 1948. *Human Knowledge: Its Scope and Limits*. London: Allen and Unwin.

- 1956. *Logic and Knowledge*. Edited by R.C. Marsh. London: Allen and Unwin.

- (1912) 1982. *The Problems of Philosophy*. Oxford: Oxford University Press.

Ryle, G. 1949. *The Concept of Mind*. London: Hutchinson.

Salmon, W. 1989. *Four Decades of Scientific Explanation*. Minneapolis: University of Minnesota Press.

Schaffner, K.F. 1972. *Nineteenth-Century Aether Theories*. Oxford: Pergamon.

Schwartz, B. 1987. *The Battle for Human Nature*. New York: W.W. Norton.

Shank, J. B. 2008. *The Newtonian Wars and the Beginning of the French Enlightenment*. Chicago: University of Chicago Press.

Shankland, R. 1963. "Conversations with Albert Einstein." *American Journal of Physics* 31: 37–47.

Shapin, S. 1998. *The Scientific Revolution*. Chicago: University of Chicago Press.

Sellars, W.F. 1963. *Science, Perception and Reality*. London: Routledge and Kegan Paul.

Simpson, G.G. 1953. "The Baldwin Effect." *Evolution* 7: 110–7.

Singer, P. 1995. *Animal Liberation*. London: Pimlico.

Smart, J.J.C. 1963. *Philosophy and Scientific Realism*. London: Routledge and Kegan Paul.

Smith, D. 2003. *The Atlas of War and Peace*. London: Earthscan.

Smith, G.E. 2002. "The Methodology of the *Principia*." In *The Cambridge Companion to Newton*, edited by I.B. Cohen and G.E. Smith, 138–73. Cambridge: Cambridge University Press.

Smolin, L. 2000. *Three Roads to Quantum Gravity*. London: Weidenfeld and Nicolson.

– 2006. *The Trouble with Physics*. New York: Houghton Mifflin.

Sokal, A. and J. Bricmont. 1998. *Intellectual Impostures*. London: Profile Books.

Spinoza, B. 1955. *On the Improvement of the Understanding. The Ethics. Correspondence*. New York: Dover.

Squires, E. 1989. "A Comment on Maxwell's Resolution of the Wave/Particle Dilemma." *British Journal for the Philosophy of Science* 40: 413–17.

Swain, M., ed. 1970. *Induction, Acceptance, and Rational Belief*. Dordrecht: Reidel.

Terrall, M. 2002. *The Man Who Flattened the Earth*. Chicago: University of Chicago Press.

Tichý, P. 1974. "On Popper's Definition of Verisimilitude." *British Journal for the Philosophy of Science* 25: 155–60.

van Fraassen, B. 1980. *The Scientific Image*. Oxford: Clarendon Press.

– 1985. "Empiricism in the Philosophy of Science." In *Images of Science*, edited by P.M. Churchland and C.A. Hooker, 259–60. Chicago: University of Chicago Press.

Vicente, A. 2010. "An Enlightened Revolt: On the Philosophy of Nicholas Maxwell." *Philosophia* 38 (4): 631–48.

Voltaire. 1964. *Lettres Philosophiques*. Paris: Editions Garnier Freres.

Wallace, D. 2012. *The Emergent Multiverse*. Oxford: Oxford University Press.

Watkins, J.W.N. 1984. *Science and Scepticism*. Princeton: Princeton University Press.

Westfall, R.S. 1977. *The Construction of Modern Science*. Cambridge: Cambridge University Press.

Whitehead, 1932. *Science and the Modern World*. Cambridge: Cambridge University Press.

Wigner, E.P. 1967. *Symmetries and Reflections*. Cambridge, MA: MIT Press.

Wittgenstein, L. 1958. *Philosophical Investigations*. Oxford: Blackwell.

– (1922) 1960. *Tractatus Logico-Philosophicus*. London: Routledge and Kegan Paul.

Woit, P. 2006. *Not Even Wrong: The Failure of String Theory and the Continuing Challenge to Unify the Laws of Physics*. London: Jonathan Cape.

Worrall, J. 1989. "Why Both Popper and Watkins Fail to Solve the Problem of Induction." In *Freedom and Rationality: Essays in Honour of John Watkins*, edited by F. D'Agostino and I. Jarvie, 257–96. Dordrecht: Kluwer.

Index